DOCUMENTS AND NARRATIVES

Concerning the

DISCOVERY & CONQUEST
OF LATIN AMERICA

NEW SERIES

NUMBER FIVE

THE CORTÉS SOCIETY

BANCROFT LIBRARY, BERKELEY, CALIFORNIA

Photograph by James N. Doolittle

HENRY RAUP WAGNER, IN HIS EIGHTIES

Engraving by Tomás López Enguidanos

BARTOLOMÉ DE LAS CASAS, IN HIS EIGHTIES

THE LIFE
AND WRITINGS OF
BARTOLOMÉ de las CASAS

by Henry Raup Wagner with
the collaboration of
Helen Rand
Parish

Published for
THE CORTÉS SOCIETY
by

THE UNIVERSITY OF NEW MEXICO PRESS

ALBUQUERQUE

First Edition

Library of Congress Catalog Card No. 66-29983

© THE UNIVERSITY OF NEW MEXICO PRESS, 1967

ALL RIGHTS RESERVED

MANUFACTURED IN THE UNITED STATES OF AMERICA

BY THE UNIVERSITY OF NEW MEXICO

PRINTING PLANT

CONTENTS

vii

HENRY RAUP WAGNER, 1862-1957

THE FIRST TIME I MET HENRY R. WAGNER was in the Bancroft Library in 1921, according to my recollection. I was then but a graduate student, never dreaming I would one day become Director of the Bancroft. It was a chance meeting, but one that was to have a profound influence on my life.[1] Wagner had come to look up some references, to call on Herbert E. Bolton, the Director, and on Herbert I. Priestley and Joseph J. Hill, preparatory to his projected trip to Spain in 1922, once he had extricated himself from the world of business—he was then one of the leading officials in the Guggenheim organization. On my part, the meeting was wholly casual, for I had not yet learned of his distinguished achievements, nor of his historical and bibliographical investigations, and knew but little of his plan to cut himself off from business and devote himself to the history and bibliography of New Mexico and the western United States.

Wagner's background was typically American. His father, Jacob Frederick Wagner (1816-1892) had migrated to Philadelphia from Germany and become a manufacturer. His mother, Eliza (Kemp) Wagner, was of English descent, her ancestors coming from Yorkshire. Their son, baptized Henry Raup Wagner, was born September 27, 1862, in Philadelphia.

In 1921 Wagner had passed his fifty-ninth birthday, an age at which but few men would think of embarking on a career in a field entirely divorced from previous experience. He had, however, a remarkable though unconventional preparation for his new work, as may be inferred from even a cursory glance at his activities.

Graduated from Yale University in the class of 1884 and from its Law School in 1886, he turned to the West to launch his career. For him, this meant Kansas City and later Denver, where he engaged in various business affairs, especially mining, and made many friends. A sociable and gregarious bachelor, he helped form a University Club in Kansas City in 1887 and another in Denver in 1891. In his business life and in the companionship of these social circles he met kindred spirits, formed friendships, and got the feel of the frontier, which even then exhibited many of the characteristics which had made it famous. At that time the buffalo had but recently vanished before the onslaught of hunter and settler. Free or cheap land was still available, and European immigrants were pouring into the region beyond the Mississippi. Mining was an important business, though the fever that

---

1. With the exception of a few paragraphs, this sketch appeared originally in the *Hispanic American Historical Review*, XXXVII, 486-489.

had characterized the California Gold Rush in 1849 and the Comstock Lode in 1859 had subsided. Wagner's own pursuits drew him more and more into mining, chiefly in New Mexico and Colorado, where he learned ore sampling and other phases of the business.

In 1890-1891 Wagner was connected with the Census Bureau, collecting mining statistics in Denver and New York, and for the next two years he was associated with the Globe Smelting and Refining Company in Denver. Then, in 1894, he was invited to go to Mexico to manage a branch office for a mining machinery firm, E. P. Allis & Co., and in the course of the year he became acquainted with American experts in the mining and smelting field. This was not his first visit to Mexico, for he had gone there in 1892 on an ore-buying mission for the Globe firm, and again the next year on a similar project. For a time he lived at Durango and Zacatecas, both ancient mining centers, and became so interested in the old patio process of extracting the bullion from the ore that he studied the subject and collected books on it, with the idea of writing the history of its development by the Spaniards. This plan never materialized, but Wagner had begun the collecting of books and the study of Spain's contribution to the development of the New World, interests which came eventually to dominate his life and to give him his greatest satisfaction.

From 1895 to 1898 Wagner was in Denver, Spokane, and other parts of the West, still engaged in mining, and when, in 1898, he received an offer from Simon Guggenheim to become an ore buyer for the Guggenheim interests, he accepted. This appointment took him to Chile for the greater part of four years, and later to New York and London. It was in March, 1903, that he went to work in London, where, as his avocation, he sought out books on mining and metallurgy and "inhaled about a ton of dust looking through bookstores for them." Here he built up a collection on Irish economics, later presented to the Yale University Library, and gathered extensively in the fields of mining, metallurgy, and Chilean and Peruvian history. By the time Wagner left London at Christmas time in 1906, he had been thoroughly infected with the book-collecting fever.

Wagner's mother had accompanied him to London, where she provided a home for him. She died in 1916, at the age of eighty-seven.

For the next decade or so, after the London experience, Wagner made Mexico his home, as a representative of the Guggenheims. At first he was in charge of the El Paso office, with frequent trips to Aguas Calientes, but about 1910, when he was made general manager of the company's Mexican affairs, he moved the general office to Mexico City and remained there till 1915. He was in the capital during the Revolution, knew personally many

of its leaders, and observed at first hand the stirring events of this remarkable decade.

After ten exciting years in Mexico, during which he not only carried
on important business functions but collected books and manuscripts with
zest, he was transferred to Santiago, Chile, remaining there for two years
in charge of the Guggenheim interests, which by then were very large. As
always, Wagner mixed business with the pursuit of books, an avocation for
which he had a special opportunity in Chile since it was the home of José
Toribio Medina, famous Chilean historian and bibliographer. Wagner
spent many pleasant hours in this famous historian's home, and under his
inspiration, conceived the idea of extracting from Medina's bibliographical
works descriptions of the books in his library relating to the Spanish Southwest—material which was to be of inestimable value to Wagner in the compilation of his own bibliography, *The Spanish Southwest.*

Before his term of duty in Chile had come to an end—a term he had
limited to two years by previous agreement with the Guggenheims—Wagner
determined to sever all business connections with the firm in order to devote
his full attention, unhampered by worldly affairs, to the study and writing
of history. This decision found little favor with his employers, who obviously
did not wish to lose Wagner's valuable services, but eventually, though not
till about 1921, he freed himself entirely from these mundane preoccupa-
tions. From then on, he apparently never gave another thought to the making of money (except from the sale of books—never from his own publications), nor had he any desire to return to the old pursuits. At least, during
the years I knew him, he never talked about business and rarely ever mentioned his old associations. On the contrary, he was so deeply immersed in
research topics on Spanish colonial history, especially New Spain and its
conquerors, that he had little time for anything else. Indeed, it was an inspiration to visit with him, which I did often during the year we spent
together in the Archives of the Indies in Spain, and later in Los Angeles
in the early 1930's and on occasions for many years thereafter.

In the meantime, at this point of transition, Wagner's life had changed
in another respect. While he was making the big break with mining in
exchange for a literary career, he also gave up his days of bachelorhood and
married an artist, Miss Blanche Henriette Collet, the daughter of a French
sculptor and architect. The ceremony took place in Oakland, California,
July 17, 1917.

Wagner's most active book-collecting years began with his stay in
London and continued unabated till the early 1920's. As usually happens
to the private collector, he eventually ran out of shelf space, and perhaps

cast an apprehensive eye, too, on the size of his investment, housed as it was
in a private home and subject to the hazards of fire. At any rate, in 1915
Wagner decided to dispose of his Mexican collection and sold it to the Yale
University Library, where he had placed his material on Irish economics.
Four years later he sold to Yale another chunk of his library, his Midwest-
ern books, including those on the Mississippi Valley and Texas, and in
1936 made a donation to Yale of his Irish collection. This left him only his
California section, which he sold to Henry E. Huntington in 1922, and with
this sale went the last of his great, major collections. He never entirely ceased
the purchase and sale of old books, but from the time of his trip to Europe
in 1922-1923 his life interest was research and writing, rather than book
acquisition, a career in which he was successful beyond measure. His an-
notated bibliography, *The Spanish Southwest, 1542-1794,* and his *Nueva
bibliografía mexicana del siglo XVI* (supplementing the work of García
Icazbalceta, Toribio Medina, and Nicolás León), have become classics. His
works on Spanish voyages and the cartography of the northwest coast of
America remain fundamental in their fields. All these, and his many studies
in the history of New Spain in the sixteenth century, endowed him with
a remarkable background for his last work, the present posthumous volume.[2]

Wagner looked upon *The Life and Writings of Bartolomé de las Casas,*
as his chief contribution to scholarship. At the time of his death, he was
supervising the literary revision of this work by Helen Rand Parish, who
undertook the task at my invitation, after Wagner had dumped it in my lap.
With half the book in finished form, she was called East and could not return to California for a number of years. In her absence, Wagner died on
March 27, 1957, at the age of ninety-four years and six months. I did not
wish to entrust his last work to anyone else, but preferred to wait until Miss
Parish's return to California so that the book could be prepared for the press
in the manner that he had approved. Fortunate is the scholar who, like Casas,
had a torchbearer—in his case a Fray Alonso de la Veracruz—to carry on his
unfinished tasks, or like Wagner, a Helen Rand Parish—proficient linguist
and able writer, to prepare his final study for publication.

—GEORGE P. HAMMOND

2. A number of bibliographies of Wagner's writings were issued during his
lifetime, notably those in his autobiography, *Bullion to Books* (Los Angeles, 1942),
and in the Zamorano Club publication, *The Published Writings of Henry Raup
Wagner* (Los Angeles, 1955). A select bibliography of his contributions in the Latin-
American field, prepared by Jerry E. Patterson, appeared in the *Hispanic American
Historical Review,* XXXVII, 489-494.

WHEN THE LATE HENRY R. WAGNER began his research on Bartolomé de las Casas, the current scholarly rage over the "Protector of the Indians" had not gotten under way, or anyhow it had not gotten into print. The last full-scale life of Casas was then MacNutt's dating from 1909. No thorough biographical study had been made of the volumes of Casas documents or his two major writings—the *Historia de las Indias* and the *Apologética*—that were published at last in the nineteenth century. In his eighties, Wagner set himself to the task, working with only a single assistant in his well-stocked library and in the sunny garden of his home in San Marino, California.[1]

Since that time a flood of new books on Casas has appeared, mostly in the 1950's and 1960's. Yet today, as a part of the fourth centennial of Fray Bartolomé's death in 1566, the University of New Mexico Press, in conjunction with the Cortés Society, is publishing Wagner's *Life and Writings of Casas,* on which I have had the honor to collaborate. For this posthumous work by an old, brilliant, and most original scholar—Wagner himself died in 1957—this posthumous masterpiece stands up very well beside the combined output of all these younger "Lascasistas."

Let me give a couple of striking examples. Dr. Lewis Hanke, who really started the current vogue, completed his work with a useful four-hundred-page *Bibliografía crítica y cuerpo de materiales* on Casas' life, writings, and career, and the related subsequent controversies.[2] How then

---

1. Mrs. Ruth Axe was Henry R. Wagner's secretary for many years.

2. Lewis Hanke and Manuel Giménez Fernández, *Bartolomé de las Casas, 1474-1566: Bibliografía crítica y cuerpo de materiales para el estudio de su vida, escritos, actuación y polémicas que suscitaron durante cuatro siglos,* Santiago, Chile, 1954. Dr. Hanke's other Lascasiana embrace several small volumes of lectures, including *Bartolomé de las Casas, Bookman, Scholar and Propagandist,* Philadelphia, 1952; a group of unpublished Casas writings and the first edition of a large fragment of *Del único modo;* and solid monographic introductions to this work and the *Historia de las Indias.* In addition, Casas is the central figure in Dr. Hanke's *The Spanish Struggle for Justice in the Conquest of America,* Philadelphia, 1949.

can Wagner's "Narrative and Critical Catalogue of Casas' Writings" contribute anything new? But the *Bibliografía crítica* contains, apart from Casas' own writings, an enormous amount of other sixteenth-century material and later publications; and since this is all arranged chronologically, Casas' works appear interspersed among these countless items, thus giving the reader no over-all picture of them. Wagner's "Narrative and Critical Catalogue," on the other hand, is a classic production by a master bibliographer—a complete and comprehensive study of Casas' own vast literary production, showing its relation to the events of his life, establishing important datings, inserting valuable discussions on the manuscripts and their contemporary copies. It is thus, *per se,* a significant new picture of Bartolomé de las Casas as a man of letters.

Again, Professor Manuel Giménez Fernández of the University of Seville has recently published a monumental book of 700 pages on Casas and the famous Hieronymite mission to the Indies.[3] Where, then, is the contribution of Wagner's two short chapters on this topic? The scholarly reader is in for a stunning surprise. Professor Giménez, absorbed in his own recreation of the intrigues of the era, and his institutional analysis of the instructions to the Hieronymite commissioners, has somehow forgotten to discuss the most important Casas document relating to the whole business. The truth is that Bartolomé de las Casas gave the Regent, Cardinal Ximénez de Cisneros, an elaborate written proposal that served as a basis for a large part of the reform instructions. Casas tells us so himself; and the actual document, in his own handwriting, was discovered by Juan Bautista Muñoz in the archives in the eighteenth century. Since then, however, this document has had a long career of misfortune. First printed under a defective heading that caused much confusion, it has been misdated and misattributed and generally neglected. Giménez Fernández' slip is only one of the latest: he rightly recognizes the document as Casas' "memorial of remedies" presented to the Cardinal Regent, and promises to discuss its contents in connection with the actual instructions; but later on, he wrongly identifies a variant text of the instructions themselves, copied in Casas' *Historia,* as the "anteproyecto," and discusses it instead. So in the end, Professor Giménez never gets around to discussing the crucial memorial at all.

Wagner, however, rightly makes this long-neglected memorial the cornerstone of Casas' entire early career. First he relates how Casas presented

---

3. Manuel Giménez Fernández, *Bartolomé de las Casas, I: Delegado de Cisneros para la reformación de las Indias, 1516-1517,* Seville, 1953. Cf. pp. 126-128 and 178-180, and especially note 508.

it at court, having previously prepared it in the Indies. Then, dubbing the document "the community scheme," Wagner analyzes its contents in full and critical detail. Subsequently, he gives a comparative analysis of the Hieronymite instructions, showing just how much was borrowed from Casas' memorial, what was not borrowed, and what was altered. The significance of Wagner's contribution is immediately apparent, almost tragically so. For Giménez Fernández' omission has lately led Ramón Menéndez Pidal to claim Casas had a "protagonist mania" for saying he had a major hand in the writing of the Hieronymite instructions.

Similar examples of Wagner's contributions could be multiplied.[4] But they all raise one intriguing question. How could Wagner make so many biographical discoveries overlooked by the younger "Lascasistas?"

The answer lies partly in the fact that these other eminent scholars were students of institutions and ideas, and not primarily biographers. Most of them have been interested in interpreting Casas according to a particular point of view. Dr. Hanke's main concern was the theoretical background of the reform movement, and he portrayed Casas in that light. Professor Giménez Fernández was busy rebuilding the corrupt Flemish court and the venal colonial bureaucracy, and he placed Casas in that setting. These were pro-Casas writers, as was Father Manuel María Martínez, who wanted to vindicate his fellow Dominican.[5] Notable in the opposite camp, the "debunkers," have been Professor Marcel Bataillon, so intent on the ideological tapestry of the age that he belittles Casas' roles as missionary and bishop and reformer;[6] and most recently Menéndez Pidal, who has tarnished his own

---

4.   For instance, a sterile argument has raged for four centuries about why Fray Bartolomé accepted a bishopric. Wagner, instead, re-dates Casas' antislavery memorial and then uses it in a provocative study of how the new bishop viewed his duties. Again, before finally leaving America, Bishop Casas attended a meeting of bishops in Mexico City in 1546. Wagner alone reconstructs the proceedings from the surviving documents, and in the process demolishes a patently erroneous seventeenth-century version that is still being repeated by contemporary scholars.

5.   Manuel María Martínez, O.P., *Fray Bartolomé de las Casas, el gran calumniado*, Madrid, 1955, and *Fray Bartolomé de las Casas, padre de América; estudio biográfico-crítico*, Madrid, 1958. Sor María Rosa Miranda's oversize popular biography is also pro-Casas; and scholarly contributions, on the pro-side, have been made among others by Father Benno M. Biermann, diligent searcher for Casas manuscripts, the noted paleographer Agustín Millares Carlo, and Juan Friede, a penetrating student of the "movimiento indigenista."

6.   Marcel Bataillon's thoughtful *Etudes sur Bartolomé de las Casas*, Paris, 1965, add many new details despite somewhat negative views. So do Angel Losada's edition of Casas' *De Thesauris* and study of Casas' adversary, Sepúlveda.

great reputation by an attack on Casas as a paranoiac.[7] Serving as a bridge between the two groups, Juan Pérez de Tudela Bueso has made a valuable summary of much of this interpretative work, and added expositions of his own.[8]

Vis-à-vis all this interpretation, the Wagner *Life and Writings of Casas* is a dramatic contrast. The essential quality of Wagner's scholarship, in history or biography or bibliography, was always a stubborn insistence on his own original study of primary sources.[9] So he gives us here a meticulous exposition of facts, as he himself extracted them from reading all of Casas' writings and the documents about him. This rich material is neither buried in notes to bolster a thesis, nor quoted in extenso to fill up text. Rather, it is spread before us by a skilled miner who knew how to extract precious metal from his ore.

With Henry R. Wagner, the intensive reading of a document was an intricate and loving ritual. All its aspects fascinated him: the document's provenance, who had owned it, how it had changed hands in various sales; the date, and if that was lacking, a tireless search for internal and external evidence to establish it; the writer's identity and life and background; the circumstances under which the document was written and its purpose; and finally an analysis of the contents and his own evaluation and comment. It was his lifelong habit to read sources, in depth, and record all the facts as

---

7. Ramón Menéndez Pidal, *El padre Las Casas, su doble personalidad,* Madrid, 1963. Based on no original study of sources, this work contains both ancient and modern anti-Casas opinion and studies. Menéndez Pidal suffers from the familiar madness that afflicts some patriotic Spaniards at the mere mention of Casas' name; he fails to realize that most colonial powers have produced a Black Legend, but Spain produced a humanitarian, Bartolomé de las Casas, who championed the victims of colonialism.

8. See the critical résumés, *passim,* in Juan Pérez de Tudela Bueso's informative monograph, "Significado histórico de la vida y escritos del Padre Las Casas," printed as the prologue to the latest edition of Casas' *Obras,* Biblioteca de Autores Españoles, XCV (Madrid, 1957), ix-clxxxviii.

9. Wagner ignored the work of other scholars to an absolute fault. If there is a nearly perfect reference work, it is the Marqués de Foronda's *Estancias y viajes del Emperador Carlos V*—the immense folio volume that documents with full quotations exactly where Charles was on every day of his life (all but the "lost two weeks" finally "found" by Alice B. Gould). Yet Wagner, when he wished to date certain events of Casas' life by means of Charles's movements, would not look them up in Foronda's masterpiece. Instead, he himself worked out the data he needed from the original sources. This unflinching method had one amusing consequence. Though the whole world says "Las Casas," Wagner alone stubbornly said "Casas," that being the name Fray Bartolomé called himself; I have, of course, followed Wagner's usage.

he found them, and only then to venture an opinion afterwards—an approach ideally suited to this final magnum opus.

For Wagner's unique method of working from the documents outward has produced a refreshing study of Bartolomé de las Casas, a book completely unbiased and free from preconceptions, either pro or con. More accurately, Wagner's work is free from every preconception save one, which he had derived from his own study of the material. He felt strongly that Casas' life and writings were inseparable; you simply could not discuss one without the other.

So Wagner has given us the first full-scale narrative *Life and Writings*, with all of Casas' works presented in the context in which he wrote them— a narrative that should be read from start to finish for its cumulative effect. This presentation changes the whole story. Not since Fray Antonio de Remesal first wrote the full life of Casas in a seventeenth-century chronicle have its main factual outlines been so drastically altered. From Remesal's time to ours there have been countless small emendations and isolated contributions, and the same old major distortion—the overblown early period, the foreshortened ending. Wagner, instead, spreads out Casas' life as it happened, with the proportions guided by the importance of the events, and what a different view we get. Casas' early reform try, always given too much space ever since he himself recounted it at such length, is told briskly but with new critical acumen—a welcome contrast to Professor Giménez Fernàndez' diffuse two thousand pages.[10] Next, we witness the events of Casas' climactic second effort, which resulted in the famous New Laws; some Lascasistas have tried to minimize Fray Bartolomé's role, but Wagner convincingly lays out the contemporary evidence. And finally, for the first time in any biography, we see that remarkable last phase of Casas' career, with the writings discussed alongside the events. "Viejo y acabado," Casas returns to court, engages in the great disputation with the humanist Sepúlveda, and then settles down for another decade and a half to do some of his most important work; the famous printed tracts, the *History of the Indies*, the perpetuity fight, the farewell treatises—they are all here in detail in these amazing later years. I particularly like the picture of Casas at the age of

---

10. Casas' own unfinished *Historia de las Indias* devoted hundreds of pages to his first reform efforts, much of this being copied by Herrera and other chroniclers. Quantities of documents on the same episodes were located by Muñoz, and verified and printed by later researchers. Now all this material, plus a still larger mass of background data, has been incorporated in the text of Giménez Fernández' lengthy study cited in note 3 above, and in his *Bartolomé de las Casas, II: Capellán de S. M. Carlos I, poblador de Cumaná, 1517-1523*, Seville, 1960—1,354 pages.

ninety, surrounded by his "last collaborators." That is quite new, and it reminds me vividly that Wagner himself was nearing ninety when he finished this work.

Which brings me to the final and personal reason why Wagner was able to give us Casas-in-full, while the younger Lascasistas have been like the blind men describing the elephant. Every biographer, even the most objective, will tend to put something of himself into his subject. And this book is, above all, Wagner's own highly original picture of Bartolomé de las Casas—a man at first a bit commercial and ambitious, not really a missionary, but singleminded and wonderfully persevering in devotion to his life's work, a writer of impressive proportions, completing his *History of the Indies* around the age of eighty-seven and speaking posthumously in his great cause. Do I detect a resemblance to the late Henry R. Wagner?

—HELEN RAND PARISH

FOREWORD
MY ORIGINAL PLAN CHANGES

W<small>HY HAVE</small> I <small>UNDERTAKEN</small> the first wholly new biography of Bartolomé de las Casas since the seventeenth century? This was not my original intention. But I found that a major distortion had grown up around him these three hundred years—a mounting interest in his prolific writings, and a corresponding neglect of his colossal career.

It is a curious fact that Casas, a great man of action in his own times, has been chiefly remembered by succeeding generations as a sensational man of letters. For a prolonged period after his death, the *Very Brief Account of the Destruction of the Indies* was what made him famous, or notorious, throughout the world. Translated into the main European languages and illustrated with lurid woodcuts, the *Brevissima relación* was a phenomenal *succès de scandale* in the late sixteenth century and particularly throughout the seventeenth, when anti-Spanish feelings ran high. Another prolonged scandal, if it may be called that, concerned the manuscript of his monumental *Historia de las Indias,* which was first plagiarized extensively by Antonio de Herrera and then withheld from public view for more than three centuries. Conversely, after the French Revolution of the eighteenth century, radical ideas on liberty became the rage and Casas' polemical works began to enjoy a new vogue.

In the nineteenth century, this worldwide craze for Casas' writings extended even to his manuscripts. Two important ones were found in the library of the Kings of France; and in 1822 a pro-Napoleon Spaniard, Juan Antonio Llorente, featured them in a new collection of Casas' miscellaneous works, freely rendered in Spanish and French. In 1854 the Vermonter Henry Stevens printed in London four separates of miscellaneous pieces by Casas that he had picked up in Spain. In 1866 the Mexican scholar Joaquín García Icazbalceta incorporated in the second volume of his document collection a group of Casas' writings transcribed for him in Paris. Spain was not to be outdone. In 1867, volume VII of the official collection of *"inedited documents"* from the Archives of the Indies was mainly devoted to Casas and included a number of hitherto unpublished papers by him. Still more were printed in 1879, by Antonio María Fabié, in the volume of appendices to his life of Casas commissioned by the Real Academia.[1]

During this same period the older editions of Casas' short works became a great desiderata of collectors, especially in the United States. American collecting started early—Thomas Jefferson had in his library one original printing and several translations of tracts by Bartolomé de las Casas. Impetus was given the demand by Sabin's *Dictionary of Books Relating to America*, which appeared in 1870 and contained a list of Casas' works. Thomas W. Field's *Essay Towards an Indian Bibliography* came out in New York in 1873 and further whetted the appetite of collectors. They bought mainly the translations of Casas' tracts—some sixty of these, especially the *Brevissima*, had been issued in foreign languages, mostly as propaganda in Holland and England, apart from numerous Spanish reprints. Such translations now cumber the shelves of many libraries in this country, though fortunately they are small volumes and occupy little space. The choicest item, to be sure, was the original set of Casas' eight tracts which he himself had printed in Seville in 1552-1553. A few complete sets will be found in our leading libraries, but they were hard to get and expensive when located.[2]

At the crest of this wave, Casas' two most important writings were at long last brought to light. His *Historia de las Indias* was published in five volumes by the Real Academia in 1875-1876, with a portion of his *Apologética Historia* in Volume V. The complete *Apologética* was finally printed in 1909 by Serrano y Sanz, who followed it in 1918 with a collection of documents from Casas' early career.

Curiously, all this resurgence of interest and these new publications did not lead to any drastic revision in Casas' biography. Modern writers ignored the fresh documents, avoided critical study, and clung to precon-

---

1. See the "List of Locations and Abbreviations" at the close of my Catalogue, for an index locating Casas' writings in these and other publications, as well as in manuscript repositories. On the Llorente episode, and its relation to the Negro slavery controversy, see my Conclusion, note 7.

2. Cf., in addition to Sabin and Field, the Catalogues of the Church Collection now in the Huntington Library, and of the John Carter Brown Library in Brown University. Descriptions of the tracts will also be found in José Toribio Medina's *Biblioteca Hispano-americana (1493-1810)*, I and II, Santiago de Chile, 1898.

In my Catalogue, I am concerned primarily with the date and circumstances of composition, and the differences in Casas' original texts and the texts as he printed them. His eight tracts will be found indexed in my preliminary remarks to "V. Polemicist at Court, 1548-1552."

ceived positions, pro- or anti-Casas. As a result, the outlines of his life remained more or less as they had been fixed by his first biographer, Fray Antonio de Remesal, whose life of Casas was interspersed in a chronicle published in 1619.

Remesal went to Guatemala in 1613 and worked diligently in the archives of the audiencia and of the Dominican convents in that country and in Chiapa; he also examined Casas' manuscript works then preserved in Valladolid and in New Spain. For its time, his book was remarkably well documented. Most of the important statements were backed up by references to documents, and a great many of these were quoted in full. But Remesal had no access to government archives in Spain and he found firsthand narratives for only two parts of Casas' life, his early career and his troubles as a bishop. The result was, naturally, a badly distorted and at times quite mistaken story. Casas' early reform try was exaggerated out of proportion to the rest of his life, his extremely important later years were hardly treated at all, and a number of areas were pieced together with wildly wrong guesses. Nonetheless, Remesal's was a signal achievement, and for centuries it remained the basis of all subsequent biographies.[3] The surprising thing is that his over-all distortion and specific flaws persisted long after the appearance of material sufficient to correct them.

And I must confess that I myself did not set out to revise the story of Casas's life, or even to write his biography at all. As a collector and bibliographer, my original interest was in his writings. Many of the miscellaneous

---

3. Remesal's biography is woven into his voluminous *Historia de la Provincia de S. Vicente de Chyapa y Guatemala de la Orden de ñro glorioso padre Sancto Domingo,* Madrid, 1619. (See "List of Abbreviations" for the retitled modern edition.) Since this work is arranged chronologically, Casas' story is sometimes interrupted by other events, but it is all there, as far as Remesal's information goes. The chronicler's chief source for the early career is Casas' own manuscript *Historia,* libs. I and II, plus Herrera's version of Casas' lib. III. For the travails of the Bishop of Chiapa, Remesal had the manuscript work of Fray Tomás de la Torre, first official historiographer of the Chiapa Dominicans. Remesal's narrative is inaccurate for Casas' "blank" years as a friar, since he misconstrued and misattributed a number of documents.

Around 1721-1722, Fray Francisco Ximénez wrote another history of the same Province. His lib. II, from the conquest to 1550, contributes the verbatim text of the Torre diary, and thus serves as a supplement to Remesal's magnum opus. Ximénez promised his own life of Casas, and presumably included it in his lib. III, 1550-1600, but this alone of his seven "libros" is now missing. (See the "Abbreviations" for a modern edition of Fray Francisco's chronicle.)

Finally, it should be noted that Remesal was *not* Casas' first biographer. Fray Agustín Dávila Padilla's *Historia de la fundación y discurso de la Provincia de*

ones were undated and had not been catalogued properly, and I began to search his *Historia* and *Apologética* and other books for clues. I was soon embarked on a thorough study of all Casas' writings, and though I do not claim to have read every word he ever wrote, I have very nearly done so. The more I studied, the more I came to realize that *Casas' life and writings were really inseparable*. I found that a great many of his occasional pieces and even his larger works could not really be understood without a thorough knowledge of the circumstances in which he wrote them. Conversely, his writings seemed to me to shed much light on the events of his life, which had hitherto passed unnoticed. A striking example is the memorial I have named his "community scheme"—a key production of his early career, and recognized as such two centuries ago, yet completely ignored by all his biographers. Indeed, I was struck by the fact that modern writers on Casas used secondary sources and continued to copy old errors as if they had not been exposed.

There was, I saw, a need for a wholly fresh biography of Bartolomé de las Casas—a documented and critical study of his life and writings, utilizing all the materials now available. These would include the masses of Casas documents published in the nineteenth-century craze but not used in his life, the new twentieth-century finds, many related documents (such as those from New Spain) not previously connected with him, and even a number of sixteenth- and seventeenth century chronicles not employed properly, in my estimation. But above all, I hoped to use his own writings to illustrate his biography in a way never attempted before.

In undertaking such a study, I realized that I was tackling what was supposed to be a controversial subject. But competent scholars had already written about the encomienda which Casas attacked so long—that much-disputed system of exploration, whereby the Indians of conquered regions were

---

Santiago de México de la Orden de Predicadores, Madrid, 1596, contained a "Vida de F. Bartolome de las Casas ò Casaus, Obispo de Chiapa," caps. 97-107. Writing before 1592, this Mexican Dominican used a manuscript history by Fray Andrés de Moguer, amplified by Fray Domingo de la Anunciación and Fray Vicente de las Casas, the latter a close friend of Fray Bartolomé's and probably a relative. Possibly, too, Dávilla Padilla was in Spain before finishing his work, but his harvest of information on Casas was scanty and he drew his story mainly from the printed tracts. This sketch was translated into Italian by Fray Michele Pio, who published it in Pavia in 1613, with accounts of other illustrious men; a reprint, the first separate life of Casas, appeared in Antipoli [Antibes] in 1621. I have examined a copy of this extremely rare pamphlet in the Huntington Library, and it follows Dávila Padilla's text closely.

parceled out by royal grant to individual Spaniards, and compelled to render them forced labor in their fields and in the mines—and I had no desire to enlarge on these authorities. Furthermore, most of the past controversies about Casas struck me as unfounded and meaningless today, and it seemed to me quite unnecessary to defend Casas, either.

Juan Bautista Muñoz, the tireless researcher and organizer of the Archives of the Indies, felt that the discovery and conquest and administration of the New World was an epic so vast that Spain needed no defense, just the truth. That has been my position on Casas. His was a life so large as to defy the imagination. It spanned nearly a century—his father coming to the Antilles on Columbus' second voyage, he himself arriving not long afterward, then seeing Ferdinand the Catholic on his deathbed, becoming an adviser to Cardinal Ximénez and Charles and Philip, serving as instigator of the New Laws and Bishop of Chiapa, and working for "fifty mortal years" in the defense of the Indians. At the same time, he was a prolific and sensational writer, and a most important historian besides. I felt that here was a veritable Sphinx buried in the sands of legend, controversy, and scholarly neglect for centuries. So I set out patiently, grain by grain of sand, simply to uncover the full outline of this tremendous figure and to see what I would find.

—HENRY R. WAGNER

EARLY YEARS OF CASAS

ANCESTRY AND FAMILY

Bartolomé de las Casas was born, according to his biographers, in Seville in 1474. For the date there are no documents, either baptismal certificate or firsthand record. But about the place Casas himself remarked, in an unpublished dedication to Philip II, that he had been born in Seville and was descended from one of the ancient Christians who settled in that town.[1]

This simple fact, apparently well known in his lifetime, plus the way he had his name printed as "Casas or Casaus" on his tracts, has led to considerable genealogical investigation. Not all of it is convincing or even correct. His first biographer, Remesal, merely identified the family as French, noble, originally called Casaus, and settling in Seville in St. Ferdinand's reign [1217-1252].[2] But later genealogists and annalists have grafted Bartolomé de las Casas gratuitously onto various aristocratic family trees.[3] Most recently, MacNutt was told by the Royal College of Heralds in Madrid that Bartolomé was the grandson of Alonso de las Casas, an alderman of Seville in 1409, whose children were Guillén, Isabel, Juan, Pedro, and Francisco. The filiation is wrong,[4] though several of these forenames did run

---

1. Casas to Philip, January 1564, presenting his last treatise, *Doce dudas*, JCBL MS, fol. 135 verso. See my Catalogue of Casas' writings, no. 74, for a description of this manuscript.

2. Remesal, I, 95.

3. See Fabié, *Vida y escritos de Casas*, I, 10-12 and app. I. These genealogical documents seem far afield, since by Casas' time the lineal descendants of the first settlers noted by Remesal should have numbered thousands.

4. MacNutt, *Bartholomew de las Casas*, 3-4, but this is erroneous, as Pedro is described as Dean of Seville and Francisco as Casas' father.

in his immediate family. Casas himself in his *Historia de las Indias*, tells of his father Pedro and his uncle Francisco; legal documents show he had a nephew Francisco and a sister Isabel; and there are a couple of Guilléns worth noting. One Guillén de las Casas was a Seville regidor in 1418, and some evidence suggests that a man of this name might possibly have been Bartolomé's great-uncle.

At least, that is the inference I draw from the lengthy account of the title to Canary Islands which Casas inserts in book I of his *Historia*. Beginning with the discovery by the Frenchman Betancour, he traces the descent of this involved title and the Portuguese troubles about it, transcribing several relevant letters by Juan II of Spain (d. 1454), which "came into my hands." Then he tells how a Castilian gentleman, Fernán Perraza, went to Portugal and demanded possession of these islands, having bought them from a Seville citizen named Guillén de las Casas who had meantime acquired the rights. Finally, two islands were inherited by the present Perraza, who was made Count of Gomera, "and I was the first to give him the news thereof." Casas explains his long digression by stating there was no Spanish or Latin version available. But the space and attention he devotes to this involved title leads me to suspect that the Sevillian Guillén was a distant relative.[5]

Concerning his father, Pedro de las Casas, and some other connections, we have bits of information from the Notarial Archives of Seville. The five published volumes of the *Catálogo de fondos americanos* give entries for a number of people with the Casas surname: Bartolomé, Diego, Fernando, Pedro, and one Casaus, Guillén. This Pedro definitely is the right one. For on February 13, 1512, a man issued a power of attorney to collect from his father-in-law, Pedro, the still-unpaid dowry of his deceased wife; and a similar document of February 25, 1525, makes the positive identification. The merchant Pedro de las Casas was the father of Bartolomé de las Casas; his daughter Isabel de Sosa (Bartolomé's sister) married Cristóbal Ferrandes, a Seville carpenter; they had a son, Francisco, who had also died. As dowry, Pedro gave his son-in-law some houses in the Corral de

---

5. Cf. *Historia de las Indias*, lib. I, caps. 17-21. Perhaps Casas retained some of these records. For in *Documentos inéditos de Indias*, XXXVIII, 26-30, is printed a cedula of June 23, 1433, confirming to one *Guillén de Casaus* a grant of the Canaries that had been made to his father Alonso on August 29, 1420. Incidentally, this seems further evidence that the name was originally Casaus. Gómara, in his long account of these islands makes no mention of this man. In 1569 another Guillén de Casaus (any relation?) was governor of Yucatán.

Moradores, in Seville's San Lorenzo ward; after Isabel's death, Ferrandes tried to collect the tax on them as well as some small sums he had loaned Bartolomé.[6]

In addition, I have determined that Casas did have another sister. But we can barely glean who she was from the correspondence of others with him in his latter years. On March 9, 1549, Fray Luis Cáncer wrote from Seville—on the eve of setting out for New Spain and the fatal attempt to convert the Florida Indians—and advised the aging Bishop Casas: "I received the account of Your Reverence's sister. I put it with the other."[7] At first reading this sounds as if the sister were in New Spain; but Cáncer was leaving that day to go downstream, and I think it more likely that she lived in San Lúcar at the river's mouth. She was, I believe, the Doña María Díaz mentioned as "still in San Lúcar" by a 1560 correspondent, Fuentes Manrique.[8] For in yet another Seville missive of this same period, Fray Vicente de las Casas, apparently a relative himself, sent along letters of "la señora doña María."[9]

Beyond these few relatives, we know little about Casas' family. He himself seldom refers to them, only once (if I remember rightly), saying that he stayed at their house in Seville. Scant as it is, this familial and genealogical data fits well with his own assertions about a father named Pedro, a Seville birthplace, an ancestry of "ancient Christians." But Remesal's claim of nobility seems overemphasized. And though MacNutt states the family had the right to use the title "don," that seems most improbable. In the early fifteenth century, only the highest nobles carried this indication of rank, and nowhere can I find that Bartolomé was so addressed, nor indeed that he ever used the "don" till his elevation to a bishopric. On the contrary, Casas' kin were apparently ordinary people, and he himself merely said he came from "good old stock."

---

6. *Fondos americanos*, IV, no. 126, and V, no. 541. I have called the carpenter "Cristóbal Ferrandes" as in the earlier document; the later transcription ("Cristóbal Rodríguez") is apparently an error, since the child is given there as "Francisco Fernández."

7. *DII*, VII, 200.

8. *DII*, VII, 216.

9. *DII*, VII, 210-211. Though it bears no year, this letter was apparently written c. 1550, since a postscript refers to the *Doctrina* sent by Fray Domingo de la Anunciacíon; this was probably one published in Mexico in 1548 or 1550. From Fray Vicente's general tone, and his reference to Casas' plan for his own interment, I gather that he was a relative.

Settler in Española and Cuba

The family's real distinction was that they were among the early settlers of the New World. Pedro de las Casas, the merchant father, went out on Columbus' second expedition with the very first colonists—to Española, *la isla española,* the Spanish Isle, as the island of Haiti was then called. He came back to Spain in 1498, then returned to Española and evidently made his home there. Pedro's soldier brother, Francisco de Peñalosa, also went on Columbus' second voyage; he too returned to Europe, but died soon afterwards fighting the Moors in Africa. Casas gives us these brief details in the *Historia.*[10]

It is widely believed that at this time young Bartolomé was a student at Salamanca, and received the degree of Licentiate in law within a few years. I have been quite unable to substantiate this, and have found no mention by Casas himself of any stay in Salamanca. No doubt he had a university education, as his later erudition testifies. But whether he studied Roman or canon law, or another course, and where and when he may have been graduated, is up to some future investigator of academic records to discover. Indeed, there is a question as to whether he was a licentiate at all.[11]

Anyway, his father had probably acquired some property on Española during his first stay there, because Bartolomé says he himself went out to the island in 1502 with Nicolás de Ovando, the knight commander. The

---

10. *Hist.,* I, 498, and II, 340.

11. I have not found sufficient evidence to support the oft-repeated assertion about Casas' education. It apparently rests on two statements: (1) Remesal, writing in 1619, asserts (I, 95) that Casas studied law at Salamanca and graduated as a licentiate. Though a much younger man, Remesal does have the qualifications of a reliable witness. He himself studied at the College of San Esteban at Salamanca, where he took the habit in the Dominican convent; and he certainly had relations with the monastery of San Gregorio in Valladolid, where Casas spent his latter years. (2) Casas himself (*Hist.,* II, 474) refers to the Indian slave that his father brought from Española for him in 1498, and simply says that this slave was with him for a few days in Castile. From this remark, plus Remesal's it has been inferred that Casas was then studying at Salamanca and took the degree of licentiate in law at that time.

But nowhere in Casas' writings have I found any statement that he was a licentiate or that he had studied in Salamanca. If he were a licentiate in 1510, he had a golden opportunity to assert it in writing of himself; instead, he said merely that he was a cleric and celebrated his new mass at that time (*Hist.,* III, 278). Afterwards, he always alluded to himself as a cleric until he became a friar.

Yet it is evident from Oviedo's *Historia general y natural de las Indias* of 1535 that Casas did call himself a licentiate. Oviedo refers to him as "licentiate" and continues to do so even after Casas entered the Dominican Order. (Gómara at first calls

Historia de las Indias relates many incidents that took place in Española during the following ten years, but Casas speaks only incidentally of himself and his activities.[12] In 1503 he participated in the campaign on the east end of Española, and at different times he was in several Indian hunting expeditions. I find no mention of his being engaged in gold mining at this period. Apparently he was an agriculturist, for he repeatedly refers to himself in such a role. He certainly had Indians working under him, and undoubtedly had some sort of encomienda, a fact he afterwards admitted with shame. But details on his life as a planter are scant and confused. For instance, a curious error appears in the *Apologética* passage about the region of his estates; speaking of the city of Concepción and the nearby Vega he says that "it was so fertile that in a matter of two leagues I had crops of the bread of the country which were worth each year more than 100,000 castellanos." Either "I had" is an error for "there was" or 100,000 castellanos is an error for 100,000 maravedis, more likely the latter.[13]

In 1510 he was apparently ordained a priest, for he tells of celebrating his new mass that year. In September, Fray Pedro de Córdoba had come out from Spain with a few Dominicans to found a convent in Española. This friar went to La Vega about November and preached a sermon which Casas heard with great devotion; and it was "in these same days" that a priest named Bartolomé de las Casas sang the first new mass in the Indies.[14] His

---

him a licentiate but later drops the title; cf. *Historia*, 205.) The interesting thing is that Oviedo, though employing the term, seems to cast doubts on Casas' right to use the title. Of course, Oviedo had his clashes with Casas, but his testimony here is suggestive. Could it be that Casas had studied law a while without taking a degree? Perhaps, if he did receive the distinction, it was after 1519 when Oviedo knew him at court, and not earlier as has been generally assumed; for in some documents of 1518-1519, Casas is called bachelor [of laws]. See *DII*, VII, 90, note, citing vol. LXXVI [old numbering] of the Muñoz Collection.

Finally, Dávila Padilla, writing in 1592, says that Casas studied canon law, having determined to become an ecclesiastic; Dávila makes no mention of Salamanca, leaving us to infer that these studies were at Seville. Nor does he call him a licentiate or speak of any such degree, referring to him simply as "fray." Certainly Casas knew canon law, as his later knowledge of the decretals testifies. But his repeated references to his long study of "derecho" in connection with the rights of the Indians, from his 1514 conversion onward, indicate extensive reading of legal authorities and not necessarily academic studies. See *Hist.*, IV, 254, and Catalogue, nos. 43 and 70.

12. See *Hist.*, lib. II: cap. 3, his arrival; caps. 15-18, the second Higuey campaign; cap. 9, his receiving as a slave one of the fugitives of the Anacaona massacre.

13. *Apologética*, 24.

14. *Hist.*, lib. II, cap. 54.

implied ordination at this time has puzzled scholars, since there were then no bishops in America. But no doubt he was ordained by Fray Pedro, who had probably brought faculties from the Pope to perform such a cere- mony. Casas says that everybody was then in La Vega as it was smelting time, and since there were no gold coins in circulation they made castellanos and ducats out of gold that was then being melted. A quantity of these, as well as the silver reals then in use, were presented to the newly ordained priest who gave most of them to his godfather (whoever he was). As a cleric, Casas continued to labor in La Vega for the following year and a half, the balance of his stay on the island.

Sometime in the early part of 1512—he does not give the exact time— Casas joined Diego Velásquez in the conquest of Cuba. This caballero's previous Española exploits are chronicled in the *Historia*; they had not been exactly on the divine side, but Casas evidently had a good opinion of him, and as far as I can recall always spoke well of him. In "Fernandina," Velas- quez' first task was to pacify a number of Indians who had fled across from the western province of Española to the northeast tip of Cuba. So he estab- lished his first settlement nearby at Baracoa, and soon subdued the rebels by capturing and burning their chief Hatuey. Casas was not present, but learned the story afterwards from a Franciscan friar who had offered baptism to the condemned chieftain—only to have Hatuey decline heaven because the Spaniards would be there.[15]

Soon Velásquez expanded his staff; he had the reinforcement of Cap- tain Narváez from Jamaica, and he sent for Casas, who came at once, simply for friendship's sake. For the next two years, the priest accompanied Narváez on the westward march across Cuba. The ill-armed Cuban natives could do nothing against the invading Spanish force; besides, Casas assures us that they were a kind, hospitable, and peaceful people. Only one massacre oc- curred near the center of the island, the slaughter of hundreds of Indians started by a crazed Spaniard; Casas was a horrified eyewitness. During most of this march of conquest, Velásquez remained in Baracoa (where the inci- dent took place of which Cortés was the unlucky victim, as related in my *Rise of Fernando Cortés*). Early in 1513 Velásquez married María de Cuellar, who died shortly; then late in the year he too set out westward, joining forces with the triumphant Narváez at Xagua, the modern Cien- fuegos, on the south shore of the island.

---

15. *Hist.*, lib. III, cap. 25, the Hatuey story.

Now followed the founding of towns: Trinidad, ten leagues to the east, Espíritu Santo, farther inland, others along the north coast. In each settlement land and Indians were distributed to the expeditionaries.[16]

Casas, too, received his share. A great friend of his, Pablo de la Rentería, had come with the governor to the rendezvous; and Velásquez gave the two men a "good, big" encomienda on the nearby Ariamo River, the richest in gold yet discovered. Of the partners, Rentería was given to prayer and eschewed practical matters; so it devolved on Casas to work the Indians, planting crops and washing the sands for gold. In fact, he later acknowledged that he took more care of this than of teaching them the faith, though he did feed them well and treat them kindly and commiserate with them.[17]

But though he was an encomendero as formerly, Casas' views were suffering a change. It is impossible to make out just what was going through his mind at this period, since the *Historia* is not in the form of a diary but was written many years later as a chronicle of events. Yet he does tell us some of the scenes that must have affected him. In traveling about Cuba he would go into the native villages, asking how the Indians were, and always getting the same answer, "Hungry, hungry, hungry!" All the able-bodied men were off working at the gold mines, and those he found would be hardly able to stand on their feet. The women with younger babies had so little to eat that their milk dried up and their infants died. In this way, Casas says, seven thousand children died in three months; and all these facts, "a man of credit" (himself) investigated and [later] wrote to the King.[18]

Insensibility was not one of Casas' weaknesses, and the horrible sights he witnessed daily must have been preying on his mind. So I gather that the accumulation of outrages committed by the Spaniards was slowly arousing his conscience to the fact that the encomienda was wrong and he himself was a sinner against the Indians. It was not an original idea; he himself had rejected it some years before.

THE BURGOS DISCUSSIONS

The whole system of holding Indians had already been denounced by reformers. Back in Española the Dominicans, headed by that selfsame Pedro

---

16. *Hist.*, lib. III, cap. 26, Casas' arrival; caps 29-31, the westward march; cap. 32, the towns.

17. *Hist.*, IV, 38. He says he was then as blind as his Spanish parishioners to the prime duty of converting the Indians.

18. *Hist.*, IV, 251. For the identification of this memorial, see Catalogue, no. 2.

de Córdoba, had raised a great clamor against the practice and set in motion a train of events that was ultimately to influence Casas' career.

On December 20, 1511, Fray Antonio Montesino had preached a violent sermon in Santo Domingo against the cruelties of the Spaniards and their mistreatment of the Indians. This so alarmed the colonists that they sent to Spain in 1512 a Franciscan, Alonso del Espinal, to offset the preacher's doctrine. For their part, the Dominicans dispatched Fray Antonio, and both friars appeared before Ferdinand. Meantime, the King had summoned the Dominican provincial to complain about these sermons against the royal service, and the provincial had written Fray Pedro and the others, warning them to take care what they said and retract their words if advisable —this is Casas' version.[19] The reproof by Provincial Alfonso de Loaysa is printed in Serrano's *Orígenes,* unfortunately with no date, but in it Loaysa says the Council's decision to recall the Indies Dominicans was told him on March 16, obviously 1512. Serrano asserts that the sermons had denied the right of Spain to conquer the Indies; this is not mentioned in the letter or the *Historia.*[20] But the admonition must have been communicated to Fray Antonio when he reached court.

Undaunted, Montesino gave the King such a shocking account of conditions that Ferdinand immediately called a junta to consider the matter. Casas is our chief source for its deliberations. Seven of the members were jurists, Juan Rodríguez de Fonseca, Hernando de Vega, Licentiate Luis Zapata, Licentiate Santiago, Doctor Palacios Rubios, Licentiate Mújica, Licentiate Sosa; three others were theologians, the Dominicans Fray Tomás Durán and Master Fray Pedro de Covarrubias, and a cleric named Licentiate Gregorio; also, after several rebuffs, Montesino succeeded in having Fray Matías de Paz included in the group. This body finally formulated seven conclusions to the following effect:

1. The Indians are free.
2. They should be instructed in the faith with all possible diligence.
3. The Indians can be obliged to work, but in such a manner as not to impede their religious instruction and to be useful to themselves, the republic, and the King; and this is by reason of the King's lordship and the service due him to maintain them in the faith and in justice.
4. This labor should be such as they can stand, with time to rest every day and all through the year at convenient times.

---

19. *Hist.,* III, 361-377.

20. Cf. Serrano y Sanz, *Orígenes,* 349. This scholar's documents are superior to his opinions—see *infra,* chapter II, note 10.

5. They should have houses and property of their own, such as seem fit to those who govern them now and henceforward, and they should be allowed time to farm and keep their property in their own manner.
6. It should be provided for them always to have contact with the settlers, so that they may be better and more rapidly instructed in the holy faith.
7. They should be given suitable wages, not in money but in clothing and other things for their houses.[21]

While these conclusions said nothing specifically about encomiendas, the system was clearly implied throughout. On further reflection, Fray Matías de Paz composed in fifteen days a Latin treatise assailing the idea of Indian servitude. He denied the right to exact service from the natives, who should be governed as free people, and claimed that since encomiendas were despotic the Spaniards were bound to render full restitution of all they had acquired in this way. This was the genesis of Casas' own insistence on restitution, a doctrine to which he would later devote much attention.[22]

But Fray Matías was the lone dissident voice. Written opinions supporting servitude were given the King by two other members of the junta: Licenciate Gregorio, and particularly Fray Bernardo de Mesa, a Dominican who did not belong to the school of Montesino or Córdoba but took a "realistic" stand. Mesa's seven propositions generally echoed the junta's conclusions: the Indians were liable to personal services as vassals of the King; they must be converted, not worked too hard, given houses and property, etc. But in some points he held further that the natives had to serve because of their incapacity:

2. The Indians are not slaves by war, purchase, or birth. The only reason for [their] servitude is a natural lack of understanding and capacity and perseverance in the faith and good customs, and perchance the nature of the country (there are some lands which the aspect of the heavens makes servile). They cannot be called slaves, but for their own sake must be ruled in some sort of servitude.

---

21. *Hist.,* III, 381-382, and 388-389. Casas was not certain whether Vega and Mújica participated, or whether he had omitted anyone.

22. *Hist.,* III, 390. Yet in his remarks on Fray Matías' views, Casas pointed out the impossibility of belated restitution: "Which of them, even if the King aided him with his property, could restore the damage which the innumerable people who were on this island received from the Spaniards—since, on account of [Spanish] greed, they have all perished on account of their labors and bitter and inhuman treatment, in the mines and other pestilential occupations?"

The treatise has finally been published: Matías de Paz, "De dominio regum Hispaniae super Indos," edited by Vicente Beltrán de Heredia, *Archivum Fratrum Praedicatorum,* III (1933), 133-181.

4-5. The Indians were given to the King for their own good, and idleness is their worst possible vice (and all others flow from it). So the King should with great care order them occupied in spiritual and corporal exercises, and to this end he may apportion them among the faithful of good conscience and customs.[23]

In expounding his stand, Fray Bernardo stressed this notion of depravity: The natives must be treated kindly as long as this did not interfere with their conversion, but absolute liberty was bad for them on account of their evil intentions. These people were able to receive the faith and had virtue enough for salvation, yet they had so little natural inclination to it and such inconstancy (as islanders subject to lunar influence) that it was essential to keep them in some form of servitude.[24]

Even stronger views on Indian incapacity were then being advanced at court by agents of the colonies. At this time Francisco de Garay, Juan Ponce de León, and Pedro García de Carrión, the latter a merchant, were representatives of the settlers to ask for encomiendas in perpetuity or at least for three lives. These men, or some of them, were the first to allege that the Indians were not able to rule themselves and needed tutors, and even that the natives were incapable of receiving the faith and were like beasts.[25] It was from such informants—rather than from Montesino—that Mesa and Gregorio and the other members of the junta took their opinions on the American aborigines.

So it was not surprising that the junta's conclusions upholding servitude were finally translated in the first royal confirmation of the encomienda system—the Laws of Burgos, promulgated on December 27, 1512.[26] These laws,

---

23. Hist., III, 392.

24. Hist. III, 406. Understandably, in lib. III, caps. 10 and 11, Casas makes some rather sharp comments about Mesa's propositions. The good father, he says, looked on the Indians as savages to be divided up like cattle; and when he met him afterwards, he should have asked him about parceling out the English, Sicilians, and other islanders!

25. Hist., III, 386-387. Casas says this opinion still persisted in 1559, the year he was writing.

26. See Hist., lib. III, caps.13-16, Casas' summary and discussion of these laws. For their actual text, see Rafael Altamira's transcript, Revista de Historia de América, 1938, no. 4, 22-25. Previously there had been only tacit approval of forced Indian labor, as in the secret instructions and cedula to Ovando, March 29 and December 20, 1503. (DII, XXXI, 174-179, 209-212.) Casas alleged the encomienda system had been contrary to the expressed wish of Queen Isabella in the codicil of her will; it is true that she made no mention of such a system, but Columbus had first instituted forced labor.

plus a Clarification added the following year through the personal efforts of Fray Pedro de Córdoba, did contain regulatory provisions. And in 1514, Rodrigo de Alburquerque was sent to Española to allot the Indians to individuals under the new ordinances, giving to each encomendero a paper stating that his charges were to be taught the holy Catholic faith.[27] But in practice, no attention was paid to these rules. Indian laborers continued to die in the mines, and by now the custom of kidnapping peaceful natives from the Lucayos (Bahamas) and other small islands was in full swing.[28]

That was the sum of the first protest against the encomienda: Montesino had preached, a junta had deliberated, the Laws of Burgos had been proclaimed, and the lot of the natives was no better than before.

CASAS DECIDES TO CHAMPION THE INDIANS

In Cuba in 1514, however, Bartolomé de las Casas changed his mind and finally decided to join the cause. In a famous passage, he himself tells the details of his belated conversion.

Reflecting on the scenes of native misery he had witnessed, the priest was preparing to preach to the Spaniards at Espíritu Santo on Pentecost, June 4. As he scanned the Scriptures for a text, he was struck by this passage in the thirty-fourth chapter of Ecclesiasticus: "Stained is the offering of him that sacrificeth from a thing wrongfully gotten . . ." Now memories began to crowd his mind. He recalled how the Española Dominicans had denounced Indian servitude, and he had not accepted their opinion. Once he had wanted to go to confession to one of them, and the friar had refused on the grounds that Casas was an encomendero who held natives; he had argued, then given in out of respect, but he had not changed his mind nor abandoned the practice. Next he remembered how he himself had often confessed people who held Indians, and he thought of his own continuing danger as he still held them like the others. For days he searched his books, pictured what he had seen. Finally, the hour came when the veil of ignorance

---

27. The distribution of Indians made by Alburquerque is printed in *DII*, I, 50-236. Casas gives estimates in round numbers of the Indians held by functionaries in Spain (*Hist.*, lib. III, opening of cap. 19); the list substantiates his picture. Herrera (*Historia general de los hechos de los castellanos*, dec. I, lib. X, cap. 12) says that when Pasamonte came to Española in 1508 there were 60,000 Indians alive, and when Alburquerque came there were only 14,000—the same figures as Casas, but Herrera had access to official records.

28. In *Hist.*, lib. III, cap. 37, Casas relates many abuses and evasions under this assignment of encomiendas; traffic is detailed in lib. II, caps. 43-45.

was lifted and he saw "the same truth" at last. Everything that had been done to the Indians—the whole system of allotments or encomiendas—was unjust and tyrannical. He, too, would denounce it in sermons.

But to preach freely, he must first give up his own Indians. So he went to Diego Velásquez and privately communicated his resolve. The astounded Velásquez tried to persuade him to think it over for fifteen days, saying he wished to see him prosperous. Casas declined, but asked Velásquez not to dispose of the Indians till his friend and partner in the grant, Rentería, returned from a trip to Jamaica. Perhaps because of this delay, it appears Casas did not preach his views on June 4. But on August 15 he delivered a sermon that was the public turning point of his life: he set forth the sin in which the Spaniards were living by holding Indians and the restitution to which they were bound, and he announced dramatically that he was giving up his own encomienda.[29]

This was only the first of several sermons in which Casas repeated his new convictions, but to no avail. Finally, seeing that the way things were going, Cuba would be destroyed as Española had been, he made a momentous decision. He must go to Spain and expose the facts to the King. Accordingly he sent for Rentería, and on his partner's return it was agreed that Casas should go and their property be sold. During this period of preparation, Fray Pedro de Córdoba had sent over four friars to help in the conversion of the Cubans. They arrived on March 21, 1515, and promptly joined Casas in preaching against the encomienda. The Dominicans preached several times during Holy Week; then, a week after Easter, Casas preached and held forth on his new views; and on June 2, Fray Bernardo de Santo Domingo delivered such a menacing sermon that it made Casas' flesh quiver. But no one was converted to give up his Indians, and the friars decided that Fray Gutierre de Ampudia should return to Santo Domingo with Casas, as nothing could be accomplished in Cuba.

Before leaving, Casas prepared an "Información ad perpetuam rei memoriam" of his services in Cuba; this proceeding was usually for the purpose of seeking preferment or promotion, but Casas says it was to strengthen him against expected criticism when he launched his attack on the encomienda. The document has never appeared, and I think it likely that after he became a friar he destroyed it.[30] Anyway, Casas gave out that he was going to Paris

---

29. *Hist.*, lib. III, cap. 79. The restitution doctrine had been preached by the Dominicans before this, and Casas himself, in his later proofs of it in his own works, harks back to the fathers of the church.

30. *Hist.*, lib. III, caps. 80-81. For his "Información" of services, see my Catalogue of Casas' writings, no. 1.

to study, so as to avoid being detained by Velásquez. But Velásquez was not deceived and, understanding the situation, sent Pánfilo de Narváez and Antonio Velásquez to Spain on behalf of the colonists[31] at just about the time Casas and two Dominicans left Cuba.

Casas' plan was to go first to Española with the friars and there consult Fray Pedro de Córdoba, but accidents beset the trip. The three crossed over together to Xaragua or Verapaz. Then as Fray Gutierre was ill, he and a companion started ahead overland to the capital, leaving Casas to proceed by another road. On the way, Fray Gutierre died. When Casas finally reached Santo Domingo, he learned that Fray Pedro had already set out for Tierra Firme. Shortly, however, Fray Pedro returned because of contrary winds, and the interview between the two reformers finally took place.

Casas at once declared what he proposed to do in Spain. Fray Pedro praised his intention, but warned him: "Father, you will not lose your labors, for God will take them into good account, but be assured that while the King lives you will not suceed in what you and I desire." Casas, however, was not dismayed, because it seemed to him that God had endowed him with the zeal and perseverance to secure the relief of the unfortunate Indians. So he answered Fray Pedro thus: "Father, I shall try in every way I can, and will undergo all the labor necessary to accomplish the goal I have embarked upon, and I hope Our Lord will aid me; but should I not attain it, I will have done what I ought as a Christian; and may your Reverence commend me to God, now and always."

Fray Pedro did even more. To aid Casas and obtain a grant for building a monastery, and perhaps to sustain the Dominicans' prior right in having proclaimed the reform principles, he sent a suitable friar along with him. In September of 1515, Bartolomé de las Casas, the new champion of the Indians, and Fray Antonio, the first spokesman of the cause, set sail together for Spain.[32]

---

31. *Hist.*, IV, 267. Casas says their chief mission was to solicit perpetual encomiendas and to get Velásquez appointed governor. But they were also prepared to answer Casas' charges and to attack him personally. Cf. *DII*, VII, 12-13.

32. *Hist.*, IV, 273-274.

❦[II]❦

CASAS' WORK BEGINS
WITH THE COMMUNITY SCHEME

THE ENCOMIENDA AND CASAS IN 1515

Now, let us pause briefly to examine the task confronting Casas, and the qualities he possessed for his forthcoming labors.

As Fray Pedro had warned him, the task was indeed a formidable one. Spain was a desperately poor country, and the gold of the Indies was a godsend to her. Gold mining was then the principal business of the West Indies, or at any rate the one which provided the exports. By 1515 the period of Santo Domingo's greatest gold output had probably passed. In 1517 the total amount produced at the smelting plants there was 118,524 pesos, giving the Crown a revenue of 26,317 pesos, no great sum to be sure.[1] But more gold was being found in Cuba; one smelting alone in 1515 on that island yielded 60,000 pesos. The heaviest shipments at this time were coming from the Darien district, though this was almost exclusively gold stolen from natives and much of it never reached the royal treasury. All told, the impoverished Spanish government had a very large stake in this business, which by all accounts could not be maintained without the use of forced native labor—i.e., the encomienda.

Added to this overriding interest in Indies gold, every individual of consequence—from the insatiable King right on down—had a direct hand in the encomienda business by which it was obtained. Ferdinand himself was the largest holder of Indians. In America the encomenderos included the royal officials, the Columbus family, and the old or prominent settlers. While in the administration back in Spain, the men of sufficient power or influence

---

1. *DII*, XI, 254.

already had encomiendas in at least Santo Domingo, Puerto Rico, and Cuba. These included, in particular, the two functionaries who had complete charge of American affiairs, Secretary Lope Conchillos and Juan Rodríguez de Fonseca, Bishop of Burgos. Of the two, Fonseca was the dominant figure. A bold, active, and intelligent prelate, he had fitted out the expedition of Columbus when still Archdeacon of Seville. From then on he had risen progressively in ecclesiastical circles, as bishop, in turn, of Badajoz, Córdoba, and Palencia (with the title of count), to his recent rank as Bishop of Burgos, and was then or shortly afterwards elevated to titular Archbishop of Rosano. Meantime he had attained chief authority over Indies matters, and both he and Conchillos had been awarded large encomiendas by Alburquerque in 1514, the very year before Casas' arrival.

This was the entrenched situation Casas faced when he reached Spain —yet he proposed to change the whole setup to save the Indians!

For Casas' main object at the start of his career was to get rid of the encomienda system. Later on he would claim that, once freed, the natives could be more readily converted.[2] But in 1515, this form of servitude was the sole target of his complaints; someone has observed that he was less interested in teaching the Indians the holy Catholic faith than in relieving them of their intolerable burdens and halting their extermination. This "destruction of the Indies" (to use the term he was to make famous) had already reached appalling proportions on Santo Domingo. The best account of the frightful conditions there is to be found in a letter written a few years later by the Española Dominicans to one of King Charles's Flemings, M. de Chièvres.[3] The friars alleged that under the brutal system the native population of the island had diminished from an estimated 1,100,000 to less than 18,000 by 1516; even then the surrounding Bahamas islands were being systematically raided, and their inhabitants brought to Española, where they soon died from the change and the unaccustomed hard labor; and the introduction of Negro slaves, to replace the dwindling natives, was about to begin. Casas himself at first used this same figure of 1,100,000, though he afterwards raised it to 3

---

2. I am inclined to agree, but such a system obviously did not suit the Spaniards, as it destroyed the possibility of making a profit from the Indians. The settlers held to the idea later defended by Juan Ginés de Sepúlveda that it was lawful to make war on the natives in order to spread the faith, which would be more readily accomplished by their prior subjection. (See *infra*, chapter XV, last section.) This seemed plausible to them, and though the doctrine was not accepted by the Crown in 1550, it was the one the Spaniards had followed and continued to follow.

3. *DII*, VII, 397-430. The name of this man was Guillaume de Croy.

million; Bishop Fonseca once asserted that originally there were only 600,-000, and this seems likelier than the larger estimates. Regardless of the figure, the mortality was enormous, and it was Casas' purpose to check it—by abolishing the encomienda.

What sort of person was Bartolomé de las Casas when he embarked on this tremendous task that was to occupy him for the next fifty years? Before his conversion, as we have seen, he had been much more of a businessman than a cleric. He had a reputation for diligence, but that was all; no contemporary mention of him in Santo Domingo or Cuba has been found. But from his later career, we can plainly see that he was a bundle of energy, of a penetrating mind, and phenomenal physical endurance. Bold to the point of temerity, sharp-witted and eloquent, he was always to command respect, though in the case of his numerous enemies this was sometimes mingled with fear. From the very beginning, he was self-confident and had a good opinion of himself. He started out with enough money to last him two years, and afterwards, though at times alleging poverty, he always found sufficient funds for his needs.

Beyond this, we scarcely know what he looked like. In the *Apologética,* I have found only a couple of indirect references to his physical appearance. Discussing the effects of the varying temperaments—choleric, phlegmatic, sanguine, and melancholic—he tells us that choleric men are more intellectual than the others and generally tall, though accidentally some small men are disposed to learning. Again, describing a certain Española tree, he remarks that contact with the leaves would poison a person who was very white or reddish; and "the branches struck me in the face many times but did me no harm because I am neither very white nor phlegmatic." These passages indicate that Casas was of an olive complexion and probably of medium stature.[4] A portrait of him, engraved by Tomás López Enguidanos, originally appeared in a book of *Retratos de los españoles illustres* published in Madrid in 1791; it has been frequently reproduced, but there is nothing to indicate its authenticity.[5]

Altogether, this is not a very full likeness. For a more satisfying picture we must turn rather to the actions of the man himself as he began his lifetime crusade for the American Indians.

---

4. *Apol.,* 37, and cf. 82-83 on the four types.
5. Taken from this lavish collection of folio plates by Carmona and other 18th-century engravers, the portrait of Casas has been reprinted as a frontispiece in all degrees of fidelity—from MacNutt's faithful reproduction to the considerably altered picture in both of Llorente's editions of Casas' works, Paris, 1822.

FIRST FERDINAND, THEN THE REGENTS

The cleric Casas, accompanied by Fray Antonio, reached Seville around November of 1515 after a propitious voyage. Here the friar went to a convent of his Order, while Casas stayed briefly at the house of his relatives before going on to see the King. At this time, Ferdinand was in southern Spain, very ill, and traveling to Seville by slow stages; Casas would need aid in order to obtain an audience. So at Fray Antonio's instance the Archbishop of Seville, Fray Diego de Deza, gave the cleric letters to His Majesty and members of the court.[6] Thus armed, Casas set out and reached the royal residence at Plasencia a few days before Christmas.

There, on Christmas Eve of 1515, Bartolomé de las Casas at last had his conference with the King. He related his purpose and described conditions in the West Indies at some length; and Ferdinand promised to hear him again during the holiday season in Seville. Next Casas went to the royal confessor, Fray Tomás de Matienzo, and again related his story. Fray Tomás spoke on his behalf to the monarch, and obtained a repeated promise that the King would hear him in Seville, whither His Majesty was bound on the twenty-eighth. As a necessary preliminary, Fray Tomás advised the priest to see Bishop Fonseca and Secretary Conchillos, since the matter would eventually have to come before them. So far, Casas had studiously avoided these officials because they were interested parties. But now he went first to Conchillos, who treated him so courteously that Casas suspected the secretary would have given him anything he asked for, i.e., to buy him off. (Here in the *Historia* Casas declares his belief that God had chosen him for this service, and freed him from mundane ambition. It is perhaps his first statement on the subject of predestination, which he maintained to the end of his life.) Following this interview, Casas saw Fonseca and presented a written memorial about the cruelties he had witnessed in Cuba and the death of seven thousand children in three months.[7] His report was received with cold scorn.

Casas was now confirmed in his belief that nothing could be expected from these two. Accordingly he returned to Seville, resolved to show the King in their presence that the bishop and the secretary were to blame for all the deaths and outrages in the Indies, as they had governed everything. Thus, from the very start, Casas had chosen the policy of imputing the blame for

---

6. *Hist.*, IV, 274-275.

7. *Hist.*, IV, 279-280. This memorial is very probably the one printed in summary in *DII*, VII, 5-11. See Catalogue, no. 2, for a description of the document. A rebuttal by the Cuban agents at court is printed in *DII*, VII, 12-13.

bad conditions to the King's agents rather than to the King himself. He was always to follow this line, though in later years he was so outspoken to Charles that the Emperor might well have taken the criticism personally. To be sure, it was really the King who was responsible, but Casas was too crafty to go that far. His audience never took place, for Ferdinand the Catholic became too ill and died on January 25, 1516.

Now the government devolved on the Cardinal of Spain, Fray Francisco Ximénez de Cisneros (whom I shall hereafter call Ximénez in the English style). In advance of the King's death, the heir Prince Charles, then in the Low Countries, had sent as ambassador Adrian, dean of the University of Louvain, and given him secret powers to rule the kingdom. Both men forthwith commenced to govern in Madrid, but Casas assures us that the cardinal was in reality the sole governor and Adrian merely co-signed the provisions and dispatches but knew nothing of official business.

What was Casas to do in this new state of affairs? He tells us that he had made up his mind to go to Flanders to see Charles. But before doing so, he stopped at Madrid and presented to the two Regents his written tale about the wrongs of the Indians; this he gave separately to the cardinal in Spanish and to Adrian in Latin. The foreigner Adrian was deeply shocked; and Cardinal Ximénez for his part advised Casas he should not go on to Flanders as they would attend to the business there.[8]

In my opinion, it was in response to this promise that Casas now proceeded to write out the remarkable project which I have dubbed his "community scheme." But it may be that Casas first presented to the cardinal yet another memorial, his paper containing an attack on the nefarious activities of Conchillos and others. The anti-Conchillos document is undated, but the editors of the Documentos inéditos de Indias say it is addressed to the cardinal; as the main object is to have the officials in Castile deprived of their encomiendas, and as this was actually accomplished early in 1517, it follows that the paper must have been presented in 1516.[9] But whether this document came first or not, Casas' far more important memorial containing his plan for the American Indians was certainly handed to Ximénez before mid-1516.

Bartolomé de las Casas' "community scheme" is a most extraordinary production, and had the greatest significance at the start of his career. Yet I have never seen any mention of it by his biographers. It did receive a slight notice by Serrano, but he expressses some doubt as to whether Casas was the

---

8. Hist., IV, 281; and see Catalogue, no. 3, for the memorials to the Regents.
9. DII, I, 253-264, and see Catalogue, no. 4.

author, and in what I consider a flagrant if not a deliberate error he assigns it to a later year.[10] But there is no doubt that Casas was the father of the scheme and presented it now, for the manuscript is entirely in his handwriting and addressed to the cardinal ("vuestra reverendissima señoría"). Also, it could hardly have come from any other source than the small committee appointed by Cardinal Ximénez to formulate some remedies for the Indians in the islands. Casas says that this committee, consisting of Doctor Palacios Rubios, Fray Antonio Montesino and "the cleric Casas," drew up a memorial of which he himself was the virtual author.[11]

So Casas certainly presented this project to Cardinal Francisco Ximénez in 1516. But I am convinced that he had actually thought it out in Cuba after his conversion in 1514. The execution of the main plan was devised for the island of Cuba, with a subordinate one recommended for the other islands. Furthermore, the scheme provided for an over-all administrator, and I cannot help thinking that Casas expected to get the post himself, although I do not find that he ever said this in so many words. But there is an obvious possibility that his "Información" of services in the conquest and settlement of Cuba may have been made with that in mind.

The plan itself is of such inherent interest, as a revelation of Casas' first proposals for the American Indians, that it deserves to be examined in some detail.

---

10. See Catalogue, no. 5, for the correct date of this document and the evidence fully establishing Casas' sole authorship. For the misplacing of it in 1517, see Manuel Serrano y Sanz, "El gobierno de las Indias por frailes jerónimos, años 1516 to 1518," 399 and note 2. (This monograph is the third in his *Orígenes de la dominación española en América*.) Serrano's text, notes, and appendices contain a large number of documents from the Archives of the Indies, but his work is marred by violent antagonism towards Casas, whom he constantly accused of errors. The errors that I have detected are Serrano's own.

11. *Hist.*, IV, 284 *et seq*. Casas says that Montesino merely approved what he wrote, as did Palacios Rubios who "improved" the style (cf. Catalogue, no. 5). Montesino's endorsement was just moral support from the first reform effort, for Casas' Indies background was vast by comparison.

Juan López de Palacios Rubios, noted jurist and councilor, had sat on the Burgos junta and then began to write his treatise *Libellus de insulis oceani*. The only surviving manuscript, in the Biblioteca Nacional, Madrid, belonged to Casas, as a portion is in his handwriting. In the committee memorial, Casas recommended printing this work, along with Matías de Paz's dissenting Burgos treatise, for distribution in the Indies, though he afterwards criticized it for containing the error of Hostiensis. Cf. *Hist.*, lib. III, cap. 7.

A UTOPIAN PLAN

By a curious coincidence, Sir Thomas More published his *Utopia* in Latin in 1516—exactly the same year that Casas produced his own far different grand piece of Utopia.

Casas' "community scheme"[12] is a perfect example of total regimentation, in a typically Spanish style of town planning. Though the towns of Spain then enjoyed a large measure of self-government, and though the people generally were individualistic to a marked degree, the government was perpetually interfering with the freedom of action of both private persons and corporate bodies; the same tendency was to reappear, time and time again, in the legislation of the Indies. In Casas' plan, this regimentation is minute indeed. Every detail of the Indians' lives is regulated in a way that is most startling; every possible contingency is provided for. Nevertheless, his project is in no sense communistic. There are certain usual features of joint ownership (communal lands, etc.) and a new device of joint repartimientos; but the emphasis is on the development of private property among the natives and the distribution of profits to individual Spaniards somewhat in the manner of a stock company.

Briefly, Casas' idea was to form "communities" consisting of a Spanish town and a group of annexed Indian villages. First of all, the Indians should be granted a vacation to give them a chance to recover some strength. Then all the repartimientos in a given island were to be thrown into a common pool—Spaniards being assigned a certain number of Indians but no particular ones. These natives were then to be brought into large new settlements of a thousand souls each, near the mines, and fifteen or twenty leagues away from the parent Spanish towns. As shareholders in the communities, the Spaniards would surrender to the new native villages suitable farming and grazing land. The villages were also to have beasts of burden, and to be provided with cows, pigs, sheep, and mares, as well as necessary farming tools. Each community was even to boast its own hospital, located in the Spanish center town; Casas gives the method of building one with two hundred beds.

Details for the management and profitable operation of these communities are elaborate. The native villages were to be ruled by majordomos with no pecuniary interest in them, assisted by the caciques; and a chief administrator was to be in charge of all the communities of a single island. A complete staff of Spanish officials and artisans was specified to direct and in-

---

12. *DII*, VII, 14-65. The heading should be disregarded, as it is an incorrect addition by the editors.

struct the Indians, including priests to minister to their religious requirements, and even a bachelor of letters (*bachiller de gramática*) to teach reading and writing and Spanish. Above all, the work of the natives was most
carefully regulated, some men being set aside to wash gold and others to
raise food. Compared to existing conditions, a veritable labor paradise was
planned, with limited working hours, plenty of food, ample vacations. Thus,
no Indians could be taken away to mine gold more than fifteen or twenty
leagues from their houses, and each man must have his own hammock for
sleeping in at the mines. Also, new metal implements were to be brought
from Spain for the Indians to use in farming, since they had only wooden
hoes at that time.

But all through these humanitarian provisions, Casas makes it clear
that he is trying to increase the revenues of the Crown. He even gives precise
figures showing how it would be possible to do so. In Cuba, he says, there
could be four gold-mining communities; and he itemizes a sample balance
sheet for one community, showing all the salaries and other expenses. Incidentally, he puts the office of Cuban chief administrator, the post he was
probably hoping to get, at four hundred castellanos a year, one hundred
from each community. These four communities of Cuba should produce at
least a hundred thousand pesos annually in gold, and as they became organized this would surely mount to more than two hundred thousand, giving a
rich royal fifth to the King and good net profits to the Spanish shareholders.
In time, he declared, the Indians would learn how to live and govern themselves, and serve the King as free vassals.

Casas also makes suggestions for compensating the encomenderos who
would lose their Indians. These settlers were to be allowed four natives
apiece to work for them, so-called *naborías*, and those few Spaniards who had
treated their natives well could have up to six, whom they could readily take
care of and teach. Such *naborías* were not to be put to any hard work, and
were to be dressed like Christians; and if in time they proved able to live by
themselves and pay a tribute to the King, they too were to be given their
freedom.

In addition to his communities, Casas further offers an alternate plan
for Española, where the natives were already decimated. The King was to
send out forty Spanish peasants to each Spanish town; and to every peasant
family, four Indian families were to be allotted. These were to form a company, with the Spaniards teaching the Indians how to work in the European
manner, the proceeds to be divided among all of them after the payment of
taxes. In time the natives would become civilized, intermarriages would take
place, and the population would thus prosper and increase. Apart from this

"peasant scheme," Casas also devotes much space to an idea for bringing in Indians from the Bahamas and other islands to Cuba; these natives, after a year's training by friars, should be assigned to peasants, either in companies or communities.

In conclusion, Casas asserts how necessary and useful his "community scheme" is to save the Indians from extermination and also—he does not omit to say—to provide "perpetual rent to the King which each day will be increased. If all this is not done, we can abandon any thought of the Indies as if they had never existed, not only those that have been discovered and are already destroyed, but those to be discovered which will also be destroyed. For it is certain, as long experience has shown, that there will be no hope of relieving the Indians or preventing the great offenses to God which take place there, nor will His Highness ever have the rents that he should, save by three remedies: to form these communities, to give all the Indians to the farmers as set forth in the third remedy, or to leave them at liberty as they were previously."[13]

SOME AFTEREFFECTS

This grand Utopian scheme is referred to only briefly in Casas' *Historia*, nor does he afterwards allude to it in any of his writings. Yet numerous aftereffects of the original memorial can be clearly traced in Casas' own subsequent activities and in the later policies of the Spanish Crown.

Certain minor features were to recur in the cleric's other proposals during the next few years. For instance, the alternate "peasants" plan would form the basis of an aided-emigration project that was to occupy him for quite awhile. This same plan also served, in part, as prototype for the colonies he later offered to implant in Cumaná. But both of these were to be exclusively settlements of Spaniards.

Another proposal, slavery, merits special comment. In place of their lost encomiendas, Casas had suggested that some settlers (and the King, too) might hold slaves: "If necessary white and black slaves can be brought from Castile, to keep herds and build sugar mills, wash gold, and engage in other things which they understand or at which they can be occupied."[14] Here we have one of the earliest passages in which Casas is alleged to have promoted the slave trade. Many words have been written in attempts to absolve

---

13. *DII*, VII, 64.

14. *DII*, VII, 41, where Casas says that if the Indians are not taken out of Spanish hands, the remnant will be exterminated. (He had also recommended 20 royal slaves in each community; cf. *ibid.*, 23.)

Casas from blame for such proposals, but he definitely did make them in this period. Slavery was then common in Portugal and especially in southern Spain, where he came from, and no one thought there was any harm in it. Not till much later did Casas gradually awake to a realization that Negro slavery was just as contrary to the will of God as Indian slavery.

As for the "community scheme" proper, many of its details were incorporated a decade later in a most curious undertaking—Lewis Hanke has dubbed it one of the "first social experiments" in America.[15] This was the famous "experiencia" or "experiencia del indio." Succinctly, the idea was to implant in the islands supervised Indian villages much on the model of Casas' communities. A number of intervening attempts to set up such native villages in Española had proved abortive, and we have only fragmentary information about them. But in 1526 a model settlement of "free Indians" was actually tried out in Cuba, and documents from the archives in Seville give us a rather full picture of it. Casas himself was immured in a monastery at the time, and his writings give no hint that he had anything to do with this particular project.[16] Yet it did strikingly resemble his original plan.

The experiment began on September 14, 1526, when Pedro Mexía, Franciscan provincial in Española, was ordered to depart for Cuba and put at liberty all Indians without encomenderos as well as those whose masters might die in the following six months. Also, some of the more capable native children were to be sent to Spain for education. The Governor of Cuba was now Gonzalo de Guzmán, one of Velásquez' followers, and he did everything possible to prevent the inauguration of the scheme, and then to delay it—a common attitude among colonial officials in those days. Thus, Guzmán

---

15. See his *The First Social Experiments in America: A Study in the Development of Spanish Indian Policy in the Sixteenth Century* (Cambridge, 1935), 56-58 and appendix C. A number of documents on the progress of this experiment were printed in *Documentos inéditos de ultramar,* I and IV; these and many more were located by Dr. Hanke in the Archives of the Indies.

16. I think, however, that Casas' denunciation of Indian mistreatment had left its mark on the officials in Spain; and despite the Crown's utilitarian methods, the King still had a conscience. The royal conscience, and the near-extinction of the West Indian natives, probably led to the "experiencia" rather than any discussion of theories on Indian liberty or capacity. Dr. Hanke feels the decision was made despite Tomás Ortiz's speech to the Council in 1525 on Indian bestiality—see the text in Peter Martyr, *De orbe novo,* MacNutt edition (New York, 1912), II, 274-275. But Ortiz's opening words show he was making a "cannibal" declaration about the Tierra Firme Indians, a standard preliminary for authorizing slave raids, so I do not see any connection. See *infra,* chapter IX, note 36, for the resulting slaving cedulas; and chapter XVII, note 28, for Casas' account of Ortiz.

was ordered to proceed at once with the "experiencia"; but five years passed before he finally collected about 180 natives left free by the death of their encomenderos, and talked to the chiefs about the King's interest in their salvation and desire for them to enjoy a "different" kind of liberty. To this the caciques agreed, and a start was made at nearby Bayamo.

Here, an administrator was charged to teach the Indians how to raise cotton, maize, and so on, in the manner of Spanish farmers. With these products they had to dress and feed themselves, pay their tithes and a tax to the King. In connection with their labors, they were to be instructed in the essentials of Christianity. Their native dances were to be permitted, provided they did not paint themselves. These, generally, were the instructions from "an uninterested governor to an unscrupulous administrator." It is hardly surprising that nothing went well with this Indian village, though its existence dragged on for a number of years. A full account of its vicissitudes may be found in Dr. Hanke's work. All through the pathetic story, the natives themselves showed scant pleasure in their freedom and did little or nothing to help the experiment. If there ever had been any real intention of following Casas' plan, the purpose was entirely defeated by the apathy or outright opposition of the colonial officials.

But of course, the most conspicious and immediate result of Casas' "community scheme" was the one that followed its original presentation in 1516. The joint memorial was submitted by the Regents to a junta consisting of themselves, the Bishop of Ávila, Licentiate Zapata, Doctor Carvajal, and Doctor Palacios Rubios.[17] As a direct consequence, Cardinal Ximénez decided to send some friars to oversee the government of the islands and reform the condition of the Indians. This was the origin of the celebrated Hieronymite mission, one of the most amazing episodes in the entire history of the New World.

---

17. *Hist.*, IV, 284.

THE HIERONYMITE MISSION

THE INSTRUCTIONS

Bartolomé de las Casas played a significant part in the dispatching of the famous Hieronymite mission. He largely drafted its instructions, and (if we may trust his narrative) even helped in the choice of the high commissioners themselves.

When the Regent was ready to pick his reformers, Casas wrote a memorandum describing the various qualities and conditions of the persons who should be sent. Cardinal Ximénez thought the friars of St. Jerome would best fill the requirements, because of the old friction between Franciscans and Dominicans on Española. In the ensuing negotiations with the Order, the cleric took some part, being sent to Lupiana to see the father general—a journey for which Ximénez insisted on paying the expenses. Casas at first refused the money, but the cardinal insisted, "Go on, father, I am richer than you are!" Three Hieronymite priors were finally selected: Luís de Figueroa, Bernardino de Manzanedo, and Alonso de Santo Domingo.[1]

For their mission to the Indies, an elaborate set of instructions was prepared. Casas says he wrote these in substance, though they were altered by the Council. We can verify that a very substantial part of the Hieronymite

---

1. *Hist.*, lib. III, caps. 86-87, and Catalogue, no. 6. The first documents concerning this mission appear to be dated from Madrid on July 8: a letter to the general of the Hieronymites to give credence to the treasurer Baza, with an instruction to Baza to ask for two friars to go to the Indies. Serrano y Sanz, *Orígenes*, 346-347. Also see *DII*, VII, 438-450, where this preliminary is followed by further exchanges between the cardinal and the Order and other papers relating to the mission, extracted by Muñoz. The cardinal refers indirectly to both Casas and Montesino, telling how a report was made to Ferdinand during his last illness, and afterwards persons from the Indies, including friars, came "here" with complaints. *DII*, VII, 442-443.

instructions was actually taken from Casas' "community scheme." This was pointed out by the editors of the *Documentos inéditos de Indias*, but Serrano seems to have been unaware of it.

Under these instructions, plus further powers and orders, the Hieronymites were to proceed in three main directions. First, they were to take away the Indians held by all royal officials, both absentees on the Peninsula and administrators on the scene. Likewise, the standard investigation was to be made of the Española functionaries, and for this purpose Licentiate Alonso de Zuazo was to join the mission as judge of inquiry.

Next the friars were to function as a commission of inquiry on the whole Indian problem. They were to assemble the colonists and select three or four of the most reliable for consultation. Similarly, through Franciscan and Dominican interpreters, they were to confer with the caciques, advising them of the royal wish to put an end to the mistreatment of the past. All this was to gather information and see whether some arrangements agreeable to Spaniards and Indians might be worked out. Incidentally, they were to investigate whether any individual natives had the ability to live alone and govern themselves.

Then, if feasible, the Hieronymites were to concentrate the natives into supervised towns replacing the repartimientos. This was the major feature of their instructions and most of the details were lifted bodily from Casas' communities. Thus, after inspecting the countryside, they were to choose sites accessible to the gold mines, and settle the Indians in towns of three hundred families each, making them understand this was for their own good. In these villages should be built a church, plaza, streets, houses, and a hospital for the poor, old, and sick. Every resident was to have a plot of ground to raise food, and the remaining land was to be held by the community for farming and grazing.

Each village would be in charge of the principal cacique, together with a friar or cleric who was to collect tithes and perform religious functions. Spaniards would be encouraged to marry chiefs' daughters, so that finally many caciques would be mestizos. A Spanish administrator was to have charge of each neighboring group of villages, his salary to be paid half by the towns and half by the King. This official, a married man, should live in a stone house, and generally oversee the life of the Indians. He was to keep a book with a record of each Indian, and see that his charges slept in beds, had only one wife, did not eat on the ground, and took care of their tools and other property. The natives were not to be allowed to give or gamble away their belongings, or to exchange or sell them, except for food, save by license of the religious or administrator. Also, every effort was to be made to have the Indians taught Spanish.

Special directions were given about mining, at which one-third of the Indian men from twenty to fifty years of age must always be engaged. Curiously, if a woman wished to work with them, she was to be counted as a man. These mine workers were to set out at sunrise, have three hours to eat at midday, and return home at sunset. In addition, the cacique was to send a native foreman with the party, as experience had shown a Spanish miner was not desirable. The mine shift was to change every two months, and those Indians not at the mines, as well as the women and children, were to be compelled to work in the fields.

Profits of the venture, and funds to establish it, would come from the gold mining. Thus, to initiate the project, the Hieronymites were empowered to take haciendas, which would be paid for from the first smelting. Cattle, hogs, and horses were to be provided similarly, and minute details were given about their handling, including the meat ration per Indian. And instructions for the distribution of proceeds were most elaborate. All the gold mined was to be taken over by the foreman every night. At smelting time he, with the administrator, was to see to the division, one-third going to the King and the rest to the Indians. From their share, land payments were to be met first, and then all the expenses of the community; the remainder was to be distributed equally among each native householder, but with six parts for the cacique and two for the foreman.

As for the dispossessed Spaniards, some could sell their lands, others be employed by the administrators as salaried mining prospectors, etc. Provision was further made for allowing two or three slaves for each Spanish resident, and for assisting the settlers to go on Carib slave-raiding expeditions to the mainland.[2]

In the *Historia*, Casas afterwards objected to some of these regulations, such as making one-third of the Indians always work at the mines, and having land and stock paid for instead of given outright. The King, he claimed, was obliged to satisfy the Indians for the harm done them by the Spaniards, even though this was against his will. Furthermore, he insisted that the

---

2. The Hieronymite instructions have been printed a number of times: *DII*, XI, 258-276, and XXIII, 310-331; also *DIU*, IX, 53-74. In *Hist.*, lib. III, caps. 88-89, Casas copied the prologue and the two parts of "la instrucción que llevaron los frailes hierónimos." His is not a continuous copy, but is intespersed with comments; the opening formalities are omitted and there are minor variants in the first portion, as Serrano y Sanz noted.

clauses about enslaving Caribs were unjust, since these Indians had never heard of the faith nor been preached to. But his main complaint was that the removal of the Indians from repartimientos to towns was not compulsory. For the Hieronymites were given an alternate instruction permitting them to retain the encomiendas with some modification of the Laws of Burgos, and their powers allowed them to decide as they saw fit. Casas tells us that he was responsible for these revisions, too, including repeal of the law that ordered Spaniards to have communication with the natives. He felt that the amendments would at least alleviate the oppression under which the Indians suffered.[3]

Apparently, however, Casas did expect the commissioners would remove the Indians from their encomenderos. He admits he was too timid to insist on this when the instructions were being formulated in the Council but he thought he had accomplished it. His hope, we shall see, was to prove entirely unfounded.

THE CLERIC AND THE COMMISSIONERS

Perhaps as a reward for his work on the instructions, Casas was now given an official post to accompany the Hieronymites to America. He himself, he tells us, had offered the earliest suggestion for the appointment of some man of knowledge and conscience to look after Indian rights at court, and had also urged the aided emigration of Castilian peasants to the islands. These matters were dropped, he says, as he was the only one to negotiate for the universal good of the Indies. Nevertheless, on September 17, 1516, the cardinal issued an order for him to go to America to inform the commissioners about native welfare and send reports back to Spain. Other cedulas the same day authorized payment of his passage, and made him "Protector of the Indians" at a salary of a hundred pesos a year. This sum, he comments, was "not so little, as the hell of Peru had not yet been discovered, which

---

3. *Hist.* IV, 314-315. But is should be remembered that the *Historia* was written in final form between 1551 and 1561, when Casas' own opinions had undergone a change. Thus, originally, and perhaps down to the time of the Tuzulutlán experiment, Casas favored concentrating the Indians into towns; he was probably responsible for the insertion of this part of the scheme in the instructions to the Hieronymites, although writing later he says he opposed it. Similarly, in 1516 he favored mixing Spaniards with Indians, but in 1560 he did not, since experience had demonstrated the harmful effects on the Indians of such intercourse.

with its multitudinous quintals of gold has impoverished and destroyed Spain."[4]

All this while the agents of the colonies had been busy at court, protesting any changes. Having failed to forestall the reform, they now began to frequent the society of the Hieronymites and to slander Casas. As a result, at sailing time the commissioners refused to have the protector of the Indians go along in the same boat. This is according to Casas, but it seems apparent such attacks had persuaded the new overseers that it might be prudent to arrive alone. At any rate, there was some compensation, as he says; he embarked on a better ship where he was more comfortable.

So, on November 11, 1516, Casas and the Hieronymites sailed from San Lúcar on separate vessels. Casas reached Santo Domingo thirteen days after the Hieronymites, who had made port at the end of December. Their divided arrival was almost an omen, for differences were due to increase between the protector and the commissioners.

On the crossing, Casas' vessel had stopped at Puerto Rico, where he learned about one of those astounding outrages which were perpetrated daily in the Indies. He tells the story with considerable indignation: a certain Juan Bono (no more "good" than a Negro is "white") had made an assault on the inhabitants of Trinidad Island, on the theory that they were cannibals. These Indians received him well, but Juan *Malo* succeeded in kidnapping 185 of them; in the accompanying fight a house was set afire and all the people in it were burned to death. When Casas landed in Santo Domingo he related the incident to the Hieronymites, but they disregarded it.[5]

In the months that followed, the commissioners paid virtually no attention to any of the protector's other protests of Indian maltreatment. It did not take long for the disagreements between them to reach an impasse. The Hieronymites' position was hardly enviable. On one side, urging them to further reforms, was the fiery cleric. On the other, protesting any reforms, were all the Spanish inhabitants of the island. This was the sort of situation that afterwards arose frequently in the Indies; faced by the threat of a popular upheaval, there was nothing the royal envoys could do but refuse to carry out those instructions that were certain to be resisted. Accordingly, the Hieronymites merely took away the Indians from the absentees in Spain,

---

4. *Hist.*, IV, 316-317. The cedula to pay his passage, with four servants and his goods, is given by Fabié in app. III.

5. *Hist.*, lib. III, cap. 91. This Juan Bono was Bono de Quexo, who cut some figure in the conquest of Mexico.

conducted an inquiry, and generally tried to see to it that the natives were well treated. In the *Historia*, of course, Casas insists that they did nothing to improve the lot of the Indians. But his real criticism of the commissioners was doubtless based on their refusal to release the Indians from the encomenderos.

By spring, the break between Casas and the Hieronymites had reached the stage of open incidents. About three months after the arrival of the original party, the judge of inquiry, Alonso de Zuazo, reached Santo Domingo and proceeded to proclaim the investigation of the royal judges and officials. Casas in person made a "terrible accusation" against them, charging them with having been implicated in the kidnapping of the Lucayos Indians. This, he says, greatly upset the Hieronymite friars.[6]

Public resentment against Casas had meanwhile risen so high that the Dominicans took him into their monastery, where he was at least safe at night. Throughout this period they were his major partisans. As the first to denounce the encomienda, the Black Friars naturally held the same views as the protector. In fact, their spokesman, Fray Bernardo de Santo Domingo—one of the initial group that had come to Española in 1510—prepared an outspoken Latin memorial denouncing the allotment of Indians. Fray Bernardo declared that encomiendas put not only their holders in mortal sin, but also the priests who absolved them, and even the Hieronymites themselves! Not even the Laws of Burgos, he insisted, nor any further laws however just they might be, could serve to justify encomiendas because of the insatiable cupidity of the Spaniards. The document was signed by most of the Dominicans and handed to the commissioners, who of course paid it no heed.[7]

Around this time the embattled protector did gain new friends in the persons of fourteen Franciscans from French Flanders who arrived in Santo Domingo. Fray Pedro de Córdoba, who had gone to Spain to recruit friars, also returned to Española and reaffirmed his support of Casas. But these monastic allies, and even the kind interest of Judge Zuazo, availed him little in his campaign to free the Indians.

It was now clear to Casas that he could do nothing under the Hieronymite regime, and he resolved to return to Spain and complain directly to the Regent. As a matter of fact, the original cedula ordering the cleric to

---

6. *Hist.*, lib. III, cap. 93.

7. *Hist.*, lib. III, cap. 94 (and *DII*, XI, 211-215, for an abridged version). It was signed by most of the Dominicans and is as good an example as can be found of arguments advanced against encomiendas.

America had directed him to come back to court if he found this advisable. There is also evidence that, on the complaints of the commissioners about him, orders were sent out to ship him back to Spain, under arrest if necessary. About this, however, partial obscurity persists, though it seems that something to that effect was written in July; but a cedula summoning him back was certainly issued on July 22.[8] At all events, these recall orders must have arrived after his departure.

For in May of 1517, the protector of the Indians, convinced that all his work so far had been nullified by the high commissioners, set sail once more for Spain.[9]

WHAT DID THE REFORM ACCOMPLISH?

But we cannot dismiss the entire episode quite so easily. Before following the cleric on his return to court, let us pause for a more critical examination of its biographical and historical meaning.

The Hieronymite mission, to say it plainly, was the first reform instigated by Bartolomé de las Casas. His efforts had been in large measure responsible for the sending of the friars; he personally had made the major contribution to their instructions. To be sure, his main goal, the abolition of the encomienda, was not realized. Yet the commissioners did accomplish quite a number of things, even some that he had urged, though Casas would be the last to admit this.

For an objective evaluation of their work, we can turn to sources other than Casas' firsthand narrative. The history of this mission was detailed at some length by the chronicler, Fray Joseph de Sigüenza, from documents of the Sisla Hieronymite monastery in Toledo.[10] In addition, we have other papers and correspondence from the three Hieronymite priors themselves, and a number of relevant cedulas and on-the-spot documents.

---

8. Fabié, app. III, cites this cedula as July 17, 1517, in a Muñoz digest. But Dr. Hanke, summarizing the documents in the archives, dates it positively as July 22 —*First Social Experiments*, 37, note 33. According to Casas himself, he should have been back in Spain before that date.

9. See *Hist.*, lib. III, cap. 95, for the final events of Casas' stay in Española. Apparently he sailed at the very end of May, since on May 28 Fray Pedro de Córdoba wrote: "and now he [Casas] is returning there." DII, XI, 221.

10. *Tercera parte de la historia de la Orden de San Gerónimo*, Madrid, 1605 (in Medina, *Bib. hisp.-am.*, I, 59 et seq.). Sigüenza never once mentions Casas in connection with the mission—further evidence of the break between the cleric and the commissioners.

From this data, it is quite certain that soon after their arrival, the commissioners did revoke the encomiendas of the officials in Spain. Thus, a 1519 report of the Santo Domingo audiencia stated that on January 5 the factor had charged himself five thousand pesos obtained in 1517 with the Española Indians taken away from caballeros in Castile; these cavaliers are named, and they include the chief absentee encomenderos.[11] Besides this, there is evidence that properties belonging to the Bishop of Burgos and other court personages had also been sold. Sigüenza informs us that this action created so much opposition in Spain that a royal order was issued directing the return of these Indians to their holders, but Judge Zuazo overruled it. And cedulas were finally issued to the Hieronymites to pay Almazán, Cabrera, Vega, and Zapata what their Indian allotments had been worth.[12] So it appears obvious that Casas had actually obtained very prompt results from his campaign against members of the Council and other courtiers holding Indians in the islands.

With rather less promptness, the commissioners also did conduct a broad inquiry into the question of what to do with the Indians. In April of 1517, seven questions were put to more than a dozen witnesses; these included the oldest inhabitants, local officials, and Dominican and Franciscan friars. The caciques, however, were not consulted as the formal instructions had directed. The questions considered a number of possibilities, like releasing the natives from encomiendas and concentrating them into villages. But much of the testimony was directed to the problem of whether the Indians had sufficient capacity to be given complete liberty. Could they live in civilized fashion (*políticamente*) like the Spaniards, supporting themselves by their own efforts, mining gold and tilling the soil, keeping what they acquired and purchasing only necessities?

There was, naturally, almost complete uniformity in the answers; nearly all those questioned were encomenderos. In consensus, the Indians were described as prodigal (most of them were, for that matter); these natives didn't save anything for a rainy day; they had no interest in mining gold, would not even pay the small gold tribute that had once been imposed on them, did not in fact dig for gold unless forced to do so. Very few

---

11. *DII*, I, 370. And cf. the Hieronymites' January 20, 1517, letter relating the colonists' glee at their actions—*DII*, I, 269-270.

12. Cf. the March 30, 1519, orders to pay Vega and Zapata, in Serrano y Sanz, *Orígenes*, apps. LXXVI-LXXVII. On December 9, 1518, Licentiate Figueroa, the new judge of inquiry, was given final and categorical instructions to take away all Indians from absentees and officials—*ibid.*, app. LXXII.

witnesses even suggested that the Indians had any capacity for freedom. Nevertheless, one settler admitted the aborigines had some ability, because they had raised crops, built houses, and made other things before the Spaniards came; also, the caciques seemed to have some good method of taking care of their people. But the only strong divergent note came from Fray Bernardo de Santo Domingo, again speaking for the Black Friars, who claimed the Indians were quite ready for liberty. He was virtually drowned out, however, by a chorus of witnesses insisting on Indian incapacity and the need for continued servitude.

These anti-Indian conclusions were more or less what could have been expected, but the interrogatory itself was a valuable reflection of public opinion among the Spanish residents. And the matter of settler reaction was naturally a great concern to the reform commission. So it is hardly surprising that, after the inquiry was over and all the evidence had been received, the Hieronymites decided to put at liberty only a single Indian.[13]

It is somewhat more difficult to make out just what the high commissioners contemplated in the third main step undertaken by their administration, their so-called native "towns." They did write officially that they were preparing sites to collect all the Española Indians into villages under administrators and friars.[14] But that there was any real intent of carrying out Casas' plan, as it appeared in their instructions, I am strongly inclined to doubt. Apparently this was to have been very much of a compromise, combining some sort of relocation with the existing encomiendas. But the Hieronymites themselves, and their chronicler Sigüenza, lamented their inability to carry out the project, attributing the failure to an epidemic of smallpox that swept Española and wiped out many of the remaining natives. This unsuccessful Hieronymite attempt to establish Indian towns took place months after Casas was back in Spain, and he must have heard about it from court officials. Yet he mentions it only scornfully in the *Historia*, in connection with an opinion of the court preachers, completely omitting it where he tells in detail of the smallpox epidemic that all but exterminated

---

13. *DII*, XXXIV, 201-229, a summary of replies to the first six questions; also *DII*, XI, 147-152, the Franciscan opinion. For the dissenting Dominican opinion, see *supra*, note 7. Dr. Hanke located the manuscript of the interrogatory in the archives and summarized the answers to question 3 on Indian capacity; he identifies the liberated Indian as the "very good Christian" Don Rodrigo. *The First Social Experiments*, 28-37.

14. The Hieronymite commissioners to the King, February 15, 1518, *DII*, XXXIV, 279-286.

the Española natives. Indeed, Casas' narrative hardly refers to the Hieronymites again, and then but scathingly—saying, for instance, that on their
arrival at Charles's court they were unable to obtain a royal audience.[15]

The three high commissioners finally did come back to Spain in 1520,
after trying for several years to be relieved of their burdensome position.[16]
Following Casas' departure they had sent back one of their number, Fray
Bernardino de Manzanedo, chiefly, I believe, to seek permission for their
return. Sigüenza quotes his instruction to this effect, as well as Manzanedo's
own petition to the King after Cardinal Ximénez's death. On the whole, I
think, the Hieronymites had done their best with an assignment they had
been most reluctant to accept in the first place. They had put through one
administrative reform of consequence, an end to absentee repartimientos of
councilors and courtiers. On the other hand, the adverse results of their
interrogatory would long be used by enemies of further reform. Their
tentative measures had come too late to save the Española Indians, but it
is doubtful if anything more drastic could have been enforced against the
opposition of the settlers. All in all, they had struggled with a thankless
task and they excite our sympathy.

But to Bartolomé de las Casas, the Hieronymite mission seemed a
total failure, a betrayal of his first reform effort. And he abandoned it completely in May of 1517—when he sailed from Santo Domingo to start all
over again on his own crusade for the American Indians.

---

15. Writing to the King on January 10, 1519, the Hieronymite commissioners
reported that in one month the epidemic had wiped out one-third of the natives, and
if it continued another month no gold could be mined that year. *DII*, I, 366-368. In
Hist., lib. III, cap. 128, Casas tells how the smallpox epidemic carried off all but 1,000
of the Española natives. This finished the mining and led to the introduction of sugar
cane. In *ibid.*, cap. 155, he describes the commissioners' frustrating return to Spain in
1520 and Fray Luis de Figueroa's subsequent death.

16. As early as the summer of 1518, they wrote that they would return in the
first ship after Christmas if no other order came from Spain. *DII*, I, 347-353. This
letter is undated, but the time of writing can be fixed by a reference to Licentiate
Zuazo's arrival a year and a half before.

PEASANT EMIGRATION

CASAS' RETURN TO FAVOR

Back in Spain, Casas found himself in disfavor with the dying Cardinal Ximénez, and it was not till the following year that he was presenting reform plans once more at the behest of the young King. His rise at the new Flemish court, as he relates it in the *Historia*, reveals him in the novel role of skilled courtier. But the chronology of this interlude and even some of its events are hard to establish.

For instance, Casas tells us he left Española in May and arrived in fifty-two days at Aranda de Duero, where he saw the Regent. This would place the interview in July, a clear error since Ximénez did not leave Madrid for Aranda till August. Casas' narrative therefore contains a mistake about the place or the dates. Either he saw the cardinal in Madrid, or he did not see him till late August or even September.

At any rate, the aged Cardinal Ximénez was now mortally ill, and angry at the cleric besides. As Casas says, his own letters from Santo Domingo had never got through, having been confiscated by the Hieronymites in Española or the House of Trade officials in Seville; whereas the commissioners' complaints against him had reached and impressed the cardinal. Casas saw that he could do no further business with the ailing Regent, and resolved to address himself instead to the new ruler who was then expected in Spain.

Waiting for the youthful King took months, but at least Casas was no longer alone on his mission. The cleric's plan was to go to Valladolid, staying there through September to await the royal coming, and if the King did not come, going on to Flanders to see him. A brother of Fray Antonio Montesino, Fray Reginaldo by name, offered to accompany him on the long journey, and even obtained the provincial's permission. But while the two were still in Valladolid, Charles landed on the Basque coast on September 17.

The youthful monarch lingered about, visited his mother in Tordesillas, never saw Ximénez (who died on November 8), and finally reached Valladolid on November 25.

What had Casas been doing in the meantime? He gives us only an anecdote about Fray Reginaldo, who was told one day by an old-time Indies councilor that the American natives were incapable of receiving the faith; Fray Reginaldo challenged this, and wrote to consult the celebrated Fray Juan Hurtado, then prior of San Esteban in Salamanca. This Dominican prior thereupon convoked some thirteen university theologians, and after discussing the matter they sent four or five authorized conclusions, the last of which was that those who maintained such an opinion should be proceeded against and burned at the stake as heretics. Casas says he saw and copied the document; "and I would put it here verbatim save that, with other writings, it was stolen from me on a certain journey."[1]

Did he make the journey during this interval, and if so where did he go? In the *Apologética*, there is evidence that Casas took a trip to Rome about which almost nothing is known. He discusses the Inca highways and mentions seeing fragments of old Roman roads in Spain and Italy. Elsewhere, speaking of the ancient Roman masques, he says cryptically: "the vestiges of these dances I have myself seen during the days in the year '07, I mean five hundred and seven, when from these Indies I went to Rome."[2] Now we have absolutely no evidence that he went to Rome from Santo Domingo in that year, or even to Spain. But we do know he came back to Spain from America in 1517, so perhaps this is the year he meant; and he could have gone to Rome in the idle months from August to November. There is, however, no indication that he had any good reason for doing so, nor does he mention any such voyage in his *Historia;* also, the dances he describes apparently took place between the Epiphany and carnival time, a different season altogether. So a Roman journey in this interim is only a dubious possibility.[3]

Anyway, with the arrival of the young King, the cleric's waiting was over and he was soon winning the ear of the new Flemish courtiers. Three of these Flemings, in particular, were to become Casas' chief supporters in all his struggles for the next few years. One was Chancellor Jean le

---

1. *Hist.,* IV, 365.

2. *Apol.,* 483, and cf. 683, the roads.

3. But in 1517, Fray Hierónimo Peñafiel, Prior of San Pablo de Valladolid, did tell Casas about going to Rome and informing Cardinal Cayetano, the Dominican general, of the oppression of the Indians. Cf. *Hist.,* IV, 63.

Sauvage, a most prudent and excellent man of great capacity and authority, to whom Charles entrusted all the business of the kingdom. Another was Monsieur de Chièvres, whom Charles had brought along as his chief chamberlain; this high functionary had charge of all the King's private affairs, and all grants which did not involve the justice department. The third was Monsieur de La Chaux, or as the Spaniards wrote his name, Laxao—the influential chamberlain who slept in the royal bedchamber.

Easily the most powerful was Chancellor Sauvage, and Casas lost no time getting in touch with this personage. The cleric presented letters of introduction that the Española Dominicans and Franciscans had written for him, and it turned out that some of the Flanders friars were well known to the chancellor.[4] So Sauvage was quite willing to listen to what this priest had to say, all the more so as there was widespread ignorance about American affairs at the new court.

Casas immediately launched a vigorous attack on Bishop Fonseca, Secretary Conchillos, and the members of the Council—blaming them for the misgovernment of the Indies, insisting they did not care whether the natives died or not. And the chancellor gave such credit to the cleric's charges that he actually suspended the Council's business for a while. Casas tells us, however, that this body continued to carry on secretly; and the agents of the colonists importuned the King till he finally ordered Fonseca and Conchillos to get on with their work. These colonial representatives, Casas says, had only one real business, the same that occupied them from the discovery clear down to 1560, namely "to keep the Indians in terrible and mortal servitude"—i.e., they wanted perpetual encomiendas. But the resumption of the Council did not get far. The King, instead of sanctioning any requests, had them turned over to his chancellor, who delayed answering them. In this impasse, Secretary Conchillos—who still had the lucrative privileges of appointing notaries in the Indies, and receiving fees for the smelting and marking of gold—went to Sauvage and tried to get the dispatches signed. "Get out of here!" cried the chancellor, "You have destroyed the Indies!" So dejected was Conchillos over losing the favor he had enjoyed with Ferdinand that he withdrew from court to his home in Toledo; and he was finally replaced as secretary by Francisco de los Cobos, a long-

---

4. Cf. the Latin letter to Cardinal Ximénez from the Dominicans and Flanders Franciscans, dated at Santo Domingo, May 28, 1517—José María Chacón y Calvo, *Cartas censorias de la conquista* (Havana, 1938), 18-27. Casas had a similar Spanish letter of endorsement of the same date from Fray Pedro de Córdoba to the King. *DII*, XI, 216-224.

time Council employee who had gone to Flanders and gotten into the good graces of Chièvres. Conchillos' fall was afterwards blamed on Casas, one more proof of the influence the priest had attained with Sauvage.[5]

By this time, the cleric Casas had become the chancellor's trusted adviser on American matters. Many petitions about the Indies were then being presented, many letters were coming from the Indies addressed to the new King. All these the chancellor handed to Casas, to translate into Latin and return with a written comment. Indeed, Sauvage now had such a good opinion of Casas that he even lauded him to the King, telling Charles about the cleric's experience, ability, knowledge of the New World, and praising his good intentions for the natives. Young King Charles responded by directing Sauvage to get together with Casas and devise a reform for the Indians.

NEW COLONIZATION PROPOSALS

To Bartolomé de las Casas, it seemed as if for the second time God was placing "the remedy and liberty and welfare" of the American natives in his hands.[6] Sauvage had transmitted the royal request with the Latin words: "Faciatis vestra memorialia." Accordingly the cleric proceeded to "prepare his memorials" aplenty. These have not come down to us, or at least they have not been found; but we have a petition of his to the King, written before the middle of 1518, that summarizes them rather fully.[7]

To save the remaining island Indians, Casas again proposed releasing them from encomiendas and resettling them in towns where they would become tribute-paying vassals. In Española, there were now only eight or nine thousand natives left, and it was urgent to let them rest for awhile. Then, bit by bit, they should be brought into villages near the mines and seaports, closer to the gold and Spanish goods. After they had been living quietly in these towns, each married man could pay a castellano in tribute, and in time perhaps more. Only thus would their extermination cease and these natives again multiply and populate the island. "They must be taken out of the hands of the Christians, because otherwise they will be killed and

---

5. Casas relates his new rise to favor in *Hist.*, lib. III, caps. 99-100. During the period of the "surreptitious or irregular" provisions, Bishop Fonseca sent some orders to Diego Velásquez as "governor"—an affront to Diego Columbus, whose "lieutenant" he was. Someone saw the dispatch and advised the Second Admiral, who complained to the King and chancellor. Was the informant Casas, who afterwards did report another such infraction to Admiral Columbus? Cf. *ibid.*, cap. 101.

6. *Hist.*, IV, 373.

7. *DII*, VII, 101-109, and see Catalogue, no. 7. This is undated, but internal evidence places it approximately at the summer of 1518.

the country destroyed even though the King puts into effect many laws and penalties."

Casas' major attention, however, was now devoted to new forms of colonization and means of livelihood for the Spanish settlers, so they might prosper without using forced native labor. For the largely unsettled mainland, he outlined an ambitious new system for a chain of forts and trading posts to be established along the coast. For the older settlers, he suggested a variety of miscellaneous aids, including reduction of the royal fifth (from gold) to one-tenth only; and permission for the importation of African slaves —each resident to be allowed two Negro men and women apiece. But his chief new proposal for the West Indies was a system to foment colonization by Spanish farmers. A similar idea had already been advanced in his memorial to Cardinal Ximénez, via the alternative proposal for peasant-Indian "companies." But now he dwelt on peasant emigration per se, elaborating perhaps the most important contribution of this memorializing period.

Casas wanted what he called quiet peasants to be sent out to the islands, though, recognizing their unwillingness to work, he advised sending along some slaves who presumably would perform a good part of the actual labor under the supervision of their masters. His basic idea appears to have been quite sound, for the islands were extremely fertile and the climate was excellent, and I see no reason why Spanish farmers could not have settled there. He took great pains to work out every practical detail of the scheme. Thus, the King was to proclaim through all his kingdoms, and even in foreign lands, that Indies settlers would have many privileges, including free passage, and laborers could be offered wages of ten or twelve thousand maravedis a year. But above all, many peasants should be persuaded to emigrate; as inducements, prizes should be promised for the raising of new crops—silk and cinnamon, pepper and cloves, and ginger, wheat, and wine grapes. Also, sugar mills should be encouraged, and those who built them might take twenty Negro slaves. Furthermore, Casas gave full specifications for establishing these rural settlers in the Indies—we learn the details from a chapter of his history where he also reviews these memorials.[8] The peasants with their families were to be transported from their homes to the islands, and there provided with land, animals and farming tools, and also granted a year's supply of food from the royal granaries, so as to give them time to raise crops to sustain themselves. Of all his new plans, he seems to have felt this was the most urgent.

8. *Hist.*, lib. III, cap. 102.

What resulted from all these "memorialia" now presented by Bartolomé de las Casas? There were a few minor and negative consequences, and one major success, as we learn in part from the same *Historia* chapter. Rejected outright, apparently, was the mainland scheme, which he would revive in after years as his famous Tierra Firme project. This is the only inference possible from his long lament over its non-adoption and the blindness of the Council. In addition, several of his proposals were enacted later that year, but never got beyond the paper stage.

For instance, he speaks of redrafting the villages plan given the Hieronymites, but says nothing about any fresh measures for the island Indians. As a matter of fact, both supervised towns and freedom with tribute were included in the instructions of Licentiate Rodrigo de Figueroa, newly named judge of inquiry for Española; and cedulas of September 20 even directed Casas himself to cooperate with Figueroa (and vice versa) in trying out his new tribute scheme with the natives. But the cleric subsequently withdrew from the project and the new judge did not leave till 1519; so presumably Casas intended to discuss all this in the next "decade" of history.[9]

Again, Casas' advice for the importation of Negro slaves was not carried out the way he counseled. The cleric had recommended individual licenses; instead, a monopoly to ship four thousand Negroes was granted to a Flemish court favorite who sold it to Genoese merchants, with Casas pro-

---

9. See Serrano y Sanz, *Orígenes*, 428-429, the Casas cedulas, and app. LXXI, the Figueroa instructions of December 9, 1518. These instructions contain a reference to the cleric's report that the Trinidad Indians were not cannibals and should not be enslaved, the only portion referred to by Casas. See *Hist.*, lib. III, cap. 104, where he tells of transmitting a letter from Fray Pedro de Córdoba on a Trinidad outrage (cf. *infra*, the beginning of my chapter V).

The Figueroa instructions also cite a petition by Fray Pedro de San Martín, Dominican agent at court, complaining about Spanish raiders on the Pearl Coast. The complaint appears in *Orígenes*, app. XLVIII—a petition read to the Council on December 11, 1517, by "el fraile dominico . . . procurador de los dichos indios." It closely parallels Casas' proposals of this period (the community scheme, peasant emigration, and the new tribute plan) and appears to be written in support of them.

Figueroa's basic instructions were accompanied by a number of implementing documents of the same date of December 9, 1518. See *Orígenes*, apps. LXIX-LXX, powers to free the qualified Indians and impose tribute; app. LXXII, directions to remove Indians from absentees; app. LXXIII, ordinances for the treatment of encomienda Indians, i.e., the Laws of Burgos further revised, particularly as to religious indoctrination and adequate food for the natives. These amended ordinances are also printed in Santa Cruz's *Crónica*, I, 188-191. The total effect of the Figueroa instructions was nil. The Indians were not removed from the encomenderos, save

testing the transaction. This is the incident that led, centuries later, to the controversy over Bartolomé de las Casas' alleged responsibility for the inauguration of the slave trade. The charge is somewhat afield, for the sending of slaves was then being urged by many others—the Hieronymite commissioners, friars, and officials on both sides of the Atlantic. It was around this time, too, that the raising of sugar cane began in the Antilles; and as the Indians were dying out, and most of those left were engaged in washing gold, a great demand arose from the settlers for Negroes. These pressures ultimately led to the opening of large-scale traffic, and within a few decades the islands (except Puerto Rico) were to become virtual colonies of African slaves working for a handful of landlords, with the raising of sugar the principal industry. None of this, however, occurred in the years immediately following Casas' suggestion nor in any way as a result of it.

On the other hand, perhaps his most important notion definitely was adopted in 1518, and very much as he had proposed. His plan for aided emigration to the islands was promptly taken up by the Council that spring, and finally enacted despite a whole series of obstacles that held it up for months. First, Bishop Fonseca returned to a position of power in American affairs (some said by bribery), and "moderately" opposed the plan, which had the support of the chancellor. Then negotiations were interrupted by the cleric's illness and afterwards by the bishop's. And on July 7, the worst blow fell: Casas' patron Sauvage unexpectedly died, and the cleric found himself suddenly "deprived of all favor." But he speedily obtained the aid of two Flemings, Monsieur de la Mure and his uncle, the influential Monsieur de Laxao (La Chaux), as well as the support of Cardinal Adrian.[10] Before fall his new peasants' scheme became a reality at long last.

THE RECRUITING DRIVE FAILS

On September 10, 1518, the Crown issued a sweeping royal provision promising all sorts of "privileges and franchises" for farmers emigrating to the Indies.[11] It was the second time—the Hieronymite instructions had been

---

for a handful under subsequent orders, and apparently all died off. Figueroa himself issued his famous "cannibal" declaration, authorizing settlers to enslave mainland Indians, but in a few years these were dead too, and Negro slaves replaced the vanished race.

10. *Hist.*, IV, 366-376. Peter Martyr was in Zaragoza at the time. He first speaks of the chancellor's death in a letter of July 15, but does not mention it in a previous one of July 4. See his *Opus epistolarum* [1530], Amsterdam, 1670, nos. 621 and 622.

11. Serrano y Sanz, *Orígenes*, app. LXI, and *DIU*, IX, 77-83.

the first—that a major reform idea of the cleric Casas had received official sanction.

This general order of September 10 granted practically all that Casas had recommended: free passage, free land and farm animals and seed, free maintenance for the peasants from the royal estates till they could live on their own crops, assistance from Indians to build homes, prizes for the first farmers to produce certain new products, tax exemptions, and so on. In addition, the cleric himself was (at least implicitly) put in charge of the scheme. Instructions to Casas were promulgated the same day, setting down the procedure he was to follow in recruiting emigrants.[12] In addition, he tells us, "many letters and provisions were issued, all that the cleric asked": letters for civil authorities and justices, letters for bishops and religious, accrediting his person and asking these dignitaries to aid him in the campaign; a cedula for the House of Trade in Seville to provide maintenance and supplies and passage to America for as many farmers as he might send; directions to the island officials to look after the settlement of the emigrants on their arrival. Many of these actual orders have been printed. Fabié listed an instruction, two dispatches, and a bonus, though only in the form of Muñoz extracts without dates. But Serrano copied a number in full from the archives, some from a first batch issued that same September 10, and others from a later "second dispatch."[13]

On top of this, Casas explains that he was given "persons who should accompany him and by whom he was to be aided," all on royal salary. For these, too, we have quite a few of the actual records. Serrano found two commissions: on September 10, a certain Juan de Salaya was assigned to join Casas in his work, and on October 12 a Captain Luis de Berrio was ordered to go along under the cleric's orders. On October 18 also, an advance of twelve ducats apiece was paid to Casas and to this Berrio, who served from October 12 at least through May 12.[14] As for Casas himself, he afterwards received twenty-five thousand maravedis to complete the pay due him for having spent two hundred days proclaiming the "franchises and privileges" for peasants wishing to go to the Indies.[15]

---

12. *DIU,* IX, 83-88.

13. *Hist.,* IV, 398; Fabié, app. III; Serrano y Sanz, *Orígenes,* 431-432, and apps. LXII-LXV and LXVIII; and *DIU,* IX, 94-95 and 109-114.

14. Serrano y Sanz, *Orígenes,* 430-431, and app. LXV, the commissions; *DII,* VII, 90, note 1, the advance and term.

15. The back-pay order is in Fabié, app. XVIII, item from fol. 95. Casas and Berrio both received the same salary of 150 maravedis a day; cf. their appointments in Serrano y Sanz, *Orígenes,* 430 and app. LXVII ("450 maravedis" in *Hist.,* IV, 399 is

Despite all these provisions and appointments, the campaign to recruit peasant emigrants was ultimately to prove a failure. Casas' own rather full account of the events may be read in chapter 105 of book III of his history. Leaving Zaragoza, the cleric and his assistants traveled through old Castile, with Casas reading the King's proclamation and making speeches in the rural villages. The peasants were enthusiastic, and a great many signed on to go to America. The enlistment of emigrants was as promising as he had forecast, but unexpected difficulties began to arise.

Powerful opposition to the scheme was soon manifested by the great landowners, who disliked the idea of losing their tenants. A chief scene of trouble was Berlanga, near the Aragon border. This town was the property of the Fernández de Velasco family, then headed by Iñigo, fourth Count of Haro and Lord High Constable of Castile, one of the most powerful grandees in Spain. His hostility was a considerable obstacle; the peasants had to enroll secretly, and the lord constable threatened confiscation for any attempt of would-be emigrants to sell their belongings.

In addition, Casas was now confronted with defection in his own staff. It seems that his aide Berrio had, before leaving court, gone secretly to the Bishop of Burgos; and the hostile prelate had changed this assistant's dispatches to read "do what you think best" instead of "do what he [Casas] tells you." During the Castile recruiting, Berrio had asked repeatedly for permission to go to Andalusia, which the cleric had refused; but one day he presented himself, booted and spurred, exhibited his altered papers, and coolly went off on his own.[16]

To counter these mounting difficulties, Casas now returned to Zaragoza, exhibiting his large enrollments and seeking further royal backing. Nothing could be done, however, as the King set out shortly for Barcelona. There

---

a misprint). But Casas was to receive 100 pesos of "ayuda de costa" in Española on bringing a good number of emigrants (*Orígenes*, 432) and further financial assistance in Spain—cf. *Hist.*, V, 34. In addition, a cedula was issued on September 24, directing Diego Velásquez to pay Casas for his 2½ year's Cuban service—*DIU*, I, 77-78. No amount is specified.

16. See *Hist.*, IV, 399-403; This account is amply supported. Thus, Serrano y Sanz, *Orígenes*, 430-432, prints a number of Berrio's documents, mistakenly concluding that they impugn Casas' version whereas they confirm it: Berrio's October 12 appointment specifically tells him to do what Casas "os dixere"; the annexed "introduction" cedulas bear the date of September 10, and are hence mere "blanks" issued at the time of Casas' (not Berrio's) appointment; and Berrio's lack of authorization showed up at the House of Trade. Casas' account implies the emendation was made in Berrio's own copy of his commission.

the cleric resumed his efforts, only to encounter new and fatal obstacles to all his plans. Word had been received that the Española Indians were all but wiped out by smallpox, so there was no chance of his tribute scheme saving the remnant. In addition, the Hieronymites had sold the royal estates on Española, the very ones that were to support his peasants till their crops were established. So he therefore demanded a new cedula, to guarantee the colonists a year's maintenance in fulfillment of the King's promise. But this was flatly refused. I am of the opinion, though I know of no documentary proof, that the lord constable and some of the other mighty landlords had complained to the King and induced him to withdraw his support. Anyway, as a result, Casas now abandoned the scheme, despite the fact that four hundred ducats were already being provided for his expenses, and strongly warned that sending emigrants under these terms would expose them to hardship and death.[17]

This dire prediction was shortly fulfilled, for his former insubordinate aide actually attempted to carry on without safeguards. Casas tells us that Berrio proceeded to recruit two hundred unfit persons in Antequera, and that they subsequently went to the Indies where they suffered great privations. We learn something of their fate from the new judge of inquiry, Licentiate Rodrigo de Figueroa. On May 13, 1519, Figueroa—then about to sail for America—wrote from Seville that some peasants had arrived with a certain Luis de Berrio, who was asking the House of Trade to give them passage, but the officials did not know what to do with them. Eventually they were put on a ship with supplies and sent over to Española; and on July 6, 1520, Figueroa reported from Santo Domingo that thirty-seven of Berrio's peasant families had arrived in poor shape. On September 16, he wrote again that the peasants were ill and destitute, and some had died, and nothing could be accomplished by this means.[18] Casas belatedly learned of their plight and persuaded the King to have some wine and flour sent to Santo Domingo for them, but when the succor arrived they had all scattered and none could be found.[19]

---

17. *Hist.*, IV, 403-404 and V, 33-34.

18. *DII*, VII, 91, note, and Fabié, app. III, the 1519 letter; *DII*, I, 420 and 416, the 1520 letters. All are extracts only, presumably by Muñoz.

19. See *Hist.*, lib. III, cap. 155, where this incident occurs in May 1520, at La Coruña. Berrio and his emigrants had finally sailed on April 15, 1520; his recruiting salary had been continued till the end of 1519, and 93,750 maravedis were spent on their costs besides supplies, but they had no provision for maintenance in Española. See the rest of Muñoz's note (*DII*, VII, 90-91) printed in Alejandro Tapia y Rivera, *Biblioteca histórica de Puerto Rico* (Puerto Rico, 1854), 163.

Such was the tragic outcome of Bartolomé de las Casas' second big venture into reform. Long afterwards he would lament its failure and insist on the soundness of peasant emigration; he was still urging it twenty-five years later, and after forty years he claimed that if the original plan had been carried out, there would by then have been two hundred thousand citizens on Española.[20] But when he abandoned the scheme in 1519, he wasted no time on these recriminations. Instead, he now flung himself with renewed energy into the most ambitious of all his proposals so far—his grand design for the settlement of Tierra Firme.

---

20. These are his concluding words on the affair in the *Historia* account. See also Fabié, app. XXXI, section headed "Cerca de la vivienda de los españoles" (cf. Catalogue, no. 21, for the date); and Casas' February 20, 1559, letter to the King—Catalogue, no. 60.

A TIERRA FIRME GRANT

The initial mainland idea

Casas' new Tierra Firme venture proved the most extensive of his early career. It occupied him full time for the next three years, from 1519 to 1522: first a prolonged fight to win a grant of his own, then a heartbreaking struggle to carry out the terms in America. And the origins of the idea went back a whole year before that.

He had first offered his mainland plan among the memorials for Sauvage. Unlike the others, however, this one did not derive from his earlier "community scheme," but was suggested by a recent communication from the Indies. Casas himself tells us the source.

Near the middle of 1518 he received a letter from his friend, Fray Pedro de Córdoba, relating a new outrage committed by Juan Bono on the people of Trinidad, and complaining about other raiders in the vicinity of the Pearl Coast missions.[1] On the northern shore of Venezuela, the Dominicans then had a small monastery at Chiribichi, and the Franciscans another at Cumaná, not very far to the east. Unfortunately, both sites were near Cubagua, the pearl island, a rendezvous for Indian stealers and a general line of reprobates; the lack of water on Cubagua gave the pearl fishers a constant excuse for visits to the Cumaná river and raids along the coast. These slavers had already made trouble for the adjoining missionaries, and Fray Pedro was determined to recall his friars to Santo Domingo if the scandalous incursions could not be stopped. So he begged Casas to try to secure a concession for one hundred leagues of Tierra Firme, including the town of Cumaná, where the King should with great penalties exclude all

---

1. *Hist.*, IV, 393-396. Casas says that after reading this letter he felt strongly moved to go to Tierra Firme and labor alongside the friars, though as a cleric.

other Spaniards and leave the area free for preaching by the Franciscans and the Dominicans. If Casas could not get a hundred leagues, he should take ten, and if not ten he should try to get some small islands fifteen or twenty leagues to the west where the friars might collect the Indians who fled from Spanish persecution and instruct them and save their souls. In pursuit of Fray Pedro's request, the cleric showed this letter to the Council, only to have the Bishop of Burgos scoff at the idea of the King granting a hundred leagues to friars without advantage to himself.[2]

It was therefore after this rebuff that Casas offered his mainland plan, summarized in his mid-1518 petition to the King.[3] His scheme embodied Fray Pedro's goals—the suppression of slave raids and conversion of natives along the coast—but it dwelt heavily on profits for the royal treasury.

Casas proposed that on one thousand leagues of Tierra Firme, the King should cause to be erected ten fortresses, one every hundred leagues, each with a town of Christians consisting of a royal captain and at least a hundred men. (The cost would not be more than a thousand ducats per settlement.) These inhabitants should have strict orders to make no raids on the Indians; for the natives had been injured by the great outrages perpetrated against them and would no longer trust words but only deeds. So the first step was to return to that country all the Indians who had been kidnapped and taken to the islands and to Spain as slaves. After this had been done and the local Indians had regained their confidence, they could then be induced to trade gold and pearls for Spanish goods of little value. "With every 500 ducats worth of goods, I affirm your Highness can receive 30,000 castellanos."[4] To be sure, inducements would have to be offered the Spaniards to live there, and they could also trade individually, but methods could be followed by which nearly all the gold would come to the King.

As for the natives, after everything was quiet they could then be told they would be obliged to pay tribute, and this could be imposed on each married man up to the amount of gold he could pay. "As there are many Indians, Your Highness will have marvelous rents from that coast." Furthermore, "the King should appoint a Bishop for each fortress, taken from friars

---

2. *Hist.*, IV, 396-397.

3. *DII*, VII, 102-106; Fabié, app. IV. (Cf Catalogue, no. 7, for the date.) This is a slightly different version from the summary he gives at the same point in his own narrative, where he speaks of 30 men per fort. *Hist.*, IV, 379-380.

4. In my résumé, I have corrected an obvious misprint in the printed text. The cost per fort should read 1,000 ducats, as in subsequent estimates, and not 100; this is verified by Casas' closing figure of 15,000 ducats as the total cost, i.e., for 10 forts and miscellaneous expenses, such as barter goods, maintenance of friars, etc.

of Santo Domingo and San Francisco and the like . . . for they will have to work to pacify the Indians and keep them in towns. . . . Likewise many Franciscans and Dominican friars should be sent, as they will greatly aid the bishops, for in assuring the land one friar is worth more than 200 men-at-arms."

To finance all this without the King putting up any money, Casas advocated a system of restitution:

> As the Christians have done Your Highness great damage in destroying a large part of that country . . . you could very well make them restore it by surrendering at least one-fifth of the gold and pearls they have received—because they obtained it very unjustly and are obliged to restore it all, . . . so even if the King took all of it he would not commit any sin. If the fifth part is not sufficient, Your Highness can take one-third. . . . This is nothing new in the Indies, for when Ovando came to Española he ordered the inhabitants to pay to the King one-third of all the gold they had collected. If, however, you wish to treat more kindly with them, you could consider the money borrowed and order it repaid, as time goes on, out of the products of the land. . . . Altogether it would not take more than 15,000 ducats to apply this remedy and you could easily obtain 20,000 castellanos.[5]

This was Casas' first Tierra Firme plan—with its emphasis on lucrative barter and tribute, rather than on native missionary work. Anyone reading it without a knowledge of his character might imagine he was putting up a moneymaking scheme to the King; apparently, after the rejection of the Dominican request, he had learned that something of the sort was necessary.

His promise of wealth from the mainland seems to have been inspired by the discovery of Yucatán, which was then creating a sensation at court. Everyone was impressed with the finding of a new civilization only a short distance from the West Indies, complete with stone buildings, paved streets, some kind of organized religion, and of course treasure. Early in 1518, Casas told the Flemings about profits to be expected from the new-found territory, and unintentionally helped set off a scheme by the Admiral of Flanders to colonize it. (But the cleric reported this to Diego Columbus who got the grant cancelled.[6]) Then around midyear, in Zaragoza, Casas

---

5. *DII*, VII, 105-106.

6. *Hist.*, lib. III, cap. 101. The King made the grant "just as if it were a piece of pasture," says Casas; and four or five months later five boatloads of Flemish farmer-emigrants arrived at San Lúcar. But meantime, forewarned by Casas, Diego Columbus complained to the King and Chièvres and Gattinara. They suspended the concession, pending decision of his suit over the privileges granted his father—especially as it was

received a letter from "a very good friend," Francisco Hernández de Córdoba, the discoverer himself. We do not know its full contents, but it gave details on the expedition and perhaps also on the gold obtained from the natives for Spanish trinkets.[7] All this surely contributed to Casas' original plan.

Again the following year, when he gave up his peasant assignment, the American mainland was a center of interest. About the end of 1518 or the beginning of 1519, the gold and other objects obtained by Grijalva, in barter and gifts, reached court. Many of the articles were hollow, and their value was probably much less than generally believed. Though Casas nowhere mentions seeing them, he gives an account of Grijalva's expedition; and in my opinion the arrival of these presents more or less synchronized with his new project.[8] After all, if gold could be had in such quantities in New Spain, why not along the Spanish Main? Plenty had already been obtained in the Darién region midway between the two. The whole atmosphere of the time was full of schemes aiming at mainland discoveries and settlements; Casas' proposal was only one of a number.

Sometime in the spring of 1519, Bartolomé de las Casas resubmitted his Tierra Firme scheme. But now he asked one thousand leagues as a grant for himself, undertook to finance the venture with the aid of fifty share-holders, and promised large royal revenues—clearly he shared the common golden vision of the Spanish Main.[9]

CASAS' FIGHT AT COURT: FOES AND A FRIEND

Casas' battle to win his own grant was a fantastic struggle that took an entire year. In the course of it, he faced a battery of opponents: most of the

---

connected with the government of Cuba, which was legally in the hands of the Columbus family.

7. In *Hist.*, lib. III, cap. 98, the last of three chapters relating this discovery, Casas speaks of the barter and closes with a mention of the letter written him by Francisco Hernández shortly before his death.

8. *Hist.*, lib. III, caps. 109-113; and cf. the opening of the next chapter, where Casas tells of the cleric Benito Martín's reaching Barcelona with these objects. Casas minutely calculates the small value of the clothing and articles given by Grijalva in exchange for gold and other precious objects of great value from the Indians (cf. *ibid.*, IV, 431, 437-438, and 441-442). This strikingly resembles the similar remarks in his own petition about obtaining 30,000 castellanos for every 500 ducats of trinkets.

9. *Hist.*, lib. III, cap 131, the financing; and *DII*, VII, 94, the original territory asked and revenue offered. Casas did not begin to seek his own grant till he was "already free from the care" of the emigration scheme; his 200 days on that assignment were over at the end of April.

colonial agents at court, directed by Bishop Fonseca; also Oviedo, the future chronicler of the Indies; and Bishop Quevedo of Tierra Firme. On the other hand, Casas had the support of Flemish courtiers, the new Chancellor Gattinara, and one powerful ally—Diego Columbus, the second Admiral of the Indies.

An ingenious device of the opposition was to ask concessions in the same district he had applied for, promising greater returns to the King. One petitioner asked one hundred leagues and offered sixty thousand ducats of rent within the time Casas offered thirty thousand; and there were several other such offers. These were submitted to Bishop Fonseca's limited council for Indies affairs and passed on to the Chancellor and the King, temporarily bringing the cleric's business to a halt. But Charles referred the matter back to an enlarged junta, including sympathetic Flemish councilors, which had previously determined to concede the land to Casas. They were amazed at Bishop Fonseca's persistence, and summoned the cleric, who again repeated the charges of misgovernment by Fonseca and his associates. It was a stormy session, marked by a verbal clash between the American priest and Antonio Fonseca, the bishop's brother; and at the end, many of those present once more voted in Casas' favor.[10]

But the controversy did not end there. As a culmination, the bishop's special council prepared a written report containing thirty charges against the cleric. With Gattinara's help, however, Casas managed to see this document and had no difficulty in composing a rebuttal; he himself tells us some of the accusations as well as his replies. First, it was claimed that since he was a priest the King had no jurisdiction over him; second, that he had been "escandaloso" in Cuba (i.e., a disturber of the peace); then, that he had deceived the cardinal, that he would steal treasures and flee to Venice or Genoa, and so on. The last charge was a secret one that he never learned—perhaps it had something to do with his character.[11] (In the course of Casas' troubled career, there would be several intimations that his life in the islands had not been beyond reproach, but it is unlikely that any charge could have

---

10. *Hist.*, lib. III, cap. 139. For the councilors who met with the Bishop of Burgos, see the opening of cap. 134. For the expanded group, to which had been added Juan Manuel, Alonso Téllez, the Marquis of Aguilar, and Licentiate Vargas, with the Flemings also taking part and sometimes Adrian, see cap. 138.

11. *Hist.*, V, 90. Casas does not list the other charges and says he had burned them and his answers 40 years before. But he adds that there were "many others" designed to justify the tyrannies in Darien. Herrera, dec. II, lib. IV, cap. 3, gives a few of the charges in a slightly different version, showing he may have had access to the documents.

been at all serious.) Anyway, his answers were voluminous and well supported. Thus, he answered the first point by offering a bond from the Marquis of Aguilar in the amount of twenty or thirty thousand ducats. And for the second, he produced his "Información ad perpetuam rei memoriam," the notarized account of his services prepared in Cuba before his departure in 1515.[12]

After all was finished, Chancellor Gattinara called a further meeting of the enlarged assembly, at which Casas' documents were read. Only Fonseca offered any challenge, saying that the royal preachers must have prepared these answers for him. At which the chancellor, in whose apartments Casas had drawn up the reply, struck back: "Do you hold *micer* Bartolomé [as the Flemings called the cleric] so lacking in reason and discretion that he has to go out and find somebody to answer for him? As I understand it he is quite capable of that and much more." The results of this session were relayed to the King, who ordered that negotiations on Casas' grant should proceed and the rival petitioners be disregarded.[13]

In this whole maneuver, Oviedo seems to have had a large hand—we shall examine his role later. An independent controversy also developed between the cleric and the condescending Bishop Juan Quevedo from Darien, which resulted in a formal royal audience where Casas, Quevedo, and others aired their views on the Indians. Casas devotes a number of chapters to this dispute, exhibiting his own ready wit and self-complacency, and attacking Quevedo's Aristotelian concept that the natives were servile by nature.[14] But as a matter of fact, Quevedo himself had complaints to make about the actions of Pedrarias Dávila, whom he wanted to get removed; and after the debate, he related as frightful a tale of Indian mistreatment as any Casas ever wrote, and substantially acknowledged that the cleric was right.

---

12. In *Hist.*, lib. III, caps. 140-141, Casas relates this episode at great length, describing how he worked at his answers on four successive nights from eleven to midnight in the apartments of Grand Chancellor Gattinara. See Catalogue, no. 8, for a description of the resulting long document.

13. *Hist.*, V, 98. A few days before this victorious meeting, Casas saw Bishop Fonseca and said sarcastically to his face: "On my faith, sir, you've sold me the gospel neatly, and now that someone's outbidding me, give it to him!" This is but one of many sharp interchanges that Casas records; on the occasion of a previous favorable vote he had engaged in wordy warfare with Antonio Fonseca, the bishop's brother (*ibid.*, 88).

14. *Hist.*, lib. III, caps. 148-149 and 152. In relating the dispute proper, Casas takes the opportunity to describe the King's method of handling business in private meetings.

During his many court battles, Casas had supporters too—ranging from the court preachers, who harangued the Council at his instigation, to Flemings like La Chaux and Chièvres, who sponsored him openly, to one prominent ally who offered to back his request for a grant.[15]

Some time near the end of 1519, Casas enlisted the support of Diego Columbus for this scheme. Relating the episode in the *Historia,* Casas says that Columbus conferred with his brother Hernando, who advised him to ask perpetual dominion over the territory requested. As this was a point at issue in the courts between Columbus and the government, Casas opposed including it; but Hernando's advice prevailed, with the result that the offer was turned down by the Council. Columbus' actual petition was turned up and printed in the last century by Henry Stevens, who ascribed it to 1520. The date should be late 1519, as Casas implies; for the document refers to concessions already made to Casas, but many of its conditions were afterwards changed in the final grant.[16] The text gives us an unusual glimpse of some of the "asking terms."

This provisional contract, formulated by Columbus and Casas, very closely followed the lines of Casas' original petition. But there were more details. They asked for a specific stretch of country between the Boca del Drago and Cabo Gracias á Dios. They agreed that within three years after Columbus reached Española he would erect three towns in this territory, and in each succeeding triennium three more, to a total of nine. In these towns, Columbus agreed to maintain settlers without cost to the King, who was, however, to grant them certain privileges. Thus, there were several clauses regarding tax exemptions, permission to take salt, freedom to barter for necessary food. Furthermore, African slaves were to be introduced; a license was requested to take, at Columbus' expense, twenty Negroes each three years to furnish labor for building the towns, and five hundred Negroes to be divided among the settlers. Also, the settlers would be rewarded with land grants—no specific rules would be made for the distribution of land and house lots, as everything woud depend on the usefulness of the people.

---

15. Starting out with an account of his Flemish supporters, Casas spends four chapters on the court preachers—*Hist.*, lib. III, caps. 134-137. He tells how he conferred with them, and gives the text of their speech denouncing the encomienda and advocating the relocation of the Indians into supervised towns. In a spirit of hindsight, Casas criticizes this.

16. See *Hist.*, V, 156-158. In the provisional contract itself (printed in London, 1854), I see no specific clause about perpetual dominion, unless it may be inferred from Columbus' insistence on his privileges. See Catalogue, no. 9, for the correct dating of this document.

Finally, power was asked to satisfy them in the name of His Majesty by profits, as well as by various honors, including knighthood.

For the Indians of the area, the provisions were sweeping. The King was to grant no encomiendas whatever; and a principal stipulation was that no outsiders should be allowed to trade there or take anything from the natives, except passing ships in need of wood and water. Indian relations would be in charge of Casas and a group of religious; a papal bull should be obtained granting absolution to all who might die on the expedition, also a license for twenty Franciscan and Dominican friars (these Columbus would maintain). In addition, the King was to put at liberty all the Tierra Firme Indians then in the islands, and have them delivered to Columbus, so Casas and the missionaries might return them to their own land. Ten island natives were also to accompany the friars as interpreters.

Columbus himself would finance the enterprise, and hold criminal and civil jurisdiction over the area according to his privileges (the ones in dispute). But His Majesty was to contribute twenty thousand ducats from island smeltings in the first two years. Subsequently all expenses would be repaid out of revenue; and, after the deduction of what was due the Admiral under his grants, the entire net profits were to go to the King.

From this petition, it seems clear that the territory asked was excessive, and it was substantially reduced in Casas' actual contract the following year. But before we study those final terms, let us pause for a postscript to the cleric's long battle at court—the role of Gonzalo Fernández de Oviedo.

OVIEDO'S VERSION

Oviedo was one of those who opposed Casas' plans as fantastic and visionary; whereas to the cleric, Oviedo was a Darien encomendero who had held slaves and was hence in the category of the damned. At the time the two men clashed at court, Oviedo had been in Spain a couple of years trying to get Pedrarias removed as governor of Castilla del Oro. He had originally gone out with the governor in 1514, in the capacity of inspector of gold smelting and with various other appointments. Like Casas, he complained to the Council about the ruining of the Indies, but he only wanted the officials changed. Casas himself rather pithily recounts Oviedo's part in the intrigues against him:

"The bishop [Fonseca] stirred up against the cleric all the agents of the colonists . . . He arranged it in this wise: In those days, Oviedo had arrived from Tierra Firme whither he had gone as royal smelting inspector (he owed his position to the bishop)—and he was a good talker and knew very well how to state things he wished to put across. Also, he was one of the greatest enemies the Indians have had and has done them the worst harm, for he was blinder than others in not knowing the truth, perhaps because of his greater cupidity and ambition, qualities and customs which have destroyed the Indies. This man was the first instigated by the bishop; he sent him to the grand chancellor with one of that functionary's own retainers, whom he instructed: 'Tell the chancellor that this hidalgo, a servant of the King, who has now come from the Indies, will inform him very well about Tierra Firme.' This was so that Oviedo could tell him how much deceitful information (in his opinion) he was receiving from the cleric, giving credit to his false stories; and that he, as a royal official who had come from Tierra Firme, would advise him that what the cleric said was not true, and that the enterprise he proposed was in great disservice to the King and damage to his royal rents. Of this he would give him ample information, along with many Spaniards at court; and they would all together offer to serve the King with much greater revenue and profits than the cleric promised. Finally, he told him all he could to convince him and destroy his partiality for the cleric, and dissuade him from granting the concession that had been [tentatively] accorded him. But this contrary argument did not much move the grand chancellor from his intent, because he had already understood the bishop's prejudice and the malice of those who spoke against the cleric; rather, he seemed to be confirmed in his affection and favor for the cleric."[17] Casas goes on to explain that it was actually Oviedo who arranged to have the conflicting offers presented—in all, quite an insidious role!

Oviedo gives his own version in his *Historia general y natural de las Indias.* The chief chronicler is worth quoting in full, for his is a rare picture, the cleric's battle at court as seen through hostile eyes:

"In the year 1519, at the time that news of his election as King of the Romans and future Emperor reached Don Charles in Barcelona . . . I was at that court of his, on certain business about Tierra Firme. And a reverend father, a secular priest who called himself Licentiate Bartolomé de las Casas, was there soliciting from His Majesty and the gentlemen of his Council of the Indies the government of Cumaná and of the Pearl Coast. In this he was favored by some Flemish cavaliers who were close to the King, and especially by Monsieur de Laxao [La Chaux], who later died while grand commander of the military Order of Alcántara, and who was one of the most accepted court favorites of Caesar. And because of this [he won favor], and also because this father promised them great things and much

---

17. *Hist.,* V, 85 *et seq.*

advantage and increase of the royal revenue. Above all he said that by the method and counsel that he was proposing he would convert to our holy Catholic faith all those lost people and idolatrous Indians; and it seemed that his aim and intention were holy. Furthermore, he obstinately maintained that the Bishop of Burgos, Hernando de la Vega, Licentiate Zapata, Secretary Lope Conchillos, and others who handled the affairs of the Indies till then, in the lifetime of the Catholic King, Don Ferdinand (of glorious memory), had erred in many things and deceived the Catholic King in many ways, profiting personally from the sweat of the Indians, and from the offices and revenues of those parts; and that these lords and councilors, in order to support what they had done and the mistakes they had committed, were opposed to him and did not find good what this father said. Thus in this design he was engaged many days, presenting memorials and petitions.

§ "But not without great opposition; for those councilors whom he blamed were on hand; and they showed for their exoneration the books and what had been decreed in the time of the Catholic King, for some years before this father undertook this fantasy of his. It all seemed holy and well done, and for the purpose of the good conservation of the land and condition of those parts, and well suited for the conversion of the Indians. So Caesar was satisfied, and considered himself well served by those whom this father blamed; and they played a great part in the negotiations to hinder the cleric in what he asked. Thus the cleric's persistence was put off for some months. When he saw that those of the Council could not be injured by him, he said that although they might have decreed well, all had been badly understood and carried out worse.§

["Thus he continued presenting petitions], saying that the people who were to be sent with him should not be soldiers nor killers, nor bloodthirsty men, nor eager for war, but very peaceful and quiet peasants—and these to be made nobles and knights of the Golden Spur, and given passage and ship stores, and made tax exempt and aided in founding settlements, along with many other privileges which he asked for them as it occurred to him. All this was granted to him, even though the gentlemen of the Council—or at least the Bishop of Burgos, Don Juan Rodríguez de Fonseca, and others who shared his opinion—opposed him, and notwithstanding that some Spaniards, men of substance, who were at that time in the court from those parts and should have been believed, tried to undeceive the King and his Council in this matter. They said that the father, desirous of being in command, promised what he could not perform, nor could it be in the manner that he said, for he talked about a land that he did not know, nor had ever seen nor set foot upon; and they condemned as folly all that the cleric affirmed, and said that the King would spend his money in vain, and that those who might accompany the father would go into great risk and danger. But as I have said, Laxao weighed more than all that was said in opposition."[18]

Casas was naturally incensed when this unflattering account appeared in 1535 (there was still more, a garbled tale of the expedition itself, which we shall take up later). He retaliated very strongly in his own history, correcting the misstatements—e.g., the knighthood was designed for his shareholders and not the peasants—and devoting chapters 142 to 146 of his book III to an attack on Oviedo and his *Historia general,* answering alleged slanders against the Indians and sharply examining the inspector's relations with the Darien natives. Yet we are indebted to the chief chronicler. Possibly his words provoked Casas to relate the story at such length—besides giving us a choice hostile picture of the cleric's long battle for his grant.

FINAL TERMS

Casas' concession was finally approved on May 19, 1520, but it was for Cumaná only and not the whole of Tierra Firme. Much negotiation had been required to cut down his original vast scheme to these more modest dimensions; and we have a petition from the cleric to the chancellor that reviews the whole process.

In this letter, evidently written near the end of 1519, Casas protests the removal of Cenú from his territory, for the following reasons:

First, when he began to negotiate about this enterprise he asked for a thousand leagues of country, where he would construct ten fortified substantial towns and provide fifty thousand ducats of revenue for the King in three years. But when the business came before the Council, the thousand leagues was reduced to six hundred or less; and the only remaining gold was in two provinces, Cenú and Santa Marta, together only some hundred leagues in extent.

Second, he had asked for the pearl fishery in Paria and the exclusion of Spanish traders; but they took away the fishery, and he agreed that all traders might come, so as to conclude the contract.

Third, without the promise of gold, he will have difficulty finding persons to invest in the venture and go with him.

---

18. Oviedo, *Historia general y natural,* primera parte, lib. XIX, cap. 5. I have quoted this from the 1851 Real Academia edition (I, 599-600). It should be noted that the passage between section marks (§) was not in the book when Oviedo first printed it in 1535, nor in the 1547 reprinting, which Casas allegedly interfered with. (Cf. *infra,* chapter XVII, note 29.) This is Oviedo's later and doubtless piqued addition to his manuscript, so I have made it a separate paragraph in my translation.

Fourth, he needs to land in Paria, because it is necessary for him to have the help of the Franciscans and Dominicans already in that province, as well as of those he will take with him; and he must start making peace with the natives from that point.

Fifth, without Cenú, Lope de Sosa [the new governor of Castilla del Oro] would still have plenty of gold-bearing country from Darien westward; and with his twelve hundred men he is bound to do great damage to the Indians.

So now Casas begs for the inclusion of Cenú in his grant, or at least that it be divided between him and Sosa; and the other limit should be the Río Dulce, east of Paria, in order to include the missions. Finally, if he loses Cenú, that would cut his territory down to three hundred fifty leagues, so the original promise of revenue ought to be cut down. Also, as chances of profit would be less, more liberal terms should be allowed for his fifty shareholders—their "twelfth" should begin with the first payment to the King and last for eight heirs instead of five.

At the end of the document is a note by Chancellor [Mercurino Arborio de] Gattinara to Don García [de Padilla] to reduce the cleric's obligation in proportion to the reduced territory.[19]

Apparently, however, little was done at this time, for in January of 1520, Charles left Barcelona, and Casas no doubt traveled with the court on the slow journey across Spain. It was not until May at La Coruña that the closing negotiations took place, and the King at last signed the concession on the nineteenth, the very day before he sailed for Flanders.[20] A supplement, granting a few privileges to the other settlers besides the shareholders, was signed by the Queen after Charles had left.

Casas' final "contract and stipulation" still followed the outlines of his original plan, but the final cuts had been very drastic. He had lost not only Cenú but Santa Marta as well, and his territory had shrunk to two hundred sixty leagues along the coast, though it was unlimited in the interior. In three years he was to produce fiteen thousand ducats of revenue in different things, increasing to sixty thousand by the end of ten years; and within five years, he was to erect three Christian towns of forty or fifty settlers each.

---

19. See Henry Stevens' edition of 1854, which contains the added note of Gattinara—cf. Catalogue, no. 10. This is omitted in *DII*, VII, 93-100, where the text is further disfigured by the misprinting of Cenú as Zebú, wildly identified by the editors as an island of the Philippines.

20. See *Hist.*, V, 161. Casas implies the favorable atmosphere was influenced by a speech of Adrian's, which led to a formal declaration that the Indians should be free and treated as such, and their conversion should be by peaceful means.

In return, a number of privileges were granted to the cleric and the fifty picked men who were to accompany him: one-twelfth of the revenue, inheritable only to the fourth generation; the right to barter for pearls at the fishery with payment of the usual fifth, but this would be reduced to a seventh after payment of the fifteen thousand ducats. These men would be made knights of the Golden Spur, but for the first three years they could use their exemptions and privileges only in the Indies, though after that and payment of the fifteen thousand ducats, they could use them elsewhere. (The caballeros were also to have other distinctions and exemptions.) Similarly, after the first town was built, Casas and each of the fifty men could bring in three Negro slaves, half of them women and half men, and seven Negroes apiece after the three towns were finished. Further, they were granted exemptions from import duties, the salt monopoly, etc.; and Casas was to assign land to them and his other settlers, for whose benefit the royal fifth from gold mining was cut to a tenth the first year, returning to normal after five. Casas was also to appoint commanders for the fortresses and town officials; an accountant, treasurer, and judge were to be named by the King.

For the Indians, there were a number of clauses that Casas had requested. The King agreed not to give any encomiendas in the territory; and to secure a papal bull so Casas might bring in a dozen Franciscan and Dominican friars to convert the natives. All unjustly held Tierra Firme Indians in the islands were to be freed and delivered to Casas to return to their country; and he was allowed to take ten island Indians along for a period of ten years. But Spanish trading ships were specifically permitted in the area, though strict orders were to be given that no trader in Casas' territory should maltreat the Indians, nor trade arms nor take anything from them by force. Within the first two years, Casas was to have pacified ten thousand tribute-paying natives.

The King was to pay none of the initial expense. But out of the revenue, when received, he would build and maintain a hospital, and make some repayment of costs: two thousand ducats a year for the first ten years, for barter goods and other expenses in pacifying the country; maintenance for eight months of Casas and his fifty men and the friars; and a total of three thousand ducats in ten years for the cost of the fortresses.[21]

---

21. *DII*, VII, 65-89, the grant; 89-92, the supplement. Herrera (dec. II, lib. IX, cap. 8) says the territory granted extended along some 260 leagues of coastline; the editors of the *DII* estimate 260 or 270 leagues. In the supplement, one limit of Casas' concession is wrongly printed as Santa Marta "inclusive," instead of "exclusive," as in the grant proper.

So much for the final terms of the grant. In many respects it was simi-lar to others issued in those times, especially in the King's refusal to pay any part of the expenses except from revenues received. The Crown had the habit, too, of giving concessionaires large salaries, payable always from profits to be realized; but Casas did not even get this. Save for the license itself, the only royal contribution was in relief from import taxes and the salt monopoly.

Still, Bartolomé de las Casas had won his year-long battle: he had a grant from the King authorizing him to found a model colony on Tierra Firme. But what this document really meant—and what happened when he tried to carry it out—would be a tragic sequel to the story.

THE CUMANÁ FIASCO

LAUNCHING AN IMPOSSIBLE VENTURE

During the next two years, Casas struggled desperately and in vain to establish a colony at Cumaná on the Venezuela coast. It was one of the great fiascos of his life, all the more pathetic because he should never have tried.

A sharp second look convinces one that this venture was impossible from the start. Failure lay in its very essence, and in fact the whole scheme was an indictment of Casas' good judgment. What could have induced him to undertake it? In the first place he should have known that he could not obtain fifty men to go and work without pay for three years, still less if he expected them to put up two hundred ducats apiece, as set out in the initial project. Furthermore, it is assumed in the contract that these men would be recruited in the islands, something Casas must have known was absolutely beyond the realm of possibility. Whether he actually found any shareholder in Spain or not is a moot question; there is proof he did take over a contingent of peasants, but nowhere can I find mention of a single knight of the Golden Spur.

Not only was the plan basically unsound, but it even throws somewhat of a stain on Casas' character. The transactions had all the aspects of a commercial speculation. True, the conversion of the Indians was mentioned, but little stress was laid on that. Far more attention was given to a quite worldly idea, the plan of erecting towns and fortresses in the territory chosen.

These forts are a curious feature for Casas to have included. Fray Pedro's letter, which started the affair, contained no suggestion for making any Spanish settlements on the coast. Yet in Casas' first mainland scheme, and throughout the negotiations for his grant, there is talk of founding settlements—they are called now towns, now fortresses. Regardless of the designation, fortifications are always implied, for if there was any necessity whatever for building them, this need would remain constantly operative. Even to the untutored savages who inhabited the region, the building of a fortified town in their territory would have an obvious significance. And though Casas had not yet expounded the doctrine of peaceful conversion later elaborated in his *Del único modo,* yet he had already given indications he thought peaceful conquest was the only line to pursue. Why then did he propose forts? Their object, incidentally, seems to have been the one hinted in his original Tierra Firme plan: they were intended to be centers for penetrating the interior in search for gold, which gives a still greater appearance of commercial enterprise to the whole project.

A couple of explanations suggest themselves. Did Casas perhaps envision these forts to defend the missionaries? Certainly, he was aware that at this time there were two religious establishments on Tierra Firme, a Franciscan one at Cumaná and a Dominican one at Chiribichi. But there is no evidence he had in view any military protection for either. These were strictly evangelical enterprises, of the sort he afterwards argued for so strongly. It is a fact that both missions were destroyed later by the Indians, but this happened some time in 1520, well after the concession had been made and around the time Casas sailed for America. So there is nothing to show he anticipated any need for armed support for the friars.[1] I think it more likely that the forts idea might have originated with the Council, perhaps in the oral discussions of Fray Pedro's original request. The strong commercialism of his plan (Casas tells us) was developed in consequence of that first refusal; and it may be that this whole provision for the erection of towns or fortresses was also inserted to secure Council approval. I have no authority to support this theory, but I cannot otherwise account for the inclusion of such clauses in Casas' contract, in view of his well-known opinion.

Another main clause definitely was put in by the Council, and it was to have tragic consequences. The proviso that Spanish ships could come to the coast to "trade" with the natives was bound to be fatal to the enterprise, and so indeed it turned out to be. Here, too, Casas showed a lack of foresight. He was planning to start his colony near the Pearl Coast missions, in order to have the help of the friars. Yet the presence of a mob of rascals on Cubagua, only thirty miles or less from Cumaná, was a known menace, and

---

1. It is, however, true that more than a decade later Casas again supported a somewhat similar proposition, a combination of ecclesiastical-military government for a series of forts to be erected at strategic points along the coast. See his January 20, 1531, Memorial to the Council of the Indies, Fabié, app. V (II, 76-78). By that time, however, he had perhaps become convinced that some military protection was necessary for the missionaries.

it stood to reason the location would also be risky for the infant colony. Strict exclusion was necessary and had been requested by Fray Pedro, Diego Columbus, and Casas himself; so this admission clause added an element of danger to a scheme that was already impossible.

Nevertheless, during the rest of 1520, Casas set to work to prepare for his hopeless venture. The summer was occupied in getting issued the numerous cedulas necessary for every contract of this sort. Most, if not all of these are available to us, usually in the form of digests made by Muñoz. In addition, we have a number of staff appointments. Miguel de Castellanos was named royal accountant on May 20; Hernando de Almonacid was appointed treasurer on July 7; but the post of judge was never filled.[2] Then, on October 12, 1520, one Blas Hernández, a priest, contracted with Casas to go along as chaplain for three years, at an annual salary of twenty thousand maravedis. In this contract Casas is referred to as chaplain of the King and administrator of the Indians of Tierra Firme.[3]

Casas himself had meantime gone to Seville to arrange for the voyage. There he borrowed some money, including 6,980 maravedis from his brother-in-law, as he had spent his total capital at court; and friends gave him some beads and other small articles for the Indians.[4] He tells us that he set sail at last from San Lúcar on St. Martin's day, November 11, 1520, with a group of peasants to help build the towns he was to found. This is confirmed by the documents—though Casas' date seems to be an error, as the departure actually took place in mid-December, apparently on two vessels. On December 15, a payment of some twenty thousand maravedis was made to the storekeeper of the "San Juan" for maintenance of ninety-eight persons who were with Casas till December 14, the day the ship sailed; and her captain afterwards received one hundred forty thousand maravedis for the safe passage of seventy of them.[5]

---

2. Fabié, app. III.

3. *Fondos americanos,* IV, no. 734. This "capellan" part of the title appears in the supplement to the capitulation (*DII,* VII, 89); and Casas himself, speaking of the signing of his grant, says it was decided "that the cleric be given charge of the conversion of the natives" of that part of Tierra Firme (*Hist.,* V, 161).

4. See *Fondos americanos,* V, no. 541, on Ferrandes' later attempt to collect the loan, which was for Indian trading goods.

5. Fabié, app. XVIII, items from fols. 86 and 93. Casas gives the sailing date in *Hist.,* V, 165. I believe this is a simple confusion with his previous sailing to America at the time of the Hieronymite Mission—it was on St. Martin's day, November 11, 1516. Herrera, dec. II, lib. IX, cap. 9, says Casas had 200 peasants in three ships.

This modest expedition was afterwards exaggerated and ridiculed by contemporary chroniclers. Gómara, for instance, wrote that it consisted of three hundred peasants who wore crosses. The reference was to an insignia like that of Calatrava, which Casas had designed for the outer garments of his knights to show the Indians they were different from other Spaniards; but no one, he says, ever wore the costume except himself.[6] Oviedo started this canard about the ennobled peasants, but did give details on their equipment and sailing: "The King, our lord, therefore ordered him [Casas] to be dispatched and provided for. Under this order the Council and the officials at Seville dispatched him in the manner that he knew how to request; and so he set out for Tierra Firme with up to [blank] men, large and small, farmers, to whom they gave good ships and supplies, and everything necessary, and trade goods for bartering with the Indians, all of which cost His Majesty many thousands of ducats."[7]

BAD NEWS, BAD BARGAIN

Casas and his peasants reached San Juan de Puerto Rico the second week in February, 1521, and here the cleric received a stunning blow. He was told that the coastal Indians had destroyed the Dominican convent at Chiribichi and killed two of the friars, and a punitive armada was already under way from Santo Domingo to the very territory of his concession!

Briefly, this was the bad news, as Casas himself afterwards repeated it in his *Historia* and his *Apologética* (the latter account passing into several monastic chronicles).[8] The Dominican monastery was then five or six years

---

6. Cf. Gómara, *Historia*, 205, and Casas' answer in *Hist.*, lib. III, cap. 160; also his previous description and explanation of the device in cap. 131. He was adapting a type of reward customary in New World ventures.

7. Oviedo, primera parte, lib. XIX, cap. 5.

8. *Hist.*, lib. III, cap. 156, and *Apol.*, cap. 246. This chapter of the *Apologética* was copied by Fray Jerónimo de Mendieta in his *Historia eclesiástica indiana*, caps. 9-10. See Catalogue, no. 64, "Contemporary MSS [of the *Apologética*] and their users."

Since Mendieta did not see Casas' MS *Historia*, he could give only a garbled version of the previous history of the Pearl Coast missions: an initial massacre of two Franciscans in 1516; a subsequent mission of three Dominicans, also martyred; and a further Dominican foundation. But in *Hist.*, lib. III, caps. 33-34 and 83, Casas tells the full story, obviously learned at first hand. Fray Pedro de Córdoba obtained royal provisions for this venture in Spain in 1513. Returning to Española, he sent three missionaries to Tierra Firme—one became ill and remained at Puerto Rico, and two others (a friar and a lay brother) went on to the Pearl Coast and were later martyred because of the kidnapping of an Indian chief. Then, after September 1515, Fray

old and had gathered much fruit in the work of conversion. Unfortunately, as we know, the pearl-fishing resort of Cubagua was nearby, inhabited by a lot of desperados. One of these men, Alonso de Hojeda, had decided to make a raid for slaves on the mainland and had implicated the mission. With fifteen or twenty companions he went to Chiribichi, where the friars regaled them. Hojeda then summoned the local chief, and began to ask him, before the scribe, if there were any cannibals [the legal pretext for slaving]. Much enraged, the chief shouted "No! No!" and departed. Hojeda then went to Maracapana, some four leagues farther west, where he landed and succeeded in kidnapping thirty or thirty-five Indians. A day or two later, Hojeda again landed with ten or twelve men; but this time the Indians attacked them and killed all but a few. The following Sunday, September 3 [2], 1520, natives killed two Dominicans at the mission; two other friars were at Cubagua, and so escaped.

An official report of the affair, written on November 14, 1520, tells a quite different story.[9] The Santo Domingo officials insist the massacre at the mission was without provocation and Hojeda only landed at Maracapana the day after; they go on to tell of other Spanish landing parties that afterwards suffered the same fate. But Casas undoubtedly obtained his account from the Dominicans; if it was true, the Indians were fully justified in killing the Spaniards, though it was certainly tragic that blameless friars should be included in the affair. Some time after this massacre the Franciscan convent at Cumaná was also destroyed, but those friars had apparently gone to Cubagua, though the chronicler Mendieta says a Fray Dionisio was killed.

As word of the situation reached Santo Domingo, the officials resolved to send a small war-fleet to punish the Indians and build palisaded forts at Cubagua and Cumaná. Gonzalo de Ocampo was appointed captain, first with one hundred men and later with two hundred, after they heard of the destruction of the Franciscan monastery. These details are given in the audiencia letter just cited (it was also signed by Columbus, who had arrived after the report was written). Instructions to Ocampo were issued on January 20, 1521. These ordered him to proceed to Santa Fé, the place the Dominicans had built at Chiribichi, and arrest the chief; if the Indians resisted, he

---

Pedro himself went to Tierra Firme and founded the Chiribichi mission; at the same time, some Picardy Franciscans founded the Cumaná mission ten leagues away. Casas mentions no previous Franciscan massacre, and it may be apocryphal. Besides, the early Dominican martyr, a lay brother named Juan Garcés, could readily be confused with the later Fray Juan Garceto and the martyred lay brother of 1520.

9. *DII,* I, 422-427.

was to make war on them. At Cumaná, he was directed to follow the advice of the Franciscan, Fray Juan Garceto, who was going with him.

This, in sum, was the tragic tale that Casas learned when he reached San Juan. As Ocampo was due to stop at that island shortly, on his way to the Pearl Coast, the cleric decided to wait for him there. In a few days the armada arrived, and Casas formally read his powers to Captain Ocampo, and demanded that the soldiers should not proceed to Tierra Firme as the King had granted that land to him. Ocampo replied with the standard "obedezco pero no cumplo" formula used by Spaniards for unwelcome royal orders. He acknowledged Casas' provisions but would not comply with them because the audiencia had ordered him to go to that coast and would therefore "hold him safe." At this point, I feel, Casas made a grave mistake. He ought to have accompanied Ocampo to the mainland, taking the peasants along, and there endeavored to turn the war venture into a peace-making and colonizing expedition. Instead, he decided to go to Santo Domingo and complain to the audiencia about the violation of his grant. Accordingly, he purchased a ship for five hundred pesos on credit—many San Juan people, seeing what they considered a wonderful opportunity to get rich, offered to lend him money. Also, he distributed his peasants among the residents to be looked after till his return. Then he sailed off, not to Tierra Firme but to Española.[10]

Once in Santo Domingo, Casas presented his credentials to the authorities—a group of some ten functionaries, consisting of the admiral, the judges, and the royal officials, then known as the *Consulta*, or Conference. They agreed to have his provisions proclaimed publicly, including the order that no one was to harm Indians in his territory. But his major demand, that they recall the Ocampo expedition, brought no action. Instead, it was debated for many days, and finally the audiencia thought up a scheme to outwit Casas. A calker, who had made money in the slave business, was charging publicly that Casas' ship was unseaworthy. This individual and others of his kind were now appointed on a commission to examine the vessel, and of course condemned her, leaving the cleric in a precarious financial position. To make matters worse, by this time some of Ocampo's ships began to return with cargoes of slaves from Maracapana. Casas, raging, went to the audiencia and threatened to return to Castile and have the judges punished by the King; and they knew he was capable of accomplishing it.

---

10. *Hist.*, V, 166. Also see Licentiate Gama to the King, Puerto Rico, February 15, 1521, on Casas' confusion at learning of the armada. *DII*, XL, 52-54.

So now began a tug-of-war between a man with "powers" and no authority, and the officials who had no legal papers but all the authority. In the end, the Conference came up with a compromise, proposing to combine their venture with the cleric's. They made up a pool and offered to furnish Casas with ships and supplies and the aid of Ocampo and one hundred twenty of his men; in return, they were to receive one-half of the profits, one-quarter being reserved for the King, and one-quarter for Casas and his fifty knights. In this contract, they had four objects in view: the pearl fishing at Cubagua; bartering for gold all along the coast; the taking of many slaves; and finally, squaring themselves for their unauthorized expedition at royal expense, by helping Casas gain some revenue for the King. One of the clauses actually provided that the cleric should decide which tribes were cannibals or unwilling to receive the faith; and then these could be captured as slaves. This, says Casas, was the principal hope of the Conference, and the reason they offered him such terms. It was a strange and unsavory bargain, yet under the circumstances, Casas had to accept.

All this seems to have taken months. Casas tells us that he finally got underway some time in July. He sailed with two ships, well stocked with provisions and trade goods, and stopped off at Mona Island to take on a thousand loads of cassava, weighing fifty pounds each. From there he proceeded to Puerto Rico, expecting to pick up his peasants, but they had all gone off on Indian raids, and he found none to take along. And so—with no colonists for his colony, his territory ravaged for five months by a Spanish force, his hard-won grant replaced by a strange new contract—Bartolomé de las Casas at long last sailed on to Tierra Firme.[11]

THE OUTPOST AND THE TRAGEDY

Some time in July or August of 1521, Casas went ashore in the vicinity of the Cumaná River. Here he found the Ocampo expedition engaged in constructing a settlement named Toledo, and a few Franciscan friars who rejoiced at his coming. The surrounding region was almost deserted, as the terrified coastal Indians had fled to the interior. Without natives to prey on, the Spanish soldiers were hungry and close to mutiny, and in no mood for the cleric's new arrangements. Not one was willing to remain with him, so Ocampo and all his men abandoned the enterprise and sailed back to Santo Domingo.

Casas was left at the Cumaná outpost, with only the friars, Accountant Castellanos (who had joined him in Santo Domingo), and a few salaried

---

11. *Hist.*, lib. III, cap. 157 and the beginning of cap. 158.

employees. We know comparatively little about his life there, and most of it is rather negative. In the *Apologética* he says he was at Cumaná five months. But in his *Historia* narrative he does not even mention the length of his stay or give any description of the abandoned Spanish settlement, speaking only of the fine monastery garden.

He did, however, build a storehouse to hold his trade goods; and a native woman named María, who understood a little Spanish, was instrumental in communicating with some Indians, to whom Casas made gifts and announced his kind intentions.[12] But there is no indication that the cleric obtained any revenue in gold or in barter trade during his months at Cumaná. The subsequent failure of the enterprise prevents us from ever knowing what its monetary achievements might have been.

Nor do we have any evidence that his Indian relations went beyond this preliminary stage, or that he obtained any firsthand knowledge of the natives. In telling of his Cumaná stay, in the *Historia*, Casas does not speak of the land or the customs of the people; and in the *Apologética*, he confesses that although he spent some time in that country, he never learned the natives' method of government. Several chapters of the *Apologética* are devoted to the Cumaná Indians, but Casas acknowledges that he did not know much about them; aside from his remarks on their personal appearance, most of his information seems to have been derived from the missionaries. Thus, he says that the friars had seen the native remedy for poisoned arrows; it was not a complete cure, for the victim had to abstain for life from certain foods and drinks and from hard labor, but the Spaniards knew no remedy at all. Again, he tells of the native religion, saying that like most Indians they had temples, idols, and sacrifices, but he knew little of their practices; and in speaking of their priests, called *piachas*, he gives a long account of Fray Pedro de Córdoba's experience with one of them.[13] In other chapters, he tells how women performed men's tasks even in war and were bosses at home, and also describes funeral customs rather elaborately, but this, too, is apparently taken from monastic sources.[14] Elsewhere in the *Apologética*, Casas does occasionally allude to what he saw in Cumaná; but he also says

---

12. *Hist.*, V, 180-182. Virtually the same picture is given in a later report by Castellanos to the King—*DII*, X, 32-34. This was written in Spain when news of the 1522 "uprising" had been received but not verified.

13. *Apol.*, cap. 245, with repeated references to "our religious" and Fray Pedro.

14. *Apol.*, caps. 245 and 247. In the latter chapter he also discusses interments along the rest of the coast, with special reference to the gold treasures found in the tombs of the Cenú chiefs. This recalls his rejected request for the inclusion of Cenú in his own grant because of the gold.

frankly that most of his Indian information in this book was obtained from friars, as they were the only ones to learn the native languages.[15]

Most of Casas' own Cumaná narrative is devoted instead to an account of his troubles with his Spanish neighbors. Just as he might have foreseen, the rascals on Cubagua soon proved an open menace to his tiny establishment. Since these islanders lacked fresh water and came to the mainland to get it, Casas had decided to build a fortress at the mouth of the river to control the water supply and prevent the raiding. He therefore hired a mason on Cubagua; but the Spaniards, understanding what was in the wind, persuaded or bribed the man not to come. Before long the pearl fishers began appearing on the coast—abusing the Indians, trading with them for slaves, giving them wine so that they got drunk and started to fight among themselves. Casas went over to Cubagua and read the riot act to the mayor, but nothing availed.

For the cleric's difficulties with the Cubaguans, we have a witness, Accountant Miguel de Castellanos, who later wrote his own reports. Castellanos attributed the trouble to the fact that the King had not sent a judge to handle civil and criminal affairs in Cumaná, as agreed in the contract; instead, Casas had to contend with hostile officials on the pearl island, including a judge who claimed jurisdiction over the coast. Seeing that nothing was to be achieved under these circumstances, Accountant Castellanos went back to Santo Domingo, in order to persuade the audiencia to send some relief to the cleric. Of course, none was forthcoming; and the discouraged accountant thereupon returned to Spain.[16]

Casas meanwhile was growing more and more disheartened in his outpost. He was powerless to stop the raids, and there was much evidence that the Indians were going to attack the tiny settlement. The prudent Franciscan prior, Fray Juan Garceto, finally persuaded Casas to go to Santo Domingo in person and complain to the authorities. It took a month of worry and

---

15. *Apol.*, 176. But Casas also says he used the accounts of others if they seemed true. In writing of the Pearl Coast, he gives credit to Peter Martyr's *De orbe novo* for material taken literally from decs. VIII and IX, but refutes the dec. VII story of the Chiribichi massacre; cf. *Apol.*, 643.

16. *Hist.*, V, 182-184. And see Castellanos' two relations, *DII*, X, 33-39 and VII, 109-116, the latter written after receiving letters about the destruction of the settlement. The hostile Cubagua official is identified as one Francisco de Vallejo.

In the second relation, Castellanos says he sailed from Santo Domingo for Spain "about the middle of last February"—i.e., of 1522, because Casas had not yet returned. At the close, Castellanos asks payment of his salary for the two years since he originally left Spain; as he came over a bit after Casas (who sailed in mid-December, 1520), this places the writing of his report at the very end of 1522 or early in 1523.

prayer to reach this decision. But in the end Casas gave in, much against his will. He placed in charge a certain Francisco de Soto, whom he had brought with him from Spain, with strict instructions not to allow the two small vessels left in port to go away under any pretext. Then, beset by deep misgivings, Casas left his "colony" early in 1522; he sailed on a salt ship bound for Española, taking only a chest of clothing and another of books.

After the cleric's departure, Soto promptly sent off the two vessels, one east and the other west, to try to trade for gold and pearls. No sooner were these escape ships gone than the Indians decided to wipe out the settlement. The attack came at dawn, fifteen days later. All the friars, except a lay brother, escaped in a canoe, but several of the servants were killed. Pursued by native warriors in a swifter pirogue, the members of the small fleeing party ran their canoe ashore and took refuge in a thorny thicket. Here the Indians, being naked, could not get at them and finally went away. The Spaniards at length made their way to a nearby vessel that was loading salt. Soto, who had been wounded by a poisoned arrow, was found and brought aboard still alive, but then as a result of drinking water he became violently ill and died. In the melee, the Indians had set fire to the warehouse, and they subsequently burned the rest of the buildings and killed the lay brother who was left behind. The remaining survivors were taken to Santo Domingo, with word of the total destruction of Casas' settlement.[17]

For a couple of months, Casas himself knew nothing of all this. The pilot of his vessel had overrun the port of Santo Domingo and was unable to get out of the currents near the west end of the island. So the cleric was finally obliged to go ashore and walk back to the capital—it must have been in February or March of 1522. On the way some travelers chanced to give him the news, including the rumor that he himself had been killed. Of course, Bartolomé de las Casas was still alive, but his great Tierra Firme venture had ended in such complete tragedy that it was to change the whole course of his life.

---

17. Casas tells the denoument in *Hist.*, IV, 184-190. He says that the property lost, some of which belonged to the King, was worth 50,000 pesos.

CASAS AS A DOMINICAN

His monastery years

As a result of the Cumaná tragedy, Bartolomé de las Casas entered the Dominican Order. I cannot but think that he made a great mistake in becoming a friar. He was in no way fitted for the monastic life. Rather, his temperament was that of a fighter, and his new state gave him little opportunity to effect his chief purpose, the liberation of the Indians.

But, evidently, Casas was too discouraged to do anything else. When he finally reached Santo Domingo after the massacre, his few friends tried to comfort him and even offered to lend him four or five thousand ducats to start over again. Casas, however, felt the outcome was a divine punishment for his having joined with the members of the Conference, who cared only for riches and not for gaining souls; perhaps God was offended by his having mixed a spiritual affair with base worldliness, though he humbly believed that the Lord did consider his good intention and so saved him from death.[1] This was poor consolation, and he had no heart to return to court. Instead, he went to stay at the Dominican monastery, and was finally persuaded by Fray Domingo de Betanzos to ask for the habit.[2]

Casas' novitiate began in 1522 and he took the vows as a Dominican in 1523. These are Remesal's dates and are the most probable under all the circumstances. Some remarks in the *Historia* seem to indicate Casas became a friar in 1522; and Accountant Castellanos refers to his joining the Dominican Order in a report written at the end of 1522 or the beginning of 1523.[3]

---

1. *Hist.*, lib. III, cap. 160.

2. Cf. Rem., I, 145. The vice provincial was then Fray Tomás de Berlanga.

3. *Hist.*, V, 200; and cf. *DII*, VII, 115. Castellanos says the King has doubtless heard that Casas withdrew to Española and "became a friar with the Dominicans," so

For a long time after his profession Casas was dead to the world, so to speak, and we have little data with which to follow him for the next decade.[4] According to Remesal, Casas was present at the death of Fray Pedro de Córdoba on St. Peter [Martyr's] day (April 29), 1525. But this year is only the first of Remesal's numerous slips for the ensuing obscure period. Casas himself tells us categorically that Fray Pedro died on the eve of St. Catherine's day (i.e., on April 29), 1521, and even gives the text of the funeral oration.[5] We may be certain, however, that the memory of Fray Pedro was important to Casas when he himself began to follow the rule his friend had instituted. In the *Apologética* and the *Historia*, he pays warm tributes to this valued associate and counselor; for Pedro de Córdoba, as I have demonstrated, first raised the question in 1511 of the mistreatment of the Indians by the Spaniards, and was in truth Casas' spiritual father.

Remesal also allegedly learned from an elderly friar of the Province of Santa Cruz de la Española that Casas served as prior of the Santo Domingo convent. In confirmation he quotes a statement from the *Apologética* that Casas gave the habit to a Spaniard who had been with Hojeda, though Casas actually says *"we* gave." Anyway, Casas did, by his own account,

---

he is speaking of entering and not profession. Herrera (dec. III, lib. II, cap. 5) includes the event in 1521, though not dating it; but this is merely because he places it at the close of three successive chapters on the Cumaná fiasco.

4. His own words are "the cleric, now friar, Fray Bartolomé de las Casas, slept as it seems for some years"—and he says there will be much more to tell later. But the *Historia* breaks off after just a few more chapters, which yield but one incident in his life. In lib. III, cap. 166, relating the kidnapping of Chief Higoroto from a Cumaná town, Casas does say he arrived at San Juan just when the Indian slaves were brought in and sold. As he places the event here, rather than earlier, he may have seen it in 1522 when he was returning to Española.

5. Cf. Remesal, I, 145-146, where he tells that Casas and Betanzos were at the deathbed. But *Hist.*, lib. III, cap. 158, opens with the following solemn words: "In these days, a few before May, the year of 1521, on the eve of St. Catherine of Siena, died that servant of God, father Fray Pedro de Córdoba." The year 1521 is doubly confirmed. Casas places the event just before his sailing to his own colony in July 1521, and says Fray Pedro died at the age of thirty-eight. And the young vicar was twenty-eight when he brought the first Dominicans to Española in 1510. (Cf. *Hist.*, lib. II, cap. 54, which also contains the rule and a tribute. The other tribute is in *Apol.*, cap 245.) The month and day of April 29 are also doubly confirmed: Casas describing the *funeral* on the following day, Sunday, St. Catherine's; and Remesal the *death* on St. Peter's, i.e., Peter Martyr's or Catherine's eve. Fabié, I, 124, misconstrued it as St. Peter Apostle's, July 28; and many writers have misread Casas' passage as May.

build the monastery at Puerto de Plata on the north coast of the island. And, as we shall see, there is documentary proof that he was prior there.

More important, it was at Puerto de Plata that Casas undertook the lasting contribution of this monastic retirement. In 1527 he commenced what would turn into a lifelong literary endeavor: his vast *Historia general de las Indias,* covering the Spanish history, natural history, and ethnography of the New World. Perhaps originally spurred by the publication of Oviedo's *Natural historia* in 1526, Fray Bartolomé worked at the task all through these Española years.[6] In a later chapter on Casas as a historian, I shall reconstruct the "first draft" which he produced on the island. At this point, we need only observe that writing history merely filled an interlude, and he was eager to resume his interrupted career.

From Puerto de Plata, on January 20, 1531, Casas at last broke his long silence with a big memorial on behalf of the Indians. This letter to the Council of the Indies was probably directed to García Manrique, Count of Osorno, then substituting as president for Cardinal García de Loaysa;[7] and in it Casas recalls the nearly six years when he appeared in person before that body. Now he again returns to the cause, calling on the Council to do its duty and also expatiating on the obligation of the Emperor—evidently he had heard of Charles's coronation in Bologna in 1529.

This duty, he insists, is to convert the natives and stop their extermination. On the conversion requirement, he cites the Bull of Donation by Alexander VI, saying in a postscript that he encloses a copy "which I had printed." But he really warms to his favorite subjejct. Already multitudes have died without the faith. On Española alone, two millions [one million and one hundred thousand] have been burned to death, thrown to dogs, and stabbed, regardless of age or sex! These horrors he has seen for thirty years, and for more than fifteen he has studied the remedies necessary. Now he offers a twofold plan to correct the intolerable situation.

First of all, the officials who have been sucking the blood of the Indians must be put out of office. Then a new system of colonization must be implanted—his familiar idea of fortified mainland settlements supported

---

6. *Hist.,* II. 121, the monastery, and I, 32, the start of the history. *Oviedo de la natural historia de las Indias* (usually called the Sumario, from its subtitle) appeared in Toledo on February 25, 1526.

7. The paths of Casas and the Count of Osorno were to converge in 1542, during the New Laws period: Santa Cruz tells how Casas advised His Majesty of the laxness of some councilors in accepting money from governors and others; he adds that the Count of Osorno, then heading the Council in place of the Cardinal, had advised the Emperor to the same effect. *Crónica,* IV, 221.

by bishops and friars. Men of good conscience and customs are to be put in charge; each is to have the aid of twelve, fifteen, or twenty friars, and of bishops appointed with suitable jurisdictions; and every caballero is to have a hundred soldiers (in some places fifty), first to build a fortress and then to guard it and perform other tasks appropriate to the conversion. These forts should be at convenient places on the seacoast—they could be built of mud in twenty or thirty days, then covered with tiles and lime brought from Española. The King is to pay the captain's salary, from the proceeds of barter trade; and after the natives have been brought to the faith, they are to pay tribute or services to the King.

The whole scheme resembles Casas' own former Cumaná plan, and is even closer to his original Tierra Firme scheme. For here he emphasizes the bishops who would in practice be the real rulers; and although he specifically renounces all compensation for his good advice and the time he took to prepare it, one cannot help wondering whether he did not have his eye on a bishopric. Anyway, the entire program is just such a curious mixture of spiritual and temporal interests as Casas had elaborated a dozen years before. But now there is an even more marked insistence on the great advantage to the monarch in increased revenue. Thus, Casas says openly that the Indians would be more willing to pay tribute to the King through friars than through the hated secular officials. So, after ten cloistered years, Fray Bartolomé still urges his old fortress scheme—and indeed, he was to reiterate it after another ten years, in the remedies suggested to Charles in 1542.

Likewise, his proposals for the islands show little change in this letter. He once more repeats that the only remedy for the surviving Indians is to take them out of the hands of the Spaniards; and he again suggests Negro slavery as a means to this end. The King, he says, could well lend gratuitously five or six hundred Negroes to each island, to be distributed among the citizens according to their services, and they could give bond to pay for these slaves in three years. In his conclusion, he actually laments that for the last ten or eleven years licenses for importing Negroes have not been freely given—though he had obtained the privilege from the King, but certainly not to see it sold to court favorites and Genoese. This brings forth one final reference to his withdrawal: at that time Heaven had placed the remedy of the oppressed Indians in his hands, but then he had no longer attended to [worldly] affairs, "God having taken me for my greater security."[8]

This memorial from Puerto de Plata apparently marked Fray Bartolomé's return to the cause. For in 1533, the Española audiencia forwarded to

---

8. Fabié, app. V. See Catalogue, no. 12, for the correct date of this memorial.

Spain a complaint that Casas, while Dominican prior in that town, had preached sermons against the encomienda and engaged in other activities harmful to the royal service and the welfare of the residents. As a result, the King sent a cedula reprimanding him.[9] To clear himself, Casas wrote a letter to the Council on April 30, 1534, which gives us more details on the matter.

Fray Bartolomé begins by citing his past services to the Crown: his five years at court, working for the welfare of the Indians, and the previous years he had spent pacifying Cuba and subjecting it to royal authority. He further recalls the communication he had sent from Puerto de Plata, about the unspeakable crimes perpetrated against the natives, contrary to all law, human or divine. Then he takes up the audiencia complaints, point by point. One charge was that he had interfered in a death-bed confession, and forced a dying man to make the will he dictated. In rebuttal, Casas points out he has been preaching and confessing twenty-eight years and would do no such thing; furthermore, the property never came into his hands but into those of the town officials. Another difficulty, he says, had arisen because the civil authorities seized from the monastery a man who had taken sanctuary there, just as if it were a mosque and not a Christian church. As for his "opinions," he was merely affirming that the offenses against God in these lands—the destruction of so many native souls and bodies—offend no one more than the Emperor himself, destroying his vassals and wealth and putting his conscience in danger.[10]

Certainly in this letter, as in the long memorial that preceded it, we can see the old Bartolomé de las Casas stirring again even in the cloister.

THE ENRIQUILLO STORY

One dramatic episode does stand out near the close of Casas' monastery years: his part in the "pacification" of the famous Indian rebel Enriquillo. The story of this chief is most interesting. Some facts come from the *Historia*, others from official documents, and we shall review them here before establishing Fray Bartolomé's own role.[11]

---

9. The judges to the King, June 7, 1533—Fabié, app. V. We know of the cedula from the opening of Casas' own letter cited in the following note.

10. Casas to the Council of the Indies, Santo Domingo, April 30, 1534. *Archivum Fratrum Praedicatorum,* IV, 197-202. See Catalogue, no. 13, for a description of this document.

11. In *Hist.*, lib. III, caps. 125-127, Casas tells the Enriquillo story clear to the San Miguel truce, ca. 1528.

As a youth, Enriquillo had been brought up in the Franciscan monastery of Verapaz; he was a devout Christian, spoke Spanish very well, and could read and write. When of age, he returned to his people in the province of Baoruco, where he was married in the church to a young Indian woman of good lineage named Lucía. With his Indians, he served a certain Spaniard, who first took his mare from him and then raped his wife. When Enriquillo protested to this Spaniard, he was given a beating; next, the chief complained to a magistrate in the Spanish town, and was thrown in jail. After his release he betook himself and his plaints to the audiencia, but the authorities merely sent him back to the same official who had mistreated him; and his master showered him with threats and further punishment.

Enriquillo dissimulated for a while, then fled to the mountains with a few followers. This made him a rebel, and the Spaniard came with eleven soldiers to bring him back. But the Indians were armed; and after an altercation, with the encomendero calling the chieftain "dog" and attacking him, there was a skirmish in which two Spaniards were killed and the rest routed.[12] The audiencia now sent seventy or eighty soldiers to subjugate the Indian, but these too were driven off, with some dead and wounded.

As the news of these exploits spread throughout Española, many Indians escaped to join Chief Enriquillo, until his forces numbered some three hundred. This guerrilla band he ruled with great skill. He instructed his men to kill no Spaniards save in self-defense, but always to take their arms and release them. (A few of his band, however, killed some Spaniards who had come from Tierra Firme, and seized their gold.) In this fashion he seems to have accumulated a supply of weapons that made him a formidable foe; and he also took remarkable precautions for the safety of his people. All the old folks, children, and sick persons were hidden away in a secret place in the mountains where he raised crops; with them he kept about fifty warriors as a guard, leaving the rest of his force under a captain to mount a lookout for Spaniards. When a few men were sent out hunting or fishing, he at once moved to another place, so that even if these individuals were captured and tortured they could not reveal his hiding place. Above all, he maintained great mobility, repeatedly exhausting the numerous Spanish expeditions sent against him.

The first serious attempt to recapture Enriquillo took place in 1525, when a formal expedition was sent out under Licentiate Badillo and Jacomé

---

12. Casas gives Enriquillo's exact words: "Be glad I did not kill you; go away and come no more!" Oviedo (I, 140) says that this happened in 1519.

de Castellón. Over eight thousand pesos were spent with no result. Again, in late 1527 or early 1528, another effort was made by Captain Fernando de San Miguel and eighty soldiers. A Franciscan named Fray Remigio, one of the early missionaries and probably, Casas thought, a former teacher of Enriquillo's, offered to go along with the party as an emissary. This friar was put ashore near where the rebel was supposed to be, and was shortly discovered by some of Enriquillo's scouts, who took him for a spy. Fray Remigio stated his peaceful and conciliatory errand; whereupon the scouts spared his life, but stripped off his garments except his underclothes, and departed with his message. Enriquillo came at once, apologized to the friar for their conduct, but declined Fray Remigio's invitation to establish friendship with the Spaniards. They had killed his father and grandfather and all the lords of Xaragua province, and greatly affronted him, and he wished to see none of them. Finally, however, the two sides did encounter each other and Enriquillo and San Miguel talked across a deep barranca—the Captain offering to conclude an official peace and Enriquillo to give back the gold he had captured. They agreed to meet at an appointed place on the coast, with eight men each. The chief did have a shelter erected and the gold placed therein, but he became suspicious because the Spaniards were arriving in force; so he disappeared in the forest and did not keep the rendezvous, though his men duly delivered the gold. The expedition, according to the official account, cost ten thousand pesos and recovered only fifteen hundred pesos in gold.[13] Chagrined at the outcome, San Miguel returned to Santo Domingo; but anyway, says Casas, this truce lasted four or five years.

Finally, the government decided to conclude the matter. Dissatisfied with the state of affairs on Española, the Council of the Indies organized an armada of two hundred men to go to America and capture or kill or make peace with Enriquillo. Francisco de Barrionuevo was named commander under an order dated July 4, 1532; the following February he appeared in Santo Domingo and presented his credentials and instructions. At once the audiencia held a strategy meeting, and after long consideration decided that his soldiers were not fitted for a guerrilla campaign and he should take a smaller and more experienced force. Accordingly, on May 8, 1533, Barrionuevo left port in a small caravel with thirty-two men and some Indians.

After two months' search, Barrionuevo at last succeeded in meeting with Enriquillo and concluding a peace. He gave the chief a provision

---

13. The judges to the King, March 30, 1528, with an appended March 31 statement of costs and special taxes—*DII*, XXXVII, 389-396, 397-400. The taxes kept ships away from Española; cf. Herrera, *Historia general*, dec. IV, lib. IV, cap. 11.

from the Emperor, a full pardon, and no doubt also the title of "don," which the Indian bore thereafter. For his part, Don Enrique agreed to come in, though he remained somewhat mistrustful of the Spaniards. So he sent back an Indian with Barrionuevo, probably as a spy. Then in August, the chief himself came down with some of his men to within two leagues of Azúa, where a number of the inhabitants had gathered to meet him, in all some twenty-five or thirty horsemen and forty or fifty foot soldiers. But his envoy had not yet returned from Santo Domingo, and though he and the Spaniards celebrated the new peace, he was still suspicious in the presence of so many armed men, and finally returned to his mountain fastness.[14]

It was at this point, with the peace still precarious, that Fray Bartholomé in person took a hand. There has been confusion about his role for a long time, ever since Remesal mistakenly attributed to him both the earlier truce brought about by Captain San Miguel and the final peace officially negotiated by Barrionuevo.[15] But Casas himself, in his 1534 letter to the Council, tells us what really happened:

"I went—with only the grace of God and a companion friar, whom the Order furnished me—I went to Baoruco, and reassured Don Enrique and confirmed him in the service of the Emperor, our lord. I was with him a month, and confessed him and his wife and all his captains, and relieved them of all their very just fears. I would not come away from there, till I took him with me to the town of Azúa, where he was embraced by the citizenry and made merry [with them]; and I left him with the course agreed that he was to follow, [namely] to go and be entertained at the other Spanish towns, and to bring to the service of His Majesty certain captains and people in rebellion, and particularly to establish his town seven leagues from Azúa; and he is to provide all that region with bread and other supplies. All of this he is actually fulfilling gladly. And in truth, noble sirs, had the Dominican Order not sent me, to serve God and His Majesty, and had I not gone there, it might be a hundred years before Don Enrique would be

---

14. *DII*, I, 481-505. Oviedo, primera parte, lib. V, cap. 9, gives details on the Azúa visit.

15. See Rem., I, 147-155, and 161-163. Remesal (I, 468) says he did not have access to lib. III of Casas' history; he must therefore have taken his very similar narrative of the events to the truce from Herrera's version, which is lifted whole from Casas. In the truce story, Remesal gives Fray Remigio a secondary role, and in the final pacification he does not mention Barrionuevo at all.

Why did Remesal erroneously insert Casas into these events? I believe he misunderstood some papers of Licentiate Cerrato, which he says he found in the Guatemalan archives and which doubtless referred to Casas' subsequent visit to the chief.

seen outside the impregnable peaks and highlands where he was born and possesses his patrimony. Because even though Francisco de Barrionuevo went there and commenced the peace, and it is not right he should be defrauded of what he did, yet he was there only one night and part of a midday, and then he came back; and this was not sufficient in a situation where such a capital and justly undertaken war had gone on for so many years previous. Since I saw the great harm and destruction of this island, and the inestimable good that would accrue to all the land from security and peace with Don Enrique, and the long experience that I have in these matters, I persuaded the Superior to send me; and it was necessary to keep my going a secret from the royal judges, on account of the hostile attitude which I knew they had towards me. So I went, and I reassured him; and I left him firmer in the service of His Majesty than the peak of Martos, and may it please God that they know how to keep him thus."[16] Parenthetically, little more is known of Don Enrique, save that the peace was kept and he died in about a year.

This is the Enriquillo story as we have it from Casas himself and audiencia reports. Oviedo, in his account, follows the same general lines and also gives us the reaction of the authorities to Casas' exploit. Telling of some religious and other customs of Enriquillo's followers, he adds: "Who told this was Fray Bartolomé, as they informed me; and he also told many other things in praise of this cacique, saying that he was far advanced in the faith and a good Christian. The judges of the audiencia were very angry about his visit to these Indians and to Don Enrique without their knowledge and license, fearing that the natives might be stirred up on account of the newness of the recent peace. Since, however, his visit had been so productive, as I have said, they were pleased at his success and thanked him for his labors."[17]

ALLEGED JOURNEYS

Hitherto we have covered the known and documented events of Casas' first decade as a friar. We turn now to dubious ground—two journeys he is

---

16. Casas to the Council, April 30, 1534, *Archivum Fratrum Praedicatorum*, IV, 199-200. Martos was in Jaén, Andalusia.

17. Oviedo, I, 158. His account was gathered in Santo Domingo, and he departed for Spain about January 1534. The "recent peace" he mentions was Barrionuevo's whose August 1553 meeting with Enriquillo he has previously narrated in great detail. So we can fix Casas' visit to the chieftain between these two dates—i.e., in the latter part of 1533 or at the very beginning of 1534. Oviedo's version of the Enriquillo story (primera parte, lib. V, caps. 5-11) contains no mention of either San Miguel or Fray Remigio.

alleged to have made, one to Spain in 1530 and one to Peru early in 1532, with visits to Central America in between. These journeys have been accepted by most of Casas' biographers, but I find no good evidence that he ever made them.

So far as I can see, the story rests entirely on the authority of Remesal. According to this chronicler, the reason for Fray Bartolomé's journey to Spain was the news of new lands discovered by Francisco Pizarro in Túmbez. Casas, this version goes, was alarmed lest the invasion of Peru be accompanied by acts of violence like those committed in Guatemala and New Spain. So he went to court and obtained a cedula to Pizarro and Almagro forbidding them to make any slaves and directing them to leave the Indians free. The cedula, says Remesal, is contained in the first book of the four printed by royal decree. With this order Casas allegedly returned to Española; thence he accompanied Fray Francisco de San Miguel to New Spain; from there he went overland to Santiago de Guatemala, and then with Fray Pedro de Ángulo he proceeded to Realejo in Nicaragua. A ship was ready and Casas and two other friars embarked on her and went to Peru, where they communicated the cedula to the two captains, who at once proclaimed it. Casas also had a commission to found Dominican convents in Peru, but on the advice of Fray Vicente de Valverde, who was with Pizarro, he desisted and returned to Nicaragua in February or March 1532.[18]

Such is Remesal's account, and in my opinion the whole story is fanciful. Thus, it is quite certain that Fray Bartolomé did not return to Europe in this period, for in his 1534 letter he declared that his greatest wish was to stand once more before the Council of the Indies, pleading the cause of the unhappy island Indians and presenting efficacious remedies. To me this seems positive evidence that Casas had not been in Spain since 1520. Furthermore, in another letter the following year, he speaks of having already written of his desire to go to court; and he adds plainly that ever since he subjected himself to the decision of others by promising obedience, he has not dared request the permission, as it should be given without his instigation. Also, speaking of some others going to Spain, he exclaims: "Would to God I were going!"[19]

---

18. Rem., I, 155-159. One of the friars who accompanied him, says Remesal, was Fray Bernardino de Minaya. Minaya himself later wrote an account of how he went to Peru, perhaps about 1532-1533, and read the cedula about slaves to Pizarro. His memorial is printed in Dr. Lewis Hanke's "Pope Paul III and the American Indians," app. II, *Harvard Theological Review*, XXX, 99-101.

19. Cf. Casas to the Council, April 30, 1534; also Casas to a courtier, from Granada, Nicaragua, October 15, 1535. *Archivum Fratrum Praedicatorum*, IV, 202,

As for the alleged Peru trip, I cannot find that Casas ever stated he had been in that country. Two of his writings dealing exclusively with Peru have survived and can be studied: his letter to Carranza de Miranda of 1555, and his answer to questions about Peruvian affairs written in 1564. In neither of these does he evince any personal knowledge of the country nor mention any incident he saw there, apparent proof he had never been in Peru. And the question can be settled categorically by his own remark in the *Apologética*, where he speaks of handsome Indian men and women he has seen in various parts of the New World. He refers to "those of the kingdoms of New Spain around Mexico, and the province of Xalisco, those of Nicaragua, Tierra Firme toward Cumaná, and the kingdom of Yucatán, and those of the whole seacoast of Guatemala, which are the lands I have visited, and others of which I do not speak, and those of the kingdom of Peru, and the people of Florida, and the last to be discovered, that is, of Cíbola."[20]

So Casas definitely was never in Peru, nor did he make a trip to Spain in this period. The only document cited in Remesal's apocryphal account, the 1530 cedula, is really beside the point. The issuance of this order can be established; but it was unnecesary that Casas should have personally attempted to deliver it. In fact, the document must have been delivered long before 1532, perhaps even to Pizarro himself. For this conquistador appeared in Spain in 1529, and Santacruz says he only left there in 1530.[21]

The real truth of the matter lies in an attempt to go to Peru, which Casas actually made a few years later. This frustrated or incomplete journey is related sketchily by Remesal in a later passage and also by Motolinía in his celebrated January 1555 letter to the Emperor. As Motolinía tells it, Casas was bound for Peru, but could not reach that country and so stopped in Nicaragua, going from there to Guatemala and thence to Oaxaca and on to Mexico City. Evidently he is speaking of Casas' first visit to Mexico in 1538.[22] Remesal gives more particulars, though with some confusion. By mid-1534, he claims, Casas was once more in Nicaragua and, harkening to many pleas, he again embarked in Realejo for Peru. But storms arose and after many days the ship returned to Realejo; and about this voyage, says Remesal, Casas told an anecdote in his *Historia*. He then paraphrases a pass-

---

210, and cf. 205. (See Catalogue, no. 14, for a description of the 1535 letter.) Also in his later writings, Casas several times speaks of not being in Spain in 1529.

20. *Apol.*, 88.

21. Santa Cruz, *Crónica*, III, 124.

22. Icazbalceta, *Docs.*, I, 251.

age in the *Apologética*, where Casas tells of encountering contrary winds on a sea voyage bound for Peru, and of a soldier who wept for joy when they decided to try to press on.[23]

Of course, Casas was bound for Peru, but he never reached there. What actually occurred is detailed for us in letters by Casas himself and by Fray Tomás de Berlanga, with whom he traveled. Writing to an unnamed courtier in 1535, Casas describes the unlucky voyage: "A short while after sending you that letter, perhaps two or three months, I left Santo Domingo to go to Peru with my companions, in the company of the Bishop of Panama, our former father provincial [Berlanga]. Having arrived at Panama, on account of the hunger and sickness there, the Bishop sent us ahead to await him in the land of Peru, as he could not leave so promptly because all of his household were ill. When we left Panama, our Lord God disposed something different from what we expected; for after two months and a half, with three hundred men nearly dead from thirst and hunger at sea, by divine blessing four of us friars and some eight or ten men landed here at Nicaragua in a bark which we found. We fear that all the others who were returning to Panama may have perished, if they experienced but four days of calm out of the fifty or more that we had, for we left them near death from hunger."[24]

Such hardships, to be sure, were not unusual on the troublesome southward passage from Panama to Peru by sail. After a ship left the Gulf of Panama, the southeasterly wind made a southwesterly course necessary, and soon a region of dangerous calms was reached. Bishop Berlanga, in a letter from Puerto Viejo, gives a harrowing account of his own experiences in that area. He and his party left Panama on February 23, and after a long while some islands were sighted, obviously the Galápagos. They were out of water, but could find none on the first island. On another, however, they took on enough, they thought, to last them to the Ecuador mainland—some eight hundred miles, which they evidently expected to make in eight days. After ten days they still saw no land, and their water supply was gone; finally, they were reduced to drinking wine. In this letter, Berlanga makes no mention of the Dominicans who had traveled with him, but in an earlier one from Panama, written on February 22, he speaks of friars on their way to Peru without licenses.[25]

---

23. Rem., I, 164, and cf. *Apol.*, cap. 180.

24. Casas to a courtier, Granada, Nicaragua, October 15, 1535. *Archivum Fratrum Praedicatorum*, IV, 203-204.

25. DII, XLI, 538 *et seq*. Berlanga was in Valladolid in 1533, and was named Bishop of Panama.

From this I conclude that the entire group must have sailed from Santo Domingo late in 1534, and Casas and the friars left Panama in February 1535, on their unsuccessful attempt to reach Peru. But as Casas wrote afterwards, Peru was then in such turmoil that nothing could be accomplished there. So perhaps, judging from the events that followed, the hazardous voyage that brought Fray Bartolomé to Central America instead was a fortunate accident after all.

LAND OF WAR

Nicaragua and Guatemala

Casas' coming to Central America was to lead to his celebrated Tierra de Guerra, or Land of War, missionary experiment. But that venture did not begin till May of 1537. Before he and his fellow friars launched upon it, Fray Bartolomé spent a couple of restless preliminary years in Nicaragua and Guatemala.

For the events of his Nicaraguan stay we have, in addition to Remesal's somewhat garbled account, Casas' own letter of 1535 to a court personage, already cited. Furthermore, some documents about his doings in 1536 were found in the archives of Seville and published in 1867. From these papers, it seems that Fray Bartolomé had scant success in Nicaragua, either in working with the Indians or in rousing the consciences of the Spaniards, an activity that resulted in a new brush with the colonial authorities.

As to the natives, his letter is largely devoted to a recital of their destruction in that region during the past dozen years. He says that from Nicaragua some twenty-seven thousand slaves had been sent off to Peru and another twenty-five thousand to Panama, and that this land—the finest he had ever seen—is now desolate and depopulated. Sorrowfully, he recounts the total lack of missionary work among the Indians, and his attempt to start some with his small band of religious. The Dominicans with him, it afterwards appeared, were Rodrigo de Ladrada, Pedro de Ángulo, and another unnamed; Remesal also includes Luís Cáncer. They lodged in the abandoned Franciscan convent in Granada, and soon clashed with the townspeople. For Casas complains that the Spaniards flogged those Indians who took time to come to catechism conducted by the friars.[1]

---

1. Casas to a courtier, Granada, Nicaragua, October 15, 1535, *Archivum Fratrum Praedicatorum,* IV, 204-209; also 211-212 on the slave shipments, which he says are recorded in "the books of the King."

But it was on another score that Fray Bartolomé got into conflict with the Governor of Nicaragua, Rodrigo de Contreras. We know what happened from three juridical investigations instituted by this official to show that Casas had made remarks in the pulpit and out of it "in disservice to God and the King and against the tenor of His Majesty's instructions." Substantially, the charge was that Contreras had been preparing a military expedition into the interior, and Casas had attacked it, presumably as a slave raid and march-of-conquest, and hampered it in various ways.

Contreras' first "Información," instituted on March 23, 1536, before Bishop Diego Álvarez Osorio, gives particulars. The governor alleges that he was enlisting men for an expedition, and admonished them to try in every way to attract the natives peacefully and not to do them any harm or damage; he even asked Fray Bartolomé to accompany them. Casas refused, saying that if he went he would have to be given fifty men without any captain. When this was denied, Casas preached and spoke against the expedition so strenuously that many men mutinied and were afraid to go. Further, when some of the would-be expeditionaries went to Casas to confess, he told them that if they went on the journey he would not confess or absolve them, and this created a great disturbance in the city. These were Contreras' assertions, and he had little difficulty proving them. One witness, for instance, testified that Fray Rodrigo had said that if Fray Bartolomé were given the fifty men he would go and do better than anyone else. But while the questioning was in progress, the bishop died, and the matter was postponed.

Accordingly, a second inquiry was conducted on June 30 and July 5; it went over the same ground and added rumors about Fray Bartolomé's previous rebuke for his preaching on Española. The ninth question asked whether the witness knew that Casas had delivered very harmful and trouble-making sermons there, and that the Audiencia of Santo Domingo had forbidden him to preach. To this a Mercedarian, Fray Lázaro de Guido, replied that when he was in Santo Domingo he heard that the audiencia had ordered Fray Bartolomé to desist from preaching; and the witness remained there two more years, and to his knowledge Casas did not preach again. Incidentally, if there is any truth to this story, it furnishes us with a reason why Casas left Santo Domingo.

Finally, on August 23, Contreras started a third "Información"—this one designed to add the data that Casas and his companions had departed from the Franciscan convent in León, though the town officials had asked them to stay. It appears that the friars had left about two months before, taking with them all the holy pictures and sacred objects, and they had gone "as persons desirous of changes and novelties, without cause or reason."[2]

As a matter of fact, Casas and his band had gone on to Guatemala. The Bishop of Santiago, it seems, had written urging them to come, and finally paying their expenses for the journey. For these transitional events we must depend on Remesal, despite some obvious errors in his narrative. Thus, he declares that the friars reached Santiago at the end of 1535; but the third "Información" shows they could not have arrived before July 1536. Once there, the party took possession of the Dominican convent which had been built by Fray Domingo de Betanzos. With them was Fray Luís Cáncer, who already knew the Nahuatl language then spoken in part of Guatemala, though where he learned it is a mystery. In addition, all the friars took lessons in Quiché from Bishop Francisco de Marroquín, who was well versed in that language and later wrote a catechism in it. Such study, of course, was in preparation for the Indian mission they now hoped to undertake in Guatemala.[3]

This raises the question of whether Bartolomé de las Casas ever learned any native language well enough to preach in it. I can only recall one reference to the subject in his writings. Explaining the general Spanish ignorance of the Indian tongues of Española, he says: "This was not because they were very difficult to learn, but because no one, ecclesiastic or layman, took any care . . . to teach the doctrine or the knowledge of God to these people but merely to make use of them. For this purpose they learned no more words in the [Indian] languages than 'hand over bread,' 'go to the mines,' 'take out gold,' or such as were needed for serving and obeying the Spaniards."[4] Evidently Casas included himself in this category, for he proceeds to single out Fray Ramón [Pane] as having learned enough to teach the Indians the Ave María and the Paternoster. So it appears that in his thirteen years on Española and Cuba, Casas had not acquired a knowledge of the native language. Indeed, Motolinía, in his letter of 1555, claims Casas never learned any Indian languages nor taught the natives.

---

2. All three "Informaciones" are printed in *DII*, VII, 116-146. Herrera (dec. VI, lib., I, cap. 8) refers at some length to Fray Bartolomé's controversy with Contreras. This is one of the most striking indications that he made use of official documents in telling Casas' life, for the 1534 episode is not in Casas' *Historia*, which Herrera used and which ends around 1520.

3. Rem., I, 165-166, 173.

4. *Apol.*, 322; and cf. *ibid.*, 447, where Casas says that "daca" meant "I."

This casts some doubt on Remesal's assertion that Fray Bartolomé now mastered the Quiché tongue of Guatemala.[5]

Nevertheless, Casas was preparing to try out his missionary ideas in that country. Unlike Nicaragua, he found here a favorable ecclesiastical and administrative climate for the purpose. A royal cedula of March 30, 1536, had arrived in Santiago, designed to promote the Christianizing of the natives; chiefs were to be summoned by the bishop and governor, assisted by friars, to hear the royal provisions on tribute and good treatment, and a memorial about observances expected of new converts. Remesal could not locate this paper; but he did discover a related one setting forth fasts and feasts for Christian Indians, which he alleges Casas had been urging since 1530. Anyway, says Remesal, Fray Bartolomé backed these rules anew, and they were approved by the Bishops of Guatemala, Mexico, and Tlaxcala, and incorporated in the basic papal brief for the regulation of "this new Indian church."[6] It was against this favorable background that Fray Bartolomé now proceeded to embark on a remarkable mission experiment for which he secured the backing of both Bishop Marroquín and Licentiate Maldonado, the acting governor of Guatemala.

THE TUZULUTLÁN PROJECT

Briefly, Casas undertook to go into Tuzulutlán, the unconquered Land of War, with only his small band of friars, and convert the natives by loving kindness and bring them peacefully to Spanish domination. This project was to have great significance in his career, and it seems worthwhile to sketch what we know of its antecedents.

Remesal tells us that Casas had brought with him to Guatemala the manuscript of his first book, *De unico vocationis modo—On the Only Way of Attracting All Peoples to the True Faith*—in which he expounded his theory of peaceful conversion. This does not seem exact, since the extant text of the work quotes the bull, "Sublimis Deus," issued on June 2, 1537, which could hardly have reached Santiago before that September. Of course, the work might have been under way, and Paul III's famous bull arrived in time to be incorporated, but I doubt this. Certainly the papal doctrine proclaimed—that the Indians were rational, endowed with liberty and free will and able to receive the faith—was one Casas had upheld from the first, and

---

5. Remesal (I, 184) makes the astounding statement that all four friars knew well the language of Guatemala. Cf. *ibid.*, II, 54, where he later describes Bishop Casas answering Indians in this tongue.

6. Rem., I, 174-176; Catalogue, no. 11.

I feel his efforts had a notable effect; but the Dominicans had said so earlier, and one of them, Bernardino de Minaya, had actually gone to Rome and secured the bull.[7] Besides, by the time it reached Guatemala, Casas had already embarked on his missionary experiment.

So Fray Bartolomé apparently did not write his book beforehand, as Remesal claims. Yet I am confident that Casas had formulated its two basic propositions by this time: (1) Preach the gospel to all men and do not treat the Indians in an unjust or tyrannical way; and those who have taken anything from them are obliged to make restitution. (2) It is not merely illegal to employ force to convert them, but a quite unnecessary evil.

We can therefore accept the chronicler's statement that Casas now proclaimed these principles of his publicly—"in the pulpit and outside it." To be sure, he was not the first to have advocated this idea. Fray Pedro de Córdoba had originally urged conversion by friars alone, without other Spaniards, along the Pearl Coast. And a Franciscan, Fray Jacobo de Testera, had already tried out the same system in Yucatán in 1534, with considerable success.[8] Furthermore, Casas' own Cumaná attempt of 1521 had been planned along similar lines, though he had taken Spanish colonists with him too, and he had even proposed soldiers and forts on Tierra Firme as well as missionaries. But it is quite evident that he now preached and spoke in favor of reducing the Indians to the faith without any armed force at all. This, Remesal asserts, led to gibes from the Spanish residents of Santiago. Casas, for his part, offered to test his theory in the one remaining unconquered region of Guatemala: Tuzulutlán.

Tuzulutlán, then known as the Land of War, certainly was not under Spanish control at this time. Casas says the government had never subdued

---

7. Cf. Rem., I, 177 and 181, for the assertion about *Del único modo* and the Santiago conquistadors laughing at it.

Remesal prints the bull, "Sublimis Deus," in Latin and Spanish (*ibid.*, 207-209); MacNutt gives an English translation in his app. II. For the circumstances surrounding it, see Lewis Hanke's "Pope Paul III and the American Indians," *Harvard Theological Review*, XXX, 65-102. This bull is dated on the Fourth of the Nones of June, which is June 2 and not either June 10, as stated by Remesal, or June 9, as stated by Dr. Hanke.

While no one today could be found to deny the truth set forth in this bull, it created a sensation in its day because one school of thought held that the Indians, if not beasts, were slaves by nature and incapable of receiving the evangel.

8. Casas himself had presented Fray Pedro's original request to the Council, and he was later to present information on Fray Jacobo's experiment to the same body. Cf. Catalogue, no. 30.

it, and probably this was because the region did not offer much in the way of material benefits. Bishop Marroquín afterwards alleged that it had once been reduced by Diego de Alvarado, but the adelantado and all his men had then left for Peru. Remesal explains that the Spaniards had made three futile attempts to conquer it, and had nicknamed it because of the ferocity of its inhabitants.

At all events, Tuzulutlán, the Land of War of that day and the modern Verapaz, is the northeastern part of Guatemala, adjoining Chiapas, and on the north side of the main sierra. There is no precise agreement among ancient writers as to its boundary. In a 1574 report by Dominican missionaries, Verapaz is described as separated from the province of Guatemala by the Zacapulas River; the distance from that stream to the Golfo Dulce is estimated at about forty-eight leagues, and the greatest width at some twenty-seven leagues. The inhabited portion was then only one-third or one-fourth of the area, for the friars had collected the Indians into towns and established a system of commerce.[9] At the period of these reports the northern portion, a wild and heavily wooded country was, as it still is, inhabited by wild tribes, being a refuge for fugitive Indians from Yucatán. It is not clear just when this migration began. In Casas' time, the native Indians evidently spoke Quiché, because we are told that Bishop Marroquín talked to Don Juan, one of the chiefs, in that language. Quiché was a Mayan dialect, and since the Lacandón Indians to the west of Verapaz also spoke Maya, it appears likely that this entire territory was inhabited by tribes using that tongue. Nowadays, Verapaz is largely, if not entirely, inhabited by Chols, who also speak a Mayan dialect. This tribe extends over the border into Chiapas.

As to the culture of these natives, it appears not to have been of a very high order. Dr. Eduard Seler in 1895 published an article on them in his *Antiquities of Guatemala*, embodying results of some fieldwork by Erwin P. Dieseldorff and Carl Sapper. No ruin of any note seems to have been found in this region. It further appears that Casas' Indians were fairly primitive; they had no idols and used only sacrifices of birds, animals, and their own blood.[10] Casas himself, in chapters 234 to 240 of the *Apologética*, gives a short account of laws and customs among Indians in Guatemala and Verapaz. Of the Verapaz natives, he says they made slaves of their war prisoners, and the principal ones were sacrificed and then eaten, so as to put fear into

---

9. Squier MSS, XIV, 3, from tomo XXXIX of the Muñoz Collection.

10. See the edition of this study by the Smithsonian Institution, Washington, 1904.

the hearts of their enemies. He asserts, too, that these Indians had books and that he had seen works of Christian doctrine written in their characters, though most of their history was handed down orally. Even about Verapaz, however, Casas admits most of his information was not gathered at firsthand but obtained from Dominican missionaries; but he does mention a number of incidents in which he personally intervened.[11]

The chief native and mission settlements were in two distinct areas, which perhaps accounts for some looseness in colonial references to the Tierra de Guerra or Verapaz. Rabinal, founded by Casas in 1538, was apparently at the Indian town of Tequisistlán, but I have not been able positively to identify it. In 1525 Cortés passed through this country but apparently crossed the Río Dulce farther down. On that river, I believe, was the other major center of native population: Cobán, whose inhabitants spoke a different dialect from those in Rabinal. In Casas' period, the friars' center of operation was undoubtedly Zacapulas, on the upper reaches of the Lacandón River, a tributary of the Usumascinta. Rabinal is now only some twelve miles north of this place, and both are on the northern declivity of the sierra. So Remesal, concentrating on the early phase of the story, places the beginning of the Land of War in this area, relatively near Santiago, in fact just over the top of the range. Whether this was the real province, or only its approaches, is doubtful. Cobán, farther north, appears to have been the center of the region; and in 1545, Cobán was the chief seat of the Dominicans in the territory and perhaps the most important town. Ancient and later writers agree that the Cobán vicinity was the Tierra de Guerra, "properly called." But the missionary venture always included the entire territory, and reports and chronicles stress continuity rather than any definite demarcation between the two districts.

This, then, was the Tuzulutlán area which Casas now proposed to convert—a vaguely defined Northeastern region, over the sierra from Santiago, known as the Land of War because it had not been brought under Spanish rule. Casas undertook to bring these Indians to the faith and the royal service with friars alone and asked for certain conditions. Accordingly, the acting Governor of Guatemala, Alonso de Maldonado, drew up a contract with Fray Bartolomé, by which he agreed that if the venture was successful he would not give the land and natives in encomiendas. Further,

---

11. Three chapters of the *Apologética* are devoted exclusively to the Verapaz Indians: cap. 237 on tribal government, markets and useful arts, and child rearing; cap. 239 on laws of crime and punishment; and cap. 240 on burial customs. Other material appears *passim* in the Guatemala chapters.

he ordered that no Spaniard should enter the country for a period of five years, excepting only the governor in person, in the company of Dominicans. (At the time of signing, Casas was acting protector of the Guatemala Indians, substituting for Marroquín who had gone to Mexico City.) The friars mentioned as taking part were Casas, Ladrada, and Ángulo; evidently Fray Luís Cáncer was absent. The document itself bore the date of May 2, 1537, the official beginning of the Tuzulutlán project.[12]

TWO NARRATIVES OF THE CONVERSION

Fray Bartolomé's personal direction of this Land of War experiment lasted only a year, but in that time a solid start seems to have been made. The mission was launched in gradual stages, which included establishing a consolidated Indian town on the hither reaches of the province, and penetrating the wilder interior, all with the help of friendly chiefs. There are brief references to this beginning in subsequent documents. But our major knowledge of the early conversion comes from two chroniclers, Remesal and Ximénez.

Fray Antonio de Remesal tells most of the story, taking it apparently from a manuscript work in the Guatemalan tongue by Fray Salvador de San Cipriano. Another Dominican, Fray Francisco Ximénez, though writing a century later and substantially repeating Remesal's account, points out a notable error and contributes a number of details, especially about Indians, places, tribes, and chieftains. Ximénez had the advantage of having lived in the country a long time and learned three of the local languages; and in 1710 he himself had been a curate in Rabinal and so knew the Land of War thoroughly. Here, then, is a summary of the Remesal narrative, with the additions by Ximénez.[13]

To start their work, the friars devised an ingenious stratagem. They composed some verses in the Quiché tongue, reciting the creation of the world, the fall of man, his banishment from paradise, the life and miracles of Christ, His death and resurrection and ascent into heaven, and how He

---

12. DII, VII, 149-156. This contains not only a copy of the original agreement, but its confirmation by the Audiencia of Mexico on February 6, 1539, and by the Council of the Indies on November 14, 1540. Also see Marroquín's letter of May 10, 1537, on leaving Fray Bartolomé his "poder." Cartas de Indias, 417.

13. Ximénez, Historia de la Provincia de San Vicente de Chiapa y Guatemala, lib. II, caps. 12-14; Remesal, Historia de Chiapa y Guatemala, lib. III, caps. 10-11 and 15-18. Remesal (I, 429) had San Ciprian's MS, on the idols of Zacapula province, translated for his use, as it contained the history of the entry made by Cáncer, Casas, and Ángulo.

was to come again to judge men and punish the bad and reward the good. All this was very long, and Remesal alleges the stanzas were the first ever invented in that Indian language. Next Casas found four Indian merchants who traveled frequently to Zacapulas and Quiché; and these men, who were Christians, were carefully taught the religious poetry, which was even set to music so they could sing it to the accompaniment of native instruments. In addition, Casas supplied them with an extra stock of Spanish trinkets, which were sure to delight their Indian customers.

On this preliminary entry, the merchants went no farther than Zacapulas, the town of a cacique on the border between Guatemala and the start of the Land of War. Their sacred concert was a great success; in all, they sang and answered questions for eight evenings, after which the chief sent his brother back with them to invite the friars to come to his town. Fray Luís Cáncer was sent; and at Zacapulas a church was built, and the chief was converted and baptized Juan.[14] Thereupon, a missionary friar visited the district, especially the cacique's other towns, and then reported back to the waiting Dominicans in Santiago at the end of October. Left unshepherded, Chief Juan now demonstrated the strength of his new beliefs by refusing to permit sacrifices of birds and other animals at fiestas for the marriage of his brother with the daughter of the cacique of Cobán.

Meantime, the rains having ended, Casas and Fray Pedro de Ángulo set out for Zacapulas, where the cacique received them hospitably in December. The church had been burnt (either by his own people, or more likely by the Cobán visitors), but it was now rebuilt by Chief Juan. The friars said mass, preached in the fields, and visited the entire vicinity in great safety.

In time—after many days and many converts, adds Ximénez, growing more explicit—Fray Bartolomé wished to go on and explore further territory. The cacique, however, objected, saying he feared that the Indians of the Land of War might kill him, that is, the Cobán people. But finally, the chief gave the friars a guard of seventy warriors, with whom they toured most of the area effectively; their escort sent messengers ahead, and the friars were everywhere well received, returning to Zacapulas at the beginning of 1538.

In addition, according to Ximénez, Fray Bartolomé had become acquainted with the nearby towns in the hilly region of Sacabajá and Cubulco, as far as Tzamaniel, where the Rabinal Indians lived—about eight leagues from the present town of Rabinal. In Tzamaniel, the Indians had

---

14. Xim., I, 190-194; Rem., I, 184-185 and 200-204.

the houses of their idols, and all the inhabitants lived scattered around in the ravines. Casas now endeavored to have these small detachments brought together so they could learn the faith and civilized customs. The intelligent cacique agreed and they built a town in the nearby well-watered and wooded plain of their cocoa plantations. The settlement was called Rabinal, after the tribe; and some twelve minor village chieftains joined together with their people to establish it. This entailed difficulties—some petty chiefs withdrew to San Lucas near Guatemala—but more Indians were attracted to the new town from the Miau and Nicumbul mountains. These geographical particulars, and more, are all given by Ximénez.[15]

Remesal, instead, expounds Casas' views on the need of "congregating" the Indians into larger settlements, as stated in his 1542 memorial to the Emperor. On the founding of Rabinal, the earlier chronicler is much less precise: The scattered native settlements of "that province" were tiny, no more than a half-dozen houses each and no farther than a musket-shot from one another. The Tecosistlán or Rabinal Indians were picked as the likeliest to congregate, and Chief Juan tried to persuade the Indians, but there was much opposition. Finally, bit by bit they did collect about a hundred families in a town with their tribal name of Rabinal, a league below the site of the present town. Here the friars built a church, said daily mass and preached, and instructed the natives in manual arts and taught them to wash and dress. The neighboring Cobán Indians kept coming covertly to spy with curiosity on this new mode of life; and Casas sent for Fray Luís Cáncer, who went farther into the interior to Cobán and some of its little towns, where the Indians gladly heard him tell of the faith.[16]

In the early part of 1538—Ximénez now takes up the tale—Casas and Ángulo decided to return to Santiago, bringing Chief Juan with them. Accordingly, they summoned Fray Rodrigo de Ladrada to come and take their place. It appears from this account that Ladrada had been preaching in the region of Atitlán and Tecpan Atitlán, "which the Dominicans had already converted to the faith." Here we meet for the first time the Christian chiefs who were made "dons" by the Emperor a few years later: Don Juan, cacique of Atitlán, Don Jorge of Tecpan Atitlán, and Don Miguel of Chichicastenango. These chiefs now decided to accompany Fray Rodrigo on his journey. Ximénez explains that they were some of the twenty-four lords of the kingdom of Quiché who had escaped at the time of the conquest, and that the caciques of Zacapulas, Rabinal, and Cobán were of the same group,

---

15. Xim., I, 195-196.
16. Rem., I, 204-206, 211-212.

and hence old friends whom they had not seen in many years. (Don Gaspar is here identified as the cacique of Rabinal.)

Upon the arrival of Fray Rodrigo and his attendant chiefs at Zacapulas, Casas and Fray Pedro returned to Santiago, taking along Chief Juan, who received a festive welcome from the authorities, the bishop, and all the townspeople. At this point, Ximénez calls attention to Remesal's error in having Alvarado come to greet the chief—an impossibility, as the adelantado was not yet back in Guatemala. Chief Juan now returned to his town, and Fray Bartolomé personally continued the conversion of the Land of War, penetrating to Cobán and "pacifying all the land that faced it" with the aid of the caciques just mentioned (of Don Miguel and Don Pedro, says Remesal, adding a new name).[17] The missionary assistance of these chiefs in the actual Tuzulutlán territory was acknowledged a couple of years later in letters from the Emperor, no doubt at Casas' request, thanking the following:

Juan, cacique of Atitán [Atitlán]

Jorge, cacique of Tecpan Atititán [Tecpán Atitlán]

Miguel, cacique of Zizicastenango [Chichicastenango]

Gaspar, cacique of Tequizistlán [Tequisistlán][18]

Royal recognition was afterwards given to Don Diego and Don Pedro, who had apparently come from their more distant town of Zacatepeque to help in the evangelical labor.[19]

All told, it was a promising start. But then a series of events, in 1538 and 1539, interrupted the conversion of the Land of War and eventually brought Fray Bartolomé de las Casas to a much wider field.

---

17. Xim., I, 197-198. Cf. Rem., I, 213-214, mainly on the Santiago visit. Remesal's narrative source apparently gave out at this point, where he makes his error.

18. Ximénez (I, 216) copies the October 17, 1540, letter to Don Juan, and says the other three were identical. Remesal (I, 227-228) could find only the similar letter to Don Jorge.

On January 28, 1541, a cedula was issued to the Governor of Guatemala not to interfere with these four caciques if they wished to go to Tuzulutlán. Cf. Xim. and Rem., *locs. cit.*

19. These two chiefs (Don Diego and Don Pedro), along with three of the aforementioned ones (Don Jorge, Don Gaspar, and Don Miguel), were granted coats-of-arms on June 30, 1543. *Nobiliario de conquistadores de Indias* (Madrid, 1892), nos. 249, 265, 267, and cf. plate XXXVIII. (Don Juan's is missing.) Their town of Zacatepeque is not even on the road to the Tierra de Guerra. For the later events of this mission, see *infra*, my chapter XII, last section, "Visit to Verapaz."

FRAY BARTOLOMÉ'S ROAD BACK

CASAS' FIRST VISIT TO MEXICO

Within the next couple of years Casas achieved a wish of long stand-ing: a return to Spain after an absence of two decades. He finally went as a Dominican missions procurator, entrusted with numerous other missionary errands by church and monastic authorities in Central America. The inter-vening circumstances, which took him from the wild Cobán Indians back to the imperial court at last, all revolved around his first visit to Mexico.

In the spring of 1538, the Tuzulutlán conversion was unexpectedly broken off for that journey. Bishop Marroquín, it seems, had recalled Fray Bartolomé from the Land of War to confer on over-all mission matters in Santiago at the beginning of May. This prelate wanted to send to Spain for spiritual reinforcements, offered to provide the money necessary, and sought the assistance of Casas and his band.[1] According to Remesal, Marroquín had made some efforts the year previous when he was in Mexico for his consecration; these are confirmed in a letter of his from there on July 25, 1537, saying he had expected to go to Castile himself but instead had sent money to one Juan Galvarro in Seville to pay the passage of new friars.[2] But this Galvarro, Ximénez explains, left for the Indies and could not attend to the business. So Bishop Marroquín now asked the Dominicans to send one of their number to Spain for the purpose.[3]

The proposal was most timely. Casas himself needed more helpers for

1. Rem., I, 215.
2. Arévalo, Docs., 187. Though it bears no date, this letter to the Guatemala town council was written on Santiago's day [July 25], shortly after Marroquín's con-secration on April 7, 1537.
3. Xim., I, 199-200.

Tuzulutlán and the rest of Guatemala; and it had already been decided to bring this up at the Dominican provincial chapter which two of the friars had to attend in Mexico that August. So they now resolved that all four friars would proceed to Mexico: Cáncer and Ángulo to serve as representatives at the chapter, and Casas, as the best known at court, to go on to Spain with Ladrada, after obtaining due authorization.[4]

Accordingly, all four Dominicans left Santiago on May 20, bound for Mexico City. Ximénez denies this, insisting that two friars stayed in Guatemala. But from a petition written by Casas in 1539, it is quite apparent that the entire group went.[5] About their journey, Remesal gives us some particulars. Cáncer and Ángulo took the west coast route through Soconusco, while Casas and Ladrada traveled via Rabinal and Cobán to advise the Indians of their journey. The cacique, Don Juan, begged Fray Bartolomé not to leave them alone, since they had made many enemies by becoming Christians; the fathers consoled him as best they could and promised that the friars would return soon. Casas and his comrade then went on through Chiapas, and the four Dominicans continued together towards Mexico.[6]

Remesal does not say whether Fray Bartolomé walked or rode on this journey, though Ximénez insists that Casas and the friars made the whole trip on foot. This I am inclined to reject. Years later, in 1545, when Bartolomé de las Casas was a bishop, an eyewitness friar made an ambiguous reference to his walking in his own diocese of Chiapa.[7] Yet the Bishop himself writing from Gracias á Dios in Honduras, spoke of having paid fifty pesos for horseshoes.[8] To me, this is a plain indication that Bishop Casas rode horseback on the journey from his see to Honduras and did not walk, as many of his biographers maintain; and it also suggests that he rode when traveling from Chiapa to Mexico at that period. That he rode a horse on this journey to Mexico in 1538, when he was still a friar, cannot be proved. But considering the distance, about 900 miles, I doubt that he walked. Certainly

---

4. Rem., I, 215-216.

5. Xim., I, 200-201. But the petition states that the friars left the monastery empty (*ibid.*, 146, and cf. *infra*, note 26, on this document). Remesal even gives the name of the caretaker, Agustín de Salablanca.

6. Rem., I, 216-217.

7. Xim., I, 201. And see *ibid.*, 389-390, Fray Tomás de la Torre's diary, relating Spanish attacks on Bishop Casas and commenting: "I have wished to tell this as the travails of the sainted Bishop, not his going on foot in his old age through this land, or eating no meat, or having never an hour of repose."

8. Casas to Prince Philip, November 9, 1545, *Cartas de Indias*, no. V, 32.

he had ridden in Nicaragua; that is clear from his interesting account of his ascent of the volcano Masaya.[9] At all events, by foot or by horse, Casas and his three companions finally arrived at Mexico City, to be warmly received by Fray Domingo de Betanzos, the retiring provincial.

Just when did Casas reach Mexico, how long did he stay, and what towns did he see? These external limits of his first Mexican visit are somewhat hard to establish. We have verification of Remesal's statement that the friars arrived in time to attend the provincial chapter that was held on August 24, 1538.[10] This allows at least two months for the journey, which seems to me correct, in view of Casas' age, the Land of War stopover, the bad weather, and the route followed.[11] But the widely accepted belief that Casas left for Spain in 1539 is apparently erroneous, for we have a letter from Bishop Zumárraga, written in Mexico as late as April 17, 1540, and recommending Fray Bartolomé de las Casas and the Franciscan Jacobo de Testera (the one who had been in Yucatán), both of whom were bound for Spain to bring friars of their Orders.[12]

So Casas was in Mexico between the years of 1538 and 1540, though

---

9. *Apol.*, cap. 112. Casas did not descend into the crater. Later, in Mexico, he received a letter from a friar who actually did. This friar had himself let down safely in a cage and tried in vain to collect some molten lava.

10. Rem., I, 217. See also Casas' confirming statement in the 1539 petition, Xim., I, 146.

11. My estimate is based on a careful study of the *Relación* of Fray Alonso Ponce's overland journey from Santiago de Guatemala to Mexico City in 1586, written by his secretary and printed at Madrid in 1873.

This narrative, the only early account of such a journey that I have seen, is a very detailed one. The outward trip took about a month, from March 18 to April 19, and followed the road by Tehuantepec and through Soconusco; it was the dry season and this was the shorter route. On the way back they passed by Comitán and Chiapa; this return trip took almost forty days, from August 27 to October 3, being on the longer and harder route and in the rainy season. Save for a few deviations, they followed the main road both ways. Although many place-to-place distances are given, enough are missing so that the entire distance cannot be established; the secretary intimated the round trip covered 800 leagues, but that seems excessive. Nor is it always easy to determine the distance covered in any given day, though I do not think they averaged more than eight leagues or 25 miles. They traveled very fast, usually starting before daybreak and riding till four or five in the afternoon and sometimes later.

In my judgment, Casas at 64 could not have performed the journey in anything like the time of Ponce's party; two months seems more reasonable.

12. Joaquín García Icazbalceta, *Don Fray Juan de Zumárraga, primer obispo y arzobispo de México* (Mexico, 1881), app. 27, closing paragraphs. Zumárraga im-

nowhere have we any connected account of this visit. His own personal narrative in the *Historia* does not go beyond 1521 or 1522, when he became a Dominican; but in the *Apologética* there are numerous references to Mexico, some with firsthand allusions. Since Fray Bartolomé was in the country at least twice—on this first occasion, and then afterwards in 1546—it is not always easy to tell which stay these passages refer to. Incidents that happened after 1540 must have been learned of on his second visit, but data on some earlier events might also have been gathered at the later period. Anyway, we learn that Casas was in Texcoco, Tlaxcala, and Tepeaca—the latter evidently while en route to or from Guatemala, or possibly on his trip to Veracruz to embark. He does relate a number of episodes which probably occurred in 1538 or 1539, notably an account of the pageant held in Mexico in January 1539 to celebrate the peace signed at Aguas Muertas the previous June between Charles V and Francis I.[13] Here and elsewhere, he praises the ingenuity of the Mexican Indians, citing several cases he himself observed. He was especially interested in the Mexicans' capacity for imitation, a trait still common with them. Thus, he speaks of their wonderful goldsmith's work and tells of finding an Indian slave with a guitar so well made it seemed to have come from Spain. But mostly he devotes space to Mexico City at the time of the conquest, copying his material, he says, from a letter of Cortés and failing to give us any picture of the city during his own visits.[14]

But the events of Fray Bartolomé's early stay in Mexico can be sketched in from other sources. First, of course, came the decisions of the provincial chapter—Remesal gives these from private papers. To carry on Casas' interrupted Guatemalan missions, Fray Pedro de Ángulo was named vicar and assigned three friars and two novices, though for some reason they delayed their return, not reaching Santiago till around April 1539.[15] As for Casas

---

plies they have just left; whereas several recommendations of Casas written from Guatemala in late 1539, doubtless obtained by Ángulo, only say that Fray Bartolomé is going to Spain. Cf. *DII*, XXIV, 337-338, 342.

13. See *Apol.*, caps. 62-64, *passim*, especially pages 165-166, a description of the festival in the plaza of Mexico City. (It was held on January 23.) Also cf. *ibid.*, 374, for a possible reference to the ecclesiastical junta of 1539 described in my next section, though more likely this refers to the bishops' junta of 1546—*infra*, chapter XIV.

14. *Apol.*, caps. 49-51, and cf. page 130.

15. Rem., I, 221-222. Remesal says they left after the profession of one of Ángulo's companions on November 21, 1538, and reached Santiago almost at the same time that Alvarado landed in Honduras, i.e., April 2, 1539. Just previously (*ibid.*, 213-214) Remesal had mistakenly referred to Alvarado as being in Santiago in early 1538; cf. *supra*, chapter VIII, note 17.

himself, he was given license to go to Spain with Ladrada and Cáncer to recruit more friars; but their departure too was delayed. Apparently Fray Bartolomé stayed on in Mexico City because of a religious meeting to be held there the following year on mission problems, and the rest of his Mexican visit seems to have been largely occupied in writing and talking about the conversion of the American natives. This activity deserves to be examined in some detail. It was an interesting intellectual interlude between his fieldwork in Tuzulutlán and his forthcoming return to court.

"Del único modo" and Motolinía

In Mexico, between 1538 and 1540, Bartolomé de las Casas made two contributions to the theory and rules of Indian missions. He wrote his first book, *Del único modo*, expounding his own principles of peaceful conversion, and he got into the current controversy on the adult baptism of natives. Evidently this won him the enmity of the famous Franciscan, Toribio de Benavente, better known as "Motolinía."[16]

This problem of adult Indian baptism was a major topic discussed at the Mexican ecclesiastical junta of 1539, with a view of making missionary practice obey the papal decision on the matter. We know both the formal antecedents of this meeting and the background situation. Briefly, on November 30, 1537, the three bishops in Mexico had answered an imperial request for information with a lengthy report on church affairs and the difficulties regarding adult baptism. The Emperor's reply of August 23, 1538, told Zumárraga to conform to the bull of Paul III which ordered henceforth a strict observance of the customary baptismal ceremonies of the church.[17] This amounted to a prohibition of the wholesale baptism of Indian adults as practised by Motolinía and other Franciscan missionaries. Accordingly, on April 27, 1539, a formal meeting of ecclesiastics was held in Mexico to discuss further instructions on this point and other conversion matters, which the Emperor had sent to Viceroy Mendoza. The three bishops had prepared a set of regulations which they submitted to members of the three mendicant Orders, and the discussion was mainly directed to the baptism and marriage of the Indians. The conclusions of the meeting, of which we have the full

---

16. See José Fernando Ramírez' "Noticias de la vida y escritos de fray Toribio de Benavente, o Motolinía," first printed in Icazbalceta, *Docs.*, I (1858).

17. See Icazbalceta, *Zumárraga*, app. 21. The bull was "Altitudo divini consilii," issued on June 1, 1537. It was printed as a broadside; cf. Quaritch Catalogue of 1885 for a copy.

text, appear to have been aimed in the first place at stamping out the mass baptisms.[18]

We do not have any record of what part Fray Bartolomé may have played in this meeting, though he doubtless attended it. But he emphatically did support the majority view upholding the papal bull and criticizing those engaged in the mass baptisms. This is clear from his own subsequent complaints at court, which included obvious references to Motolinía and led to the practice being condemned by a group of Salamanca theologians. On the other side, the Franciscans could hardly have accepted the Mexican junta's decision with good grace; and as a matter of fact, they did not. Motolinía himself continued baptizing Indians en masse despite the decrees. Fray Toribio even boasted of having baptized with a companion as many as fourteen thousand Indians in Quechola at one time, contrary to the prohibition the bishops had just issued pursuant to the papal bull.[19] So I consider it probable that Motolinía's later adverse opinion of Casas, expressed in such unbecoming terms in Fray Toribio's well-known letter to the Emperor of January 1555,[20] may have had its beginning in their disagreement during the meeting in Mexico.

We do have evidence of Motolinía's antagonism towards Casas right at this early period, as well as hints that this was the cause.[21] In the celebrated diatribe, Fray Toribio caustically tells of his first acquaintance with Fray Bartolomé, making liberal allusions to the adult-baptism controversy. He relates how Casas came to Tlaxcala with either twenty-seven or thirty-seven Indians, and how at this time the junta had "imposed silence upon us that we should not baptize adult Indians." So Fray Toribio and others asked Casas to baptize an Indian who came from afar, seeking baptism and "well

---

18. Icazbalceta, *Zumárraga*, 98 *et seq.* and app. 26. The privileges of the mendicant orders were aired at some length.

19. *Historia de los indios de la Nueva España,* tratado II, cap. 4—Icazbalceta, *Docs.,* I, 114-115.

20. Icazbalceta, *Docs.,* I, 253-277; also printed in *DII,* VII, 254-289, and XX, 175-213.

21. Perhaps before the junta, they seem to have been on good terms. For each gave the other material for his writings. Motolinía, in cap. 68 of his *Memoriales* (Luis García Pimentel, ed., Mexico, 1903, pages 220-221 and note 1), tells Casas' ascent of Masaya volcano and adds the information about the friar who descended into the crater; so Casas evidently showed him this friar's letter when it came—cf. *supra,* note 9. Similarly, Casas (*Apol.,* caps. 63-64) copies a description of a notable Corpus Christi pageant in Tlaxcala, given him by Motolinía—cf. *infra,* chapter XVII, note 19.

prepared" for it. This Casas at first agreed to do, but at the last minute changed his mind. Whereupon Fray Toribio said to him: "How is it, father, that all this zeal and love you say you have for the Indians ends in bringing them in with loads on their backs and in going about writing of the lives of Spaniards? . . . And since you don't baptize or teach an Indian, it would be well if you paid all those you brought loaded and weary."[22] This sounds as though their initial disagreement went very deep indeed; Motolinía evidently considered himself a successful practical missionary who had converted multitudes, and resented theological criticism of his methods by Casas who allegedly just wrote and talked about the Indians. But of course, many other Franciscans, like Bishop Zumárraga, and Testera from Yucatán, and Fray Marcos de Niza of later renown—all were good friends of Casas' and agreed with his mission theories.[23]

---

22. Icazbalceta, *Docs.,* I, 258.

23. Casas' relations with Fray Marcos de Niza are interesting, though the evidence is scanty. The two men must have met in Santiago de Guatemala, where Fray Marcos stopped on his return from Peru. For Niza was definitely there on September 25, 1536, when he gave testimony about his experiences with Alvarado in Peru. See the document from AGI, 2-2-1, in my article on Niza, *New Mexico Historical Review,* IX (1934), 194-198. Apparently Bishop Zumárraga summoned Niza to Mexico, where he arrived before April 4, 1537; for on that day Zumárraga wrote of Niza's writing a report for him about Peru, a copy of which he gave Viceroy Mendoza. Cuevas, *Docs.,* 83-84.

Naturally, Casas too was interested in Niza's story. In his own *Brevissima relación* he later inserted a long letter from Fray Marcos about Spanish enormities against the Peruvian Indians, perhaps the same report.

Casas' influence on Niza's famous journey is problematical. Bishop Zumárraga had adopted Casas' views about converting Indians peacefully, having perhaps already reached the same opinion himself. He suggested that new conquests be entrusted to Mendoza: soldiers should accompany the friars, but be prohibited from entering towns; instead, they should build a fort and trade with the natives. As is well known, Mendoza gave Niza instructions for the trip in search of the Seven Cities either in October or very early November 1538. Casas was already in Mexico and may have been the moving factor in Niza's journey. But Niza was then in Nueva Galicia, so perhaps the trip was already anticipated. For Coronado's letter of July 15, 1539, says the friar was sent to him by Mendoza to make the journey of discovery— see George P. Hammond and Agapito Rey, *Narratives of the Coronado Expedition* (Albuquerque, 1940), 45-49.

Anyway, no soldiers accompanied Fray Marcos de Niza. So at least that feature of Casas' plan was carried out, though there was no conversion of Indians. And in the *Apologética,* Casas speaks of knowing Niza well and relates part of his journey to the north.

Which brings us to Fray Bartolomé's other main activity of this Mexican stay: the production of his extensive treatise on what he considered the only true missionary method. I think it likely that Casas' *Del único modo* was written at this time. Only a portion of the work has come down to us, and as previously noted, this fragment contains a copy of the bull, "Sublimis Deus," not received in America till the fall of 1537. Casas must therefore have written his bulky treatise after that date; but he could hardly have done so during the rest of 1537 and 1538, when he was directing the Tuzulutlán venture and then making the long trip to Mexico. It is, however, evident that Casas was still a friar when he wrote the last of these chapters; he opens it with a criticism of bishops as well as friars for punishing the Indians' pre-baptismal sins by whippings, and at the end he asks his "hermanos" to re-volve in their minds a thousand and one times a certain quotation from St. Prosper. From all this I conclude that *Del único modo* was written after 1537 but before Casas became a bishop, and most probably in Mexico in 1539 and 1540. This would also serve to account for how he spent part of his time between the 1538 provincial chapter and his departure for Spain in 1540.

For the contents of the book, we must still depend upon Remesal's chronicle. The extant part of *Del único modo* consists only of chapters 5, 6, and 7 of book III; and Casas himself tells us a little more in his *Historia*—e.g., that he treated of restitution in books I and II.[24] But Remesal gives a full digest of the entire work, summarizing its thesis as follows: First, Casas discussed predestined salvation and how the Indians were included in it. "He proved how, by the works of Christ, all the predestined of all nations are to be called together . . . and so the same must be understood, believed and affirmed of the nations and peoples of this New World . . . Nor is this predestination impeded by their sins, however many . . . nor can the whole of any people be lacking sufficient understanding for the Gospel . . ." Next he proceeded to the topic of Indian capacity, showing that among the American natives there were different degrees of understanding, as in the rest of the world. "But all of them were ingenious, and even more so than other peoples in the government of human life . . ." This he proved by the "universal reasons," manifest effects such as the favorable influence of the celestial bodies in the mild climate of their lands, their good physical proportions, their excellent foodstuffs; and likewise by the "specific natural causes," the temperament of their "humors," their inner faculties like com-

---

24. *Hist.*, V, 154.

mon sense, imagination, fantasy, memory; and also by the "accidental causes," temperance, continence, indifference to temporal things, marvelous skill in the mechanical arts, etc. Finally Casas returned to predestination to make his main point on the way the chosen ones must be called to the faith of Christ: "One and one only is the method that Divine Providence instituted in all the world and at all times to teach men the true religion, namely that which persuades the understanding with reason and gently attracts the will; and this is common to all men without any difference because of errors, sects, or corruption of customs."[25]

This conclusion, Remesal says, Casas proved with thirty-six very long paragraphs citing scripture, church fathers, papal decrees. Then, in another eight paragraphs, he went on to discuss the contrary method: war and conquest. Finally, having explained the four types of infidels, Casas pointed out that the Indians are the fourth kind, i.e., removed from the Christians, whom they never harmed; therefore, any war of conquest upon them, under pretext that this will promote their conversion, is "unjust, perverse, and tyrannical."

Clearly, these views, which Casas elaborated as he prepared for his return to court, were a religious-missionary extension of the selfsame ideas that had struck him at his "conversion," when he originally decided to champion the Indians.

ERRANDS IN SPAIN

Fray Bartolomé returned to Spain at last some time in 1540. About his actual journey—by what route he reached port and when he embarked— nothing definite is known. Ximénez believes he went via Guatemala near the close of 1539, basing the notion on a document unknown to other writers. This is a petition from Casas to the Guatemalan town council, presented September 5, 1539, complaining that while the Dominican monastery was left vacant by his departure with the friars to Mexico, some townspeople had helped themselves to part of the land. Ximénez intimates this paper was written in Santiago de Guatemala, but I do not agree.[26] At Casas' age it would likely have taken him two months to travel from Mexico to Santiago, and another two months back to Mexico. As there is no intimation anywhere that he made such a trip, I have come to the conclusion that Casas simply wrote the petition from Mexico City, in response to a request from Fray

---

25. Rem., I, 177-180.
26. Xim., I, 145-146; Catalogue, no. 15.

Pedro de Ángulo in Guatemala.[27] According to Zumárraga's letter, Casas did not leave the capital till the spring of 1540, which indicates he may have sailed from Veracruz around summer and reached the Peninsula a couple of months later.

For the rest of 1540 and into 1541, Fray Bartolomé was busy in Spain with a variety of missionary errands. One of his main concerns was the Tuzulutlán mission, and he succeeded in obtaining support for it in numerous official documents. Thus, on October 17, 1540, at his instance, the Council issued a cedula prohibiting Spaniards from entering the territory for five years "by war or other means." In this order, a tribute from the Indians was also suggested, if the friars thought it advisable. On the same day, letters were sent in the Emperor's name to the governor and the friendly caciques, thanking them for their aid in the conversion. And on November 14, another cedula specifically confirmed the original contract (of May 2, 1537) between Maldonado and Casas for the Land of War venture.[28]

A side interest also occupied Fray Bartolomé at court: the missionary controversy over the baptism of adult Indians. When he left Mexico, everything there had been confusion and defiance, and Casas was apparently so upset over the situation that he complained to the Council about the lax practices. This must have been late in 1540 or at the start of the following year. As a result, the Emperor, in a letter of March 31, 1541, submitted the whole question to the famous Fray Francisco de Vitoria; on July 1, Vitoria and seven other theologians at the University of Salamanca rendered a dictum in Latin, strongly condemning the mass baptisms as sacrilegious and insisting on strict observance.[29]

But even that was not enough to stop the practice, and Fray Bartolomé afterwards renewed his protests. In a joint memorial of 1543, Casas and Ladrada again complained of those in New Spain "baptizing adult

---

27. See Catalogue, no. 15, for my conjecture on Ángulo's difficulties with the Santiago town council, and *infra*, last section of chapter XII, for his subsequent clash with this same body.

28. Remesal devotes lib. III, cap. 21, to this dispatch, transcribing most of the documents in full and including a more general one on Indian welfare. Ximénez (I, 214-219 and 246) copies a number of these and gives a few others. See *supra*, chapter VIII, note 18, for details on the royal thanks to the chiefs, and one of the implementing cedulas of early 1541. The royal confirmation is printed in *DII*, VII, 155-156 and Xim., I, 189.

29. *DIU*, XIV, 114, the consultation. *DII*, III, 543-553, the dictum; also printed by Henry Stevens in 1854.

Indians without their being first instructed in matters of the faith . . .
contrary to the express wording of the Evangel, the sacred canons and
doctrine of all the saints and the custom of the universal church . . .
The worst is that many are persisting in these errors and do not wish
to reform, but even defend them in the pulpits and in other places . . .
causing great dissension and confusion . . . very dangerous to those recently brought to the faith." So Casas then proposed the appointment of
a man eminent in letters, prudent and holy, to assume jurisdiction over the
Mexican clergy, with provisions from the Pope to put things in order![30] Undoubtedly, Casas' pursuing this matter in Spain served to inflame Motolinía's
antagonism towards him, though to Fray Bartolomé, as we have said, it was
hardly more than a side issue.

Of course, Casas' chief commission in this period was the recruitment
of missionaries. It will be remembered that Bishop Marroquín had originally asked him to go to Spain in order to obtain Franciscan and Dominican
friars for Guatemala; and indeed, the Mexican chapter had authorized his
return to court for this specific purpose. Apparently, the work of gathering
friars continued through 1540, for in January 1541, we find Casas in
Seville to assist at the embarcation of quite a contingent. The party consisted of a group of Franciscans—Remesal names six of them—and also Fray
Luís Cáncer, who was to take back the Tuzulutlán cedulas and provisions.
In order to make these better known, Casas actually had them proclaimed
from the steps of the Seville cathedral on January 21. A number of Dominicans had been recruited also, but they did not sail; for by now Casas'
own departure had been postponed, and it was thought best that they should
wait and travel with him as their vicar.[31]

Achieving this postponement was the climactic event of Casas' 1540-
1541 stint as missions procurator at court. For though Fray Bartolomé performed all his commissions diligently, even brilliantly—and in the years just
ahead he would recruit an even more impressive number of Dominicans
for Guatemala—right now his aim was to put aside the missionary role for
more vital affairs of state. Remesal says it was Cardinal García de Loaysa,
head of the Council of the Indies, who ordered Casas to stay on in Spain so
as to participate in upcoming discussions of American affairs. But that is
only part of the story. Casas had personally sought the order in a letter to
the Emperor, sent by the hand of Fray Jacobo de Testera. This communica-

---

30. Hanke, "Festón de docs.," *Revista Cubana*, XVI, 193-194.

31. Rem., I, 232-233. See *infra,* chapter XII, last section, "Visit to Verapaz," for
Cáncer's return with the dispatch.

ion makes it clear that Casas had interrupted the Land of War conversion and come to Spain, not on miscellaneous missionary errands, but to resume his life's crusade for the Indians.

Before we examine this notable document, let us look very briefly at the reform situation Casas had found in Spain after an absence of two decades. Meetings had been held intermittently about the rights of the Indians, and he was now busy summarizing their pronouncements, though not their full contradictory character.[32] Thus, in 1523, when Casas was taking his final vows, a junta at Valladolid had formulated instructions to Cortés forbidding encomiendas;[33] but in 1526, at Granada, another gathering prepared a definitive ordinance regulating conquests and permitting encomiendas.[34] Then, after the tragic fate of the Mexican Indians under the first audiencia, an important meeting was held at Barcelona in 1529. Conquistadors stressed their services and the depravity of the natives; while reforming friars, including Antonio Montesino, denounced killing and robbing and oppression, and won a decision that Indians should henceforth be free tribute-paying vassals.[35] But this was not carried out, and in the 1530's the pendulum swung the

---

32. That is, in *Entre los remedios* of 1542 (cf. Catalogue, no. 19 for the date), which he was undoubtedly preparing at this time. See Llorente, *Obras*, I, 295 and 331 *et seq.*

33. See *DIU*, IX, 67, dated June 26, 1523.

34. See *DIU*, IX, 268-280, the ordinance of November 27, 1526, on "discoveries" [conquests].

A curious printed account exists which may refer to the 1526 junta: *Por la guerra y muchos esclavos que hazia Pedrarias en las Indias, se disputaron entonces las siguientes dos questiones por los religiosos Dominicos y diversos juristas,* viz., the legality of war against the Indians, and of enslaving prisoners so taken. Maggs. Bros. of London cite the item in their Catalogue of Americana, 1922, with a note that Fernández de Enciso wrote a pamphlet on the other side (cf. *DII*, I, 441); they advise me that this printed brochure was sold to Señor Jijón y Caamaño, then living in Quito, Ecuador.

35. Apparently far more important than appears from contemporary chronicles, the deliberations of this junta are known to us from several interesting sources. Herrera, dec. IV, lib. VI, cap. 11, gives a long extract from some document relating the arguments of both sides and the conclusions. (Could this be the pamphlet cited in note 34, *supra*, which would then refer to the 1529 junta?) Casas himself gives these conclusions at some length in *Entre los remedios,* and we have a number of papers by and about the Española contingent. See the March 30, 1528, Santo Domingo letter from Licentiates Zuazo and Espinosa, reviewing the extermination of island and mainland Indians, and speaking of Dominican representatives who carry powers-of-attorney, etc. *DII*, XI, 342-346. Cf. also the pessimistic report by Montesino and a companion; and two other reports from friars. *DII*, XI, 249-252, and 252-254.

other way: a general anti-slavery ordinance was reversed in cedulas permitting slaving.[36] Even the famous Fray Francisco de Vitoria felt the change. Apparently around 1532 he had questioned the conquest as a basis for the King's title to the Indies, but in 1539 he was the target of a silencing order from the Crown for lectures on the same topic.[37] During these decades of indecision, which Casas knew well from the participating friars, the Emperor himself had long been away from Spain.

It was against this background of prolonged imperial vacillation that Casas on December 15, 1540, addressed his momentous letter to Charles V. The paper itself is a simple request, with much obviously left for the bearer to fill in orally. Casas writes that in Guatemala he had received a letter from the Emperor urging him to continue his work there, namely the pacification of the Land of War with friars, by the road of peace and love and good works, "which he had already begun." But instead he had come to Spain to report to the Emperor on certain things of far greater importance and

---

36. See Gómara, *Historia*, 290. He tells of the Emperor issuing a slaving authorization from Madrid in 1525, following Ortiz' denunciation of the Indians (cf. *supra*, chapter II, note 16), and of the 1531 [1530] ordinance, which he attributes to Minaya. Minaya himself speaks of a slaving provision resulting from Betanzos' activities at court somewhat later. *Harvard Theological Review*, XXX, 100.

37. Vitoria's famous "relectio" *De Indis* is believed to have been delivered at the University of Salamanca about the end of December 1538 or in the first weeks of 1539. (See the Madrid, 1928, edition of the *Relectios*, using the chronology of Fray Vicente Beltrán de Heredia.) On November 10, 1539, the Emperor issued an indignant directive ordering the prior of Estaban de Salamanca to collect and submit all such writings on the Crown's rights to the Indies, prevent their dissemination, and forbid further discussion of the topic without royal license. AGI, 139-1-9, printed in Luis G. Alonso Getino, *El Maestro Fray Francisco de Vitoria*, Madrid, 1914.

After reading Vitoria's *De los indios* very carefully, I have a theory that its three distinct parts (2-55, 56-139, 140-189) might originally have been three separate lectures given at different times, with at least the third added to mollify the Emperor. The first might have been delivered around 1532-1533, or anyway Vitoria enunciated similar views at that time. (For the internal and external evidence, see *infra*, chapter XIX, note 3.) In the subsequent parts, Vitoria stultifies himself by giving various reasons to justify the Spaniards reducing the Indians to the Crown, and his third part contains a number of contradictory statements.

I believe the Emperor's sudden sensitivity on this issue may be explained by the current rebellion in Ghent. The burghers had refused to pay some newly imposed taxes, citing their ancient exemptions. This news reached Spain in October 1539, and so irritated Charles that he at once went to Ghent to handle the matter personally. Obviously, if the Crown's rights in the Indies could be questioned, the same might apply to the Lowlands.

urgency for "your royal estate in all that New World"; and in consequence he had had to suspend the pacification of Tuzulutlán. In Castile, however, Casas had found His Majesty absent. So now he begged Charles to order him to stay over and await the royal coming for the sake of all the Indies, and to direct this through the Dominican provincial of Castile [Loaysa], "so that I can comply with the prelates of my Order and the obedience I promised them."[38]

The imperial command did come, apparently within the month, and he was ordered to stay on. So in 1541, after a monastic hiatus of twenty years, Fray Bartolomé de las Casas was once more to champion the cause of the Indians—with the most significant results of his entire career.

---

38. *Documentos inéditos de España*, VIII, 555-556; Fabié, app. VII. See Catalogue, no. 17, for more particulars on this document and Fray Jacobo.

THE NEW LAWS

CASAS' ROLE, ACCORDING TO THE CHRONICLERS

Casas' work for the Indians in 1541-1543 led to the famous New Laws of the Indies. Some modern writers have tried to minimize his influence, but I find it fully substantiated.

As a matter of fact, Fray Bartolomé put on a sensational campaign along three main lines. He denounced the "destruction" of the natives in lurid detail. He apparently charged members of the Council of the Indies with venality. And he presented significant proposals for reform legislation. On the "destruction" and the "remedies," his actual memorials have survived, in abbreviated form, as two of his most celebrated tracts. Furthermore, the events leading to the New Laws are reported by a number of sixteenth- and seventeenth-century chroniclers—Gómara, Herrera, León, etc.—all of whom stress Casas' decisive role.

The most elaborate contemporary account is given by Alonso de Santa Cruz, the royal cosmographer, in his *Crónica del Emperador Carlos V*. Santa Cruz begins with a special chapter *About a certain account given by a friar named Bartolomé de las Casas, concerning the destruction that the Christians had wrought on the Indians of the West Indies. And how the Emperor ordered an investigation of the members of his Council of the Indies:*[1]

"In this year [of 1542] Fray Bartolomé de las Casas, of the Order of St. Dominic, came to court. He had been more than forty years in the West Indies, from the time that Don Christopher Columbus discovered them (although he was not then a friar). And he informed His Majesty in a comprehensive summary of the great cruelties and destructions which the Christians had visited on the Indians.

---

1. Santa Cruz, *Crónica*, sexta parte, cap. 42.

"The Emperor, wishing to be more completely informed of those matters, ordered Doctor Guevara and Licentiate Figueroa, of his Council [of Castile], along with the Grand Commander of León [Francisco de los Cobos], to join with the Council of the Indies to hear what the friar had to say. This they did for many days at a fixed hour, till Casas had read to them completely a certain very copious account that he had in writing." And he also informed them orally of many things pertaining to the welfare of the Indians.

At this point Santa Cruz pauses to resume this "very copious account" at considerable length—his sketch corresponds closely to the celebrated *Brevissima relación de la destruición de las Indias* that Casas himself printed in 1552.[2] Here, in abbreviated form, is the familiar bloodcurdling tale of Indian extermination in region after region conquered by the Spaniards. But the chronicler gives details not found in the published version. Thus, in Santa Cruz's summary, the "tyrants" are carefully named—Pedrarias, Cortés, Guzmán, Alvarado, Montejo, Lerma, Heredia, Ortal—showing that Fray Bartolomé charged them personally with crimes before the Emperor's expanded Council,[3] whereas in the printed tract the names are prudently omitted. Again, near the end of the *Brevissima relación*, Casas says he finished it at Valencia on December 8, 1542. That was three weeks after the signing of the New Laws, so the date can refer only to this abridgement written after the oral presentation, and given to young Prince Philip by his tutor.[4] The original memorial, Santa Cruz informs us, was presented at the start of the proceedings in 1542.

"And after Casas had given this relation to the Emperor," Santa Cruz's narrative proceeds, "he also gave his advice about what should be ordered to remedy matters for the future. . . . He advised that all the Indians should be taken away from those Christians who held them under encomiendas, and should be put under His Majesty." Thereby the King would obtain many millions in revenue, and the natives would be well treated and instructed in the faith.

This corresponds precisely to the fundamental Eighth Remedy that Casas himself later printed as another of the 1552 tracts, *Entre los remedios*. There, Casas described the "eighth" as the essence of all the remedies,

---

2. For the *Brevissima*, see Catalogue, no. 18; also *infra*, my chapter XVI, section on "Eight famous tracts."

3. Santa Cruz, *Crónica*, IV, 217-220.

4. See Fabié, app. XXI, the opening Argument and the Prologue to the Prince.

without which none of the others would accomplish anything.[5] In brief, it was to put all the Indians under the Crown and abolish the encomienda system of private allotments. Santa Cruz evidently saw the original memorial, for he gives not only this major remedy but a number of minor ones as well: total abolition of Indian slavery; opening of roads for carts, so the Indians would not be loaded as carriers; resettlement of natives from densely to sparsely populated regions; and the erection of fortresses at specified places on the mainland, such as the Río Dulce and the Marañon, Yucatán, and Florida.[6]

In addition, the chronicle continues, Casas and other God-fearing persons charged certain councilors with venality, and Licentiate Figueroa was ordered to conduct a secret judicial inspection of the Council of the Indies.

As a result of all this, the Emperor promulgated the New Laws. Santa Cruz devotes a full chapter to the text of these famous ordinances signed at Barcelona on November 20, 1542.[7] In yet another chapter he relates how the Emperor "reformed" the Council of the Indies, dismissing and fining officials and adding new members, and also appointed a viceroy for Peru and named an inspector general to conduct an investigation of the viceroy of Mexico. "And he named as Bishop of Chiapa . . . Fray Bartolomé de las Casas, who had been the cause of the making of the ordinances and of His Majesty's being better informed on the government of the Indies." Finally, a Clarification or Amendment to the New Laws was issued on June 4, 1543— its text fittingly occupies a closing chapter.[8]

Such is the classic version from Casas' own age. In the next century, the Dominican Remesal examined Fray Bartolomé's papers at the Valladolid monastery, and added significant information.

Remesal, it will be remembered, starts his story in 1541, before the Emperor's appearance on the scene, with Cardinal Loaysa ordering Casas to stay on at court.[9] This would seem to be correct, since Charles had left Spain in November of 1539 and did not return till after the Argel campaign in 1541. The King reached Cartagena some time in December, stopped off

---

5. For this tract, with its unwieldy heading, see Catalogue, no. 19. Today it is usually called *Entre los remedios* or *El octavo remedio;* Casas himself referred to it as his "veinte razones" [against the encomienda]. The text shows it was definitely addressed to the 1542 Valladolid junta.

6. Santa Cruz, *Crónica,* IV, 220-221.

7. Santa Cruz, *Crónica,* sexta parte, cap. 43.

8. Santa Cruz, *Crónica,* séptima parte, caps. 15-16. For the assertion about Casas, see *ibid.,* IV, 320.

9. Rem., I, 232.

a few days at Toledo, and then went on to Valladolid to take charge of the government. During his absence, American affairs were entrusted to García de Loaysa, who was once again serving as president of the Council of the Indies.[10]

According to Remesal, the Cardinal initiated a full-scale review of the Indian question, and the juntas and consultations of learned men and colonials ran through all of 1541 and 1542. At first these were held before the Council, but later a special commission was named for the matter: Cardinal Loaysa and the Count of Osorno, who had previously alternated as president of the Indies Council; Bishop Fuenleal, erstwhile head of the Mexican audiencia; Juan de Zúñiga, tutor to Prince Philip; three long-time councilors of the Indies, Velásquez, Salmerón, and López; and three outsiders, Doctor Guevara of the Privy Council, Licentiate Mercado of the Council of Castile, and Doctor Arteaga of the Council of Orders of Knighthood.

Remesal describes the oral sessions, at which Fray Bartolomé emphasized to the Council of the Indies the abuses in Guatemala and Honduras and the lands southward to Peru, and suggested sending royal judges. In addition, great treatises were submitted in writing—"the one who expatiated the most was our good father, Fray Bartolomé de las Casas, who composed in a clear style a long memorial of the remedies His Majesty could and should institute." Elsewhere, Remesal calls this "a big volume containing sixteen remedies against the plague fast destroying the Indies." Here he says only that "the Father himself cites sixteen," and gives Casas' own summary of the basic Eighth Remedy that was supported by "twenty reasons." Fray Bartolomé distributed many copies of these reasons and expounded them to the members of the special commission, which finally drafted the "New Laws, so famous throughout the world." The chronicler then spends a couple of chapters extracting the ordinances, and concludes by saying that, after the Emperor had signed them, Fray Bartolomé completed his *Brevissima relación de la destruición de las Indias*.[11] (But, of course,

---

10. According to León Pinelo's *Tablas cronológicas de los reales consejos supremos y de la cámara de las Indias Occidentales* (Madrid [1645] 1892), Loaysa was president in 1524-1528 and again in 1536-1537, and the Count of Osorno from 1529-1535 and from 1538-1540.

11. See Rem., I, 276-278, the narrative; and 278-286, the laws and the closing error. He says the special commission met in the house of Pedro González de León.

Remesal apparently searched Dominican archives at San Esteban de Salamanca as well as at San Gregorio de Valladolid, for he describes great memorials, each doctor and master writing in his own manner, ordinary prose or dialogue or scholastic conclu-

this misunderstanding amounts to putting the cart before the horse, since the *Brief Account* must have been a very early gun in the battle.)

Compared to these two painstaking chroniclers, others contribute mere details. Bernal Díaz del Castillo, who was in Spain during the first half of 1540 and perhaps into 1541, describes Council meetings attended by himself and Cortés at which Casas was present; but he mentions no debate on encomiendas, showing that the reform discussion did not begin till later in 1541.[12] Herrera, though official chronicler of the Indies, gives only a sketchy story. He adds a bit of background on dissensions and complaints from America, and prints a cedula showing the Emperor began the Council inspection personally and then entrusted it to Licentiate Figueroa, the Regent of Naples; he also names three other friars who helped Fray Bartolomé de las Casas instigate the reform, but these appear to be Dominicans connected with the Land of War.[13] Similarly, Gómara adds little. He enumerates a few members of the junta, and says that as a result of Casas' efforts, Figueroa was charged with examining under oath the numerous governors, conquistadors, and religious who had been in the Indies, in order to investigate the capacity and treatment of the natives, and also because some friars [i.e., Casas] had claimed the conquest of those parts could not be made.[14]

Finally, Antonio de León Pinelo, the seventeenth-century jurist who abstracted the files of the Council of the Indies, merely repeats and confirms Remesal's version of Casas' role, contributing only some particulars on the actual drafting of the New Laws. After a closing survey by the special commission, the Emperor obtained written views from the Council of State. Finally, in Barcelona, a last meeting was held in the home of the Cardinal

---

sions—"and I have seen papers of the time in those three styles composed by Masters of the Order of St. Dominic." He may be referring to the Salamanca lectures by Vitoria and others, and the adult baptism dictum of 1541, or to works we do not know.

12. See Díaz del Castillo, *Historia veradera*, II, 427, the meetings in 1540, with names of some councilors differing slightly from those mentioned by Remesal; I, 461, his story of Miguel Díaz de Aux before the Council in 1541, though he does not say he himself was there; and II, 353, on Casas being present at the Council in 1540.

13. Herrera, dec. VII, lib. IV, cap. 17, and lib. VI, caps. 4 and 5 (the last being a summary of the New Laws). Herrera states that the Dominicans, headed by Casas, brought about the meetings of 1542 and the inspection. He names Fray Juan de Torres, Fray Matías de Paz, and Fray Pedro de Ángulo.

14. Gómara, *Historia*, 249-250; and cf. *ibid.*, 290. Gómara names Cobos and Figueroa, who may well have served ex officio, and Indies Councilor Bernal, who was removed as a result of the inspection.

of Seville: "Those who took part were Monsieur de Granvela, Doctor Guevara, Doctor Figueroa, the Emperor's confessor [Cardinal Loaysa], and [Cobos], the Grand Commander of León. All the opinions were read, with particular accounts to the Emperor, who resolved to remove the right to grant encomiendas" despite the objections of Loaysa and Cobos.[15] This is a reference to the most controversial laws—the ones based on Casas' Eighth Remedy.

For of course all the writers, sketchy or elaborate, tell the same tale of Fray Bartolomé's influence. Everyone says that Casas complained of Indian mistreatment, Casas provoked the inspection of the Council, Casas inspired the reform ordinances. Contemporaries are especially insistent on this last point. Gómara, for instance, states flatly that Casas procured the New Laws, and that all the Spaniards in the Indies blamed him for them.[16] Santa Cruz asserts virtually the same thing. Both men were in Spain at the time and are unimpeachable witnesses. So we may accept the word of the chroniclers that Bartolomé de las Casas was responsible for the "Laws and Ordinances Newly Made for the Government of the Indies and Good Treatment and Preservation of the Indians."

---

15. *Tratado de confirmaciones reales de encomiendas*, fols. 6-9 verso. León had also seen an opinion of Cobos which stated: "It seems to me that in the matter of the allotments the laws were not advisable, as I always feared that some difficulties and harm would arise from them." On the dissents of Cardinal Loaysa, the Bishop of Lugo, and Cobos, he further cites Fernández' Peruvian chronicle—see Diego Fernández ("Palentino"), *Primera parte de la Historia del Peru* [Seville, 1571], Madrid, 1913, lib. I, cap. 1.

León's sequence of events closely parallels Remesal's. But speaking of Casas' sixteen remedies, he adds: *"It is a matter of record* that this was written at the command of the Emperor and copies were given to each member." [Italics ours.] Perhaps he had found an official document, though on the other hand he does cite chroniclers.

But León was more interested in Casas' works. He speaks of "his writings, printed and manuscript, which I shall treat in my *Biblioteca,* more particularly than I treated them in its *Epitome."* (So far as I know, this fuller bibliography has not been published.) Also, in parte primera, caps. 18-20 of his *Tratado,* he reviews Casas' arguments for abolition of the encomienda, from *Entre los remedios* and elsewhere. He finds the ordinance extinguishing it to have been pious, just, and necessary; but this was non-enforceable, so its repeal was pious, just, and necessary, too. Written from the "realistic" point of view, these chapters cite later laws that ameliorated the lot of the Indians, though there is ample evidence the improvement was less than León claims. Besides, the point is not the situation in 1630, when he was writing, but in 1542.

16. Gómara, *Historia,* 249. He also gives the results of the inspection.

THE ORIGINAL ORDINANCES

As originally signed on November 20, 1542, these reform ordinances fell far short of Casas' proposals. Even so, they were epoch-making and deserve to be analyzed in some detail.[17]

They began mildly enough, with a series of measures for administrative reform. After laying down some rules for the handling of business by the Council of the Indies, the Emperor then enunciated those for the various audiencias and the rights of appeal from their judgments—instituting new audiencias for Peru and the combined region of Guatemala and Nicaragua. He also ordered the courts and audiencias to be most particular about the good treatment of the Indians and the enforcement of the ordinances to that end. And now, mounting to a crescendo, followed the reform laws dealing with the natives.

First came a flat edict forbidding all taking of Indian slaves in the future. "Furthermore: we order that henceforth, neither by war nor by any other means, even if it be under the guise of rebellion, nor by barter, nor in any other way, shall any Indian whatsoever be made a slave, and we wish them to be treated as vassals of the Crown of Castile, for such they are. No person may use the Indians as *naborías* or *tapias*, nor in any other way against their will." [*Naboría* meant a household servant, and *tapia*, a watchman.] As for existing Indian slaves, the audiencias were to make a swift inquiry: whenever owners could not show a legitimate title, the slaves should be freed, and advocates should be named at royal expense to represent the slaves at the hearings.

Furthermore, *Indians could not be used as carriers,* except in some places where this was unavoidable, and then they had to be paid and not be overloaded nor used against their will. Similarly, about *pearl fishing,* it was ordered that no Indian be taken thereto against his will.

After these preliminaries came the real bombshell—the laws abolishing the encomienda system by slow stages:

For the present, all encomiendas held by officialdom were revoked outright, and these Indians were ordered placed under the Crown at once. Thus, the following were to lose their Indians even though they might beg to keep them and resign their offices: all public officials from the viceroy down, the clergy, monasteries, hospitals, the mint, the treasury, etc., also private encomenderos who held Indians without due title or had mistreated

---

17. León counts forty ordinances, Herrera counts thirty-nine, but Santa Cruz uses no numbers, nor does the official text (see *infra,* note 30). To avoid confusion, I have used no numbers and shall refer to the laws by their subject.

them. Furthermore, in Peru, the "principal persons" involved in the recent rebellion were to be deprived of their Indians forthwith. In New Spain, the excessive encomiendas of certain persons—nine are named particularly— were to be reduced to a moderate size; and from the tribute of the Indians thus removed and placed under the Crown, some support should be paid to the "first conquistadors" without encomiendas.

For the future, all private encomiendas were to be suppressed by a gradual process—no new encomiendas could be created, and all existing ones would escheat to the Crown on the death of their holders. The crucial law was most explicit. "Furthermore: we order that from now on no viceroy, governor, or audiencia, discoverer, or any other person can put Indians in encomienda, neither by our royal provision nor by renunciation nor donation, sale nor any other form, nor by vacating title nor inheritance—*but when the person holding the said Indians dies, these shall be put under our royal Crown.*" [Italics added.] Any surviving widow or children or other heirs could, upon proper examination and report by the audiencia, be paid a moderate pension, if necessary, from the tribute of the escheated Indians.

All Indians thus put in the Crown must be well treated and instructed in the faith. In appointing their *corregidores* or Spanish superintendents, preference should be given to qualified first discoverers and married colonists.

Following this climax, the ordinances wound up with a sort of final shock wave about explorations.

There was a series of new regulations for expeditions of discovery, with special regard to the treatment and tribute of the Indians: Discoveries could be made only under license of the audiencia, and no slaves could be brought back nor anything taken from the natives except by barter. Religious must go along, and discoverers must report back and start settlements only when authorized. No viceroy or governor could take part in future discoveries. In discoveries now in progress, moderate tribute and personal services of the Indians were to be assessed forthwith, to be turned over to the encomendero where there is one. But Spaniards were expressly forbidden to have power over the Indians or to make any use of them—they must enjoy only the tribute. Those holding contracts for discovery were obliged to conform to all these new ordinances and to suitable instructions from the audiencias.

Lastly, *the surviving Indians in Española, Cuba, and Puerto Rico were to be exempted from all tribute and royal or personal services,* so that they could rest and multiply.[18]

---

18. Some other clauses, *passim,* dealt with judicial and other procedures: suits

In these "Ordinances for the Indies and Indians," it is clear that Casas' extreme position had not prevailed. His Eighth Remedy had stressed the need of immediately revoking private allotments and putting all Indians under the Crown, as a pre-condition to every other reform measure. The laws did provide for the extinction of the encomienda, but only in gradual stages over a period of decades, with milder reforms in the meantime. Also, according to Santa Cruz, Fray Bartolomé had advocated the total abolition of Indian slavery. Again this was not done, though a prohibition was decreed to future enslavement of the natives. Nevertheless, the reform ordinances quite obviously showed the influence of Bartolomé de las Casas.

His campaign for the Amendment

Apparently, Casas was not satisfied with the New Laws as originally promulgated, for he promptly embarked on a further campaign to have them amended.

On the last day of February 1543, Fray Bartolomé and his assistant, Fray Rodrigo de Ladrada, submitted an elaborate joint memorial to the Council of the Indies. This basic document—we have a complete copy, found recently in a Bolivian monastery[19]—suggested a number of steps to strengthen the ordinances protecting the Indians.

Casas began, naturally, by criticizing the gradual extinction of the encomienda, as this would leave most of the natives in private allotments. So he proposed stern measures to correct the abuses of tribute and personal services. But his major fire was concentrated on a last-ditch effort to abolish Indian slavery.

All the anti-slavery laws, he protested, were inadequate. The law freeing Indian slaves, unless their holders could produce titles, was bound to fail in the face of Spanish perjury. Besides, all slaves should be freed, as there was no just title to any. The King should particularly free the Tierra Firme Indians sent as slaves to the islands and the victims of the horrible mass enslavements in Central America, Yucatán, and Pánuco, and the many slaves newly taken in the Jalisco war. A halt must be put to the infamous traffic in Indian slaves to Havana and Spain—it was rumored there were ten thousand in Seville right then.

---

of Indians were to be promptly determined; all suits of Spaniards asking grants of Indians were not to be heard in the Indies or the Council, but sent direct to the King; requests for "mercedes" must be heard by audiencias, and sealed reports forwarded to the Council of the Indies.

19. Hanke, "Festón de docs.," *Revista Cubana*, XVI, 156-195; see Catalogue, no. 20.

Also, the law forbidding future enslavement of Indians implied that wars and conquests were to continue, but they must cease altogether. For legal reasons and for the crimes of past tyrants, all existing "contracts and stipulations" for discoveries should be revoked.

Besides these measures to strengthen the laws, new officials were needed for their enforcement. In each district or province of the Indies, a person should be appointed for the defense of the natives; and at court there should be a general procurator and defender of all the Indians, with a very good salary, which the Indians could pay if the King was unwilling to.[20]

All told, this joint petition made a strong case for amendments, and it did produce some effect. An official note, written on the petition itself on April 11, directed Casas and Ladrada to submit in a fortnight an itemized summary of the points to be considered.

This document may well be Fray Bartolomé's short set of proposals with captioned sections—"Indians," "Spanish population," "Slaves," "Conquests and discoveries"—that bears no date but is clearly from the New Laws period.[21] Much of the document is devoted to detailed plans for peaceable exploitation in place of conquest—actually, revivals of his emigration and mainland schemes of a quarter-century earlier.[22] Once again Casas insists that colonization by peasants and laborers should be encouraged, both for the conversion of the natives and the maintenance of the Spanish dominions. As for further "conquests and discoveries" on Tierra Firme, he objects to the very word "conquest." In its stead, he outlines his familiar program of opening the continent peacefully with traders and missionaries, extending it now to the coasts of the whole Spanish Main, Central America, and Peru. Captains at present waging wars of conquest should be ordered to cease and settle quietly, or withdraw to the older settlements—the King may cancel their grants, which were gained fraudulently and are destroying the land.

Related to the foregoing is a curious recommendation that we have only as a rough draft in Casas' handwriting. This, too, is undated, but Fabié

---

20. In this, and throughout the document, Casas expressed his worries about enforcement. Anticipating great fraud in the cutting down of excessive encomiendas, he proposed this be done in the full audiencia, in the presence of a Franciscan and Dominican who should send sealed reports to the Emperor. His fears were later to prove justified. Similarly, he insisted that corregidores should not interfere with the native lords; and again, there were later abuses, as he had foreseen.

21. Fabié, app. XXXI; and see Catalogue, no. 21, on the tentative dating of this document, which appears to be a draft.

22. Cf. his summary memorial of 1518, also the Puerto de Plata memorial of 1531. Fabié, apps. IV and V.

placed it in 1543 by internal evidence. From random remarks in the text, it appears that news of Diego de Alvarado (the younger) had not yet been received nor had Núñez Vela left Spain, and Núñez left in the fall of 1543. So I conclude that this document may have been presented in Valladolid about May 1 of that year, apparently by Casas and Ladrada, as it is written in the first person plural like the preceding one.[23]

The recommendation boldly proposes that the King finance the emigration scheme by confiscating half the property of the Spaniards in the Indies, though he might be kind and cut the percentage to one-fifth or one-sixth. Casas had first suggested such compulsory restitution back in 1518, to raise funds for the Tierra Firme project. Here he reiterates the idea with legalistic arguments,[24] and explains how to prevent rebellions from breaking out in protest. From each major city in Mexico and Peru, the fifteen or twenty chief troublemakers should be deported to Spain; on arrival there they should be deprived of their property, given a pension to live on, and forbidden to return to the Indies.

Apart from these two documents—the itemized proposals and the sequel—there is evidence of one more follow-up step in Fray Bartolomé's campaign for amendments. Right in the text of the joint memorial he promised to give a "long and true report" consisting of sworn evidence and legal arguments against Indian slavery.

We know of two writings by Casas on this topic. One, an anti-slavery *Treatise* that he printed in 1552, reads like the legal brief, but was written somewhat later after he became a bishop. The other, "On the Taking of Slaves in the Second Jalisco Conquest, by Order of Don Antonio de Mendoza, Viceroy of New Spain, in the year 1541," is now lost. Remesal described it as a Latin book of 272 folio pages, so it too must have been writ-

---

23. Fabié, app. XXIX; and see Catalogue, no. 22, my full reasons for assigning this document a tentative date of 1543.

Fabié (I, 349-351) describes the MS and dates it in 1543, though partly by assuming that Casas came with Ovando in 1501 [*sic* for 1502]. Fabié did, however, notice the references to Vaca de Castro, which place the document in this period.

24. See the confiscation passage from the summary memorial quoted *supra* in the first section of my chapter V, where Casas also proposed confiscating one-fifth of the gold and pearls. Here he admits that legal objections could be raised, viz., that encomiendas of Indians to wash gold were set up by royal grants; also that the Crown authorized the conquests, furnished irons to brand slaves taken in war, and received one-fifth of them. In answer, he cites his "twenty reasons" against the encomienda and alleges that all these decrees were obtained by fraud—namely the "heresy" that it was necessary to make war on the Indians to attract them to God and the King. The fraction chosen for confiscation suggests he was nudging the royal conscience.

ten afterwards.[25] But I have no doubt that Casas now presented oral information about the terrible Jalisco campaign, news of which was reaching Spain around this time.[26]

During the deliberations of 1541-1542, sensational events had taken place in the Indies: the expedition of Francisco Vásquez de Coronado in search of the Seven Cities, a great and expensive fiasco, and the related revolt of the Indians in New Galicia. This Mixtón War became so threatening that Viceroy Mendoza was obliged to take the field personally with every man he could muster. The Spaniards came near losing New Spain at this time, and all available evidence points to the fact that the rebellion was put down with the most severe punishment of the captives.[27] Discounting the stories of great cruelty, there is no doubt that a large multitude were branded and sold as slaves. Just how many has not been determined; one-fifth, as usual, were allotted to the King and sold, and the books of the accountant and treasurer should show the number, though so far as I know they have never been examined. The viceroy was accused of taking many of these slaves for himself—this was one of Cortés' charges against him in 1543, and the charge was repeated in the official inquiry into Mendoza's conduct. Mendoza answered ambiguously, though practically acknowledging that he had received a number of slaves.[28]

---

25. See Rem., II, 469, and Catalogue, no. 42.

26. In the joint memorial, Casas reviews the Indian slave trade generally—the slaving regions, the devices, the Seville traffic—and includes a long paragraph specifically about the wars and enslavements in Jalisco on the Cíbola entry. Hanke, "Festón de docs.," *Revista Cubana*, XVI, 177-181.

27. For a contemporary account of this campaign see the Acazitli relation in Icazbalceta, *Docs.*, II, 307-332. Jerónimo López, that persistent beggar and indefatigable letter-writer, makes some interesting statements about the Jalisco campaign. López was with Mendoza, and should be a trustworthy witness since he was a very intelligent man. By a miracle, he says, the Nochistlán chief, Tenamaztle, came out to make peace. Had he fought, none of the Spaniards would have been left alive, as the Indians were such great fighters. *Epis. de Nueva España*, V, no. 268, letter of January 20, 1548. On Casas' later relations with Chief Tenamaztle, see Catalogue, no. 56.

28. For Cortés' charges against Mendoza, see Cuevas, *Docs.*, no. XXXIII. In his answer, the viceroy did not deny having slaves, but declared these did not number more than 190 or 200.

For the investigation charges against Mendoza, see Icazbalceta, *Docs.*, II, nos. XXXIV-XLIII. In his interrogatory, answering charge 38, Mendoza admitted that unusual punishments were inflicted on Indians taken, but this seemed to produce no effect on the others. The first captives made at Coina were handed over to the Indians after more than 248 were branded. See Ciriaco Pérez Bustamante, *Don Antonio de Mendoza* (Santiago de Compostela, 1928), 162.

It is certain that accounts of this war reached Spain in time to receive consideration in the Council. In fact, I feel that the reform ordinances about slaves and expeditions for discovery had been inserted as a result of the Mixtón War and the Coronado expedition. Casas' oral information, probably given in May, doubtless dealt with it too.

But the total results of Fray Bartolomé's campaign for amendments were rather meager. A Clarification of the New Laws was finally issued at Valladolid on June 4, 1543,[29] but it contained nothing further about conquests or Indian slavery. There was only some tightening of the regulations on tribute, and a little more help in the direction of the "poor conquistadors"—the pensions and corregimientos were to be made available to the sons of those who had died. Perhaps this was due to Casas' efforts.

The finished New Laws, the *Ordinances Newly Made* and their Clarification, were printed in Alcalá on July 8, 1543. The original promulgation of November 20, 1542, had been ordered "printed in type" and sent to the friars to translate for the natives; the amendments were to be "printed at the foot of it." Many copies were now printed, and they were widely distributed throughout the Indies to royal officials, ecclesiastics, and others in authority.[30]

But the story of Bartolomé de las Casas and the New Laws did not end there. Still to come was a melodramatic battle over enforcement that raged in the New World and the Old. With that struggle, Casas himself would be directly concerned, not just as the known instigator of the controversial legislation, but in his new role as a reforming bishop.

---

29. Santa Cruz, *Crónica*, IV, 320-326. He says the amendments were prepared by the same councilors who had formulated the ordinances.

30. Imprints of this first edition of 1543 have become extremely rare, but a facsimile reprint was issued by Henry Stevens in 1893, and García Icazbalceta printed the text from an original copy used for public proclamation in Mexico in 1544. Icazbalceta, *Docs.*, II, 204-227.

BISHOP OF CHIAPA

Casas receives the mitre

In the wake of the New Laws, Casas was made Bishop of Chiapa. There has been controversy about this, as about every other phase of his career. But before we examine the pros and cons and his probable motives, let us review the actual story of his elevation to the episcopal dignity.

Remesal recounts his appointment.[1] Some time in the latter part of 1542, Secretary Cobos went to see Fray Bartolomé and advised him the Emperor was going to name him Bishop of Cuzco. Casas was far from pleased and refused even to consider the proposition. The authorities, however, were determined to elevate him. For the King now offered him the bishopric of Chiapa, a new Central American see created in 1538 by Paul III but still vacant. The first bishop, Juan de Arteaga, had not even left Spain till 1541, and then died at Puebla in Mexico en route to his post. Casas did not want to accept even this less important diocese but the Council of the Indies insisted, and he was finally persuaded.

The necessary three steps in Casas' elevation to the bishopric of Chiapa —nomination by the Emperor, preconization by the Pope, and final consecration—spanned a prolonged interlude. The "presentation" by Charles was evidently made in the second half of 1543, after Casas' campaign for the Amendment, as he was still a friar at that time. As for his preconization, both MacNutt and Fabié wrongly date it as pentecost [May 28], 1542. They are, however, just misreading a passage where Remesal gives the date for the election in Rome of Fray Alberto de Casaus or las Casas, "a close relative of the Bishop of Chiapa," as general of the Dominican Order. According to Muñoz's summary of the relevant document, the formalities in Rome took

---

1. Rem., I, 289-291.

place on December 19 and 20, 1543.[2] But Casas' actual consecration was not till the following spring.

This interval, the remainder of 1543 and the early part of 1544, was spent by Bishop-elect Casas in preparations for his new episcopal position. First came the assembling of Dominican missionaries to accompany him to the New World. On one of the Sundays between the octave of Easter and Ascension Day, he attended the Order's provincial chapter at Toledo and obtained a license to take along a contingent of friars.[3] At court he then secured royal cedulas for their passage and provisioning, and notified all the friars whom he had previously recruited, in 1540, to foregather at Valladolid and Salamanca in order to proceed together to the departure point of Seville.[4]

One interesting band of nineteen Dominicans set out from the convent of San Esteban de Salamanca on January 12, 1544. Among them was Fray Tomás de la Torre, whose eyewitness narrative, partly a diary, partly later recollections, gives us many events of the next few years. His manuscript was used by both Remesal and Ximénez in the archives of the Order in Chiapa or Guatemala, Remesal summarizing and making extracts from it, while Ximénez copied it in full.[5] Torre begins with the day of departure, when the brother of the great Master Vitoria told the friars they could well eat meat on account of the bad state of the road. But they refused his advice and insisted on their holy poverty, walking all the way in the rain, till they reached Seville about February 15.[6]

During this same 1543-1544 interval, Casas was also finishing up all the extra errands he had begun as missions procurator. He took time to urge

---

2. Cf. MacNutt, 213, and Fabié, I, 162, both misreading Remesal, I, 292. But see Fabié, app. IX, the closing group of extracts from tomo LXXV of the Muñoz Collection. The correct date is 1543, XIII and XIV of the Calends of [the following] January. A bishop was referred to as "elect" with reference to either "presentation"— the King's presentation of his name to the Pope, or the presentation to the Roman curia, though purists use only the latter.

3. Rem., I, 292.

4. See Rem., I, 288, 292, 316, the friars; and Xim., I, 259, the dispatch Casas secured for them. One cedula, dated February 13, 1544, is in Fabié, app. VIII (95-96).

5. See Rem., I, 13, 300, and Xim., I, 249. Remesal, however, gives the full texts of speeches and sermons, which Ximénez omits. In places, Torre's text seems to be in the form of a diary, but in others he speaks of having forgotten facts, which would indicate a later writing.

6. Torre's long account of this journey may be read in Ximénez, lib. II, caps. 24-26.

Prince Philip to continue sending more Franciscans to the Indies.[7] And he obtained a royal authorization for Bishop Zumárraga and Fray Domingo de Betanzos to set out from Mexico on the evangelization of China. Their curious project never came off, but it reflected the ideas of those times—the zeal for conversion and the scant knowledge about the Philippines and China. Only ten years before, Fray Martín de Valencia had made a similar arrangement with Cortés, and Procurator Casas himself had halfway agreed to come along on this new venture. Now, of course, he could not even go to Rome to secure a papal license for his friends, as he had promised, since he had more urgent matters to attend to.[8]

In the early months of 1544, Bishop-elect Casas was struggling with the problems of his own consecration and episcopal administration and his impending journey to America. We can follow his activities in a large batch of cedulas issued to him at Valladolid during February and his subsequent letters to Prince Philip, the new Regent.[9]

A sense of haste permeates these official documents. Casas' bulls had not yet been received from Rome, and a royal order of February 13 directs him to leave without awaiting them. This is repeated in cedula after cedula, giving them a tentative character that would later cause difficulties. There was also some indefiniteness about the territorial limits of his diocese. Several

---

7. See Casas' pleas from Seville, March 21 and May 4, 1544—Fabié, app. IX (108-109, 119-120).

8. On this curious episode, see Zumárraga and Betanzos to the King, February 21, 1545. (Icazbalceta, *Zumárraga,* app. 34.) Their joint letter does not fully explain the previous circumstances, but García Icazbalceta does so in his text (*ibid.,* 146-147).

The China project seems originally to have been Betanzos' idea; he finally convinced Zumárraga that it was an apostolic mission, and they discussed it with the viceroy, who promised to furnish a vessel. Zumárraga had to give up the bishopric of Mexico first and commissioned Casas to get the necessary papal permission, sending him 500 ducats through Juan Galvarro in Seville. As Casas could not go, the joint letter asked the King to make the request through his ambassador in Rome.

Afterwards, the Pope refused his consent, and Zumárraga, unable to go himself, gave Fray Domingo 1,000 pesos for expenses. The Dominicans granted Betanzos a license for the journey, but this was revoked by the provincial chapter of 1547, which notified him not to leave the province. Bishop Casas was in Mexico around that time, and he and Zumárraga presumably got together on the matter, to judge from their extremely cordial subsequent correspondence. See *DII,* XLI, 278-280. But Betanzos became one of Casas' critics; cf. *infra,* my Conclusion, note 4, last paragraph.

9. The Bishop-elect's dispatch is in Fabié, app. VIII; most of these cedulas are translated in MacNutt, app. III. Casas' letters from Seville are in Fabié, app. IX—see Catalogue, nos. 24-27.

provinces were provisionally added to his see, at least till the matter could be referred to the Pope, and the audiencia was instructed to assign him boundaries. In addition, a number of cedulas reveal money troubles. Casas' salary as bishop was fixed at 500,000 maravedis, but his diocese was so impoverished that the Mexican authorities were directed to make up this sum by whatever was needed beyond one-fourth of his tithes. Further to help defray the expenses of his bulls and trip, he was granted the tithes collected since the death of the former bishop. As he had no current funds, the House of Trade was to advance him two hundred fifty ducats, and the Honduras authorities two hundred more, to be deducted from his future subsidy.

All this was on paper, however, and when Casas finally reached Seville on March 20, the officials had no money and apparently had to borrow it. There was also a to-do about the number of his missionaries and the sea route to America.[10] Everything was finally settled and his bulls arrived—the officials paid the costs of 88,925 maravedis as yet another advance.[11]

So at last, on Passion Sunday, March 30, 1544, in his native town of Seville, Bartolomé de las Casas was consecrated as Bishop of Chiapa. The ceremony took place in the chapel of the Dominican monastery of San Pablo, with the local Bishop Loaysa (the cardinal's nephew) officiating, assisted by the bishops of Córdoba and Honduras.[12] It was a solemn turning point in Casas' life: he had received the mitre at about the age of seventy years.

How did the new Bishop view his duties?

Despite all the urgency, Bishop Casas could not sail for America immediately. He was delayed in Seville for several months by torrential rains that caused the Guadalquivir to overflow its banks, and held up the assembly of ships for the transatlantic crossing. This pause on the eve of his departure seems a good time to examine how he viewed his forthcoming duties as bishop. In fact, the Sevillian interlude itself sheds further light on the subject.

---

10. See Casas to Philip, March 21, 1544, Fabié, app. IX (107-109); and the answering royal cedula of April 1, Fabié, app. VIII (103-104).

11. See the "letters executorial" from the Sovereigns, dated March 7, 1544, and the related forwarding and payment papers, Fabié, app. VIII (102-105). But neither the advance of 250 ducats nor the passage for additional friars was arranged till after April 20, as Casas was still reporting difficulties on that date. Cf. Fabié, app. IX (111-112, 117-118).

12. Casas to Felipe, March 31, 1544, Fabié, app. IX (109-111); and the consecration documents, Fabié, app. XXVI.

To begin with, why did Casas accept an episcopal appointment in the first place? In 1519 he had told Charles V that he renounced all honors or favors for himself, even if sought by a third party, and a decade later he repeated it. His becoming a bishop made these protestations seem fictitious, and Remesal went to considerable lengths to justify him. The chronicler stressed Fray Bartolomé's humility in refusing the rich Cuzco bishopric and in agreeing to take the impoverished Chiapa one. He alleged, with some contradiction, that Casas feared to go to Cuzco because of the Peruvian troubles and the anticipated violent resistance to the new reforms, but was finally swayed by the Council's argument that he was needed in Guatemala to help enforce the New Laws.[13]

Casas' opponents, of course, claimed that he was simply motivated by ambition. Writing on May 1, 1547, Bishop Cristóbal de Pedraza of Honduras called Casas "ambitious for worldly honors," and asserted that he had been seeking a bishopric for thirty years or more—that is, from 1515, when he first went to court.[14] That was patently an exaggeration, as Pedraza used some rather hard language about him, but there may have been a grain of truth in the charge. If so, it was ambition of quite another sort.

In my opinion, Casas accepted the Chiapa see because he wanted to carry out a long-cherished reform plan. Back in 1531 he had outlined his grandiose project for Tierra Firme: under the tacit authority of bishops, bands of friars would convert the Indians and persuade them to pay tribute, and Spanish settlers would be controlled and kept from slaving.[15] During the New Laws period he had again urged similar ideas, and I am convinced that he intended to carry them out when he became a bishop himself.

Thus, his preparations as bishop-elect show his concern with missionary activities and particularly the "peaceful conversion" already begun in the Land of War experiment. Indeed, the proximity of that mission was probably what had induced him to accept the Chiapa post. Almost his first actions were devoted to assembling a large group of missionaries. Again, while obtaining official documents, he took pains to bring not only the Land of War itself but additional "wild" lands and Indians under his episcopal authority. As early as September 7, 1543, he obtained royal confirmation of the Tuzulutlán privileges, which were now extended to Lacandón. Two related cedulas of February 13, 1544, specified that the "bordering" provinces of Tuzulutlán and Lacandón be included in his see. He even

---

13. Rem., I, 289-291, *passim*, and II, 108.
14. Squier MSS, XXII, 24.
15. See the 1531 Puerto de Plata Memorial, Fabié, app. V (76-80).

secured an order that all Indians "in revolt" or "in flight," whom he could persuade to settle peacefully, should be in Crown towns and exempt from tribute for four years.[16] So there is little doubt that he wanted to establish in his diocese an enlarged mission area where the Indians would be direct vassals of the King.

As for the Spaniards, Bishop Casas' doings right after consecration show that he meant to control the slavers and slave-owners under his charge. During his stay in Seville he engaged in a vigorous battle to liberate the Indian slaves there. His long letter of April 20 to the Prince Regent is mostly devoted to this subject.[17] Large numbers of Indians, he complained, were still being held in slavery throughout Andalusia, despite the royal orders entrusted to Licentiate López the year before—that official had been sent to conduct a judicial inspection of the House of Trade. Casas reported numerous instances of bribery, official indifference, concealment, and intimidation, and urged Philip to take stricter measures for liberating slaves. He even related his own attempt to succor an unfortunate Indian slave from armed attack. Such incidents would later abound in the Bishop's battles with his own flock.

In addition, I believe it was during these rainy months in Seville that Casas composed his *Treatise about the Indians Who Have Been Made Slaves*, which he afterwards printed in 1552. Then he explained that, while treating "the liberty and general remedy for the Indians" before the Council, he had begged that all Indian slaves be freed, and the councilors had "charged the bishop to render in writing what he thought about the matter." We have his own statement that he did leave such a memorial with them shortly before sailing.[18]

So this was the promised anti-slavery brief, and in it Casas covers almost the same material as in the joint memorial of 1543. He lays down the basic principle that all Indians made slaves since the conquest had been unjustly and iniquitously enslaved, and those still alive were mostly held by the Spaniards with bad conscience, even if obtained from other natives. By way of proof, he reviews the grisly annals of Indian enslavement—the methods

---

16. Fabié, app. VIII (92-93, 99-100).

17. Casas to Philip, April 20, 1544, and more on the same topic, May 4—Fabié, app. IX (113-118, 120). Bishop Casas had a royal power to take the free [freed] Indians back to America; cf. his July 2, 1544, authorization. *DII*, VII, 395; Catalogue, no. 28.

18. Cf. *DII*, VII, 434-435; and see Catalogue, no. 23, my reasons for identifying the anti-slavery tract with this memorial.

of the slavers, whole provinces depopulated by slave raids—and then adduces a torrent of arguments and citations.[19] Therefore, he says, the Emperor is obliged by divine precept to put all the Indian slaves at liberty. But the principal interest of the tract lies in his Second Corollary, which defines what bishops in the Indies are obliged to do in order to liberate enslaved Indians from oppression and tyranny.[20] It seems plain that Casas was here laying down his own future course of action as a bishop. Already in Nicaragua he had refused to absolve Spaniards bound on what he called a slave-hunting expedition, and we shall see later that in Chiapa he would extend this to slave owners and traffickers generally.

These, then, were the new Bishop's goals—"peaceful conversion" of the natives in his care and stern correction of the Spanish slaveholders. To attain his ends he apparently counted on support from the colonial authorities. Casas is reported to have secured the appointment as president of the recently established Audiencia of los Confines of the selfsame Governor Maldonado with whom he had made the original Land of War contract.[21] Naturally he expected Maldonado to back him up with the settlers in his see, and to furnish aid to him and his friars, much in the manner of the old 1531 proposal. Afterwards, when Maldonado failed him, Casas became bitter and vengeful.

In this program of Casas' and its outcome, I see a striking analogy to the later situation involving Fray Junípero Serra and Governor Pedro Fages in California. Serra's plans for his 1769 enterprise resembled the Casas idea of missionary establishments. Serra did want soldiers to protect his friars, but he also wanted control over them; and Casas, too, insisted on control of the judicial branch of the government, the "aid of the secular arm," he called it. In the pinch, Maldonado refused, and so did Fages when Serra pressed the point. The parallel goes still farther. Serra made charges against Fages and had him removed. For his part, Casas preferred charges against

---

19. E.g., he denies the temporal power of the Pope, he defends the Indians against charges of human sacrifice, cannibalism, and sodomy; he mentions what he himself saw in Nicaragua; and he describes the branding of 4,650 men, women, and children in Jalisco on grounds of rebellion. This may be a reference to the Mixtón War or to the earlier activities of Nuño de Guzmán; the reference to the "Archbishop" of Mexico is one of many indications that the tract was revised around or after 1547.

20. The Third Corollary, on the friars' junta of 1546 in Mexico (see *infra*, my chapter XIV, middle section), is not part of the logical framework of the treatise.

21. See Rem., II, 59; Remesal points out that Maldonado was named in the New Laws.

Maldonado and apparently had him replaced, since López de Cerrato was shortly thereafter appointed to succeed him.[22] But by the time the new president arrived, the disillusioned Bishop had left Chiapa never to return.

In 1544, however, when he finally sailed for the New World, Bartolomé de las Casas was still hoping to carry out his sweeping program as Bishop of Chiapa.

OMINOUS VOYAGE

It took Bishop Casas nearly a year to travel the five thousand miles to his faraway diocesan seat of Cuidad Real in Chiapa. His route was marked by physical dangers, a boycott from colonists, shortage of funds, and conflict with Spanish authorities, all of them foretastes of worse to come.

The voyage itself was a series of mishaps—delays, poor ships, treacherous storms. Bishop Casas and his large entourage had assembled at San Lúcar after months of waiting. The party included some forty-five Dominican missionaries, all of them with Fray Tomás Casillas as vicar, except Ladrada who was directly under the Bishop. In addition, Casas was taking a number of priests as officials for his cathedral, and several lay retainers, including at least one Negro slave.[23] At San Lúcar they were further delayed, awaiting Doña María de Toledo, widow of Viceroy Diego Columbus who was to sail in that year's flotilla. Finally, the fleet of twenty-seven vessels, including a very heavily armed galleon, left San Lúcar on July 10, but the ship carrying the friars would not move and listed badly, and they did not

---

22. Maldonado, however, was soon appointed president of the Audiencia de Santa Domingo. See *infra*, chapter XIII, section on "The hostile president," and note 17.

23. The 45 Dominicans are conveniently listed by Remesal (I, 321-322); not all of them reached Chiapa, as a few were left en route at San Juan and Española, and some perished in a shipwreck. Casas had a papal brief of February 14, 1544, authorizing him to take Ladrada and five more Dominicans exempt from obedience to the prior (Fabié, app. IX, 122), but I find no record of any others. Also, though he had a cedula to take four Negro slaves duty-free, and left his Seville agents power to send them (*Fondos americanos*, II, app. 14), he apparently took only Juanillo—see *infra*, chapter XIII, note 32. The Bishop's lay staff was headed by Gregorio de Pesquera, who had been in the Indies, probably New Spain, as he knew the Mexican language; others were Rodrigo López and Carlos Franco, afterwards a priest in Chiapa, the peasant Luis Hernández, and a young man named Segovia, who had joined the friars near Cádiz. All these men proved of great assistance to Casas, unlike the only cleric to complete the journey, Luis de Fuente, who defected to the encomenderos. They appear, *passim*, in the Torre diary and the Tuzulutlán "Información" of July 2, 1545. For the latter, see *DII*, VII, 216-231.

get away till a day or two later.[24] They arrived at the Canaries on July 19 and left on the thirtieth, with the Bishop now aboard the righted craft, which narrowly missed a wreck and a collision when they reached Santo Domingo on September 9.

Here, no vessels were to be had, but in the end Casas chartered one for 1,262 castellanos to take his party to Yucatán. Out of this the King paid three hundred pesos for the passage of the friars and the Bishop signed a note for the balance. Before they could leave, however, the ship was embargoed for debts due by the pilot and owner, and Casas had to find someone to go bond. They finally departed on December 14, following repeated delays by the pilot, only to encounter a terrifying storm while crossing the Caribbean. At length, after further travails because the pilot was no pilot, they arrived off Campeche on January 5, 1545.[25]

Now the difficult task of reaching the capital of Chiapa confronted them. The Bishop needed money desperately; he obtained a little from the priest at Campeche and sent an envoy to Ciudad Real, where the citizens scraped up a loan of a few hundred pesos that were remitted to him.[26] Then he engaged a small vessel and sent her ahead with ten friars and most of his goods. On January 18 she set sail for the mouth of the Río Grijalva; on the twentieth, overloaded and badly managed, she foundered in a storm and nine friars and a number of other Spaniards aboard were drowned. All the goods—five thousand ducats' worth, says Ximénez—were lost, save some boxes of ruined books found later in the mud. Before Casas could leave on another vessel with the remaining friars, a courier arrived on the twenty-eighth with news of the tragedy. There was a sorrowful visit to the wreck, and then the party divided forces once more. While the Dominicans took the longer route through the inland waterways—Torre's diary details their itinerary—the Bishop and his staff hurried on by ship and river-canoe, reaching Ciudad Real the first week in March.[27]

---

24. According to a payment cedula of May 14, 1548, Casas set sail on June [*sic* for July] 11, 1544. *DII*, VII, 239-241.

25. Ximénez (lib. II, caps. 28-33) copies Torre's most interesting account of this voyage. Remesal gives the full text of the eloquent and moving speech Casas made to the friars off Yucatán. Rem., I, 343-349; and see Catalogue, no. 30, for the source of this sermon.

26. See Xim., I, 299, for the Campeche loan. For the Ciudad Real loan, see Catalogue, no. 31, based on *DII*, VII, 211-214.

27. The remainder of the friars' odyssey is related in full by Fray Tomás de la Torre—Xim., lib. II, caps. 35-40. Most of the Dominicans reached Ciudad Real on March 12; there they found the Bishop and his party, who had evidently arrived about

Storm-ridden as this journey had been, the stopovers en route were even more ominous. Already at Santo Domingo, Casas had found feeling running high against the New Laws and himself as their instigator. All the royal officials were against him except Audiencia President Cerrato. Matters were further inflamed when Fray Tomás de la Torre preached a sermon against the slavery of the Indians. The colonists actually decided to starve out the Dominicans, and might have succeeded save for the timely aid of a widow, said to be the richest on the island.[28]

In addition there was disquieting news from elsewhere—Casas wrote it to Prince Philip from Santo Domingo on September 15, 1544. Word had come that Tello de Sandoval, the royal envoy, had not put the New Laws into effect in Mexico, and twelve colonial agents were bound for Spain, with some friars among them, to seek revocation. Casas begged the Prince not to talk to these people but to postpone action till he himself could be heard, or at least until a "universal procurator" had been named to speak for the Indians. His tone was apprehensive, though still a bit incredulous.[29]

Then Bishop Casas landed in Central America and met the first signs of defiance from settlers and officials in his own diocese. In Campeche, the friars were hospitably received. But when Casas attempted to admonish the citizens about their Indians, by virtue of the laws and provisions he carried, they would not release a single slave and refused to receive him as bishop or pay him their tithes.[30] Something similar occurred at nearby Mérida, which was in his diocese, as Yucatán and Chiapa then formed a single province. His visit there is not mentioned by Remesal or Ximénez; the latter merely quotes Torre to the effect that Governor Montejo, advised of the Bishop's arrival, sent his son, the lieutenant governor, and a brother-in-law to offer horses if Casas wished to come to the city. Accordingly, Casas went and presented his credentials—he scarcely alludes to the trip in his *Apologética*, but we learn from an official source that the authorities would not accept him as bishop, much to his displeasure.[31]

---

a week before. The same date is referred to later in the narrative and is doubtless correct. Cf. Rem., I, 403.

This first portion of the Torre diary, from Salamanca to Ciudad Real, was published in Mexico in 1944-1945 by Dr. Franz Blom, with a map illustrating the overland journey.

28. Xim., I, 285-290.

29. *DII*, VII, 435-437, and see Catalogue, no. 29, for this letter.

30. Rem., I, 354-355; and Xim., I, 299.

31. Tello de Sandoval to the Prince, September 9, 1545—*Epis. de Nueva España*, IV, no. 246, page 223. Torre's lack of detail (Xim., I, 298-299) is customary for

These affronts were clear warnings of what lay ahead. Even so, it is doubtful if Bartolomé de las Casas fully anticipated the tense situation he would find in March of 1545 when he at last reached La Ciudad Real de los Llanos de Chiapa.

---

any part of the narrative where the friars were not present. Remesal elaborates Torre's account slightly, saying that Montejo himself was in Honduras at the audiencia, and his son in Mérida sent the brother-in-law to Campeche. Cf. Rem., I, 350-351.

In the *Apologética*, Casas merely says he went to Yucatán, since it was in his bishopric. But instead of relating his journey to Mérida, he comments on the conquest and discourses about an Indian who told the Campeche priest some Christian-sounding beliefs, reminding Casas of the legends that the Apostle Thomas had visited Brazil. Elsewhere he describes the stupendous ancient monuments of Yucatán, with their vast bases and sculptured figures and hieroglyphics, "buildings scarce less admirable than the pyramids, seeming as if thousands of people could not have built them in fifty years." *Apol.*, caps. 123 and 52.

AN AGGRESSIVE PRELATE

CIUDAD REAL AND THE TIDE OF OPPOSITION

Casas' brief tenure as a resident bishop, a little more than a year, was to prove stormy to the point of melodrama. No doubt some of this was because of his own inflexibility, but a great deal stemmed from the blind hatred he encountered in his cathedral town.

Despite its name, the Royal City of the Plains of Chiapa was a small settlement of sixty-odd Spanish householders, some 6,700 feet above sea level. The citizens of this highland outpost were literally seething with enmity toward their new prelate. For some time they had been receiving angry rumors of his impending arrival. Letters had come from all over the New World, inciting them with words like these: "We say here that the sins of your land must be very great indeed, when God punishes it with such an affliction as sending that anti-Christ for bishop!" Not that the residents of Ciudad Real needed any inciting. An on-the-scene informant took his oath that every man in town wished the bishop had been the one to drown on the way.[1] Such passions can be understood only against the mounting tide of antagonism to the reforms blamed on Bartolomé de las Casas.

By now, opposition to the New Laws was raging all over the Indies. Some of the statutes could be easily enforced and provoked no general objection, but the paragraphs abolishing slavery and disinheriting the families of encomenderos brought on rebellion in Peru and very nearly did so in New Spain.

Even before the proclamation of the reform ordinances, the govern-

---

1. Rem., II, 108; and *DII*, VII, 157. For the anonymous informant, see note 12 of this chapter.

ment had been warned of such consequences. Typical was the letter of Bishop Zumárraga from Mexico on October 4, 1543, commenting with alarm on the advance transcript.[2] Casas himself had pointed out the danger of uprisings, and the Crown took extraordinary measures for enforcement.

Four super-envoys were sent to America to execute the New Laws: Inspector General Tello de Sandoval for Mexico, Núñez Vela as the first viceroy for Peru, Governor Díaz de Armendariz for Tierra Firme, and Audiencia President López de Cerrato for the islands.

In Mexico there might well have been a revolt save for the moderating counsel of Viceroy Mendoza and the audiencia. Inspector General Sandoval reached port on February 12, 1544, and entered the capital city on March 8; he was to have been met by the inhabitants in mourning, and only the viceroy prevented it. On the twenty-fourth, Sandoval had the New Laws proclaimed, but he promptly suspended the controversial Law of Inheritance and set about taking an interrogatory to justify this step.[3] Even so, according to a functionary who accompanied him, resentment and panic were widespread among the colonists. The officials were much aggrieved at having their Indians taken away, and in two months some six hundred disgruntled settlers had sailed back to the Peninsula.[4] It was even feared that not enough Spaniards would remain to rule the natives and "New Spain would be lost," as the conquistador Terrazas, former majordomo of Cortés, wrote to the Emperor.[5]

In Peru, the result was far more threatening. A civil war had been going on, and with the coming of Viceroy Núñez Vela to enforce the New Laws, the land nearly was lost to Spain. Earlier, after Francisco Pizarro's

---

2. Icazbalceta, *Zumárraga*, app. 31. Zumárraga says the colonists have learned the encomiendas are to be taken away, leaving them without succor for their wives and children; he advocates perpetuity.

3. León, *Tratado*, fols. 15 verso-16; Diego Fernández, *Historia del Perú* [1571], Madrid, 1913, lib. I, caps. 2-3 and 5.

4. Gonzalo de Aranda, reporting on May 10, 1544. *Epis. de Nueva España*, IV, no. 225. He fears that not enough old conquistadors will remain to hold the country in the face of so many Indians; and though many natives seem good Christians, they are basically evil and born to be subjected.

5. Francisco de Terrazas, reporting on June 1, 1544, *Epis. de Nueva España*, IV, no. 228. In perhaps the most interesting letter from New Spain at this time, he gives a classic statement of the encomenderos' opposition argument. Terrazas claims that (a) the land will be lost to Spain; (b) the King will lose his vast revenues, since the natives will scatter; and (c) those who have shed their blood to conquer the land without cost to His Majesty will lose their due reward.

death, Vaca de Castro had been sent out as governor and had defeated
Alvarado at Charcas on September 15, 1542. When the newly appointed
viceroy arrived and at once began to put the laws into effect, Gonzalo
Pizarro refused to recognize him and war began afresh; Pizarro proclaimed
himself procurator general of Peru and appealed from the reform ordinances.
After several months of fighting, the viceroy was captured and sent on a
ship to Spain, but he was put ashore and went to Túmbez, where he penned
his famous letter to the Emperor about the recent disturbances. The future
ones would be even more terrible, including the final defeat and beheading
of the viceroy himself.[6]

Meantime, the reaction took various forms elsewhere—town meetings,
tolling bells, riots, outright revolts. Colonial agents began flocking to court
to protest the New Laws. From Mexico City alone, as Casas had heard, the
town council sent two agents, Gonzalo López and Alonso de Villanueva,
with the three reluctant provincials of the mendicant Orders.[7] From Peru,
from Tierra Firme, from every quarter, came other procurators, along with
a flood of written complaints. Every town dispatched its official paper, and
countless "old settlers" wrote personal letters to the King. The major griev-
ance, naturally, was that encomenderos were being disinherited in violation of previous royal assurances to the contrary. For there had been repeated
cedulas recognizing the rights of the conquistadors to their encomiendas
and even promising that no one would lose his Indians without court action
—not to mention the famous Law of Two Lives, giving a man the specific
right to leave his encomienda to his wife or children.[8] Equally objectionable
to the colonists were the anti-slavery laws, in view of past royal approval of
the traffic.

So from every quarter, a whirlwind was rising against the New Laws,
and it was laden with vituperation for the man who had procured them.

---

6. See León, *Tratado,* fols. 12 verso-13 verso summarizing all the major chronicles
on these well-known events, to which Fernández devotes caps. 6-54 of part I of his
Historia del Perú. Núñez Vela was forced to suspend the execution of the ordinances
for two years—too late, says León—but he put a note on the document that he signed
under duress. See Gómara, *Historia,* 253.

7. These provincials were Fray Francisco de Soto, Franciscan; Fray Domingo de
la Cruz, Dominican; and Fray Juan de San Román, Augustinian. The party left on
June 7, 1544.

8. *DII,* XLI, 198-204; and cf. Gómara, *Historia,* 250-253. On December 3, 1539,
another cedula decreed that all encomenderos must marry within a year and a half
or forfeit their grants; the implication of inheritance is clear. See Paz, *Catálogo Bib.
Nac.,* no. 32 (12).

Remesal tells us that Casas was "one of the most hated men who had ever been in the Indies, great or small, ecclesiastic or layman, and there was none who would even name him without a thousand execrations."[9]

In Ciudad Real, this hatred was concentrated against the new Bishop in person. The resentment against his coming was already smoldering in a specific direction, conditioned by the geographical and human situation of the town itself.

Founded after the second conquest of the area in 1528, and more recently designated a "city," Ciudad Real was the principal town in the province of Chiapa proper, the heart of Casas' diocese, where dwelt the main body of his Spanish flock.[10] This province, the state of Chiapas in modern Mexico, belonged physically to Guatemala on the east, as it did politically for a long time. To the west, Chiapa was separated from Oaxaca by the great trough of the Isthmus of Tehuantepec. On the south side was a dry coastal section, partly the old territory of Soconusco, and on the north were the swamps of Tabasco with Yucatán beyond. In a word, the province lay well within and was one of the Central American slave lands: Guatemala, Yucatán, and Chiapa itself. The traffic was carried on openly in Chiapa, and all or most of the Ciudad Real encomenderos also held Indian slaves whom they considered their lawful property. So the reform statutes about slavery were particularly odious to the Spaniards here.

Into this slaveholding stronghold now came, around early spring of

---

9. Rem., II, 108.

10. Originally subjected at the fall of the Aztec Empire, Chiapa was afterwards conquered twice. In 1524, Captain Luis Marín led an expedition into the province; Bernal Díaz del Castillo came along from his provisional encomienda nearby on the upper Grijalva River. Diaz' account (*Historia verdadera*, II, 211 *et seq.*) intimates that Chiapa had already been assigned into encomiendas and the natives had revolted. There were two big fights, which ended with Spanish victories and chiefs coming to make peace. Marín made grants, but could not decide about founding a settlement and finally left with his men. A more detailed report of this first conquest, by another participant named Diego de Godoy, was printed with Cortés' *Cuarta relación* (Toledo, 1525).

Remesal relates the second and permanent conquest by Diego de Mazariegos, who founded Villa Real de los Llanos in March of 1528. Named its governor, he proceeded to divide Chiapa among the conquistadors, only to be exiled by a judge of inquiry sent down by the first Mexican audiencia. Subsequently, his town was moved to a higher site and its name changed to Villaviciosa and then to San Cristóbal de los Llanos. By a cedula of July 7, 1536, it was finally created a "ciudad" and renamed Ciudad Real de los Llanos de Chiapa—the full title of Casas' bishopric. See Rem., lib. V, caps. 13-18, based on full documentation from the municipal archives.

1545, the selfsame Bartolomé de las Casas who had obtained the hated laws and was, we know, resolved to interpret the anti-slavery ones drastically. Outwardly, the citizens of Ciudad Real received their new prelate well— his critics afterwards made quite a point of this.[11] But the cordiality could hardly have been sincere, and anyhow it was only the lull before the storm.

EASTER "NOT AS AMONG CHRISTIANS"

The inevitable clash between the Bishop and his flock occurred at Easter, and there are two versions of what happened. Our main source for the events is the diary of Fray Tomás de la Torre, who is full of sympathy for the "santo viejo." On the other side, we have an unsigned and virulent report "on the arrival of Bishop Casas and his conduct in the matter of the Indian slaves."[12] But it is not necessary to reconcile the opposing accounts: they complement each other perfectly. Casas was now seventy and more stubborn than ever; he had spent half a lifetime fighting for Indian rights and had strong views about his duties as a bishop to secure them. As I understand the story, the "holy old man" was intransigent in the extreme.

The hurricane broke over Bishop Casas' attempt to liberate the Indian slaves by means of the annual "Easter duty." Eastertide was approaching, when the faithful were obliged to go to confession and receive absolution in order to take communion. It was a perfect occasion for episcopal correction. According to the hostile informant, the Bishop insisted that every slave had been illegally acquired and must be freed at once; that, to be sure, was exactly the position that Casas had maintained in all his writings. Just how Bishop Casas tried to effect this, and the wild consequences that followed, we learn chiefly from Ximénez' copy and Remesal's summary of the Torre diary.[13]

---

11. Xim., I, 339. But see *DII*, VII, 157, where the anonymous informant gives the show away, stating that most members of the town council were absent, and were afterwards much put out with the councilor and magistrate who received Casas as bishop. Motolinía later stressed Casas' good reception and the fact that the inhabitants loaned him money. Icazbalceta, *Docs.*, I, 259.

12. *DII*, VII, 156-160, and Fabié, app. XI. Undated and unsigned, this document was written from Ciudad Real during the events of 1545, since the hostile writer refers to a preceding report and says he will write further, apparently to Viceroy Mendoza.

13. In Ximénez (I, 342-345) the verbatim copy of the diary is broken on page 344, indicating a mutilation of the manuscript. The paraphrase in Remesal (I, 407-413) contains a number of additional details, either from the missing piece or from supplementary papers.

Prior to the Easter season, Casas exhorted and preached against Indian slavery to no avail. Now he carefully withdrew the right to hear confessions from all but two of the priests in town—the two officials he had found already installed in the cathedral, Dean Gil de Quintana and Canon Juan de Perera. As for the Dominican friars and the cathedral chancellor named by himself, he deemed them too new to the country; among resident ecclesiastics, the Mercedarian friars were not of his "opinion," and the three clerics in the diocese were unfit. To these two appointed confessors, the dean and the canon, Bishop Casas gave careful instructions reserving certain cases to be referred to himself: those of conspicuous slaveholding and trafficking in slaves. Canon Perera faithfully followed his instructions, but the dean gave his referrals a slip reading: "The bearer has some of the reserved cases of Your Reverence, though I do not find them reserved by [canon] law or in any authors."

Soon the townspeople were in an uproar over the denial of absolution —the angry citizen fills in some details. Everyone complained that slave owners had formerly been absolved, that no Indian would obey a Spaniard if the slave trade ceased, that the losses from releasing slaves would be tremendous. Spokesmen called on the Bishop—the dean, the Mercedarians, prominent citizens—and presented the papal Bull of Donation to justify war and slavery. Some slaveholders tried to win the Bishop over with schemes for partial or token compliance. Others "required" him, before a notary and witnesses, to authorize confessors, threatening to complain to the Archbishop of Mexico, the Pope, the King, the Council, that he was a disturber of the peace and a foe of Christians and a protector of Indian dogs.

Casas, Torre tells us, held firm and read them the New Laws on slavery. They countered that they had appealed from the ordinances, and began a campaign of slander against the Bishop. He was called a glutton and an ignorant fool; the orthodoxy of his lineage was questioned and so was that of his religion. Street urchins were trained to sing scurrilous songs as they passed his residence, and one night a harquebus without a bullet was fired outside his window. When a Dominican preached a sermon supporting him, the citizens withdrew all alms from the friars, just as the islanders had done before.

The showdown came during Easter week, with Dean Quintana openly defying the authority of the Bishop. On Palm Sunday, Holy Thursday, and Easter Sunday and Monday, the dean was seen giving communion to notorious slaveholders. Casas repeatedly summoned him to explain, but the dean refused to come; after the fifth summons, Casas sent his bailiff to arrest him. By this time most of the town had gathered outside, and as the dean emerged under arrest, he began to resist and cry out: "Help me, sirs, for I will confess all of you; get me loose and I'll absolve you." Whereupon a full-scale riot erupted. The crowd set the dean free, blockaded the Dominican monastery lest the friars try to help the Bishop, and then stormed the Bishop's house. The ringleaders got in and exchanged words with Casas himself. Luckily he was protected by some visitors who drew their swords, but the man who had fired the harquebus vowed to kill him. Then the citizens dispersed, perhaps fearing they had gone too far. As for the dean, he promptly fled the diocese, leaving a defiant statement that as commissary of crusade indulgences he had no superior save the Archbishop of Seville. The Bishop promptly excommunicated him.

In contrast to this circumstantial account, the anonymous citizen gives a sketchy description of the riot, obviously touched up to put his fellow settlers in the best possible light. But his summary could hardly be improved on: "We spent Holy Week not as among Christians."

Flamboyant versions of the tumultuous Easter soon spread afar. Someone even wrote to Inspector General Sandoval, who in turn wrote to the Prince Regent, that Bishop Casas had issued orders which created a great disturbance in Ciudad Real, as many remained unconfessed. "And now they tell me that a certain Mazariegos tried to kill him but he escaped over the walls and went to Gracias á Dios."[14]

Like most half-truths, this report was exaggerated to the point of falsehood. There were only threats on the Bishop's life, and he never fled. Bartolomé de las Casas finally did go to the audiencia at Gracias á Dios, but he went without haste and in connection with a ceremonial visitation of his diocese.

VISIT TO VERAPAZ

Bishop Casas, as Remesal tells us, only left Ciudad Real twice during his stay there. Both times he triumphantly toured native areas of his farflung see, and came up against Spanish enmity toward the missions.

On his first tour, soon after Easter, Casas visited the Indian lands of Chiapa province: the main east-west valley stretching some fifty miles along the Chiapa River, really the Grijalva River, between two high mountain ranges, with five or six different tribes living by the riverbanks or on the slopes.[15] He had been invited out to the village of Chiapa where the Do-

---

14. *Epis. de Nueva España,* IV, no. 246, page 223.
15. These were the Zoques, Chiapanecas, Mexicans, Quelenes, Tzendals, and

minicans had established their first mission, and it was a happy occasion. The elderly Bishop had a festive reception from the Zoque Indians, complete with nine floral arches in his honor, and took part in a conference about organizing the missions. Casas wanted the friars distributed among his provinces near and far. But the vicar prudently decided to concentrate most of his workers among the native towns right in this valley, with headquarters at Chiapa village where the encomendero was so helpful.[16]

Parenthetically, it was the Dominicans, not the stubborn "santo viejo," who finally got forced out of town by the citizens' boycott. The subsequent course of their Chiapa valley missions is worth mentioning here, for the light it sheds on Bishop Casas' problems. All the valley encomenderos proved hostile, probably fearing reduction of their tributes. The bitterest was Baltasar Guerra of Chiapa village, who had first feigned friendliness and then launched on a determined persecution to get rid of the missionaries. This Guerra finally wound up in the Spanish courts—Remesal found the papers of his case in the Guatemala archives and devoted a dozen chapters to the story. It appears that Casas himself must have intervened in the matter, for the Guerra encomienda was finally revoked and the village was made a Crown town.[17] But all that happened later on.

For the present, the Bishop returned to his seat, where the disturbances were resumed. So around May, a thoroughly exasperated Casas again left

---

Tzazils. In his *In Indian Mexico* (Chicago, 1908), Frederick Starr asserts that all these tribes still inhabit the country except the Quelenes, now extinct. According to Ximénez, the so-called Quelenes were actually Tloztlis Vinic and lived chiefly at Cinacatlán. Remesal says the Chiapanecas were at war with the Cinacatlán Indians, whom in one place he calls Mexicans. Apparently the Mexican Indians had originally come with Mazariegos, and many died in the conquest; in 1529 the town council made an official request for the sending of 200 Mexicans and Tlaxcaltecas with their families. They must have arrived, because in 1546 Judge Rogel had the township assign them lands for planting.

16. Rem., I, 421-423; Xim., I, 352-353. Down at around 2,000 feet, Chiapa was the main town in the west end of the valley. It was, and still is, in Zoque territory, some ten miles from the present capital of Tuxtla Gutiérrez. Ciudad Real, renamed San Cristóbal de las Casas, remained the capital till 1891, when the seat was shifted down to Tuxtla, where the westward-flowing river turns north.

17. Rem., lib. VI, caps. 13-23. Guerra's case was peculiar, as the Crown attorney's suit (1549-1552) developed that his title was fraudulent. Prior to the friars' arrival, he had given up his encomienda before the secretary of the audiencia of Mexico, and then arranged with the lieutenant governor of Chiapa to give it as vacant to his bastard mestizo son, Juan.

But the hostility was general. Guerra and his fellow Spaniards especially ob-

Ciudad Real, really bound for the audiencia in Honduras this time. But en route he was going to make an extensive tour of the most cherished of all his provinces, the Land of War, which was now in a thriving state. The "peaceful conversion" was progressing so well that the missionaries had re-named the area "Verapaz"—the Land of True Peace—and naturally they had begged their bishop and founder of the mission to come and see it. Apparently the hostile Santiago town council got word of his coming, for on May 20 they wrote to the township of Ciudad Real, bitterly attacking him and asking the Chiapa body to prevent his visit.[18]

Bishop Casas, however, was undeterred and set out for Verapaz with quite a retinue. He took along three Dominicans, one of his own cathedral officials from Spain, also Gregorio de Pesquera, Rodrigo López, and other laymen. In addition, the Indian chief of Cobán, Don Juan, had come to Ciudad Real with some of his men to escort the party.[19] Evidently they traveled through Guatemalan territory, probably via Quetzaltenango. On the way Casas met other caciques and Fray Juan de San Lucas at Zacapulas, and still others at San Juan Chamelco; also Fray Pedro de Ángulo, vicar of the Guatemala Dominicans, came to join him at Jatic.

On June 12, Casas and his cortege reached Tuzulutlán village in triumph. The friars welcomed him and the Indians brought him presents and thanked him because they had been made Christians without bloodshed. From there he proceeded to Cobán, where he enjoyed a great reception and many gifts, admired the sumptuous wooden church, and even arranged a solemn procession on Corpus Christi. Then he returned to Tuzulutlán on the second of July, meeting Bishop Marroquín of Guatemala, who had arrived on June 28. "And the Indians of the said province of Tuzulutlán greeted the said bishops with a tremendous festival."

We learn all these particulars and more in an interesting juridical "Información" that Bishop Casas had drawn up that very day with witnesses

---

jected to the missionaries telling the natives about the King of Spain. Another antagonist was Pedro de Estrada, Mazariego's half-brother and encomendero of Cinacatlán, where the Dominicans found the Indians oppressed by intolerable tribute.

Bishop Casas took a hand in both the general and the specific matters. He did succeed in having the tributes reassessed by the audiencia, and evidently he wrote to the Council at length about Guerra's interference with the missions. For the man, unable to dislodge the friars, left for Spain at the end of October 1545, and no sooner had he landed than he was summoned before that body.

18. Xim., I, 355-356.
19. Rem., II, 54.

before a notary.[20] The stated object was to preserve a record of his triumphal tour through the erstwhile Land of War, and to show its peaceful state and what could be accomplished by religious alone. But beyond that, the formal proceedings were designed to counteract a menacing situation.

From the beginning, the Land of War experiment had been opposed by the Spaniards, as it kept the Indians in Crown towns and free from encomiendas or slavery. So all during Casas' absence at court, the citizens had been waging a bitter campaign against it. Starting in 1539, the original missionary venture was threatened by violations of the contract with the friars. That year Adelantado Alvarado returned to Guatemala and gave Cobán itself in encomienda, temporarily halting the conversion.[21] No further effort was made till Fray Luís Cáncer reached Santiago in the latter part of 1541 or early in 1542, bringing the royal order that Casas had obtained in Spain, and also some Mexican Indians who knew how to play and sing music.[22] But once more the missionaries were to be impeded. By this time the original Casas-Maldonado agreement and its extension had both expired, the ones providing for non-aggression by the Spaniards for only five years; and it seems obvious that Spanish soldiers had begun invading the territory from Guatemala and making slaves as usual. For in a later letter, Fray Luis tells that the Spaniards had taken away some seven hundred slaves, and that a town of these slaves had been formed near Santiago, twice as large as the village of Tuzulutlán.[23]

Nevertheless, the missionary labors proceeded. Remesal quotes a 1543 document which indicates that Fray Pedro de Ángulo and other Dominicans had already penetrated beyond Tuzulutlán into the country of the Lacandones. And Ximénez says the interrupted conversion was fully resumed in 1544.[24] That was also the date of the next major Spanish attack on the friars and their Indian allies. On June 9 of that year, Fray Pedro presented before the Santiago town council the latest royal dispatch in support of the mission—decrees granting coats-of-arms and the title of "don" to the caciques who had assisted the friars in the conversion, and guaranteeing that their towns and those of the Land of War should be always under the

---

20. *DII*, VII, 216-231; Catalogue, no. 32. Casas' route is also disclosed by this interesting document. The witnesses included two clerics, one having come with Casas and one with Marroquín, and several other members of Bishop Casas' retinue.

21. Xim., I, 208; cf. Rem., I, 230.

22. Rem., I, 234 and 274-275; Xim., I, 236-237.

23. *DII*, VII, 233-234.

24. Rem., I, 288; Xim., I, 208-209.

Crown. In a rage, the officials snatched the documents from Fray Pedro and proceeded to compile an "Información" belittling the missionary experiment, in order to appeal to the new audiencia and the King.[25] Even so, the mission went on apace.

Now, on July 2, 1545, Bishop Casas could make his own glowing investigation "at the request of the friars" to use in a successful appeal to the Crown. The resulting batch of Tuzulutlán cedulas would extend the exclusion of Spaniards for five more years, furnish sacramental wine to the friars, and officially rename the province "Verapaz."[26] But these would not arrive till 1547, and on the day Casas had the sworn evidence drawn up, his triumph was still threatened. The Land of War was being oppressed, perhaps deliberately, with excessive Crown tribute—"that black tribute," Fray Luis called it.[27] Furthermore, the coincidental and needless presence of Bishop Marroquín, from whose diocese Tuzulutlán had been removed, gave an inkling of fresh troubles to come.

In Honduras, Bartolomé de las Casas was to face enmity from the former sponsors of his mission: the Bishop of Guatemala, now his rival, and Governor Maldonado, now president of the new audiencia.

---

25. Rem., II, 49-50; and Xim., I, 246-248. For the coats-of-arms, see *supra,* chapter VIII, note 19, and Don Miguel's patent in Xim., I, 245-246. Remesal (II, 54-55) also gives royal letters of February 23, 1544, to Don Miguel and Don Pedro, which he claims were transmitted by Casas in person.

26. See Xim., I, 189 and Fabié, app. XIII, for all these orders, dated January 15, 1547. This was in answer to Casas' September 30, 1545, report from Honduras (see Catalogue, no. 35), which apparently transmitted the Tuzulutlán "Información."

27. *DII*, VII, 233-235. There would be worse troubles for the mission in the years ahead. Already a party of Spaniards from Yucatán had ascended the Río Dulce, established a town, and begun making incursions into Verapaz. Casas was to protest in vain to the authorities—see Catalogue, no. 34. The raiders were finally removed some years later by royal provisions and an enraged audiencia. But about that time the Lacandones, on the border between Guatemala and Chiapa, invaded the territory; this led to a war, and of course halted the expansion of the mission. Nonetheless, for about 50 years, till the beginning of the 17th century, Verapaz was a missionary bishopric, gradually languishing. In these subsequent events, Bishop Casas would play no direct part save in the role of a procurator back in Spain. Cf. *infra,* the opening of chapter XV.

NO HELP FROM THE AUDIENCIA

CASAS PRESENTS HIS DEMANDS

Bishop Casas spent the next three months seeking help from the Audiencia de los Confines for his dual problem. He wanted reassessment of tributes and prevention of slaving, to protect his oppressed Indians, and he needed police power to control his truculent Spaniards. What he got in the main was further frustration and final disillusionment.

During the latter part of July or the early part of August, Casas reached Gracias á Dios in Honduras where the audiencia was sitting. The four Central American bishops had arranged to meet here for the consecration of Antonio de Valdivieso, the new Bishop of Nicaragua. Apparently Casas expected they would also join him in pleas for the natives and for the New Laws, since bishops were official "protectors" of the Indians in their dioceses. He was to be cruelly disappointed.

All the prelates did finally assemble in the little Honduran outpost. This miserable hole with just a few Spanish residents, affording not even ordinary comforts to visitors, had been chosen as audiencia seat only because it was centrally located to all the provinces of the jurisdiction: Chiapa, Tabasco, Yucatán, Guatemala, Honduras, and Nicaragua.[1] Of course, that made it central to the bishoprics, too. Bishop Valdivieso arrived first, on May 13; on July 15 he wrote that Bishop Casas was expected soon; and by

---

1. Chiapa had been under the older Audiencia of New Spain from the time of its permanent conquest in 1528 until the Audiencia of los Confines was established in the New Laws. The sessions of the new audiencia opened on May 16, 1544, with the notification of its jurisdiction as the first order of business. Cf. Rem., I, 296. (Afterwards, Chiapa was under the Captaincy General of Guatemala until the Independence period, when it passed into the control of Mexico.)

August 17 Bishop Marroquín of Guatemala made his appearance.[2] But
Bishop Pedraza of Honduras, though he had reached his diocese on August
9 and taken possession on August 11, did not join the others for nearly
three months.[3] It was November 8 when the four bishops—of Nicaragua,
Chiapa, Guatemala, and Honduras—were at last together in Gracias á Dios.
In the interval, Marroquín became openly antagonistic to Casas, and Pedraza, when he came to town, followed suit. Meantime Valdivieso, a Dominican and staunch ally, was afraid to speak out lest the other two refuse to
consecrate him.

So month after month Casas found himself presenting demands on
his own, with a whole series of petitions and unpleasant scenes before the
royal judges. To my knowledge, these petitions have never been assembled
and I therefore summarize them here.

First came his opening petition—we have it from Remesal. Each of the
bishops had prepared a memorial of complaints and requests, and all the
papers must have been delivered in late August or early September. Those
of the others dealt mainly with individual cases, but Bishop Casas demanded
enforcement of the reform ordinances for the Indians on six counts:

1. Tributes in his entire bishopric should be assessed anew and reduced
to moderate levies payable from the products of each village.

2. Roads should be built, to avoid loading the Indians with consequent
abuses.

3. Spanish encomenderos and their families should be ordered at once to
leave the Indian towns and take up residence in the depopulated capital city.

4. No encomendero should be allowed to put Indians to work in his mills,
nor to hire out Indians to work in such mills by day or still less by night.

5. No encomendero or other Spaniard should be allowed to establish
plantations in or near the Indian towns, and those having such properties should
leave them.

6. No overseer or any Spanish person, even the encomendero, should be
allowed to remain in the Indian villages more than eight days in the year.

Next followed specific recommendations for his bishopric: one Sotomayor to be named a judge, one Orduña to be punished for branding an In-

---

2. See Valdivieso's letter, Squier MSS, XXII, 107-111. Marroquín wrote to the
Emperor from Gracias á Dios on August 17— Fabié, app. XV, and Quintana, app. XI.

3. See Pedraza's letter of August 21, Squier MSS, XXII, 117-118. This bishop
had helped consecrate Casas in Seville.

dian woman. Finally, he asked the aid of "the royal arm" against erring civil functionaries in his see.[4]

This last demand was repeated by Casas in a September 30 petition to the Council or the Emperor. We know its contents only from the answer of Prince Philip on January 15, 1547. The Regent referred to various requests from Bishop Casas, who asked that the Audiencias of New Spain and los Confines be required to favor him and his ecclesiastical affairs.[5]

But far more important than these two petitions was a formal representation that Casas read solemnly to the audiencia on October 22, a document that would have severe repercussions. Fortunately, the original has been preserved, along with the answer of the president and royal judges.[6]

Prefacing his demands with a severe canonical lecture on "administrators," Bishop Casas began by asking support in his turbulent see via two measures:

> 1. Official steps to insure his full and free exercise of ecclesiastical jurisdiction.
> 2. The aid of the secular arm to punish churchmen as well as laymen who had dishonored his episcopal dignity.

Next he insisted on the native rights promised by the New Laws:

> 3. His special flock, the Indians, must be freed from excessive tribute, from being loaded like beasts, from personal services, from the slavery which many suffer unjustly, and from other tyrannies of the encomenderos that prevent the friars from teaching the faith.

Finally, to implement these rights, he demanded the following:

---

4. Rem., II, 56-58; Catalogue, no. 33. This petition speaks mainly of encomienda Indians and not of the order freeing slaves, but perhaps Casas presented another paper on that topic, as the audiencia appealed from the anti-slavery ordinance on December 30, 1545. (Fabié, app. XIV.) Casas did present a separate petition on Yucatán, now lost—Catalogue, no. 34.

5. See Catalogue, no. 35, for a summary of much of this petition, based on Philip's answer, Fabié, app. XIII. The Prince said he had referred "the rest" of Casas' letter to the Emperor—much to our regret.

6. Printed by Henry Stevens in 1854; *DII*, VII, 172-178; and Fabié, app. XII. (See Catalogue, no. 36, for a description of the MSS and printings.) Concerning the Tuzulutlán Indians (point 5), Casas speaks of giving the audiencia sworn evidence on their peaceful conversion presented before himself and the Bishop of Guatemala—probably the July 2 "Información."

4. A declaration that protection of the Indians, as well as cognizance in cases of injury to them, belongs to the ecclesiastics, and provisions thereon to the magistrates who might otherwise suppose he was usurping royal jurisdiction.

5. Prevention of wars or slave raids against the Indians of Yucatán, as such entries would destroy the natives and further make those of Tuzulutlán revolt.

6. An order that Indians in Crown towns be well treated, because now the officials oppress them to make them ask to be allotted to individuals instead.

7. Immediate placing under the Crown of Indians in encomiendas held by officials, to provide for many Spaniards and silence the false rumor that the King was dispossessing individual encomenderos.

Then he ended with a bombshell. For compliance with these seven demands, plus his former ones made alone or with the other bishops, Casas assigned a time limit of three months, under pain of major excommunication for the president and royal judges!

Four days later, the royal judges gave their indignant answer.[7] There was mostly more evasion, with only one item of compliance. Action was taken on point three: Licentiate Rogel, one of the judges, was named to reassess Indian tributes. About the Bishop's shaky authority, however, they merely admitted he had ecclesiastical jurisdiction and vaguely promised the necessary provisions and the aid of the secular justice. As for Indian rights, they saw little to do. A declaration of church jurisdiction was already provided, and a proclamation would be made against slave raids (with citation of the relevant New Laws), and they would look into alleged mistreatment of Crown Indians, though they had heard of none. But Casas' threat of excommunication brought forth a violent denial and counterblast. He had no such power and they appealed to the Pope. Besides, they had always responded to his requests and those of the other bishops and had provided for native welfare and had not usurped church jurisdiction, but Casas had tried to usurp that of His Majesty, in his demands and actions here, and they would give notice of it and of his disrespect so that the King might order him punished.

Late in December the audiencia actually did send the Emperor an official letter of complaint against Casas; only one judge, Licentiate Herrera, refused to sign it. On the twenty-fourth this dissenter wrote that Casas had good, if excessive, zeal and that the Indians were treated worse than slaves.[8]

---

7. *DII*, VII, 178-180; Fabié, app. XII.

8. See Fabié, app. XIV, first item, and Squier MSS, XXII, 126-127—a Muñoz extract, not the audiencia letter but Judge Herrera's December 24 statement about it.

But President Maldonado had the last word, assuring His Majesty on the thirty-first: "Casas has been so arrogant since he came here as a bishop, that nobody can do anything with him. He would be better in Castile in a monastery than in the Indies as a bishop."[9]

That same month Bishop Marroquín also wrote the Emperor an unfavorable report about Casas' admonishing the judges:

> We [bishops] presented certain clauses, but the Bishop of Chiapa was not content with them and said we ought to demand and protest to the audiencia and present some canonical admonitions, so that if they did not comply with any of our demands the president and judges would be excommunicated. This seemed to me to be very disrespectful and irregular; but he had more daring and fervor, relying on his propositions and principles drawn from a breast of hypocrisy, arrogance, envy, and avarice. So he presented it and made the demands and admonitions, just as this audiencia has sent you.[10]

I can find no sign of hypocrisy in Casas, but of "arrogance" there was plenty in his dealings with the audiencia, though perhaps that is not exactly the right term. Marroquín uses the word *soberbia,* which connotes both pride and presumption.

But of course this was a very biased version of the incident. Casas had been provoked by the endless delays, and it seems to me that avarice and envy were rather the traits of his new enemies, Bishop Marroquín and President Maldonado.

THE HOSTILE PRESIDENT

In these months at Gracias á Dios, Casas had ample proof of hostility from the president of the audiencia, Alonso de Maldonado, once his supporter. Licentiate Maldonado had definitely changed sides since the days when he signed the Tuzulutlán contract and wrote glowing reports about Fray Bartolomé. The underlying cause was not so much Casas' temperament as it was the change in Maldonado's personal fortunes.

I have no doubt that the old Bishop's inflexibility did irritate President Maldonado, who seems to have quite lost his self-control, for he indulged repeatedly in violent and abusive language. Once he called Casas a scoun-

---

9. Fabié, app. XIV; Squier MSS, XXII, 134. Maldonado added: "It would not be a bad idea to have him personally give the Council of the Indies an account of how the Indians are [i.e., come to be] under ecclesiastical jurisdiction. Because we did not provide this as he asked, he excommunicated the audiencia."

10. Marroquín's December 1 report, Squier MSS, XXII, 139-140.

drel, a bad man, a bad friar, a bad bishop, shameless, and worthy of punishment. His standard greeting when Casas appeared before the audiencia was
the loud cry: "Throw that lunatic out of here!" Casas' response was both
calm and cutting, a reminder that Maldonado owed him the appointment
as president. These insults finally reached such a pitch that Maldonado himself, being well versed in law, realized he was automatically excommunicated
and made a token apology.[11]

But the evidence seems clear that the real basis of Licentiate Maldonado's hostility was not temperamental. The audiencia's October 26 reply
gives an inkling of this by rejecting Casas' final demand—the immediate
suppression of encomiendas held by officials.[12] Therein, I believe, lay the
crux of the matter. While Fray Bartolomé was in Spain, Maldonado had
married the daughter of Governor Francisco de Montejo of Yucatán, thus
joining a family with one of the largest holdings of Indians in all Central
America.

Bishops Casas and Valdivieso reported the shocking details to Prince
Philip, writing collectively and separately on October 25 and November 9.[13]
They estimated that Licentiate Maldonado, for his own interests and those
of his father-in-law, son-in-law, brothers, relatives, etc., already had more
than sixty thousand Indians. At that very moment, Montejo was conducting
a second conquest of Yucatán in a most barbarous and bloodthirsty manner,
and the Montejo-Maldonado combination was amassing slaves there without number.

Furthermore, I detect indications that the Montejos and Maldonados
were antagonistic to Casas having any episcopal power. It will be recalled
that the Mérida authorities, under Montejo, had refused to accept Casas as
bishop upon his arrival. The president's December 31 letter attacking Casas

---

11. Rem., II, 59. Remesal claims that not only President Maldonado but the
three royal judges all owed their appointments to Casas. Maldonado had been a judge
of the Mexico audiencia before serving as acting governor of Guatemala.

12. The rejection is stated defensively: "Of all that is said in this item, advice
has been given to His Majesty; and in what has been done in the matter in this
audiencia, His Majesty has been well served, while in the contrary case he could
have been much disserved." *DII*, VII, 179.

13. Casas and Valdivieso to the Prince, October 25, and Casas to the Prince,
November 9, 1545—*Cartas de Indias*, no. IV, 14-27 and no. V, 28-37; Catalogue, nos.
37 and 38. In his letter Casas praises the audiencia in Mexico, especially Licenciate
Ceynos, Viceroy Nuñez Vela in Peru, and President Cerrato in Santo Domingo, as
the only good governors in the Indies.

wound up most revealingly. Maldonado recommended that Yucatán—Montejo's territory—be removed from the Chiapa diocese and made a separate bishopric.[14]

Naturally, an audiencia presided over by Alonso de Maldonado was not inclined to listen to Casas or comply with the New Laws. Indeed, the two bishops reported that the situation verged on lawlessness:

> Never in the time of Alvarado or Nuño de Guzmán, or any of the other past tyrants, have the churches or the ministers been so affronted, nor have such enormous crimes been committed as in the time of this president and judges. In contravention of the ordinances, they treat the Indians cruelly. . . . If the execution of the New Laws is not committed to the prelates, these natives will all perish. . . . Here all are as tacitly in revolt as those in Peru, without obeying any of your orders, and tomorrow they will declare their rebellion and they are preparing for it.

Whether or not this was so—and a rebellion did break out in Valdivieso's Nicaraguan see—President Maldonado certainly obstructed the laws stripping his family of huge Indian holdings. Hence, in large part, his delays and rebuffs of the stubborn old Bishop. Hence, too, his official complaint to the Emperor, which forced Casas to continue appealing to the government in Spain—a long-drawn-out process that eventually took years. Even at Gracias á Dios, the audiencia blocked his simple request for the return of his original petitions with their answers, as required.[15] Then he had to write his own letters of complaint, with the concurrence of Valdivieso and Judge Herrera. Finally, he had to present charges against Maldonado to the Council of the Indies.[16] In the end, Bishop Casas was vindicated. Governor Montejo's Indians were taken away; his daughter, Doña Carolina, later protested this was done under the New Laws, though his contract permitted perpetuity for him and his heirs. President Maldonado presumably lost his Indians, too, when he was removed from the presidency of the Audiencia

---

14. Fabié, app. XIV. Maldonado recommends Motolinía as Bishop of Yucatán; Fray Toribio was in Guatemala at this time, and friendly with Marroquín.

15. Near the end of his November 9 letter (*Cartas de Indias*, no. V, 35-36), Casas tells how they tried to make him pay for transcripts and he refused. Cf. Catalogue, no. 36, for the present whereabouts of the original and transcript.

16. See Fabié, app. XIV, last item, Maldonado's letter to the King on September 20, 1547. On the same date, Marroquín chimed in with a bitter letter accusing Casas of being a hypocrite and an obstacle to the doctrine, and of having caused disturbances: "Look what happened at Cumaná, and now we have seen it in Peru." *Cartas de Indias*, 446.

de los Confines (though he was not officially disgraced, as he changed posts with Licentiate Cerrato, President of Santo Domingo).[17] But the Council did order the audiencia not to interfere with Casas' exercise of ecclesiastical jurisdiction, told them to favor him, and sent a number of cedulas that he had requested.[18] All that, however, came in 1547, too late to be of any use to the embattled Bishop of Chiapa.

This fall of 1545, Casas and Valdivieso were almost friendless in the little town of Gracias á Dios. "We are abhorred," they wrote, "we go about alone without any layman or cleric daring to accompany us, because we adhere to God and to His Majesty!" Maldonado's hostility had infected not only the whole audiencia, except one judge, but the entire community as well. Bitterest of all was the naked enmity of a fellow prelate.

THE RIVAL BISHOP

Francisco de Marroquín, Bishop of Guatemala and another former ally and patron, had also turned openly against Casas. In Gracias á Dios he affronted him publicly from the pulpit and denounced him privately in letters to the Emperor.

In my opinion, Marroquín was piqued over Fray Bartolomé's elevation as Bishop of Chiapa and the consequent curtailment of his own position. For Casas' entire diocese had been carved out of territory removed from Bishop Marroquín's jurisdiction and was now wrapped around the Guatemalan see like an antique version of the gerrymander.

Briefly, this was the story. When Guatemala was originally made a bishopric in 1534, the province of Chiapa (which then included Yucatán) was taken from Tlaxcala and allotted to it, and the provinces of Tuzulutlán and Soconusco were original parts of it. Consecrated as first Bishop of Guatemala, Marroquín retained control of these three provinces until Casas took over—that is, despite the naming and death of Arteaga. But then the Prince Regent issued three drastic cedulas on behalf of Bishop-elect Casas; they were dated February 13, 1544, but their impact was not felt in Central America till the following year. One ordered Bishop Marroquín to stop interfering in the vacant Chiapa see contrary to canon law. Two others

---

17. See Doña Catalina Montejo's letter of November 21, 1565, from Mexico. *Epis. de Nueva España*, X, no. 565. Maldonado was replaced in Central America by Licentiate Cerrato in 1548, but was not named to the Santo Domingo post till 1552; he served there a number of years.

18. Fabié, app. XIII.

directed the audiencia to add both the Land of War and Soconusco to Bishop Casas' diocese.[19]

Marroquín's immediate resentment was expressed in letters to the King. On June 4, 1545, he requested some financial recompense for his "ten or twelve years' work" with Chiapa. Further, he objected to the assignment of Soconusco to Fray Bartolomé, as the province could only be approached via Guatemala City, and Casas' diocese stretched from sea to sea and was much too vast for one man. "If I should oppose him before the audiencia," he added caustically, "it will not be for self-interest, but because he requested more than he can fulfill."[20] On the seventeenth of August, Marroquín reported his own visit to Tuzulutlán—the one timed to coincide with Bishop Casas' triumphal entry—acknowledging the successful peaceful conversion but belittling the whole venture, questioning Fray Bartolomé's jurisdiction, and assailing him for "vainglory since he was given the mitre."[21]

By the time the two prelates met again at Gracias á Dios, Bishop Marroquín's bitter rivalry was out in the open. He unhesitatingly challenged Fray Bartolomé's episcopal authority, naming him in sermons and offering to absolve those whom Bishop Casas would not absolve. Previously he had welcomed the rebel dean into his own diocese and declined to return him to Casas. Now he actually wrote to the Soconusco residents, advising them not to receive Casas as their bishop.[22] Furthermore, in Casas' tug-of-war with the audiencia, Marroquín (as we know) openly sided with the hostile president and against his fellow bishop, and then wrote yet another uncomplimentary letter to the King.

For their part, Casas and Valdivieso duly reported Marroquín's conduct and shed some further unfavorable light upon it: "The Bishop of Guatemala . . . has always followed the wishes of the people [i.e., the encomenderos], and has been one of those most active in unjustly making an infinite number of slaves. . . . This man is held to be of suspected lineage, and his words give rise to more suspicion. He is highly harmful. He knows

---

19. Fabié, app. VIII (92-93, 100-101).

20. *Cartas de Indias*, 442.

21. Marroquín to the King, August 17, 1545, Fabié, app. XV and Quintana, app. XI. He wrote again on December 1: "The affair of Tuzulutlán is as I have said and nothing more. I know that Fray Bartolomé tells miracles about it." (Squier MSS, XXII, 140.) On June 6, 1546, Philip replied laconically, telling Marroquín to go on helping the Dominicans—Xim., I, 388.

22. Casas and Valdivieso to the Prince, October 25, 1545—*Cartas de Indias*, no. IV, 19-20, 23-24, and Squier MSS, XXII, 118-124 *passim*.

little, came here very young, and was not thirty years old when he was made a bishop."[23]

As if Marroquín's affronts were not enough, Casas had also to endure those of Bishop Pedraza of Honduras. Pedraza kept the two Dominican prelates waiting for months till he arrived to take part in Valdivieso's consecration.[24] And then he seems to have joined Marroquín in opposing Casas. The vehemence of Pedraza's attacks can be judged from his later accusation that Fray Bartolomé was "violently biased, blind with covetousness and ambition for worldly honors."[25]

All in all, it was a completely discouraging autumn for Bishop Casas, and his letters to the Prince Regent reflect this. His salary, he wrote, was woefully insufficient, leaving him poor and in debt; he had spent two hundred pesos for the trip to Honduras, and fifty for horseshoes, and there was a move to have the Mexican officials withhold his 500,000 maravedis because he was away from his diocese. Furthermore, the jurisdictional sniping from Marroquín was unwarranted: "I, Fray Bartolomé, have begged that bishops be placed in Soconusco, Yucatán, and Chiapa, leaving me with only the province of Tuzulutlán. I again beseech this, and that the rest be given to some poor friars." The same request appears repeatedly—he wanted to give up the other provinces and move his cathedral to Verapaz, so as not to have in his diocese a single Spaniard who held Indians, for they were all tyrants and not one would be saved.[26]

This was Bishop Casas' depressed state of mind as he made ready to leave Gracias á Dios. He still hoped to direct the "peaceful conversion" part of his diocese, but he despaired of ever "correcting" the Spaniards. Valdivieso had finally been consecrated on November 9 and there was nothing more to be accomplished here.[27] True, largely through Casas' efforts a royal

---

23. Cf. Casas' later denunciation of Marroquín's slave-branding activities and excessive tribute assessments, *DII*, VII, 170, where the footnote identification is erroneous. Writing against Casas and the New Laws on June 4, 1545, Marroquín admitted the need to revise tributes assessed by himself and Maldonado—*Cartas de Indias*, 434-443. On March 15, 1546, he urged the King to believe "three apostolic men from New Spain," i.e., the reluctant provincials, and guaranteed that in their presence Fray Bartolomé would not contradict them. Squier MSS, XXII, 135-136.

24. See their joint letter of October 25, 1545, *Cartas de Indias*, no. IV, 22.

25. See Pedraza's May 1, 1547, letter from Truxillo, Squier MSS, XXII, 24.

26. *Cartas de Indias*, no. IV, 20-21; no. V, 32 and 36-37; also, on reducing the diocese, cf. his letter of September 30—Catalogue, no. 35, last paragraph.

27. In his letter of November 9, Casas says that Pedraza arrived yesterday, "today we consecrated the Bishop of Nicaragua," and he himself will leave for Chiapa tomorrow. *Cartas de Indias*, no. V, 36.

judge had been named to reassess the tributes of the Chiapa Indians, but that was certain to provoke fresh turmoil.[28] The audiencia obviously was not going to grant the Bishop's main demand for the "aid of the secular arm." No stringent provisions had been or would be issued, no strong peace officer provided.[29] Without such help, how could he control the encomenderos of Ciudad Real?

A CONCLUDING RIOT

When Bartolomé de las Casas started back toward his diocese, at the approach of the 1545 Christmas season, he knew that he was heading for a dangerous showdown.

Even before leaving Honduras he had received alarming word from the Dominican missionaries and Canon Perera, whom he had left in charge, about new threats by the magistrates. Also, a vicious letter came from his own cathedral chancellor, who had now gone to Guatemala. This man swore he would seize the Bishop on the highway and send him bound to Pizarro in Peru—the wretch had been pressured into writing thus by Spaniards who hoped to dissuade the Bishop from the return journey. Nonetheless, Casas set out around November 10, probably traveling via Guatemala and Comitán, for he arrived at Copanabastla in Chiapa just before Christmas. There a further distressing report reached him.[30]

Back in Ciudad Real, it seems, things had gone from bad to worse. Still fuming about the reserved cases, the town council on September 4 had given power-of-attorney to two men to appear before Casas or his vicar general and make representations on the subject. The canon managed to put them off, despite threats and bribes, but then they heard that Bishop

28. While passing through Cinacatlán, the Chiapa Dominicans had a copy made of the town's tribute assessment and sent it to Casas at Gracias á Dios. He read it before the audiencia: it was so exorbitant that some said all Seville would have trouble paying it. This was one of the reasons the audiencia agreed to send a judge to make a new assessment. Hearing of this, the encomendero Estrada at once collected a whole year's tribute. Rem., II, 73-74.

29. In point 7 of his original demands, Casas had specifically asked that the staffs of office be taken away from the Ciudad Real magistrates and chief constable, and be given to a "faithful person" not holding Indians in encomienda or slavery nor related to the delinquents, who would administer justice and assist the Bishop. Rem., II, 57.

30. Rem., II, 60-61, 66-67; also *Cartas de Indias*, no. V, 30. Just where Copanabastla was located, I cannot discover. Modern histories of Chiapas say it has disappeared, possibly depopulated during the congregation of 1549; I suspect, however, that the present town of San Bartolomé occupies the same site.

Casas was returning with a judge to revise the tributes. So on December 15 they took more drastic action.

Convoking all the citizens, the town council had its secretary record an inflammatory resolution, to wit: Casas was exercising the office of prelate without having officially presented bulls and cedulas, yet he had reserved to himself cases appealed to the Crown, introducing new rules and usurping the royal jurisdiction. Furthermore, if the provisions and assessments he was rumored to be bringing against them should be executed, they would be impoverished and the Indians would rebel. So a demand was to be made on him to make no innovation pending the decision of their appeal, but to proceed like the other bishops of New Spain; and if he refused, they would not admit him to the office of bishop or pay his tithes till they had informed the King. Any riot or disturbance resulting from this action would be his fault, and they were making these protestations because he wouldn't shrive them the past year. Remesal, who saw the original resolution in the books of the town council, says that thirty-four citizens signed this at the time, and four days later three more, and finally the secretary. Next the townsfolk proclaimed the suspension of tithes forthwith, prepared a great stock of arms, and posted guards on the roads, intending to halt the Bishop outside town and present their demands.[31]

The prospect was truly frightening, and the friars begged Bishop Casas not to enter Ciudad Real lest he be killed. But he insisted, traveling by night and making an entry that was the wildest drama. The Torre diary gives us the incredible details. First, Casas came upon the Indian spies who had been stationed on the highway—they were no longer watching for him, as he had recalled his baggage carriers to Copanabastla. Startled, they knelt to beg his pardon, as they were only there under strict orders. To protect them from the charge of carelessness, the Bishop bound them himself with the aid of Fray Vicente Ferrer and took them along as prisoners. That night a terrible earthquake struck Ciudad Real, and one of the citizens declared it must be a warning of the Bishop's return to destroy the city. Finally, after an all-night journey on foot, Casas entered town at dawn and went straight to his cathedral.

When it was day, the Bishop sent a priest to summon the magistrates and councilors to the church, where a tense encounter took place. The town council filed in silently, accompanied by the citizens, and they all took seats as if to hear a sermon. Bishop Casas emerged from the sacristy, but no one addressed him a word. Only the clerk arose and read the paper they

---

31. Rem., II, 61-63, 67.

had meant to present at the town gate, demanding that he treat the citizens as their quality required and help them to preserve their property, in which case they would receive him as bishop. What would happen if he refused was left to his imagination. The Bishop began to answer mildly, when suddenly a councilor, without even standing or removing his hat, began to berate Casas as a private person who had presumed to call the noble town council to see him, when he should go humbly to them if he wanted anything. At this insolence, Casas rebuked the man sharply and turned back towards the sanctuary. But now the council secretary approached deferentially and handed the Bishop a petition—from the citizens, he said, begging him to assign confessors. Casas promptly assented, and turning to the company loudly announced that he was naming Canon Perera and the Dominican friars. This brought a chorus of protests: the Spaniards did not want priests of his opinion but confessors who would preserve their property. To quiet them, Casas named instead a Mercedarian friar and a certain cleric from Guatemala who was in town; he wanted time for tempers to cool and knew he could count on these two. But his companion, Fray Vicente, thought he was giving in and tugged at his cape: "Don't do such a thing, Your Reverence—better death!"

Whereupon a near riot broke out. Everyone turned on the friar, and the tumult waxed so great that they came near to maltreating him. Fortunately, at this juncture two Mercedarians entered the church; they had heard of Bishop Casas' return and promptly took him and Fray Vicente off to their house for breakfast. But by now the poor Bishop was so exhausted that he lacked the strength to eat. He took just a bite of bread in order to manage a sip of wine, and at that moment a fresh riot surrounded him. All the townspeople were shouting outside the monastery, armed to the teeth, with the bolder ones storming inside and right into the Bishop's cell. Seeing himself suddenly surrounded by drawn swords, Casas was momentarily paralyzed and almost choked.

The new uproar, it developed, had been set off by the discovery that the Bishop had seized the city's Indian spies. When Casas was able to speak, he explained quietly that he had tied the guards with his own hands, lest they be punished for failing in their assignment. This only brought on fresh abuse, which the Bishop answered with restraint. Unable to provoke him, the rioters now vented their fury outside. One of them accused Juanillo, the Bishop's servant, of tying the Indians, and gave the big Negro a pike blow that stretched him out on the ground. But the Mercedarians came to his aid and a couple of strong and spirited young friars avenged the blow so well that the mob gradually dispersed.

All this happened before nine o'clock, and as morning wore on in Ciudad Real heads began to clear. By noon, most of the citizens had visited the Bishop to kiss his hand and ask his forgiveness. Finally, the town organized a procession, the magistrates not carrying wands and the citizens leaving off their swords, and escorted him to the house of Pedro de Orozco Azebedo, a leading citizen, where lodgings had been prepared for him.[32]

From that day on, a relative calm prevailed between Casas and his flock. The citizens even made peace temporarily with the Dominicans, especially those at Cinacatlán; very possibly they felt they had gone dangerously far in opposing their prelate.[33] As for the Bishop, he had his own reasons for being conciliatory; evidently the riot had convinced him, too. Bartolomé de las Casas was thinking seriously of leaving his diocese for good.

---

32. Rem., II, 68-72. This episode contains the first mention of Casas' big Negro, Juanillo.

33. Cf. Rem., II, 79, 101, 105. From Cinacatlán, Fray Tomás de la Torre came to Ciudad Real; he was well received by the townspeople and conferred with Casas on the future establishment of a Dominican province of Chiapa and Guatemala.

FAREWELL TO AMERICA

CASAS LEAVES CHIAPA AND LEARNS OF THE REVOCATION

At the beginning of 1546, Bishop Casas was preparing publicly to travel to Mexico for a church council. But privately he was planning to give up his bishopric and go back to court. The decision did not come to him quickly or easily.

Back at Gracias á Dios, he had already contemplated it. In their joint letter, both he and Valdivieso wrote that they were determined to resign if no remedy was provided; in fact, he himself did not think he could even wait for the license he had asked to return to Spain.[1] The riot that greeted Casas' return to Ciudad Real was just one more confirmation that the step was necessary. Even so, his resolution was still tentative. It would only take final shape in the vice-regal capital under the influence of some shattering news. On October 20, 1545, the Emperor had revoked the Law of Inheritance, the most controversial of the New Laws!

From the outset, Casas' stormy time in Chiapa had come from his identification with the New Laws. This was still true at the finish. It was put to him in so many words by Licentiate Rogel, the royal judge who finally came on March 9 to reassess the Chiapa tributes. Rogel interviewed Spaniards and Indian representatives, but made no move to get on with his task. When the Bishop urged him to proceed, Rogel answered flatly that Casas himself was the obstacle:

> Your Reverence well knows that although these New Laws were made in Valladolid with the accord of great personages . . . one of the reasons that has made them abhorred in the Indies is that you had a hand in them, soliciting them and writing some of them. Deeming Your Reverence prejudiced, the

---

1. *Cartas de Indias,* no. IV, 16-17, and no. V, 32.

conquistadors do not understand that you were procuring these ordinances for the benefit of and out of love toward the natives, but think rather that it was from hatred of the Spaniards. With this suspicion, when I strip them of their property, they will resent Your Reverence's presence even more than losing their slaves. Don Francisco Tello de Sandoval has called Your Reverence for a meeting of prelates in Mexico, and you are already preparing for the journey. So I would be pleased if you would hasten your departure, for while Your Reverence is present, I can do nothing.[2]

Accordingly, Bishop Casas made haste to leave, and there were many more indications that he did not mean to return. He left around mid-March, with the leading citizens accompanying him on foot as far as Cinacatlán. There he made the Dominican Order a legal donation of the churches at Chiapa village and the adjoining sugar-mill and Cinacatlán, and also of everything he might have on sailing day, in case he went back to Spain. In addition, he left with the friars his library and household belongings, including two big clocks; they could use these as a loan, but if he never came back, the things were theirs to keep. Finally, he went over to Chiapa to pick up the elderly Fray Rodrigo de Ladrada, who would of course return to the Peninsula too; his other traveling companions were Fray Vicente Ferrer, his old co-worker Fray Luis Cáncer, and the faithful Canon Perera.[3]

So ended Casas' stay of a little less than a year in Chiapa. There was no fanfare at his going, and no disturbance either. Later legends claimed that the citizens had stoned him out of town, and that he had ascended a nearby hill and cursed Ciudad Real. But Remesal went to considerable length to disprove these calumnies.[4] The real truth is that Bartolomé de las Casas was driven out of his diocese quietly, not by stones but by public antagonism toward the author of the New Laws.

---

2. Rem., II, 95-96. Rogel had orders of August 31 and December 19, 1545, from the audiencia to investigate Casas' complaints and revise the tributes; an earlier October 23, 1543, cedula, produced by Casas, also ordered revision of the Chiapa tributes. Cf. *ibid.*, 93-94.

3. Rem., II, 101, 103, 108. On January 8, Casas gave many ornaments to the cathedral church, which offered to pay half the cost of his Mexican trip, but he never collected it. *Ibid.*, 105.

4. Cf. Rem., II, 103-105. I have been unable to determine whether the terrible epidemic then decimating the Indians of New Spain may have reached Chiapa before Casas' departure, or even whether it did so afterwards. The "cocolistle," perhaps a virulent form of influenza, was in full swing in Mexico in March of 1545 and later that year—see *infra*, my Conclusion, note 5, for details. Oaxaca was desolated, and on December 31, 1545, President Maldonado wrote that the epidemic had not yet reached Honduras. (Squier MSS, XXII, 135.) Remesal's book contains not a word

Similar antagonism awaited him in Mexico City—and similar calm. Bishop Casas and his party were cordially received by the Oaxaca Dominicans, but as he neared the capital, the populace became as excited as if an enemy was approaching. Fearing riots, the viceroy and the inspector general wrote him to wait until the Spaniards had calmed down. Yet when the aging Casas finally entered town, possibly on the eleventh of June, there was no outbreak. People just stared at him with awe, and a few even said: "There goes the holy bishop, the true father of the Indians!"[5] His arrival was an anticlimax after all. He was still the hated Fray Bartolomé who had procured the reform, but the biggest battle against the New Laws was over, and everyone in Mexico knew it. Casas himself may have had the news before he left Chiapa; if not, he certainly learned it here. And the friars at the Dominican monastery, where he stayed, must have given him the full details.

The campaign against the New Laws had been astutely organized from Mexico. At the outset, the Spanish government was handed Sandoval's extensive "Interrogatory"—a document in which not only conquistadors but Dominican and Franciscan friars insisted that the encomienda was necessary for the royal rule, the stability of the country, the support of religion, etc., and should be preserved and even made perpetual.[6] Then, when the Councils of Indies and State were convoked to review the matter, plenty of witnesses from New Spain were on hand to give more testimony of the same sort. After this mountain of data was forwarded to the Emperor in Belgium, Charles was personally besieged by the Mexican envoys.

As Casas heard the story, these men were being paid a ducat a day. They insisted on talking to His Majesty, though he told them three times not to bring up the subject. Finally, they persuaded the King and his con-

---

about it, but in 1549 the audiencia authorized a great attempt to congregate the Chiapa natives; five towns were joined in Iztapa, three in Chamula, and so on. Cf. Rem., II, 245. Though previously urged by the friars, the timing might indicate a sizeable population loss.

5. Rem., II, 108-109. A later cedula (DII, VII, 239-241) discloses that the Mexican officials paid Bishop Casas his supplementary funds to that date.

6. See DII, VII, 532-542, Sandoval's questions and the Dominican opinion of May 4, 1544; also ibid., 526-532, the Franciscan opinion. The Dominicans stressed the need for rich Spanish encomenderos to maintain the faith and provide a militia, and lauded the improved conditions under Viceroy Mendoza. The Franciscan answer was so similar as to suggest prior agreement between the two groups; they too urged perpetuity, using a line of reasoning that went back to Cortés. For conquistador opinions, see supra, chapter XII, notes 4 and 5.

fessor that the Indians would be fully protected under the encomienda if the Spaniards were merely deprived of civil and criminal jurisdiction over them.[7] (There was another version, that the agents actually offered the Emperor sums up to twenty-one million gold pesos for revocation of each of the more obnoxious laws.)[8]

In the end, neither bribes nor the elaborate Mexican campaign seems to have decided the issue. What no doubt clinched the matter was the rebellion in Peru. The letters of Núñez Vela and others must have reached the Emperor while colonial agents were urging him to revoke the most offensive New Laws. Peru was then a much more valuable asset to the Crown than New Spain, and Charles must have realized that its loss was threatened. This was no mere suspicion. Gonzalo Pizarro was the de facto ruler of Peru and seriously considered making himself king by edict.

At any rate, the accumulated pressure was overwhelming. At Malines, on October 20, 1545, Charles issued a fateful cedula revoking the Law of Inheritance: the encomienda was not to be extinguished.[9] He followed this with yet another cedula, given at Ratisbon on April 16, 1546, on the advice of the Mexican provincials and procurators, authorizing Viceroy Mendoza to grant encomiendas.[10] But the colonists' victory was only partial. Mendoza did submit an elaborate report with lists of conquistadors and Indian towns, but neither he nor his successor granted any encomiendas. The Emperor had sent secret orders not to grant them.[11] Indeed, the royal officials and others were actually deprived of their encomiendas; some (but only a few) of the most excessive allotments itemized in the New Laws were reduced; and pensions were assigned to Spaniards not holding Indians.[12]

---

7. See Fabié, app. XXVIII, the conclusion of Casas' long letter to Carranza de Miranda.

8. Juan de Solórzano Pereira, *Política indiana* (Madrid 1629-1639), lib. VI, cap. 1, no. 7.

9. Puga, *Cedulario*, I, 472-475, and see León, *Tratado*, fol. 16. This cedula left matters as before, with encomiendas for two lives.

10. Puga, I, 479-480.

11. León, *Tratado*, fols. 16-16 verso. The April cedula directed the viceroy to compile lists of towns and Indians, living conquistadors and wives and children of deceased ones, married and unmarried settlers, and then to make a division with a recommendation on tributes and pensions. The various lists made by Mendoza have been printed in *Epis. de Nueva España*, XIV-XVI, various numbers, all undated. Individual reports were abstracted and printed by Francisco A. de Icaza, *Conquistadores y pobladores de Nueva España*, Madrid, 1923.

12. León, *Tratado*, fols. 81 verso-85. León lists encomenderos who were to lose part of their holdings, and gives a long account of the pensions or "situaciones." From

Furthermore, the laws on slavery, which had brought almost as much opposition, were never revoked. Instead, supporting ones were issued and the Emperor sent out Doctor Melgarejo to supervise the liberation of slaves.

This was the full story that Bishop Casas certainly pored over in Mexico. The revocation of the Law of Inheritance had struck a major blow against the New Laws, and when it happened he himself had been thousands of miles away in Chiapa and there had been no one in Spain or in Flanders to speak on behalf of the oppressed Indians. Years later he would still ponder the bitter memory, and we cannot doubt that the news affected him right now.[13] A good part of the ordinances still held, but the question was how firmly. Clearly it was his duty to return to court and use all his energies to reinforce the breached reform.

JUNTAS IN MEXICO

First, however, Bishop Casas must do what he could in Mexico City, where he had come to attend a convocation of all the bishops of New Spain.[14] Just why this ecclesiastical junta was called in 1546 is something of a mystery. Our sources about the meeting are incomplete: Remesal's narrative, which is partly in error, and a few fragmentary references. The official proceedings have not been found, though García Icazbalceta made strenuous efforts to locate them both in Mexico and in Spain, and a contemporary allusion suggests that there may have been some secrecy about them.[15] But at least we can put together the tentative outlines of the

---

the audiencia report of June 29, 1544, it appears that there must have been cedulas qualifying the New Law on pensions; according to rank, these were set from 300 down to 150 pesos, and from 100 down to 50 pesos for children of deceased. Cf. *Epis. de Nueva España*, IV, no. 230. So far as I know, no concession for discovery was revoked, but orders were issued forbidding further expeditions by any viceroy or other citizens without license.

13. Cf. Fabié, app. XXVIII, last paragraph. This was written in August 1555.

14. In the *Apologética*, Casas tells very little about this stay in Mexico. But he evidently learned a great deal about the affairs of New Spain since his previous visit—see *infra*, chapter XVII, section on the *Apologética Historia*, and especially notes 19-21 on his informants. Doubtless he also gathered material at this time for his treatise on the Jalisco campaign. See Catalogue, no. 42.

15. See Icazbalceta, *Zumárraga*, 191. This scholar could only find a few notices of town council meetings in the latter part of the year, at which a demand was made on the Bishop for the "actas," indicating that they had not been given to that body. Zumárraga himself, writing to Sandoval on November 12, 1547, says he is sending a copy of the proceedings which he forgot to enclose in an earlier letter. Cuevas, *Docs.*, 124.

bishop's junta, in which Casas took part, and a follow-up junta convoked by him.

Apparently before March, Inspector General Sandoval had called bishops, friars, and "men of conscience" to a meeting in Mexico City. Besides Casas, the bishops of Guatemala, Oaxaca, Michoacán, and naturally of Mexico, were summoned.[16] (The see of Tlaxcala was then vacant.) The sessions, perhaps beginning in late May or early in June, lasted "many days." On July 20 they were still going on, for on that date Bishop Marroquín wrote to the Guatemala town council: "Since I arrived, we have met every day. The Bishop of Chiapa arrived somewhat late and is very subdued. He will be more so every day, although yesterday he wished to begin to object, but he was not allowed to do so."[17] As usual, Marroquín's adjective was ill chosen. Upon lodging at the Dominican convent, Casas had declined to call on the viceroy and royal judges, sending word that they were in a state of excommunication for having ordered the hand cut off a cleric in Antequera; and the dignitaries had to perform the canonical apology. But apparently Fray Bartolomé was able to accomplish little with his fellow bishops.

So we must dispose at the outset of Remesal's fanciful account of this bishops' junta, which has been accepted by all of Casas' biographers.[18] Certainly the chronicler was mistaken in thinking that the meeting was called to debate the Spanish conquest of the Indies, the lawfulness of Indian slavery, and the matter of encomiendas—topics on which Casas held strong views. There mere fact that the conclusions were unanimous indicates that no such controversial subjects were discussed. And it turns out that the so-called eight decisions, of which Remesal summarizes five, do not come from this meeting at all. They are actually the eight principles from Casas' own *Tratado de las doce dudas* of January 1564—the chronicler admits possessing a memorial of that date and gives a precise description, but is thoroughly confused about its authorship.[19]

As a matter of fact, the conversion of the natives was the principal topic discussed, according to almost all the available sources. Bishop Marroquín speaks of the bishops treating "affairs more spiritual than temporal," and Madrid's Biblioteca Nacional has an extract from the proceedings which concerns the instruction and conversion of Indians in encomienda.[20] The

16. Rem., II, 95, 109. Perhaps Sandoval called the meeting simply to comply with his instructions.

17. Xim., I, 407-409; Arévalo, *Docs.*, 189.

18. Rem., II, 95.

19. Rem., II, 109 110. But cf. *Doce dudas—infra*, chapter XIX, second section.

20. Paz, *Catálogo Bib. Nac.*, no. 34 (55).

only contemporary statement of the object is found in the instructions to Viceroy Velasco, Mendoza's successor: "The principal purpose of this meeting, and which most of us desire and pray God for, is that the Indians be well instructed and catechized in the matters of our Holy Catholic Faith and in their well being and civil status."[21]

What we know of the meeting's decisions bears this out. Licenciate Alonso de Zorita quotes the first conclusion. It stressed the royal obligation to send out many friars of the three Orders then in New Spain, as well as clerics and other ecclesiastics to minister to the great population in the Indies, and requested His Majesty to have prelates of the universities of Salamanca and Alcalá choose appropriate persons for this work.[22] The Velasco instructions add another point: "In order for them [the Indians] to be true and civilized Christians, like the reasonable men they are, it is necessary for them to be congregated into towns." To this end, the King should order audiencias and governors to prepare plans promptly, and should suspend all or part of the tribute to encomenderos during the period required for establishing the new Indian towns.[23]

In addition, the bishops' junta ordered the printing of two catechisms, a long one and a short one. We have both of these, or rather, five issued in the same period, perhaps as a result of this decree. First I would cite a pair in "the Mexican language," as the ecclesiastics called the Nahuatl tongue of the dominant Aztecs. The long catechism was definitely Fray Pedro de Córdoba's famous *Doctrina*, originally printed a few years earlier and now reprinted with a Mexican translation on January 17, 1548. The colophon states distinctly that it is the long catechism authorized by the 1546 meeting and that the short one was printed that year. This points to the *Doctrina cristiana breve*, written in Mexican by Fray Alonso de Molina and printed on June 20, 1546. A further pair of catechisms was issued simultaneously in Spanish: the longish *Regla cristiana*, printed by the end of January 1547, with a colophon saying its compilation and printing were entrusted to

---

21. Icazbalceta, *Zumárraga*, app. 37.

22. Zorita, *Historia*, 523. At the end, however, he says this was unanimously adopted and signed on July 14 by eight friars; all are named and there is no bishop in the list. So perhaps the item was repeated from the 1541 junta of regular and secular clergy that dealt with the papal concessions and the royal granting of encomiendas. Bishop Zumárraga had asked provincials and friars to spell out Spanish obligations for conversion, and they specified the encomenderos' duty to provide ministers, friars, or clerics of good example. Cf. *ibid.*, 521.

23. Icazbalceta, *Zumárraga*, app. 37. León likewise says that the council approved a resolution that Indians be congregated; cf. *Tratado*, fol. 103 verso.

Zumárraga by this meeting; and a short *Doctrina para gente sin letra*, apparently written after the junta by Zumárraga, and printed at the end of 1546 as an addition to a catechism already in press. Finally, Fray Pedro de Gante's Mexican *Doctrina* was probably printed in 1547 as well.[24]

From the foregoing, the general tenor of the bishops' junta in 1546 seems fully apparent. In all this, the not-so-subdued Bishop of Chiapa seems to have played a relatively minor part. Perhaps he engineered one of the lesser conclusions, a strong statement of ecclesiastical privileges and immunities, as he refers to it in his *Apologética*.[25]

But what Bishop Casas really accomplished was the convocation of a second junta—a meeting of friars alone, without the bishops, to deal with Indian slavery. Here we can follow Remesal's narrative safely, as there is ample confirming evidence.[26] Apparently the viceroy would not permit this subject to be discussed by the bishops when Casas tried to bring it up. Perhaps Mendoza was touchy because he himself had been criticized for making slaves during the Mixtón war. Anyhow, Casas indirectly rebuked him

---

24. For a discussion of these rare imprints, see García Icazbalceta's *Zumárraga*, 266-295, and his *Bibliografía mexicana del siglo XVI* (Mexico, 1886), nos. 10-11 and 13-15; also my *Nueva bibliografía mexicana del siglo XVI* (Mexico, 1946), nos. 10-11 and 13-15.

In the "Mexican" pair, Córdoba's *Doctrina* is well known; it was first printed in 1544 by the Dominican Order. But of the 1546 edition of Molina's *Doctrina*, only a fragment is known today—four pages identified by me in the Hispanic Society. The entire work, however, was copied in the *Códice franciscano, siglo XVI*, a document belonging to José Fernando Ramírez and printed by García Icazbalceta as volume II (1889) of his *Nueva colección de documentos*. Apparently the brief original (*ibid.*, 34-61) did not exceed thirty pages and, if printed as a result of the bishops' decision, was already in use in manuscript beforehand.

In the "Spanish" pair, the *Regla cristiana* is the better known. As for the short *Doctrina* of 1546, García Icazbalceta believed that the title page as well as the brief appended "doctrina mas facil" were both added by Zumárraga after the Bishop's junta. The main part of the book has an undated colophon, and a copy without the addition was preserved in the Biblioteca Provincial de Toledo.

Gante's *Doctrina* is known in only one copy (colophon missing), which I bought in 1922, and which is now in the Huntington Library.

25. *Apol.*, 374. He speaks of attending a Mexico City meeting of all the bishops of New Spain, where a petition on this matter was addressed to the Emperor, citing the great Aztec respect for the right of sanctuary, and asking a royal order for strict enforcement.

26. Rem., II, 111-112.

in a spirited sermon and the viceroy then permitted Casas to call a special meeting in the Dominican convent. As Marroquín tells it: "We [the bishops] agreed that the matter of slaves and personal services of the Indians should not be discussed, and that the confessors should do this by themselves."[27]

A little is known of what went on at this second meeting. Evidently the conferees—Dominicans, Franciscans, and Augustinians, according to Casas—discussed the injustice of past Indian wars. Fray Luis Cáncer read the text of the notorious "requirement," whereby Indians were bidden to submit to the Crown and then attacked as rebels; and several stories were told on the folly of the procedure and its use as a pretext for brutal enslavement. Current problems must have come up too, as profitable silver mining was then carried on with Indian slaves, and the government found slaving raids difficult to control.

Anyway, strong conclusions were reached. According to Remesal it was decided that Indian slaves were unjustly taken and should be freed, though there was some doubt about prisoners of the second Jalisco war; oppressive personal services were also condemned. Casas himself, writing soon afterwards, praised the friars for agreeing not to absolve any Spaniard holding Indian slaves until these were examined by the audiencia according to the New Laws—though an absolute decision would have been better.[28]

Bishop Casas' own part in the friars' junta is not quite clear.[29] But he did prepare a bold and uncompromising document bearing on its main theme, a document which merits our detailed attention.

---

27. Xim., I, 408.

28. See the added Third Corollary of Casas' *Tratado sobre los indios esclavos* (Catalogue, no. 23). Manuel Orozco y Berra asserts that the second council declared unanimously that all slaves were held illegally and *should be freed* no matter how obtained, and this opinion was sent all over the Indies. Cf. *Historia de la dominación española en México* (Mexico, 1849), II, 187. But Torre's diary merely indicates that the conclusions condemned personal services, and enunciated with reservations the principle that slaves were held illegally. See Xim., I, 404.

29. For example, did Casas himself appear or was Cáncer his spokesman? Even more interesting, were Negro slaves discussed, and how might this have affected Casas? Mexico had many Negroes till the epidemic of 1545, when a large number died. Even Bishop Zumárraga had such slaves, and they were then, and for many years afterwards, employed as domestic servants and mechanics. Casas had with him the big Negro Juanillo, and I feel certain someone twitted him about it at this meeting. From then on his views changed and he recognized the evil of the African slave trade—see *infra*, my Conclusion and note 8.

His "Confesionario"

Casas' celebrated *Confesionario,* his "Twelve Rules for Confessors," was his last great effort as Bishop of Chiapa, and this raises a number of questions. Had he actually drawn up these rules some years back, as Remesal says, presumably for his own use as bishop? Was this paper, or a version of it, submitted to the second junta, which treated similar ideas? Was there any prior discussion of it by the bishops at the first junta?

I have a suspicion that Casas' *Confesionario,* or at least his handling of confessions, came under fire at the bishops' meeting. His refusal to absolve the Chiapa slaveholders had created a great scandal throughout the land and had brought him harsh letters from the viceroy and the inspector general, as well as from some bishops and learned friars.[30] In view of this generally adverse attitude, I cannot accept Remesal's account of the first junta approving Casas' "formulary for confessors"—though condemnation seems unlikely, too, if the bishops' findings were unanimous.[31] Rather, both Marroquín and Casas hint at what probably happened: confessions, as well as slaves and tributes, were left to a later meeting. And I think the second junta did not approve the *Confesionario* either, since Casas' views went much farther than those of the friars.[32]

What we know for certain is that Casas did send his "Twelve Rules" back to his own diocese later that year. He had now definitely decided to go back to court, and this was his fiery farewell to Chiapa. In two formal notarized documents done in Mexico City on November 9 and 10, 1546, he appointed Canon Perera as vicar general and named certain Chiapa Dominicans as confessors for the reserved cases which were to be heard according to "twelve rules that we are sending, signed with our name and sealed with our seal." Clerics might confess such persons only in deathbed emergencies, using the same formulary, but the very existence of these rules was not to be divulged to the Spaniards.[33]

---

30. Rem., II, 102. Remesal rightly notes that most religious backed the laymen in opinions contrary to those held by Casas, and only some Dominicans agreed with his extreme position. Cf. *ibid.,* 95 and 101-102.

31. Rem., II, 110-111 and 165. But in view of Sandoval's letter of reproval, it might be argued that he wished to examine Casas personally about this and might have referred the topic to the other bishops before Casas' arrival.

32. See his commentary on the Third Corollary of the *Tratado sobre los indios esclavos.*

33. Rem., II, 164-165, and Catalogue, nos. 39 and 40.

No American copy of this manuscript *Confesionario* is known today, since all available transcripts were destroyed a few years later under official orders. But I believe that the twelve rules Casas himself afterwards published were identical, since he says they were written in the Indies and he prints his later "clarification" as an appendix.[34] These rules were to be applied to conquistadors, encomenderos, slaveholders, and all others who had made money from the Indians (including merchants who furnished supplies for the wars, and overseers of mines and plantations).

Rules 1 and 5, which Casas subsequently "clarified," created the most uproar. Before confessing, on his deathbed or in health, the penitent had to execute a legal document (enforceable in an ecclesiastical court) authorizing the confessor to dispose of all his property for restitution to the Indians. In various rules it was pointed out that none of this property was lawfully owned by the penitent, as it was not brought from Spain but had been taken from the Indians—and all the conquests and wars were crimes, all the tributes and services were received unjustly, all the slaves were acquired illegally. So the confessor was to order restitution: to any surviving victims or their descendants or their villages, or for freeing other Indian slaves and establishing new villages, or for assisting Spanish settlers and peasant immigrants. But the requirement of total restitution was to be moderated according to the means and condition of the penitent. Thus all slaves, no matter how obtained, were to be freed and pensioned. Rich encomenderos with other income might keep only a modest part of this for their families, but must use the rest for restitution and might receive no further tribute. Poor encomenderos might, until the tributes were reduced, receive enough for sustenance, provided they looked after their Indians and taught them the faith. Restitution of past tributes was stipulated for the wealthy, while poorer encomenderos should simply persuade their Indians to forgive them. No children of Spaniards had any right of inheritance to all this stolen property, but a little something could be given them out of charity or to enable them to settle in the New World.

In Fabié's opinion, these rules for confessors were equivalent to a decree of universal expropriation.[35] I do not agree. If the doctrine of restitution was

---

34. *Aqui se contienen unos avisos y reglas para los confesores;* for the 1552 printing and the known MSS, see Catalogue, no. 41. The tract consists of the 12 rules, followed by an extensive Addition relating to Rules 1 and 5. See *infra,* my chapter XV, first section.

35. Fabié, I, 308.

fitted to the case, then its execution, though drastic, was only carrying out a dogma that had been accepted for hundreds of years. Casas was able to support his views by numerous references to church authorities. The question was not the doctrine but whether or not it applied here. Under the New Laws, holding Indian slaves was illegal without proper title, and Casas claimed there was none, as all the wars and conquests were unjust. Therefore anything gained by the labor of slaves, or any damage they had suffered, had to be restored to them by their owner before he could be absolved. Encomenderos were in a somewhat different class. Of course, one of the New Laws had originally abolished encomiendas on the death of the holder, and no doubt Casas drew up his rules before he learned of its revocation at Malines. Thenceforth, to be sure, allotments could hardly be called illegal, but Casas still claimed that they were unjust and contrary to divine law and their holders were consequently delinquents. In sum, he labeled as unlawful the whole conquest and exploitation of the natives. This bold basis of his *Confesionario*—tantamount, some said, to challenging the legality of Spanish rule in the Indies—was bound to get him into trouble back at court.

Bartolomé de las Casas finally sailed for the Peninsula in 1547, probably in April, from the one oblique reference I have found to his departure date.[36] He was leaving the New World for good, and I believe he was glad to do so. Parenthetically, he had not made six or seven round-trip voyages to America, as his biographers claim, but only four that are known, though there may have been a fifth.[37] By now he seems to have realized that his

---

36. Cf. Rem., II, 168. Remesal says that Casas was detained in Veracruz for lack of a vessel; so Canon Perera, who had accompanied him on the Mexican trip, could not return to Chiapa until June 15, 1547. It thus seems that Casas did not sail before April 1. He might possibly have left with Sandoval on April 20. Motolinía says that Casas was refused a license to return to Spain but went anyway—cf. Icazbalceta, *Docs.*, I, 260.

37. The following are definite: (1) Casas came from Spain to Santo Domingo in 1502, and returned in 1515. (2) He came back to Santo Domingo in 1516, and returned in 1517. (3) In 1520 he came again to Santo Domingo and, after the Cumaná tragedy, he remained on the island till about January 1534, when he went to Central America and then returned to Spain in 1540. (4) He came to Chiapa in 1545, and then returned to Spain for good in 1547. (His letters of 1531, 1534, and 1535, prove he did not return to the Peninsula in the '30s, nor go to Peru.)

Casas may have made one further transatlantic trip, since in *Apol.*, 438, he speaks of being in Rome in the year "seven" when he returned from the Indies. In

true place was at court, and that he alone could serve as the much-needed "universal procurator" of his beloved Indians. The beleaguered Bishop probably did not foresee that he would first have to serve as procurator in his own cause.

---

the *Historia,* however, he mentions no 1507 trip, and I have already discussed the possibility of his visiting Rome in 1517. He might have done so now, when he returned to Spain in 1547 under a cloud, i.e., going to Rome to clear himself and obtain permission to resign his bishopric. But this seems unlikely, as he wrote congratulations to Archbishop Zumárraga from Aranda de Duero at the end of 1547. Cf. Zumárraga's answer of June 20, 1548—*DII,* XLI, 278.

CASAS VERSUS SEPÚLVEDA

Back in Spain, Casas found himself under fire. Charges against him had been pouring in from the Indies. At court, his opponents were launching a powerful new attack on the very principles of reform and his own position with the Crown. For the next few years he was definitely on the defensive.

Bishop Casas had left the New World with several unsettled disputes on his hands. The one with the audiencia probably did not trouble him very much, for he soon presented accusations that led to President Maldonado's removal and transfer. Similar prompt success attended his efforts for the Dominican missionaries in their struggle with the settlers. Apparently he had reached Valladolid before July 22, since on that day the Prince issued letters commending the Chiapa friars and the cacique Pedro Noti for their missionary labors, as reported by Casas, and promising protection against "vexations" by the Spaniards.[1] It is not specified that this report was given orally, but a September 14 sequel clearly stated that Casas was present, and I believe he was already there in July.[2] Anyway, he shortly obtained fresh royal support for the Verapaz mission and action against Maldonado and the Montejos; according to Remesal, he secured the appointment of one Diego Ramírez as investigating judge to look into the persecution of the friars by the Spanish residents.[3] So in these missionary and administrative conflicts, Casas soon gained the upper hand.

But the uproar caused by his refusal to absolve the Chiapa encomenderos

---

1. Rem., II, 189-190; Xim., I, 466-467.
2. Xim., I, 467-468.
3. Verapaz cedulas thanking caciques and friars, and ordering Montejo's men to keep out, were issued on October 11 and 30, 1547. Rem., II, 190, 206-207, and others

and slaveholders, unless they bound themselves to make restitution, was quite another story. Although these men numbered only sixty or thereabouts, they were supported by all others in New Spain who were in the same predicament. Certainly the members of the Ciudad Real town council had carried out their threat of appealing to the King, and perhaps to the Pope as well.[4] Even Inspector General Sandoval had an "Información" drawn up in Mexico about Casas' actions in this matter, to which he objected.[5] And the rash "Twelve Rules for Confessors" had not been kept secret. Remesal suggests the document was used by other bishops who were less careful; and of course its availability to clerics presented a danger. Within the year, many shocked laymen were passing around transcripts, and this brought a fresh crescendo of objections from America.

By some time in 1548 these complaints had piled up and taken such a serious turn that the Council was obliged to intervene. Casas was called in to explain his stand and particularly his *Confesionario*—he himself tells us so. And official steps were taken to halt its distribution.

On November 28, a royal order was issued to collect all manuscript copies in New Spain, as contrary to the royal policy forbidding circulation of ecclesiastical decrees in America without approval by the Council of the Indies.[6] The Franciscan Motolinía, entrusted with this task, gathered a large number of them and gleefully reported they had been burnt by the viceroy as containing seditious passages.[7]

Just what passed between Casas and the Council is not known. Apparently he was pressed to relax his two most stringent rules, those on the penitents' bond. For the Bishop composed an "Addition to the First and

in Xim., I, 470-471. By September 20, 1547, Maldonado had heard about Casas' charges against him (cf. Fabié, app. XIV), and Cerrato was named to replace him in the spring of 1548. Herrera (dec. VIII, lib. V, cap. 5) summarizes the new president's instructions to liberate slaves, support the episcopal authority, and prevent royal judges from engaging in gainful enterprises or expeditions; also, Yucatán was put back under the Mexican audiencia, Montejo was stripped of his Indians, and Campeche was made a crown town.

For Ramírez' appointment and activities in Chiapa, see Rem., II, 192-196. Also cf. *infra*, chapter XVI, note 19, on Casas' later influence and Ramírez in New Spain.

4. Rem., I, 410. Also, on April 22, 1547, the cabildo had sent a power to Guerra, the "encomendero" of Chiapa, to ask for a new bishop. Cf. *ibid.*, II, 160.

5. This document is said to exist among the Muñoz papers, but I have not seen it.

6. See the Prologue of Casas' *Treinta proposiciones* (*infra*, note 10) for the summons, and Rem., II, 165, for the cedula.

7. Icazbalceta, *Docs.*, I, 256.

Fifth Rules," which occupied nearly as much space as the original articles and was filled with supporting quotations from church authorities and canonical writers, mostly in Latin. He also secured approbation for these expanded rules from an impressive group of theologians: four masters, Galindo, Melchor Cano, Miranda, and Mancio, as well as two regents of the College of San Gregorio, Pedro de Sotomayor and Francisco de San Pablo.[8] But neither approbation nor confiscation seems to have satisfied the Council of the Indies.

The attack on his *Confesionario* went much further. It was alleged that, by attacking Spanish wealth obtained from the natives, Bartolomé de las Casas was in fact denying the King's title to the Indies. In short, he was charged with lese majesty.

Was the accusation well founded? Inferentially, Casas did deny the power of the Spanish kings to grant encomiendas. As Motolinía afterwards charged, Casas really ascribed the same guilt to the King as to the encomenderos, because the kings took for themselves the tribute of a great part of the conquered provinces.[9] As for slaves, the King had recently received one-fifth of those taken in the Mixtón War, and these had been branded with the royal brand and then sold. The buyers had a legal title to them, and if any crime had been committed, the King personally was the one on whom to fix it. I am convinced Casas meant to do so, though his plain speaking usually stopped short of the throne, in order to arouse the royal conscience and so prevent further crimes against the Indians. But he said nothing directly, either in the *Confesionario* or in the Addition, about the King's title. His adversaries, however, charged that he had in fact denied it. The same old charge had allegedly been made long ago against the first Dominicans who attacked the encomienda. And the Council now ordered the Bishop to present in writing his views on the rights of the Crown to the Indies.

Casas answered with the two "just title" treatises that he afterwards printed in Seville. The first, *Treinta proposiciones*, was written hastily, with-

---

8. Cf. the Argument of his *Avisos y reglas para los confesores*. Casas made much of this approval in the Twelfth Reply of his rebuttal to Sepúlveda, printed in the tract *Aquí se contienen una disputa* (see *infra*, note 24). León Pinelo, who had access to the Council's papers, says in his *Epítome* that Casas added the "clarification" because of objections to the first and fifth clauses. Cf. *Epítome de la bibliotheca oriental, y occidental, nautica y geográfica*, II (Madrid [1629], 1738), tít. 1.

9. Icazbalceta, *Docs.*, I, 256-257.

out "proof," so it could be forwarded to the Emperor. This was followed later by his longer *Tratado comprobatorio,* citing a mass of authorities.

In *Thirty Propositions,* Casas advanced the radical thesis that the royal title was based solely on Christianizing the natives and all conquests were unlawful. For his premise, he defined the respective powers of the Pope and of the Castilian kings acting under the Bull of Donation. The Pope's power extended over all men as far as their salvation was concerned, but its exercise was different for the heathen. His was the obligation to spread the faith throughout the world and see that the gospel be preached to all who would receive it, and he was bound to choose proper persons for the task. Such were Christian rulers, to whom he could distribute the lands of pagans for the sole purpose of conversion. Some incidental profit might derive from the operation, but the object was not to gain land or revenues at the expense of the natives. Native kings ruled by a just title and should not be deposed or outraged—violations of that law gave rise to injustice and cruelty. Neither pagan idolatry nor sins justified Christians in usurping their lands or seizing their goods, since no Christian tribunal had a right to punish pagans for such offenses so long as they had not opposed the propagation of the faith or refused to receive it.

Proceeding next to the specific case, Casas held that Pope Alexander VI had rightly and appropriately entrusted the conversion of the New World to Ferdinand and Isabella. So the jurisdiction of the kings of Spain over the Indies was lawful. This was something of a *non sequitur:* it had not followed from his premises. He even went on to declare inconsistently that the native rulers were obliged to submit to the protection of the Spanish kings, though he had stated earlier that to compel their obedience was to usurp their rights. Apparently he expected the Indians to receive the faith voluntarily and be baptized, after which they became bound to accept Spanish sovereignty by another title than before. Only love and kindness should be used in converting them (his own plan from *Del único modo*), for armed invasions were naturally resisted and created an obstacle to the propagation of the faith. As to previous tyrannical invasions and the giving of Indians in encomienda, the system was contrary to the counsel of Isabella. Subsequent abuses were due to the ignorance in which the present sovereign was kept by interested parties and by his frequent absences from Spain. In sum, all the armed conquests, whether by Crown officials or individuals, were illegal because they were carried out contrary to natural justice and the orders of the King.[10]

---

10. Llorente, *Obras,* I, 369 *et seq.* See Catalogue, no. 43, for the date of the

A question at once comes to mind. If this was so, then why was the King's jurisdiction legal, as stated in Proposition 17? No wonder Casas was obliged to compose subsequently his massive and almost unreadable *Tratado comprobatorio,* elucidating this tenuous "title."[11]

So both treatises were written under fire, and they were part of a counter-offensive as well. In them Bishop Casas not only defended the controversial basis of his *Confesionario*—the illegality of all conquests—but he issued a challenge to a new and powerful adversary at court.

THE GREAT DISPUTE, TOLD BY THE PRINCIPALS

Casas' formidable new antagonist was Juan Ginés de Sepúlveda, the noted humanist and translator of Aristotle. The pro-conquistador and pro-encomienda faction had at last found an intellectual of stature to argue their case. Encouraged by Cardinal Loaysa, who had opposed the New Laws, Sepúlveda had recently composed a Latin dialogue, *Democrates alter, sive de justis belli causis apud Indos,* upholding "the just causes of war against the Indians" and the consequent enslavement and encomiendas. He was seeking official approval for this work when Bishop Casas returned to court.

A personal clash between the two men was inevitable and the course of their controversy was prolonged and bitter. It started with the Bishop's successful efforts to block the publication of the *Democrates alter,* and culminated in the convocation of a special junta to hear Casas and Sepúlveda debate the legality of Spanish conquests.

The events of this great dispute are told rather fully by the protagonists themselves. Casas printed his version in 1552, as the introduction to a tract on the subject.[12] Sepúlveda retorted with a denunciation of his rival's work, and gave his own side of the story.

Casas began with a scathing account of Sepúlveda's book in "elegant" Latin. The volume, he asserted, was based on information from Spaniards guilty of destroying Indians, designed to justify conquests and encomiendas, and "colored" as a defense of the royal title to the Indies. But though Doctor Sepúlveda importuned the Council of the Indies for a license to print it, this

---

hasty composition of *Treinta proposiciones,* one of the tracts afterwards issued in Seville in 1552.

11. Cf. the Argument of the *Tratado comprobatorio,* which Casas printed in 1553. For a description of this tract, its date of writing, and a possible Latin version, see Catalogue, no. 44.

12. That is, the Argument to *Aquí se contiene una disputa.* This fundamental work is resumed in the next section of this chapter.

was denied him many times. So, through friends at the Emperor's court, he obtained a cedula referring it to the Council of Castile, which was ignorant of American affairs. At this juncture in 1547, Bishop Casas arrived from the Indies and, learning of the book, "opposed it with all the rigor he could": Since the work was mostly theological, the councilors of Castile prudently submitted it to the Universities of Salamanca and Alcalá. "These, after many and very exact disputes, decided that it should not be printed, as being of unsound doctrine." Notwithstanding all this, Doctor Sepúlveda sent his treatise to friends in Rome to print it there—though in the form of an *Apología* to the Bishop of Segovia, who had fraternally "corrected" him on the original book. Learning of this, the Emperor dispatched a cedula to have all the copies seized throughout Castile. And because the said Doctor made a Spanish *Sumario* of his work to circulate through the realm, Bishop Casas composed a Spanish *Apología* of his own, defending the Indians against it.

Sepúlveda's version of this preliminary skirmish was somewhat different and defensive.[13] The Doctor stressed the prior approval of his book and the "interference" of the Council of the Indies, and blamed Casas' supposed intrigues for an unimportant academic censure. (But his own sharp correspondence with one of the censors, Melchor Cano, belies this last.)[14] Nonetheless, Sepúlveda added many interesting details. Referring to the arrival of the three Mexican provincials to get the Law of Inheritance revoked, he told how this provoked much talk at court "over the justice of the conquest of the Indies." And Cardinal Loaysa, "hearing that Doctor Sepúlveda held the conquest to be just and holy and . . . could prove it clearly, exhorted him to write on the subject. . . . So he wrote a book in a few days, and when it had been examined and approved by all who read it

---

13. Fabié, app. XXV (544-545). On this document by Sepúlveda, attacking Casas' tract about their controversy, see *infra*, chapter XVI, second section and note 14.

14. Fabié (I, 214-215) abstracts their correspondence from the 1780 edition of Sepúlveda's *Opera*. Sepúlveda first complained to Cano in a letter from Córdoba, December 22 (?), 1548; on January 25, 1549, Cano acknowledged this and later wrote a long undated reply, to which Sepúlveda answered with a still longer letter from Valladolid, July 15, 1549. They did not specifically discuss the Indians, but rather the theological principles on which Sepúlveda based his *Democrates alter*.

Their interchange indicates that the academic criticism was in 1548; this is borne out by Sepúlveda's correspondence with Martín de Oliva, abstracted in Fabié, I, 219. In August 1548, Oliva wrote Sepúlveda about a discussion of *Democrates alter* at the Dominican provincial chapter in Córdoba. Sepúlveda replied in November that at that same time he had been discussing the matter in Valladolid (?) with famous theologians. See his *Opera*, III, 334 *et seq*.

at court, he presented it to the Royal Council of Castile, asking license to print it. It was given for examination first to Doctor Guevara of the same council, after him to Fray Diego de Vitoria,[15] and then to Doctor Moscoso, because Doctor Sepúlveda so requested, that it might be submitted to many for more authority. It was approved by each of these. While thus ready to be licensed, some persons of authority in the Council of the Indies interfered, alleging that although the book might be very good it was not then advisable to print it. In view of this obstacle, Doctor [Sepúlveda] wrote the Emperor about what had occurred and His Majesty responded very kindly and sent a cedula ordering the Royal Council [of Castile] to have the book well examined, and to license it for printing if there should appear to be no substantial reason for refusing. The book was then submitted anew to Licentiate Francisco Montalvo, who also approved it. At this juncture the Bishop of Chiapa arrived from the Indies. Finding out about it from some who disapproved of printing the book, he caused it to be submitted for examination anew, with the idea of procuring his ends with art and negotiations. It was submitted to Salamanca and Alcalá, where the Bishop, with negotiation, falsehoods, and favor accomplished his object. Thus, those of Alcalá answered that the book should not be printed, but without giving any reason although they had been ordered to do so by the letter from the Royal Council. Those at Salamanca gave the same answer, with reasons which were considered frivolous in the Council and of little weight." Despite his injured tone, however, Sepúlveda had engaged in some elaborate string-pulling himself, writing Prince Philip to have Doctors Escudero and Figueroa intercede with the Emperor against Casas' *Confesionario* and on behalf of his own *Democrates alter*.[16]

But all this was just a prelude to the climactic clash between the two men—their historic debate of 1550-1551 on the legality of conquests. Sepúlveda had merely wanted university theologians summoned to dispute with him before an expanded Council of Castile. But evidently in the latter part of 1550 the Emperor named a full-scale assembly, as recommended by the rival council: jurists from all the other councils, and four theologians, to sit in special session with the Council of the Indies in Valladolid. The attorney of the Castile Council objected and tried to get the three Dominican

---

15. Fray Diego was an elder brother of the famous Fray Francisco de Vitoria. Fray Francisco, the great authority on such questions, was still alive in August 1546, so he might conceivably have had something to do with the original denial of permission to print the book.

16. Sepúlveda to the Prince, September 23, 1549. *DE*, XLI, 130-131.

theologians replaced (as biased), or at least have Doctors Moscoso and Se-púlveda added to the judges, but in vain. It was only agreed that Sepúlveda should be heard as well as Casas.

Doctor Sepúlveda accordingly appeared at the first session of the judges and summarized the main points of his *Democrates alter*. Then, for five or six days running, Bishop Casas read all or most of his *Apología*. Afterwards one of the judges, Fray Domingo de Soto, was commissioned to prepare a summary. Obtaining a copy thereof, Sepúlveda wrote a twelve-point rebuttal, to which the Bishop replied with twelve answers. The fore-going is related by both men, and Sepúlveda adds a few particulars about the reconvening of the judges. He states that when he handed in his re-buttal it was decreed that the opinions be rendered in some months, which turned out to be six or seven; and when the judges met again, he learned of the Bishop's reply and appeared before them to dispute with the friars about the papal bulls.

In view of this sequence of events, there is ample authority that the Valladolid meeting was held in 1550-1551. Casas says the judges were con-voked in 1550; and in October 1551, Sepulveda wrote to his friend Martín de Oliva about what had occurred in his controversy with Casas in Valladolid, where he had found an eloquent defender in the Franciscan Bernardino de Arévalo.[17] Considering the delay in reconvening, it seems likely that the meeting did not conclude till late 1551, and that the later documents were presented in that year.

We are somewhat at a loss to understand the real object of this meeting. By now the conquest of the Indies was a *fait accompli;* no one could have sanctioned abandoning those lands, even had all the conquests been declared unjust. The only real question of importance was how the Indians were to be governed. Why then was the junta called?

I think it probable that Casas' *Confesionario* and his subsequent defense of it was the direct cause of the Valladolid convocation. The Emperor's conscience might have troubled him, more especially because Casas had charged him, by implication to be sure, with abuse of a title granted for the conversion of the natives. For though Casas was always careful not to hold the Emperor responsible for the actions of his subjects, declaring instead that they and chiefly the Council of the Indies were the criminals, yet the inference was plain. The Emperor had appointed these people, and if they were not proper agents he was ultimately to blame. In his relations with

---

17. Fabié, I, 219.

Casas, I believe, Charles was uncomfortable. So perhaps the Emperor was troubled enough by the current controversy over conquests to summon a junta to resolve it.

What did this junta finally decide? Before seeking an answer, let us follow the example of the judges and pause to consider the respective positions of Casas and Sepúlveda.

BOTH ARGUMENTS AND THEIR ORIGINS

Both arguments can be reviewed conveniently in the official text of the Valladolid debate. Under the title *Aquí se contiene una disputa,* Casas printed this intact the following year: namely, Soto's summary of the oral sessions, and the two written rebuttals.[18] In addition, the treatises themselves are available; Sepúlveda's *Democrates alter* has been published in modern times, and the manuscript of Casas' *Apología* has been found in the Bibliothèque Nationale in Paris and there is now a photostat in the Library of Congress.[19] But it does not seem profitable to labor through them, for the contenders approved the summary, and everything else they had to say of consequence was doubtless included in their further answers to each other. So we shall merely extract the opposing views from the printed tract and then explore their origins.

Sepúlveda, giving the gist of his treatise, justified the conquest by four main reasons: First, the gravity of the sins of the Indians, especially idolatory and the sin against nature; second, the rudeness of the natives, which made it necessary for them to serve more refined persons such as the Spaniards; third, the goal of spreading the faith, which was made easier by their previous subjugation; and fourth, the protection of the weaker ones among the Indians, who were liable to human sacrifice to false gods and the practice of cannibalism.

To these four points the Bishop of Chiapa replied in this wise: First,

---

18. See Catalogue, no. 48, for a description of this official resumé; Fray Domingo de Soto, who made the abstract, was a Dominican and generally held Casas' views on the subject. Also cf. *infra,* chapter XVI, section on "Eight famous tracts—and the Inquisition" for repercussions to the inclusion of *Aquí se contiene una disputa* in Casas' publications of 1552-1553.

19. See Catalogue, no. 45, for a discussion of the known and missing texts of Casas' *Apología,* and the date of its composition. This book should not be confounded with the *Apologética historia,* as I fear Mendieta did in describing Casas' manuscript works in the Dominican convent in Mexico. Sepúlveda's treatise, first printed in the *Boletín de la Real Academia,* XXI (1892), 257-369, was reprinted in Mexico in 1941.

Casas showed from Scripture that though war was commanded by God against certain nations, this was not against idolators in general, but only against the Canaanites and other tribes; second, he denied the rudeness of the Indians' nature and brought up plenty of evidence to prove his statement; third, he insisted that peaceful conversion was the best means, adducing his own success and that of the Dominicans in the Land of War; fourth, he insisted: "Of two evils, choose the least." Human sacrifices were a lesser evil than indiscriminate warfare.

In elaborating these answers, Casas had little difficulty with the first three, but he had the temerity of attempting to defend human sacrifice, arguing (truly enough) that such offerings were the best that the worshippers possessed. In sum, Casas maintained, Sepúlveda founded the rights of the kings of Spain to the Indies upon the Spaniards' superiority at arms. This placed the King in the position of a tyrant whereas his rights really rested "on the extension of the gospel and the good government of the natives."

Such were the opposing theses, and it is interesting to trace their genesis. Casas alleged that his rival had been "informed" by conquistadors. As a matter of fact, in Sepúlveda's points we can easily trace the two historic justifications of the conquest-and-encomienda party—the "servile nature" and "vicious sins" arguments.

In the early disquisitions on the rights of the Indians, the principle advanced to support the encomienda was that the natives were incapable of self-government and needed tutors, namely the Spaniards. Of course, the Indians of the islands were humble, simple tribes that worked no more than necessary to supply food for their own subsistence. The Spaniards wanted them to labor for foreign masters in mines and fields, and this the Indians did more or less willingly. If idolatry existed among the islanders, it was confined to worshipping some small figure like those of the Christian saints; there was no trace of human sacrifice or cannibalism, and only the mainland Caribs were accused of eating human flesh. So "rudeness" of native customs was the chief justification for imposing forced labor on the Indians in the Antilles—the theory that they were "siervos a natura."

The subsequent discovery of New Spain, and the Spaniards' first experience with a civilization comparable in many ways to their own, required a different justification for its subjugation. The natives encountered by Grijalva and Cortés could certainly not be called animals or brutes. These Indians, however maintained temples with images of gods and sacrificed human beings to them. A new excuse for conquest was thereupon offered—native idolatry and sinfulness.

Its first use occurs in an official letter from San Juan in July 1519. After pointing out these evil customs, the town councilors proposed that "Your Majesties may . . . give this account as true to our very Holy Father so that . . . His Holiness may . . . allow the wicked and rebellious, after being first admonished, to be punished and chastised as enemies of our holy Catholic faith. This will . . . put a fear in those who may be recalcitrant in receiving knowledge of the truth, and thereby the great evils they practice in the service of their devil may be avoided." The report then proceeded from insult to injury by asserting that all the natives were sodomites.[20] As a matter of fact, sodomy did not exist in New Spain, and when this letter was written Cortés and his men had seen only a few cases of alleged sacrifice and attributed the practices to all the natives of the country. In 1521, Peter Martyr published similar stories, adding the one on the sacrificial rite of eating part of the victim. Thus, a new excuse for murdering, enslaving, and robbing the natives at once supplanted the former animal, natural-slave theory.

It was on these dubious old grounds that Sepúlveda based his theory that conquests were just. So Casas was repeatedly able to tax him with misinformation. But in their discussion, the Bishop found himself in deep difficulties of his own.

Allegedly, Casas had maintained that the kings of Castile had no legitimate rights in the New World, since it was gained by conquest. Sepúlveda charged him with this, and Casas tried to exculpate himself. The wars were unjust and could not establish a solid sovereignty, but this did not contradict the King's rightful possession of the conquered provinces for their conversion. That title was based on the Bull of Donation, and the prior right of those who discovered countries to Christianize them, and the further fact that the Indians, having received the faith, willingly recognized the Spanish king. "The union of all these circumstances is sufficient to establish . . . the veritable and just title of the kings of Castile and León over the universal principality of the Indies."[21]

As this was an extension of his own "peaceful conversion" doctrine, Casas readily applied it to missionary matters. He explained Fray Luis Cáncer's unfortunate death, adduced the entire Verapaz experience, attacked the notion of papal authorization for initial bloody warfare as an aid to missionaries. And he was indignant at the suggestion of conquest to recover the

---

20. Pascual de Gayangos, ed., *Cartas y relaciones de Hernán Cortés* (Paris, 1866), 26-27.

21. Llorente, *Obras*, I, 479-480.

cost of missions. In view of the vast treasures already received from the Indies, the monarchs were bound to fulfill such duties at their own expense.

But the rub came in trying to derive a solid juridical title from this doctrine. If, as he insisted in his writings, all past conquests were a mortal sin and could not establish legitimate sovereignty to the Indies, then all Spanish acts based on the conquest were on a shaky footing. So he now felt obliged to coin a new right on which to base the Spanish title: "Sovereignty of protection."[22]

That term has a familiar sound, but I doubt if Casas sensed that it was a very limited right. The subjects might readily ask: "Protection from whom?" On his side, Sepúlveda had said that the Indian nations needed protection from each other; this proposition Casas stoutly denied, maintaining that the Indians were peaceable. Then from whom were they to be protected? From the English? From the French? Those were the only two nations who, before 1550, had been troubling the Spaniards in the Indies.

Possibly Casas obtained this idea from Fray Francisco de Vitoria's "relectio" *De Indis*. In that academic lecture, the Salamanca theologian had raised the contingency of a rush of foreigners to the New World that might hinder one another, develop quarrels to the destruction of the faith, and impede the conversion of the natives. But Vitoria did not come right out and say that preservation of Spain's rule in America demanded not only evangelization but "protection" of the natives from marauding nations. So perhaps Casas was only using a catch phrase to enable him to get out of a tight spot: the predicament of his own "conversion first" doctrine, that he had enunciated long before Vitoria lectured on the Indies.[23]

Did he succeed? There is some doubt about the outcome of the Valladolid meeting, Casas claiming that the judges agreed with him in 1550,

---

22. See Llorente, *Obras*, I, 481-482 et seq.—Casas' rebuttal to Sepúlveda, comprising his own final résumé of his position in this period.

23. Cf. Vitoria's *De Indis* (Ernest Nys, ed., Washington, 1917), 157. The whole question of Casas' personal and ideological relations with Vitoria is interesting though not fruitful. When Casas returned to Spain in 1540, Vitoria was still lecturing at Salamanca and Fray Bartolomé just might have heard him. But in Casas' writings, I have discovered only a couple of brief citations of Vitoria as a "most learned master" (in *Aquí se continene una disputa* and the *Tratado comprobatorio*). Of course there was a general correspondence between their ideas on the right of conquest by the kings of Spain and the authority of the Pope in the matter. But I find that members of the Dominican Order, who were the most active in denouncing Spanish practices in the Indies, held similar views. Vitoria's two great pronouncements—that the Emperor is not lord of the world nor the Pope the civil or temporal lord of it—harked

Sepúlveda asserting that the jurists of the commission sided with him in 1551 when a number of the theologians were absent.[24] No formal decision seems to have been made, and none could have been. The assembly could hardly annul the previous conquest of the Indies. At the same time, if the anti-reform party had hoped to obtain via Sepúlveda a revocation of the New Laws on conquests and slavery, they were frustrated. These laws all remained in effect, thanks to Casas' disputation; and there is further evidence he may also have expanded his anti-slavery tract at this time.[25]

So Bartolomé de las Casas did not win the great debate with Sepúlveda in any formal sense. But by instigating it, he regained the offensive once more, buttressing the reform laws and re-establishing himself as the outstanding defender of the American Indians.

---

back to Thomistic principles. And I believe that Casas imbibed such principles during his early years as a friar in Española, since his first formal mention of "restitution," which implies illegal possession or title, is in his 1531 memorial from the Puerto de Plata monastery. As to the possibility of some Erasmist as well as mediaeval influence in his and Vitoria's political concepts, see *infra,* chapter XVIII, note 34.

24. Probably both statements are correct. Fray Francisco de Vitoria had generally endorsed a doctrine similar to Casas', viz., that the King had no good title based on the conquest. Under his influence the Salamanca theologians seem to have been mostly upholders of this opinion. Thus, in his rebuttal Casas pointed out that they had approved his *Confesionario* but rejected Sepúlveda's *Democrates alter.* On the other hand the jurists, who comprised the various bodies having the government of the Indies in their hands, took the realistic view; whatever the basis of the King's title, Spanish interests in the New World could not be disturbed as this would mean enormous loss of royal revenue. No doubt because of this consideration, Vitoria evidently could see no prospect of putting his doctrine into effect. Nor did Casas himself advocate any immediate execution of his like doctrine, in disregard of the King's rents.

25. I have reached the conclusion that Casas' *Tratado sobre los indios esclavos,* in its printed form, is a rewriting in this period of the original anti-slavery memorial that he left with the Consejo in 1544. (See Catalogue, no. 23.) From start to finish the entire tract reads like a defense of his conduct as bishop and a plea against further modification of the reform ordinances. It also contains a number of allusions, such as one to President Cerrato in Central America, that date it here. Finally, the "Corolarium tertium," with its Latin heading and commentary on the friars' junta of 1546, reads like a later addition to the first two corrollaries with their direct statements of royal and episcopal duties. Unlike the *Brevissima* and the *Confesionario,* to which he only made additions, Casas appears to have rewritten this memorial completely.

A VIGOROUS RETIREMENT

CASAS RESIGNS AND ARRANGES HIS AFFAIRS

From the great debate till the end of his life, the aging Casas occupied at last the post he had sought since the time of his conversion—universal procurator of the Indians at the Spanish court.

No such official title was accorded him now, but none was needed. He became the government's chief adviser on Indian problems, the sponsor extraordinary of Dominican missions in America, the focal point and representative for native grievances and reform efforts from all over the New World. To fill this final role—and I think it was his true one—the 77-year-old Fray Bartolomé had first to arrange his own affairs.

Almost coincidentally with the convocation of the Valladolid junta, Casas had moved to rid himself of his onerous duties as Bishop of Chiapa. He resigned his bishopric no later than the summer of 1550. This seems certain, though his biographers have been confused about the date since he occasionally signed his name as bishop long afterward. But on September 11 of that year, the Emperor wrote from Augusta in Germany to Diego Hurtado de Mendoza, his ambassador at Rome, forwarding Casas' resignation and the nomination of Tomás de Casillas as the new bishop.[1]

The following year, retired Bishop Casas made arrangements to reside permanently in the Dominican College of San Gregorio at Valladolid. On July 21, 1551, he executed a contract with the prior, whereby he exchanged part of his episcopal pension for a base of operations at court.

The terms were interesting. On its side, the monastery agreed to keep Casas and his companion Ladrada for their lives, furnish them food and drink and clothing, and all necessities of human life in conformity with the

---

1. Fabié, app. XVII; see Catalogue, no. 47.

Bishop's age and needs. Further, the college had to give Casas three new cells for life and bury him in the sacristy, muster in a servant of his, and assign the Bishop first place in the left choir, even ahead of the prior. No obligation rested on him; he and Ladrada could come and go as they pleased, to the town or outside it, without asking a license, and if Casas had to travel or go away from the monastery, he would receive provisions for his journey.

For his part, Casas gave the college four hundred ducats in cash and sixteen hundred ducats in royal drafts on the officials in Mexico, along with 150,000 maravedis of annual pension received from the Crown. He also made donation to the college of all the books and writings he then had, under condition that they remain always in the house and not be sold or given away, but he reserved the use of them for life and stipulated that he could carry them with him for any extended absence.[2]

Dávila Padilla did not know of this transaction, but in his life of Casas, inserted in his *Historia de la fundación y discurso de la provincia de Santiago de México,* he supplied the detail that living in the monastery so independently was contrary to the rules of the Order and had to be ratified by the Pope.[3] Whether or not this was so, it was an unusual contract and most convenient for the retired Bishop.

Equally thorough were Casas' financial provisions for his living and his future court activities. He brought an ample endowment to San Gregorio; probably it was with this money that the college afterwards founded the eighteen scholarships which Remesal refers to as having been left by Casas.[4] And he later took steps to have his pension increased; it was raised to 200,000 maravedis in 1555 and to 350,000 in 1563, and orders were also given for him to be lodged at royal expense when the court was elsewhere.[5]

In addition, though surrendering the mitre, Bishop Casas retained a unique status in his own Order—"father of all the Indies," Remesal calls him.

---

2. From the Archivo de Protocolos de Valladolid, printed in the *Revista de Indias,* año I (1940), no. 2. Casas had not completely abandoned all thought of returning to America. For one clause specified that should he go to the Indies and die there, the College might sell his books and papers or bring them back to the house, etc.

3. See Dávila Padilla, lib. I, cap. 103, where he implies Casas had received the papal permission.

4. Rem., II, 470. Remesal says that at the annual St. Martin's day requiem mass for Casas, the scholarship students chanted the responses with lit tapers in their hands.

5. Quintana, *Bartolomé de las Casas,* 429, note 1, summarizes the pension increases, no doubt from Muñoz extracts. The May 1, 1555, cedula ordered payment

And it is obvious that he had powers of attorney, general or special, from the Dominicans in New Spain and in Guatemala at this period. For even as he made plans for his own future, he resumed his activities as procurator-at-large for the Central American missions.

During 1551 and 1552, the venerable Fray Bartolomé traveled throughout Spain, obtaining support from the Crown and the Order and personally recruiting and dispatching friars to the New World. On May 16, 1551, he attended the general chapter of the Dominicans at San Esteban de Salamanca. There Casas presented royal dispatches for sending friars to America, and at his solicitation a Dominican province was set up for Guatemala and Chiapa and given the name of San Vicente.[6] Also at his request, the Emperor that year granted funds to purchase ornaments, books, and so forth, for the churches and convents of the Order in Chiapa.[7] Apparently still in 1551, Casas toured Castile and parts of Andalusia, seeking workers for the Chiapa and Guatemala missions. By 1552 he had assembled some thirty or so in Seville, though after an extraordinary delay and expense only six of these finally sailed to America.

But all this while Casas had been preparing his main work, and now he seized this very delay to launch it. He himself describes the circumstances in a most interesting letter of October 25 to the Council. Altogether five or six thousand people had been waiting for the fleet to leave, some for months, as seventy-three or seventy-four ships were tied up. He himself had come to San Lúcar thirty-five days previous and had spent seven hundred ducats since reaching Seville in January.[8] Frustrating as this had been, the elderly retired Bishop had spent his time and money in the congested city to good avail. For there—his bishopric resigned, his affairs in order, his mis-

---

as usual in America, but in 1560 this was made payable in the House of Trade at Seville, and in 1563 in the list of court and council salaries.

In 1560, Casas was in Toledo, and subsequently he moved with the court to Madrid. See the letter to him that year at Toledo, *DII*, VII, 245-246; also Philip's order of December 14, to furnish him lodgings there or wherever else he might go, Fabié, app. XVIII, 1st item.

6. Rem., II, 282. See also Casas' letter to the Emperor about the dispatches, *DII*, X, 87-88; Catalogue, no. 53.

7. Rem., II, 305-306. These objects reached Santiago in 1552, and were distributed in Chiapa and Verapaz.

8. Fabié, app. XVI; Catalogue, no. 54. On the missionaries, see Rem., II, 339-340, where the six friars are named. They did not arrive till 1553, so Remesal infers the recruiting took place in 1552. But Casas' letter indicates he was in Seville a good part of that year, and Remesal himself previously refers to "six friars" as 1551 recruits.

sionaries assembling—Bartolomé de las Casas began his supreme final role
with the most daring act of his career.

EIGHT FAMOUS TRACTS—AND THE INQUISITION

In Seville during 1552-1553, while he was waiting for the fleet to sail,
the "former Bishop of Chiapa" printed the eight tracts in defense of the
Indians that would make his name famous (or notorious) to the ends of the
earth.

Before we enumerate these celebrated imprints, we may well inquire
why Casas published them at this precise juncture. The answer is suggested by the tracts themselves. In the first place, they were very carefully
printed in black-letter type, during a period that lasted nearly six months;
the first came off the press of Jacome Cromberger on August 17, 1552; the
rest were done by Sebastián Trugillo, one after another, the last on January
8, 1553.[9] Several of them were specifically dedicated or addressed to Prince
Philip, with the avowed purpose of informing him. The group as a whole
represented Casas' major polemical writings of the previous ten years, in
handy condensed form. And he issued them just when he was arranging
to spend his remaining days at court. So it seems clear to me that he deliberately chose this most effective way to summarize and consolidate all his
past arguments, and lay a foundation for his future advocacy of Indian rights
with the new administration.

Apparently to that end, Batrolomé de las Casas published the following,
each (save the Latin one) with an Argument explaining how he came
to write it. From his tremendous battle for the New Laws, he printed two
treatises: a revised version of his *Brevissima relación* on the extermination
of the Indians, with some later material added;[10] and *Entre los remedios*, a
key selection from his "remedies"—the twenty reasons for abolishing the
encomienda. From his campaign for the Amendment, he chose the powerful
Tratado sobre los indios que se han hecho esclavos. Out of his stormy tenure

---

9. Both were well-known printers. All the tracts are cuarto, without foliation
but with signatures, and all have separate title-pages, except the *Principia quedam*,
which has only a caption title. See Catalogue, nos. 18, 19, 23, 41, 43, 44, 48, and 49,
for full titles, dates of writing, and differences between the works as originally presented and as afterwards printed.

10. One addition was included in the tract proper, the other was issued as a
supplement with the title, *Lo que se sigue es un pedaço de una carta*. This is often
considered a separate publication, but I have included it in my article on the *Brevissima,* Catalogue, no. 18.

as Bishop of Chiapa came the sensational *Avisos y reglas para los confesores,* and the two "just title" treatises defending it—the brief *Treinta proposiciones* and the massive *Tratado comprobatorio.* From the great debate with Sepúlveda, he elected to print the official abridged text under the title *Aquí se contiene una disputa.* Related to this was a curious Latin work, which we shall examine later: the short *Principia quedam,* or statement of principles to be followed in [similar] disputations in order to "reveal and defend the rights of the Indians."[11]

Casas' boldness in printing these eight tracts, without any licenses, did not go unchallenged. For the former Bishop of Chiapa was actually denounced to the Inquisition, which prevented the publication of a ninth tract. Little is known of this episode and it has been ignored by his biographers. But the trouble may have been instigated by his rival Sepúlveda, since it concerned two works that were offshoots of their disputation yet apparently had not been submitted to the Council. Attention has already been called to Casas' *Principia quedam;* this was an abridgement of a longer Latin treatise, the *Erudita et elegans explicatio,* that was evidently the one suppressed.

Our only source for the incident is Juan Antonio Llorente, who spent some two years from 1811 to 1813 inspecting and digesting the archives of the Spanish Inquisition after the suppression of that body. In his *Histoire critique de L'Inquisition d'Espagne,* Llorente gives the following item in his list of persons denounced:

> Casas, D. Fray Bartolomé de las, Dominican, Bishop of Chiapa . . . resigning it to reside in Spain. Defending the rights of the American Indians he wrote many very excellent books in one of which he tries to prove that the kings had no power to dispose of the persons and liberty of their subjects, to make them vassals of another lord, by way of fiefs, encomienda, or in any other way.
>
> This work and its author were denounced to the Council of the Inquisition as contrary to the doctrine of Saint Peter and Saint Paul about the subjection of serfs and vassals to their lords and kings. The author suffered great vexation because of the threats which reached his notice; but the Council did not officially

---

11. See Catalogue, no. 49. Despite its title, this short tract deals with native rights only indirectly, and in its final corollary: The Indians are to be ruled for their own good, and whatever the Spanish King does or decrees for them must be for their universal spiritual and temporal welfare. At the end, Casas says these *Principia* were approved by Fray Pedro de Contreras and Master Fray Vicente Carrillo, Rector [of the College of San Gregorio].

intimate to him anything beyond the delivery of his work which was seized in manuscript in 1552. Afterwards it was printed . . . outside of Spain . . .[12]

So far as we know, Casas' *Erudita et elegans explicatio* was first printed posthumously in 1571, when a German named Griestetter, who had been in Spain for five years with the imperial ambassador Adam von Didrichstein, published it in Frankfurt on the Main.[13] The contents of this treatise, as well as its summary, exactly agree with Llorente's description. These works are really dissertations on the rights of kings. The whole basis of Casas' argument is that kings, although sovereign, have no illimitable power; they are the servants of nations, and the people make kings, who must rule for their good. From this general doctrine, Casas goes on to attack the grants of fiefs, denying the royal right to alienate territory or give certain fiefs without the consent of the feudatory. Therefore—this was obviously what he was driving at—encomiendas were tyrannical and the King must order restitution of unjustly acquired Spanish property in the Indies.

This was a virtual denial of the King's authority to grant encomiendas, and Casas rested it on a sweeping doctrine of popular rights. Under the "natural rights of man," he asserted, all men and their affairs are free and to be ruled only for their own benefit; royal ordinances are null when contrary to the interests of the people; and the king is the administrator of the goods of the state for the public welfare and is without power to dispose arbitrarily of personal goods or communal lands or native kingdoms.

Such ideas sound like those enunciated in the eighteenth century by Jean Jacques Rousseau, who had probably never heard of Casas or read his treatise—though we cannot be sure, since several editions had been published, mostly at places on the Rhine. Anyway, Casas took pains to couch

---

12. Llorente, *Historie de l'Inquisition* (Paris, 1817), II, 434, conformed by me to the Spanish text. This work first appeared in France in the years 1817-1818, in a supervised French translation by Alexis Pellier; Llorente's original, *Historia crítica de la Inquisición de España*, was printed in Madrid in 1822 in ten small volumes. At the crucial point, the French version goes farther: Casas "was much grieved when he learned that it was intended to prosecute him." Though valuable, Llorente's item contains a typical inaccuracy, viz., a statement that Casas was afterwards Bishop of Cuzco.

13. Llorente, *Obras*, II, 49-111; for the full title of this work in its first printing, see Catalogue, no. 50. The tract is referred to nowadays by the opening words "Learned and elegant explanation," added by the original editor, though later editions were more clearly titled, e.g., *Quaestio de imperatoria potestate*. Fabié (I, 322-324) itemizes the descriptive headings of articles 1-25; articles 26-37 refute the objections that might be raised to this doctrine.

his bold *Principia* in Latin, showing he did not intend them to be circulated to the general public but only to the privileged classes who understood that language. Even so, it was this doctrine of his that was denounced to the Inquisition.

Was Sepúlveda the accuser? I infer so from a curious writing first printed by Fabié: "Reckless, troublemaking, and heretical propositions, noted by Doctor Sepúlveda in the book . . . which Fray Bartolomé de las Casas, former Bishop of Chiapa, had printed 'without license' in Seville, the year of 1552." In this, Sepúlveda is not attacking the *Principia quedam*, but angrily refuting Casas' tract on the great disputation, particularly the Bishop's final rebuttal. The charge, however, is identical: heresy and lese majesty, and Sepúlveda quotes both Saint Peter and Saint Paul as having uttered opinions entirely contrary to those of Casas. Further, this document is followed by a "Declaración" in which Sepúlveda itemizes Casas' errors with folio references—it may well be an actual denunciation.[14]

So I think Casas was probably denounced to the Inquisition either by Sepúlveda himself or by someone who saw this censure circulated in manuscript. Charges may have been made first against *Aquí se contiene una disputa*. And then, possibly, Sepúlveda made similar charges against Casas' Latin works, indignantly regarding them as further rebuttals to the great disputation. There is a lost document which if found might throw some light on this matter. A holograph letter from Casas to Sepúlveda figured in the Fischer sale of 1869, but all my efforts to trace it have been unavailing.[15] So I can only wonder if it was his final answer to these charges.[16]

---

14. Fabié, app. XXV. N.B. This document is a later copy in three parts, which are out of order. First chronologically comes Sepúlveda's "Proposiciones temerarias" (543-559). After this should be read Sepúlveda's itemized "Declaración" (567-569). The intervening material (560-566) has no heading, but internal evidence proves it is a later summary dated October 8, 1571, of the "heresies" itemized by Sepúlveda, the "outs" in Casas' writings, and the compiler's opinion which exonerates Casas but says that Sepúlveda's doctrine was more popular.

15. See Catalogue, no. 51, for this intriguing item, no. 2953 in the sale. Also unknown today is a Latin dialogue by Casas, similar in form and subject to *Democrates alter*. Catalogue, no. 52.

16. A few years later, in March 1557, Sepúlveda paid a visit to the Emperor at Yuste. See Walter Stirling, *The Cloister Life of the Emperor Charles V*, Boston, 1853. According to Stirling, Sepúlveda was then sixty and had not seen Charles for eighteen years; the two are said to have conversed about Sepúlveda's history of the Emperor's reign. (He had been appointed official chronicler on April 15, 1536.) In view of Sepúlveda's animosity to Casas, it seems possible that he may have discussed their controversy with Charles. The possibility is heightened by the date of their

In any event, no process was instituted against Casas. And though the printing of his ninth tract was blocked, nothing was done about the others.[17] So he at once proceeded to circulate them and raised a storm on both sides of the Atlantic. In later centuries it was the controversial *Brevissima relación* that made him chiefly known to the world. But at the time, his *Confesionario* made more stir, particularly in the Indies, though all eight were received with angry outcries. Probably the most virulent contemporary attack on him —Motolinía's famous letter of 1555 to the Emperor—was provoked by the arrival of these eight small volumes in New Spain.[18] Motolinía was especially indignant over Fray Bartolomé's abandoning his bishopric, and demanded that he be shut up in a monastery. All this outcry only shows how well the sensational tactic had succeeded: Bartolomé de las Casas' fearless printed tracts enabled him to begin his work at court as the acknowledged spokesman of the Indians.

PETITIONER AND CORRESPONDENT

From then on the former Bishop of Chiapa lived at Valladolid, the usual seat of the government, and served as its chief American adviser. In a few years he became a power in the affairs of the Indies, second only, I believe, to the Emperor himself. With few exceptions, Casas was able to persuade Charles to grant his requests. Of course, this is only an inference

---

meetings. For Casas' famous letter of 1555 to Carranza de Miranda had no doubt reached Philip, for whom it was intended, and may well have been sent on to Charles, as it dealt with the contemplated sale of the reversionary rights to encomiendas in the Indies.

17. Owing to the circumstances of its posthumous printing, the authorship of Casas' ninth tract has been denied by some writers. To me its authenticity is beyond question. In addition to ample external evidence, i.e., Llorente's description and Didrichstein's stay in Spain, the treatise itself expands a position Casas had long maintained. Specifically, it controverts the views of Hostiensis. This mediaeval writer justified wars against infidels by claiming that Christ's coming produced a curious juridical effect: those who did not recognize Him or embrace His doctrine lost the ownership of their goods to the faithful Christians. Casas in his other writings—the *Historia,* the just title treatises, the *Apología* against Sepúlveda—frequently refers to and refutes the "doctrine of Hostiensis." This appears to be confirming internal evidence that Casas was indeed the author of the posthumous tract.

18. Writing on January 2, 1555, Motolinía says these tracts had just reached New Spain in the last fleet of merchant ships. He describes Casas' resigning his see as "apostasy from the very high and perfect state of episcopacy," and thinks the King should send him back to America for two or three years to work with the Indians. Cf. Icazbalceta, *Docs.,* I, 256, 260-261.

from the course of events, but we have at least one contemporary authority who illustrates my ideas.

Doctor Juan Vásquez de Arce, in a memorial to the King on October 10, 1559, paints an amazing picture of Casas' ascendancy over the Council of the Indies.[19] Describing Fray Bartolomé and his zeal for improving the treatment of the Indians, he asserts that Casas was most efficient in persuasion and so influential in the Council that he practically dictated its orders. Vásquez, who became a member of the Council himself in 1555, makes further remarkable statements. He says that Casas secured appointments of his adherents to the Council, and had judicial investigations made of those with contrary opinions. Along this same line, Dávila Padilla tells us that the Emperor gave orders that Casas should have two hours during each session of the Council of the Indies to present whatever business he had on hand.[20]

What was this day-to-day business? Casas must have presented a host of petitions, pleas, and recommendations, though we have only a sampling of them from the decade after his retirement. Thus, apart from his general work as missions procurator, he began promptly to do special court errands for Dominicans in the Indies. For instance, a power from Fray Domingo de Santa María, dated Puebla [Mexico], July 6, 1549, urges him to appear before the Council and beg for sustenance and aid in building convents.[21]

In addition, Casas also represented a number of specific Indian communities and caciques. In 1556, for instance, the principal Indians of Mexico City asked Prince Philip to appoint Casas as their official protector.[22] One of his most intriguing individual cases was that of Don Francisco Tenamaztle, a baptized Christian and chief of the Indians of Nochistlán. This chief Tenamaztle reached Spain around 1553 and went to see the former Bishop of Chiapa, who put his story and his request for freedom in a petition to the Council: Tenamaztle had been hidden in the mountains for nine years after the Mixtón War. He then went to the Bishop of New Galicia, who took him to Mexico City; but when this bishop died a year

---

19. *DII*, IV, 141-146. Specifically, Vásquez claimed that Diego Ramírez had been appointed inspector of Indian towns and tribute in New Spain, through Casas' influence as he was Casas' relative; and that the King had lost 100,000 pesos of revenue through Ramírez' reassessments. This is incorrect, as Ramírez was actually a relative of the noted Bishop Sebastián Ramírez de Fuenleal. But Vásquez' hostility makes his testimony on Casas' influence even more impressive.

20. Cf. Dávila Padilla, 324-325.

21. *DII*, VII, 236-238.

22. *Epis. de Nueva España*, VIII, no. 439, page 66, dated May 2.

later, the new viceroy, Luis de Velasco, imprisoned the Indian and sent him to Veracruz and thence to Spain. All this was told in typical Casas style, accompanied by a proposal characteristic of Fray Bartolomé. The chief offered to go and fetch some tribes hidden in the mountains—"all these I offer to bring in without lances and swords if you give me a bishop and a certain number of friars to go with me." Tenamaztle promised to do this if the Council would give him an agreement and royal provision that the Indians thus brought in should be placed under the Crown and never given in encomienda.[23] It would be interesting to know what action the Council took.

But perhaps Casas' most constant concern, during this decade of petitions, was the matter of tribute levied on Indian towns. Apparently as early as 1549, even before he resigned his see, he presented a memorial to the Council regarding a Guatemalan agent who had come to court to get some of President Cerrato's new decrees annulled. Bishop Casas scorched the encomenderos of Guatemala—nine-tenths of the natives had perished under their oppression, and these Spaniards should be removed from the province and replaced by others. He was especially indignant over the suggestion that Bishop Marroquín be given the task of reassessing the tributes, since that prelate's relatives held many Indians and the King's slave brand was in Marroquín's possession.[24]

Somewhat later on, Fray Bartolomé was equally concerned about oppressive tributes in Mexico. In an undated petition, written after his resignation, he protested the situation and said that the loudest complaints came from the two towns of Huejotzingo and Tepeaca. From internal and external evidence, this document was probably presented in late 1559, or in the first half of 1560.[25]

Later still, possibly about 1562 or 1563, Casas wrote a memorial protesting the tributes in both Mexico and Central America. It seems that the Guatemala audiencia had revoked the reasonable reductions made by Judge Alonso de Zorita. Thus, though a given town had lost fifteen hundred of its inhabitants in the past decade, its tribute assessment remained unchanged. A similar state of affairs, Casas declared, also existed in New Spain. So he repeated the request for protectors, that is to say judges, to reside in each

23. Hanke, "Festón de Docs.," *Revista Cubana*, XVI, 196-203. For a detailed summary, the date of this petition, and Casas' role in it, see Catalogue, no. 56.

24. *DII*, VII, 167-172; see Catalogue, no. 46, for the date.

25. Icazbalceta, *Docs.*, II, 228-230. See Catalogue, no. 62, for a summary of this document, and the circumstances of the period in which it was presented.

Spanish town to see that the Indians received justice. Further, he assailed a new cruel oppression of the natives in Guatemala and Mexico and elsewhere—the hiring-out system. This was a muster of Indians who were then leased out to work, at that time largely in the mines; it was operated along the same principle as the mita, or periodic draft of native laborers, in Potosí. Casas advocated instead a system of bargaining between the Indians and the Spaniards who wished to hire them. He particularly complained of the outrages against the Indians committed by a Guatemalan judge named Doctor Mexía, who was also persecuting the Dominicans to such a point that they were on the verge of abandoning the province. He asked that the man be suspended forthwith, and then submitted to an investigation.[26]

But all these memorials and petitions show us only one aspect of Casas' day-to-day activities. Behind his appearances before the Council lay a vast amount of work carried on in the privacy of his cell at the College of San Gregorio. For all through this period he was the recipient of a voluminous correspondence directed to "the former Bishop of Chiapa, at court."

"Every day," he wrote, "I receive a thousand testimonies and clamors from all the Indies!" They included "a great number of letters from many different friars of the three [mendicant] Orders and many other persons . . . advising me of the evils and aggressions and injustices which our Spaniards . . . still perpetrate against the natives of those countries . . . and exhorting me to endeavor to secure relief before the King and his Council." Only a limited number of these communications have survived, though perhaps some are still unpublished in the Archives of the Indies. The available ones range from long reports of oppression, to brief notes from old friends and co-workers, to requests for help from American officials and even old conquistadors.[27]

These last are particularly revealing. For instance, we have a letter of recommendation for an illegitimate son of Adelantado Pedro de Alvarado, who was coming to see Casas at court. This young Pedro, no doubt Luisa's son, had received a modest legacy from his father and then had lost most of

---

26. DII, VII, 162-167; see Catalogue, no. 72, for the dating of this document.

27. See the 22 miscellaneous letters to Casas printed in Fabié, app. XX; 14 from the same bundle are also in DII, VII, 180-216. For a long report to him, and Casas' petition based upon it, see Catalogue, no. 69. Some of the more important interchanges are discussed *infra,* in my chapter XVIII, section on "Discouraging postscripts." Casas own description of his correspondence is from his letter of 1562-1563 to the Dominicans of Chiapa and Guatemala, and from his will. Fabié, app. XXVII (577), and Icazbalceta, *Docs.,* II, 513.

it: "But since the King has all confidence in Your Reverence, if you will inform the gentlemen of the Council of the Indies, Alvarado and his wife and children will be succored." In much the same vein, the aging Bernal Díaz del Castillo begged Casas to get his appointment made permanent as Guatemala City inspector of markets, prices, and weights: "I don't write to the King about it as he has forgotten me, but I know that where Your Reverence takes a hand, the matter will succeed."[28]

In fact, all these letters, from friars or officials or colonists, are further evidence of the great influence Fray Bartolomé now wielded. It would be even more interesting to read his answers. A few have been preserved, addressed to brother Dominicans in America; they are quite extensive, almost small treatises. As with his petitions, there must have been many others.

But the items we have—the memorials to the Council, part of the immense correspondence—fill in our picture of the former Bishop of Chiapa at court. There are two portraits, really: Vásquez de Arce's sketch of the influential adviser, and the Enguidanos engraving of Casas in his cell with pen in hand. Both these activities, advising and writing, would be his occupations from now on; and at each, the aged Bartolomé de las Casas would reach new peaks in his first decade of "retirement."

---

28. Fabié, app. XX (191-194, 199-201).

HISTORIAN OF THE INDIES

ONE BOOK BECOMES TWO

Around 1560 and 1561, Casas was finishing his most interesting and important writings: the *Historia de las Indias* and the *Apologética historia*, completed at last after a decade in the College of San Gregorio. These two books were the fulfillment of a single great project begun long ago in his early monastery days—to write the entire history and description of the Indies.

Fray Bartolomé had started the work, he tells us repeatedly, in 1527 while at the Dominican monastery of Puerto de Plata on Española.[1] Indeed, he seems to have written large parts of it during those semi-secluded monastic years. For the continued use in his text of the words "esta" or "esta isla" for Española indicates clearly that such passages were written there; seldom does he call the island "aquesta" or say "allí" or "allá" for events recorded on it. And in 1534 he was still working on his history in the Santo Domingo monastery, according to the testimony of Oviedo who was around at the time.[2] But in that year, Fray Bartolomé laid aside writing history and returned to living it—first as a missionary in Central America, then as the instigator of the New Laws, and finally as the turbulent Bishop of Chiapa. As he himself said, he was "unable to finish this history because of my great travels and occupations," though he doubtless continued to gather material, notably during his two stays in Mexico and when he was summarizing conquests for the *Brevissima*.

Not till his final return to Spain in 1547 and his permanent residence at San Gregorio, could he resume historical writing on the grand scale. Now at last, despite his regular appearances before the Council, he had more

---

1. Cf. *Hist.*, I, 32; and *Apol.*, 8.
2. Oviedo, I, 602.

leisure than at any period since those uneventful Española years. Here in his new cell, with his books and papers around him, Bartolomé de las Casas again took up the monumental history of the Indies that he had begun in another convent cell long before.

This time he completed the *Historia* proper in three manuscript volumes, and in a further tome, the *Apologética,* or description of the Indians. I believe that these two books were separated from each other and given the form in which we now have them between 1552 and 1563.

To begin with, there are numerous internal allusions in both books that enable us to date specific passages in those years. For instance, in the Prologue to the *Historia,* Casas says in one place that "this is the year 1552," and in another that it is almost sixty-three years since he began traveling about the Indies "near" 1500.[3] Several times he refers to his sixty or nearly sixty years of personal acquaintance with the islands. Again, speaking of Oviedo, though not by name, Casas says that the rival historian was dead; since Oviedo died in the summer of 1557, this was obviously written later. Various chapters can be identified by other references as being written in 1555, 1559, and 1561.[4]

Similarly, in the *Apologética,* Casas declares it was more than fifty-five years since he had seen the Alhambra; as he reached Española in 1502, this passage must have been written after 1557. Elsewhere he says that Huanacapac died more than thirty-five years ago; the event is supposed to have occurred in 1525, which means he was writing in 1560. I could multiply such examples further, but almost all the dates bring us to the same years, from 1552 to 1563.[5]

So Casas surely wrote the final drafts of both books during that decade, and I think he also separated his *Apologética* from the larger work in the same period. Before that, as he himself tells us, his *Historia de las Indias* was a comprehensive work, "relating not only the secular or profane events of

---

3. N.B. The "near" is significant, since Casas came to America with Ovando on April 15, 1502. Cf *Hist.,* III, 18-20, for the precise date, and Catalogue, no. 43, for Casas' occasional use of this rough count.

4. The indirect reference to Oviedo is near the end of the Prologue; the letter preceding the MS is dated 1559 (see *infra,* note 37); and dates from 1555 to 1561 can be calculated for lib. I, cap. 164, lib. II, cap. 51, and lib. III, caps. 8, 100, *et passim.*

5. Cf. *Apol.,* 130 and 67. Not all dateable passages in both works were written in this San Gregorio period. A very few can be referred to the 40's; for instance, on page 176 of the *Apologética,* Casas speaks of having known the islands for forty-odd years and more. Cf. *infra,* note 22, for material that Casas collected in 1543.

my times, but also the ecclesiastical ones . . . *interspersing* something of the quality and nature of these regions . . . along with the customs, religion, rites, ceremonies, and conditions of their natives."[6] This interspersed material reached such proportions that Casas ultimately removed it into a separate volume. As he explains in a marginal note at the close of chapter 67 of the *Historia*:

> Here was to have been placed the . . . description of these islands, more especially of this one [Española], and of the other lands the Admiral discovered, and of the condition of the natives thereof, their skills and customs. *But because this material requires a great treatise, being very diffuse and scarcely less than infinite . . . I have finally decided to leave it to write separately, and it will occupy a not inconsiderable volume—whereof, by Divine grace, the greater part is already written.*[7]

As a matter of fact, the *Apologética* does begin with the erstwhile chapter 68 of the *Historia*—it formerly opened with these words:

> Because from the Golfo de las Flechas the Admiral left this island altogether and returned to Castile with his good and felicitous news [of the Discovery], let us take leave of him now, and afterward we shall pick up the thread again. . . . But first we will occupy ourselves in treating of this island . . . and of the native peoples inhabiting it.[8]

In making the separation, Casas substituted a fresh three-page lead for this passage, and renumbered the chapter as chapter I of the *Apologética*. According to Fabié, this renumbering can be followed for another 101 chapters of the manuscript, all of which were formerly in the *Historia*,[9] a clear indication of how belatedly Casas made the separation.

He did so, I believe, in the early 1550's. Up till 1552, when he wrote the Prologue to his big history, the descriptive material was still included therein; and in the Preface to the new work he confirms that he wrote it after resigning his bishopric.

---

6. *Hist.*, I, 34.

7. According to Fabié (I, 354), these words are written in Casas' hand in the margin of the Real Academia manuscript of the *Historia*. For this MS with holograph corrections, and the holograph original, see Catalogue, no. 65.

8. Fabié, I, 356; cf. *Apol.*, 3, note.

9. Fabié, I, 355. See Catalogue, no. 64, for the original manuscript of the *Apologética* in the Real Academia. The leaves of this MS are for a time numbered consecutively with those of the first 67 chapters of the *Historia*.

Let us now look more closely at these two works, the *Historia* and the *Apologética,* that Bartolomé de las Casas thus separated and completed in his semi-retired San Gregorio years.

"HISTORIA DE LAS INDIAS"

Casas' *History of the Indies,* major work though it is, must be considered an unfinished masterpiece. What he planned, according to a statement at the end of the Prologue, was a sweeping narrative of almost six decades, from 1492 to 1550, to be divided into six "books" of ten years each, save for the first that would cover the eight years from the discovery of America to the turn of the century. Just previously, however, he says he had not been able to finish it. What he actually completed was only three books, up to 1520. Fabié was of the opinion that Casas wrote more, but I do not agree.[10] The original manuscript and all contemporary copies have only three books. The last, ending with 1520, includes a few final statements of events in 1521 and an incident of 1530, which would have gone into book IV had Casas written it. Instead, I find that he stuck to his original design of writing "chiefly the first discoveries of these Indies, and what happened in this Española and its other neighboring islands."[11]

By far the most detailed portion of the work is that recounting Columbus' voyages, mostly from priceless documents and firsthand anecdotes. Casas had exceptional opportunities to learn from participants many facts, or we might say stories, that do not appear in Columbus' accounts. Furthermore, Casas was well acquainted with the Discoverer's brothers, Bartolomé and Diego, and both of his sons, Diego and Fernando. I do not find that he knew Christopher himself, though he speaks of seeing him on the return from his Second Voyage. But he had access to and quoted from an astounding number of documents relating to Columbus or written by him. Of these, Fray Bartolomé himself owned quite a few, and he had seen many more, often taking the trouble to copy them.

Most significantly, Casas copied the log of the Voyage of Discovery, and his transcript is today the only known copy of this most fabulous document in the history of America; he likewise copied Columbus' report of the Third Voyage. Casas incorporated the bulk of these accounts in his *Historia,* though with numerous additions and interpolations of all kinds, most of

---

10. Cf. Fabié, I, 359.
11. *Hist.,* I, 32.

them quite foreign to the subject of the narratives.[12] Casas also knew and used the "Proceso," a suit of Diego against the Crown's attorney, about the privileges granted to his father, the First Admiral. Occasionally, too, Casas quoted a letter from Columbus to the King and Queen, or their answers, from originals or copies in his possession. It is needless to enumerate further his documentary sources for the voyages of Columbus, as this subject has been fully aired by John Boyd Thatcher and discussed by him and Harrisse in their works on the Discoverer. But I would add a postscript to their discussion. There is no doubt whatever that Casas had a manuscript copy of the life of Columbus written by his son Hernando. He quotes continually from the book, especially about the Fourth Voyage; and these passages correspond almost word for word, barring the difference in language, with the Italian translation of Hernando's *Historia,* later printed by Alonso de Ulloa in Venice in 1571.

Second only to this rich material about Columbus, I would rank Casas' account of early times on the islands. His picture of Española draws heavily on his own reminiscences; he relates the conquest of Cuba as an eyewitness; and he writes of the other islands from personal acquaintance with principal characters like Ponce de León. This part of the work, too, is filled with documents Casas had collected, notably on early reform efforts.

About Tierra Firme, Fray Bartolomé also supplies some exclusive information. Starting with the discovery of the mainland, he investigates at length Amerigo Vespucci's claim of a voyage to America in 1497. Casas produces almost conclusive evidence that Vespucci really accompanied Alonso de Hojeda on his 1499 voyage, and Hojeda merely followed in Columbus' wake, having probably been told about the Admiral's prior voyage by Bishop Fonseca, then in charge of Indies affairs.[13] Casas goes on to give lively details about the exploration of the Spanish Main, since he knew the first navigators of that coastline personally. And on the discovery and conquest of Mexico, he tells with authority the voyages of Hernández de Córdoba and Juan de Grijalva, and the adventures of Cortés down to 1520—these captains, too, were friends of his. But he devotes most space to a well-documented account of the exploitation of Darien and its devastation by avaricious Spaniards.

All in all, with his personal knowledge and painstaking documenta-

---

12. See Catalogue, no. 66, for these MSS.
13. *Hist.,* lib. I cap. 139.

tion, Casas' *Historia de las Indias* is a notable achievement. Its literary merit is another matter. When Fray Bartolomé narrates the adventures of the Spaniards, he tells a plain and straightforward tale; and if we could eliminate his digressions on irrelevant matters—for instance, ancient ideas on the sources of the Nile—the book would make very interesting reading. As it is, the work is heavy, and worse still it is written as one continuous complaint about the encomienda system and Spanish mistreatment of the natives. To be sure, this was always the burden of Casas' song and perhaps we should not blame him for repeating it, but the result ultimately makes tiresome reading.

Nonetheless, the historical value of the work is immense, though Casas completed only the first three books. Almost all later writers have used and praised it, starting with Antonio de Herrera, the chief chronicler, who borrowed extensively from the manuscript. Even today, Fray Bartolomé's masterpiece remains a capital source on the early history of the Indies.[14]

"Apologética historia"

Somewhat less successful was the offshoot of this main work, Casas' *Apologética historia summaria de las gentes destas Indias*. Begun as a descriptive aside in the general history, it was finished as an elaborate encyclopedia to prove Indian capacity by Aristotelian principles and comparisons with antiquity.

Why did Casas chose such an unwieldy presentation? After long study of the *Apologética*, I have reached the conclusion that most of it was recast for the specific purpose of combatting the Indian-inferiority doctrine of Juan Ginés de Sepúlveda. Only the first twenty-two chapters, the description of Española, seem to belong to the original draft written on that island.[15] The rest of the book, as Casas states at the outset, is arranged to answer the slander that the natives were incapable of self-government—i.e., the Aris-

---

14. For the use of the *Historia* manuscript by Herrera and others, and its long-delayed publication, see Catalogue no. 65.

15. These first 22 chapters carry out the original purpose set forth at the end of cap. 67 of the *Historia*. Thus in the *Apologética*, caps. 1-20 describe the "provinces, quality, fertility, amenity, prosperity" of Española; cap. 21 sketches the geography and climate of the other islands and Tierra Firme; and 22 attempts to support Columbus' notion that "the western Indies are a part of India." I think it would have been wiser had Casas stuck to his original plan and left these 22 chapters in his *Historia*, as he did with 3 descriptive chapters on Cuba at a later point (cf. *Hist.*, lib. III, caps. 22-24). Then he could more suitably have begun the *Apologética* with chapter 23.

totelian theory by which Doctor Sepúlveda justified the conquest. Indeed, Fray Bartolomé called the work an *Apologética historia* or "Defensive Account" of the Indians, just as his *Apología,* read before the judges, was a defense of his own stand on the illegitimacy of conquests and the Crown's limited right to the Indies. Of course, the "slaves by nature" thesis was also held by most Spanish jurists and the colonists generally, and had been widely current ever since controversy first arose over the justice of the conquest. But Sepúlveda was its chief spokesman. And I believe that in consequence of their dispute, Bartolomé de las Casas added an Aristotelian framework to his own vast material on the American Indians.

For the remaining two hundred forty-five chapters of the book are designed to carry out the formal "defense" of the Indians outlined in its Preface. There Casas says he will demonstrate Indian capacity by first sketching the influences that produce skill and understanding among peoples, and then describing the Indian societies themselves to show that they fulfill all the Aristotelian requisites. Accordingly, with chapter 23 he begins what is virtually a new prologue, setting up his "causes" most elaborately—climate, physical factors, and so on—and giving the Indians high scores for personal traits and domestic economy.[16] Next, Casas carefully establishes his criteria and then proceeds to examine the Indian societies minutely, according to Aristotle's six points. As a preliminary, he describes their many cities, notably in the Aztec and Inca empires. After that, he discusses in turn agriculture and stock raising; industries and various kinds of artisans; militia and warfare; wealth, commerce, and markets; religion, with its priesthoods, temples, superstitions, idolatry, rites, and sacrifices; and finally, government, laws, and miscellaneous customs including the education of children, the burial of the dead, etc. In each of these categories, whether they occupy few or many chapters, Casas arranges his material in strict geographical order: first Española and the islands, and then the mainland from north to south—from Florida and Cíbola down through Mexico and Central America, to the north coast of South America, and finally the vast domain of the Peruvian Incas.[17]

In all this, unlike the *Historia,* Casas rarely writes as an eyewitness. He refers to his personal experiences only in his account of Española and of a few places in New Spain. For instance, he relates what he himself had seen of the religion of the islanders; he devotes some space to Guatemala, where

---

16. *Apol.,* caps. 23 through 44.
17. *Apol.,* caps. 45 through 261.

he says he saw remarkable ruins in Ultatlán and Verapaz; and in telling of Yucatán, he describes the magnificent buildings he no doubt saw on his way from Campeche to Mérida.[18]

But for the most part, he relies on descriptions furnished him by missionary friars, from their own books and notes and experiences. Some of this was gathered quite early. About Española, for instance, he obtained Fray Ramón Pane's pioneer account of the Indians, written at Columbus' request, and the personal reminiscences of Fray Juan del Tisín, one of the first religious in the New World.

Later, during his stays in Mexico, Casas associated with the Franciscans and obtained much information from them on the natives of New Spain. For instance, in chapters 63 and 64 he copies an account of a Corpus Christi pageant staged by the Indians at Tlaxcala in 1536, saying he took it from the writings of a Franciscan; the extract is from Motolinía's *Historia de los indios,* which was apparently not finished at the time of Casas' first visit, so perhaps Fray Toribio allowed him to copy this in 1546.[19] Another interesting passage is a long account of the Totonacos, with whom I doubt Casas ever had personal contact, though he may have seen a few in Jalapa. Casas says he got his information from a man who had been left with these Indians when the Spaniards landed and went into the interior; possibly this man afterward became a Franciscan, though Casas does not specify when and where he met him.[20] Also in Mexico, Fray Bartolomé evidently received an account of the Coronado expedition from some participant, for he records details not found in any other known account. Doubtless his informant was a Franciscan who had made the journey to Quivira and managed to return.[21]

---

18. See cap. 52 for his wonder at the Ultatlán and Maya ruins. For typical references to his own Española experiences, cf. *Apol.,* 93 and 518, his living twenty years on the island; 445 and 520, his observing and failing to observe native customs; and 516, the appearance of Indians he saw in a certain town. Also see *supra,* my chapter IX, note 13, for *Apologética* items about his first visit to Mexico.

19. Casas says he has taken it word for word. This is verified by a comparison with Motolinía's history, which incidentally contains a (copyist's?) error. The Motolinía date of 1538 for the pageant seems incorrect; Corpus Christi fell on June 20 that year, and only a few days before that Casas himself reached Tlaxcala and then officiated at the festival mass on August 15. So I think it likely that the big pageant took place in 1536, as he states in the *Apologética.*

20. *Apol.,* caps. 175-176.

21. See *Apol.,* caps. 53-54, 187, 208-210. Casas' informant cannot be identfied from the published sources. Juan de Padilla, one of the Franciscans, was killed in Quivira, and only a couple of Tarascan Indians and a Portuguese named Ocampo escaped; Casas, however, mentions none of these. But the material he obtained differs

Thus, over the years, Casas lost no opportunity to obtain material about the Indians. Even when he was busiest at court—at Valladolid in 1543, during the promulgation of the New Laws—he secured a signed translation of some laws from Aztec pictographs.[22] By the time he finally settled down at San Gregorio, he had assembled a veritable encyclopedia.

Unfortunately, in arranging it all as a "defense," he added a whole mass of extraneous data. Nearly one-fifth of the *Apologética*, I estimate, is devoted to the practices of the ancient Greeks, Romans, Egyptians, and so forth. In an effort to prove that the customs, rites, and religions of the Indians were less corrupt than those of antiquity, Casas inserted chapter after chapter on pagan orgies, sacrifices, and depravities.[23]

Nowadays this material is unreadable, but Fray Bartolomé used it to reach a daring conclusion: "I have declared and demonstrated and openly concluded, from chapter 22 to the end of this whole book, that all the people of these our Indies, so far as is possible by the natural and human way and without the light of faith—had their republics, places, towns, and cities most

---

from the extant accounts printed in George Parker Winship's *Coronado Expedition*, Washington, 1896, and in George P. Hammond and Agapito Rey's *Narratives of the Coronado Expedition, 1540-1542*, Albuquerque, 1940.

22. See *Apol.*, cap. 215, where Casas transcribes a document headed "Estas son las leyes que tenian los indios de la Nueva España," from a copy signed by the friar who took it from an Indian "book of pictures." A mansucript with the same heading, text, and statement about pictographs is in the García Icazbalceta papers in the University of Texas; it is dated Valladolid, September 10, 1543, and signed in a different hand, "Fr. Andrés de Alcobiz [?]." García Icazbalceta printed this as no. 4 of his *Nueva colección de docs.*, III (*Pomar y Zurita*, 1891), and I believe the "signature" is a copyist's error for Andrés de Olmos. The identical laws were copied in the *Historia de la Nueva España* by Alonso de Zorita, who says he took them from a book by that friar. Zorita (8) adds that Olmos had written a work in Nahuatl on the laws and customs of New Spain in the pre-conquest era [*Sobre las cosas de Nueva España y sus indios*]; this book was sent to Spain and lost, but Olmos afterwards rewrote in Spanish what he could remember of it. Casas says only that the compiling friar was most expert in the Mexican language (*Apol.*, 564).

23. See *Apol.*, caps. 75-111 and 113-119 on ancient idolatry and divinities, magic arts and apparitions; caps. 128-129 and 138-139 on pagan temples; caps. 143-165 on ancient religious sacrifices; and 200-203 on reprehensible marriage customs of the ancients. Scattered through the book are other observations on similar matters. For instance, in cap. 205 Casas cites Strabo's *Geografía*, Munster's *Cosmografía universal*, etc., on cannibalism in antiquity, in explaining why the Caribs ate human flesh while islanders with a similar climate did not. Among such data are chapters on Christian demonology along with ancient superstitions, and Casas quotes impartially from Greek and Latin writers, the Old and New Testaments, and Church Fathers.

abundant and well provided for, and did not lack anything to live politically and socially, and attain and enjoy civil happiness. . . . And they equalled many nations of this world that are renowned and considered civilized, and they surpassed many others, and to none were they inferior. Among those whom they equalled were the Greeks and Romans, and they surpassed them by many good and better customs. They surpassed also the English and French and some of the people of our own Spain; and they were incomparably superior to countless others, in having good customs and lacking many evil ones."[24]

Whether or not we accept this sweeping dictum, there is no doubt that Casas had marshalled conclusive evidence of Indian capacity. He did so in a treatise of encyclopedic dullness, much marred by extraneous material. Yet this work, too, like the *Historia de las Indias,* was a signal achievement. From the seventeenth century down to our own times, the *Apologética* has served as a prime source book for writers on the American Indians.[25]

Octogenarian

Perhaps the most remarkable feature of both these books was that Casas completed them in his late eighties.

In 1554 Fray Bartolomé is reputed to have been eighty years old. His vigor was apparently unimpaired, but he became quite deaf and no doubt his eyes were dimmed. I believe he must have employed his friend Ladrada, who lived in San Gregorio with him, as a sort of amanuensis.[26] To be sure, Casas was always a rapid thinker and writer, and the final *Historia* and *Apologética* manuscripts are in his own hand. But he could hardly have produced the prodigious writings of these advanced years without some kind of assistance from his aide and companion. Of the three cells they occupied in the Dominican college, one was obviously a study and archive for the huge

---

24. *Apol.,* cap. 263, where Casas says he has proved all this according to the Aristotelian categories, and asserts that the Indians were as capable of receiving the faith as any other people. This is the real conclusion of the book, and is followed by four supplementary chapters on the different kinds of "barbarians."

25. For early users of the manuscript *Apologética,* and its belated printing, see Catalogue, no. 64. The material on antiquity was doubtless one of the reasons why the work was not published earlier, as such chapters were omitted from the two partial printings in the 19th century.

26. Save for Ladrada's signature on the joint memorial of 1543 (cf. Catalogue, no. 20), I have seen no authentic handwriting by him, and am therefore unable to determine for which of Casas' papers he may have served as scribe.

quantities of material Fray Bartolomé was using in his great historical works. Just keeping all this in order was a big chore.

For one thing, there were shelves and shelves of books. Evidently on his return to Spain, Casas had taken pains to assemble practically every book and pamphlet on the Indies that had appeared in print since he began writing— he already owned the earlier works. We know the extent of his collection from scattered references in his own *Historia* and *Apologética* to these printed sources.

On Columbus, for instance, he quoted from the earliest and latest books of all lands giving brief versions of the discoverer's exploits. Thus, he used the Portuguese chronicle of García de Resende, and Juan de Barros' *Asia*, which had recently come out in Lisbon on March 25, 1553. But he also took material on the Discoverer's youth from Sabellicus' older Venetian chronicle of 1498 and 1504.[27]

Naturally, too, Fray Bartolomé had the books of other historians of the Indies, and used them rather severely. Among the early writers, he spoke well only of Peter Martyr, and obtained some information from his *De orbe novo*.[28] But he was especially hard on his chief rival, Oviedo, charging him with crimes against the Indians, and making long extracts from his work solely to refute what he had to say.[29] And he had nothing but condemnation for Gómara's recent *Historia y conquista* of 1552.

Casas also had all the "relations" of conquests and expeditions published from the beginning right down to this San Gregorio period. Thus, in

---

27. Cf. *Hist.*, lib. I, cap. 3, where he first cites Barros and Sabellicus (also cap. 74 for Resende). Casas' use of Barros' "Historia portuguesa" so early in his book is one of the indications that the work as we have it is a final draft. Though Casas might have seen the brief notice of Columbus in Sabellicus' part I, he repeatedly cites the fuller passage in the *Secunda pars Enneadum,* dec. X, lib. VIII.

28. *Hist.*, I, 32. But this was only for data obtained personally from Columbus, as elsewhere this author tells "many falsehoods." Thus, in cap. 246 of the *Apologética* Casas takes pains to correct Peter Martyr's story of the Chiribichi massacre evidently supplied by the embittered Fray Tomás Ortiz, former Dominican vicar at Cubagua. (Cf. Ortiz's diatribe against the Indians, and the resulting slaving provision. *De orbe novo,* MacNutt edition, II, 274-275, and Gómara, *Historia,* 290.) This Ortiz—Casas tells his story without naming him—was chosen a bishop, but such unfavorable reports were received that the Council cancelled the nomination and he lived for many years in his small hometown, alone and outside the Dominican Order.

29. Gómara even says in his *Anales* that Casas prevented the publication of Oviedo's *Historia general* in 1548. Presumably this refers to the fact that Oviedo started to reprint his book in 1547, but only got out one part.

writing of the Incas, he extracted the story of Miguel de Estete and the
abortive expedition to Cuzco from Francisco de Xérez' *Verdadera relación
de la conquista del Perú*, printed at Seville in July 1534. This is the first
known imprint on the subject, but Fray Bartolomé also seems to speak of
another account published in Salamanca, which he says was the earliest one
printed.[30] On the other hand, in discussing Florida, he gave a long section
on Indian customs taken from the *Relación* of Cabeza de Vaca, and some
data on Hernando de Soto's expedition presumably drawn from the original
Relacam verdadeira, which was not printed till 1557 in Evora, Portugal.[31]

Besides these books on the Indies, Fray Bartolomé also had in his
library any number of learned tomes: the works of ancient and mediaeval
writers who supplied the endless digressions that he wove into his *Apologética* and *Historia*, in the fashion of a man of "ciencia y consciencia."

In addition to his books, Casas' study was further filled with piles of
valuable papers that he used in writing his histories. Most important, of
course, was his extensive collection of documents, particularly on Columbus.
Noteworthy, too, were the reports that he now received constantly from his
correspondents in the New World, many of them surely transmitting data
on native customs. For instance, in the *Apologética*, Casas speaks of obtaining his extensive information on the Inca period from friars in Peru. And I
judge that much of it was sent to him at this time by his Dominican friends
there, Provincials San Martín and Santo Tomás, who were afterwards his
co-workers at court.[32] Elsewhere in the *Apologética*, he devotes two chapters
to copying the "exhortations" of Aztec parents to their children: he says
these were translated from the Nahua and sent to him from Mexico by the
Franciscan Andrés de Olmos.[33]

---

30. Cf. *Apol.*, 145 and 147; and see also the account of Cuzco before the conquest, cap. 58. I have been unable to discover where Casas obtained this description.
There is an undated copy of Xérez' *Relación* in the British Museum, but it is shorter
than the other and does not contain the passage.

31. Cf. *Apol.*, 449, and 540-543. His other sources in book form range from
the widely read letters of Cortés (cf. *Apol.*, 130) to the little-known *Barbárica* by Cristóbal de la Tobilla (cf. *Hist.*, III, 289). Casas possessed a copy of Tobilla's manuscript
work about Darien and the adventures of Balboa and Pedrarias; this book has never
been published, though I believe it may still be in existence.

32. Cf. Fray Domingo de Santo Tomás' substantial report to Casas, *DII*, VII,
371-387.

33. *Apol.*, caps. 223-224. Like the laws in cap. 215 (*supra*, note 22), these exhortations were also copied by Zorita, this time in his *Breve relación*, in a slightly
different transcription which he also credits to Olmos. See Icazbalceta, *Nueva co-*

With all these papers and books—the collection of a lifetime, and the new items coming in daily—Casas' cell in the College of San Gregorio must have resembled a fantastic historical archive. And he evidently employed Dominican students from the college at various tasks of arranging and copying; perhaps it was in recognition of these services that he left eighteen fellowships for the poorer ones. For we know from his will that "a prudent student" commenced a compilation of his voluminous correspondence, arranging the communications "in the order of the months and years in which they were sent me, and of the provinces from which they came."[34] Also, there is no doubt that Casas had several copies made of his unpublished books, probably here by students at San Gregorio. Of *Del único modo*, for instance, Remesal knew of four copies in various monasteries and private hands, although it was a large tome in Latin.[35] In the end, too, Fray Bartolomé supervised the transcribing of his great history. For we have a manuscript done by a copyist, with corrections in Casas' own hand.[36]

In this archive-cell in the Dominican College of San Gregorio, after a decade of work, Bartolomé de las Casas finally completed his *Historia de las Indias*. He deeded it to the college, to be withheld from the public for a discreet interval:

> I, Fray Bartolomé de las Casas, formerly Bishop of Chiapa, leave this book in confidence to the College of San Gregorio, begging the father rector and counselors, whoever they may be at the time, not to give it to any layman to read, either within the college or still less outside it, for forty years from this year of '60, about to begin. I charge their conscience with this. After forty years have passed, if they deem it advisable for the good of the Indians and for Spain, they may order it printed for the glory of God and principally for the manifestation of the truth. It does not seem advisable that all the students should read it,

---

lección de docs., III (*Pomar y Zurita*), 123 *et seq.* Apparently from Olmos, too, are the extracts in *Apol.*, caps. 219-220, on the rearing of children by the Mexican Indians.

Who originally recorded the Nahuatl exhortations that Olmos translated for Casas? I know of only three friars who wrote Nahuatl books so early: Olmos himself, Fray Francisco de las Navas, and Fray Bernardino de Sahagún. This particular text closely resembles a similar passage in the *Huehue-tlatolli*, a little book probably written by Sahagún. It was afterwards published in Mexico in 1601 by a Franciscan named Fray Juan Bautista—see the article on this friar in José Fernando Ramírez' *Adiciones y correcciones* to Beristain, Mexico, 1898.

34. Icazbalceta, *Docs.*, II, 513.

35. Rem., II, 469.

36. This is the Real Academia manuscript, found by Muñoz and comprising tomos XLVII-XLVIII of his collection. For a description, see Catalogue, no. 65, "Original MSS."

but only the most prudent ones so that it may not be published ahead of the time, because there is no reason therefore nor advantage therein. November, 1559. *Deo gratias.*

Bishop Fray Bartolomé de las Casas[37]

Despite the date of donation, Casas did not lay aside his histories for several more years—he was still retouching the *Apologética* in 1560 and the *Historia* in 1561 and even later.[38] That is to say, he finished them when he was about eighty-seven years old. Even more remarkable, he wrote the last drafts in the same decade when he was appearing almost daily at court as universal procurator of the Indians. In that role, too, the octogenarian Bartolomé de las Casas was to score one of the most phenomenal victories in his long public career.

---

37. This letter of donation, prefixed to the manuscript *Historia,* is reproduced in facsimile in the Real Academia edition, in MacNutt's life of Casas, and elsewhere.

38. See Catalogue, no. 64 and 65, for the "final" dates of 1560 and 1561 that I assign to these works.

PERU AND PERPETUITY

Casas enters the fight

Between his seventy-fifth and eighty-fifth year, Fray Bartolomé fought and won his last great battle for the American Indians. From 1550 to 1560, he blocked a crucial drive by Peruvian settlers to win perpetual rights to their encomiendas.

"Perpetuity," of course, was an old goal of the colonists. Even with the revocation of the most controversial New Law, encomiendas were still granted only for two lifetimes, after which they reverted to the Crown. But the holders had always wanted fiefs that could be inherited indefinitely from generation to generation. Such demands finally reached a crisis following the bloody civil wars in Peru.

As I read the history of that land from the capture of Atahualpa to 1550, I find that the constant power struggles were mainly caused by the fact that there were too many Spaniards to be maintained by the Indians. The settlers would not work and had to be supported via encomiendas or official posts, but the positions were neither numerous nor well paid and the encomiendas were too few to go around. Just how many Spaniards were living in Peru in 1550 is not known to me, but in 1555 they allegedly numbered eight thousand among whom there were only four hundred eighty encomiendas to be divided.[1] So from the start there was always a party of "Outs" much more numerous than the "Ins," a situation that underlay all the upheavals. These had been ended at last by Audiencia President Pedro

---

1. Note from a letter of the Marquis of Cañete, Seville, May 9, 1555 (*DII*, III, 561). The Peruvian situation had been aggravated by a substantial migration of non-encomenderos from New Spain to Peru after 1532. This exodus was one reason why there was less trouble in New Spain over the reform ordinances.

de la Gasca. Reaching Peru early in 1547, after the beheading of the viceroy, Licentiate Gasca brought only a handful of men and some four hundred pesos. But he promptly raised the royal standard, soldiers flocked to his army, and on April 8, 1548, Gonzalo Pizarro was finally defeated and executed. That August, Gasca made a new distribution of encomiendas by the simple process of depriving the rebels of theirs and awarding them to his own faithful followers.[2] Thus was created a triumphant coterie of "Ins," who strove for a decade to stay in power by obtaining perpetual encomiendas.

Their first effort was staged in 1550, upon President Gasca's return to Spain from pacifying Peru. At this period Gasca enjoyed great influence, as he had accomplished a signal feat, not only without expense to the King but with vast profit, bringing back a huge amount of gold and silver for the Crown. The treasure was actually taken to the Emperor in Germany by Peruvian agents, who seized the occasion to press their demands for perpetuity. Charles thereupon referred the matter to a special junta that was convened at Valladolid, a situation made to order for the defenders of the Indians.[3]

By now, Bartolomé de las Casas had been enlisted in the fight by the Peru Dominicans. Their leader, Fray Tomás de San Martín, had returned to Spain with Gasca and was then staying at Casas' own monastery of San Gregorio. This friar bore the title of regent, a position of unknown power that he must have held under the president. At the same time, San Martín was also serving his second four-year term as Peruvian provincial, an office in which he was to be succeeded by Fray Domingo de Santo Tomás. Both men were evidently warm friends of Casas; he may even have known them long before, since they went early to Española. Later they had been among the first Dominicans in Peru, though I have been unable to find any contemporary record of the date of their arrival. Remesal says they came with Valverde, and consequently with Pizarro in 1533. But I believe they came a few years afterwards, perhaps with the friars who accompanied Bishop Berlanga from Spain via Santo Domingo in 1535—Fray Bartolomé himself had set out from Española with the same party.[4] Anyway, I can hardly

---

2. Assessment of tributes was also made, after which Gasca set up a sort of arbitration board to make adjustments. Those named were Gerónimo de Loaysa, Archbishop of Lima, and the two leading Dominicans, Santo Tomás and San Martín; their reports satisfied neither Indians nor Spaniards. Gomara, *Historia*, 274.

3. Díaz, *Historia verdadera*, II, 490-491.

4. Cf. *DE, XXVI*, 195-196, for a report that Santo Tomás came ca. 1540, and San Martín earlier. Bernard Moses, in his *Spanish Colonial Literature in South America* (New York, 1922), 67-68, says San Martín took orders at San Pablo in

doubt that their stories of conditions in Peru stimulated Casas to take up the cause of the natives of that land, starting with the perpetuity junta of 1550.

Our sole source for this meeting is a long account by Bernal Díaz del Castillo, who was one of the participants.[5] I find no mention of it in any contemporary document, nor in León's *Tratado*. This was not the same assembly that heard Casas and Sepúlveda debate the legitimacy of conquests, since only the question of perpetual encomiendas was discussed before members of the Council of the Indies and other royal councils, and Díaz names no theologians as taking part. Appearing for perpetuity were agents from Peru, Mexico, and elsewhere, along with Bernal Díaz as the oldest Mexican conquistador, and the Bishop of Michoacán. But the opponents were even more formidable and included three noted prelates. First to speak, of course, was Fray Bartolomé de las Casas, former Bishop of Chiapa, assisted by his companion Ladrada. He was seconded by none other than President Gasca himself, whom the Emperor had just named Bishop of Palencia and Count of Pernia. Opposition was also voiced by two members of the Royal Council [of Castile] and finally by the Peruvian regent and Dominican provincial, Fray Tomás de San Martín, who was then (or shortly after) made Bishop of Charcas, no doubt in acknowledgment of his services to Gasca.[6]

According to Bernal Díaz, the proponents argued that the Indians would be better off in perpetual encomiendas and the system would bring administrative benefits. But the opponents questioned even the existing encomiendas, and insisted that perpetuity would provoke fresh rebellion in Peru. The results were contrary to the plan, says Díaz, largely because of

---

Córdoba, went early to Santo Domingo, returned to Spain perhaps in 1529, and went to Peru with Pizarro.

Remesal (II, 286) gives the terms of both men in the series of provincials. San Martín heads the list, named for eight years, followed by Santo Tomás from 1553 to 1557.

5. See Díaz, *Historia verdadera*, cap. 208 [211], "How in the year 1550, the court being in Valladolid, there gathered before the royal Council of the Indies certain prelates and caballeros come from New Spain and Peru as agents, and other hidalgos who were on hand, to give advice about making the encomiendas perpetual; and what was said and done in the junta, I shall relate." *Ibid., II,* 490 *et seq.*

6. San Martín was chosen as bishop of the new Diocese of La Plata de los Charcas in 1551 and consecrated, I believe, in 1552. (See *DII,* XXVI, 213, letter of March 1552.) Bernard Moses says he was named first Bishop of Charcas in 1552 and died in Lima in March 1554. But this date of death must be a mistake, since efforts to name a successor apparently did not begin till 1558.

the activities of Casas and San Martín. The Council of the Indies would take no action, on the grounds that it was best to await the Emperor's return from Germany. For several years, nothing further seems to have been done in the matter.[7]

Meantime, however, Casas continued—through the agency of his Dominican friends—to take an active interest in Peruvian affairs. It appears that Gasca, before leaving Peru in 1550, had suspended the law against personal services of Indians until he could consult the emperor. Time passed without any word from Spain and the new provincial, Fray Domingo de Santo Tomás, apparently wrote Fray Bartolomé to intercede with the Council. For Herrera tells how Santo Tomás showed the royal judges a letter from Casas criticizing the delay and advising that enforcement of the order was up to the Lima authorities.[8] Thereupon, on June 24, 1552, the audiencia promulgated the law, though without the concurrence of the viceroy, Antonio de Mendoza.[9]

This action helped to bring on a revolt against the audiencia in 1553, headed by Francisco Hernández Girón. The capital city remained in an uproar till Girón's execution on December 7, 1554; about five hundred Spaniards had been killed in the interim. The trouble, of course, was not all due to the abolition of personal services. After the departure of President Gasca, the turbulent citizens of Peru had renewed their dissensions; these stemmed from the antagonisms that had developed during twenty years, and the general dissatisfaction of the "first conquistadors" who had long wanted perpetual encomiendas.

By 1554, this old agitation and the uneasiness of the current "Ins" finally brought on a new scheme—for the present holders to buy perpetual rights to their encomiendas from the King. By now, Bishop San Martín was back in Peru and Bishop Gasca was changing his opinion.[10] So the main

---

7. Bernal Díaz closes with the Council's assurances that at the imperial arrival, the conquistadors would be well contented. But I find no evidence of royal action on this. To the contrary, a Madrid cedula of April 5, 1552, specified that on an encomendero's death his wife, sons, or daughters [an extension] should succeed him, but on their death the Indians must revert to the Crown. As León says, however, this law was "dissimulated" and encomiendas were allowed to pass to the third life, and dissimulation was finally confirmed by royal order on June 11, 1559. Cf. *Tratado,* fols. 20 verso and 21 verso.

8. Herrera, dec. VIII, lib. VII, cap. 3; Catalogue, no. 55.

9. *DII,* III, 246-247.

10. Though he had disapproved the idea before, in a 1554 memorial Gasca advocated perpetual encomiendas on the ground they would put a stop to the effort

burden of this fresh threat devolved personally on the venerable Bartolomé de las Casas soon after he turned eighty years old.

His appeal to Carranza de Miranda

On their second major try for perpetuity, the Peruvians profited by the lessons of the first. Their strategy was to get to Philip in person—he was in England and terribly pressed for funds—and make so tempting an offer that the King would agree without referring the matter to the Council in Spain. Casas had to devise a unique counterstrategy to reach Philip effectively at a distance. He did so by a famous letter, almost a "little book," to the royal confessor, the illustrious and ill-fated Bartolomé Carranza de Miranda.

Master Miranda, as he used to be called, was an old friend of Casas. A fellow Dominican, he had been at San Gregorio de Valladolid for many years in various capacities—Fray Bartolomé undoubtedly became well acquainted with him there; more recently he had approved Casas' *Confesionario* and served as a judge in the dispute with Sepúlveda. Some years later Carranza would become Archbishop of Toledo and Primate of Spain, and the victim of one of the most sensational trials of the century. But at present he was the confessor and trusted adviser of Philip who had gone to England for his marriage to Queen Mary.[11] From every standpoint, friendship, sympathies, position, Carranza was the ideal person through whom Casas could reach the King.

Reaching the King was now urgent. By this time the Peruvian settlers had dispatched their agent, one Ribera, with authority to offer His Majesty a tremendous sum for a decree of perpetuity. The entire story of this mission can only be pieced together from contemporary correspondence. I first find it mentioned in a report of March 30, 1554, from the Lima audiencia to that of Panama, announcing that the good citizens are sending to Spain as their representatives Antonio de Ribera and Pedro de Cabrera.[12] But from a letter of the Archbishop of Lima on April 12, it appears that Ribera had left for

---

of the "Outs" to get in. (MS among the Gasca papers, Huntington Library.) Perhaps this was a result of the Girón trouble.

11. Born in 1503 at Miranda, Navarra, Carranza entered the Dominican Order in 1520, was a student at the College of San Gregorio in 1523, and remained at Valladolid in various capacities for many years, being elected provincial in 1550. He attended the first two sessions of the Council of Trent. In 1554, he preceded Philip to England, where he was zealous in persecuting Protestants, continuing such activities in the Low Countries in 1557.

12. *DII*, III, 232.

Spain without Cabrera.[13] What happened next, we learn from Casas' letters and memorials written at the time and afterwards. Either late in 1554 or early 1555, Ribera went on to England, where he offered Philip some seven to nine million ducats, payable in one to four years, to purchase perpetual encomiendas. Through Carranza's intercession, Casas succeeded in having the offer referred to a special council in Spain.[14] But Ribera continued his campaign, seeking a royal decision in England and Flanders—the persistent agent was with the Emperor in December 1555, a decisive moment indeed.[15] In October, the Emperor had turned over the Netherlands to his son Philip and on January 16, 1556, he resigned the Spanish crown to him.

Certainly, the agent from Peru could hardly have picked a more propitious time for his lavish offer. Not only was Philip far from Spain and the restraining influence of the Council of the Indies, but the royal finances were in a desperate state. The Emperor's almost constant wars had resulted in heavy debts, and even the much-increased revenues from the newly discovered silver mines of Potosí in Peru and from Zacatecas in Mexico were insufficient to meet the demands for money. With his accession to the throne in 1556, Philip had to resort to extraordinary means to raise funds. He drew on the Guadalcanal mines for five hundred thousand ducats, borrowed another three hundred thousand in the Villalón fair at high interest rates, had Princess Juana pawn her dowry of excise revenues, and asked forty-three millions from the kingdom of Spain. He further gave orders to sell many offices and much vacant land, and borrowed a large lot of pepper from Portugal. According to Remesal, at this time he also considered selling the encomiendas in the Indies.[16]

Under such circumstances, Casas' appeal to Carranza de Miranda had to be especially impressive to keep Philip from accepting the Ribera offer

---

13. *DII,* III, 245.

14. See the opening paragraphs of Casas' letters to the Chiapa and Guatemala Dominicans, and to Carranza de Miranda, also his counteroffer with Santo Tomás. Fabié, apps. XXVII and XXVIII, and Icazbalceta, *Docs.,* II, 231.

15. See Charles's letter to his Empress, *DII,* III, 559-561. But the only business of Ribera that he mentions is a request to have idle Spaniards in Peru removed from the country. I have been unable to find any further data on Ribera's activities. He was, incidentally, the guardian of Francisco Pizarro's two illegitimate mestizo children.

16. Rem., II, 465-466. Leopold von Ranke tells the same story, not mentioning the year except incidentally that it occurred before 1558. Cf. *La monarquía española de los siglos XVI y XVII* (Mexico, 1946 ed.), 182-183.

outright. So it is not surprising that one of the manuscript copies of the famous letter bears the notation "parvus libellus," and Casas himself called it "esta carta o tratado."

This huge missive, written in August of 1555 to answer Carranza's inquiry on the matter, is an impassioned plea against the sale of the Peruvian encomiendas. Casas begins by pointing out the great importance of the question; the Prince and the Emperor should not decide it hastily abroad, but only after they had returned to Spain and convoked a suitable gathering. Then follows a carefully structured argument, in which Casas disposes of each point advanced by backers of the sale. Laying down his recent premises —just title for the conversion of the Indians, government for the welfare of the governed—Fray Bartolomé expounds his familiar indictment of the encomienda, but now he carries it to an extreme conclusion. The only true remedy, he insists at tremendous length, is for the King to cancel all the encomiendas, returning the Indians to their original liberty and restoring the native rulers. These restored chieftains would only need to give the Spanish king an annual token tribute, like the single jewel the King of Tunis gave the Emperor, but might voluntarily grant him rights to mines, precious stones, and salt deposits. That would suffice for a royal "salary" to pay for the conversion. As for the Spaniards in the Indies, they are needed only to maintain Spanish sovereignty, which does not require thousands of men, given the superiority of their arms. So he advocates a paid royal garrison of only three hundred men in Mexico; "and when this garrison is installed, let the King set all the Indians free, and with the joy thereof they will serve him with their blood if need be, and will give him two or three millions." As for Peru, once the rebels are subdued by war or other means, a paid garrison of five hundred men would suffice. In conclusion, he again denounces the encomienda, perpetual or temporary, and offers to submit full proof of the law and facts in this appeal.[17]

All told, the letter is one of the most forthright Casas ever composed. He says he would be pleased if Carranza would show it to the King, yet in the course of it he makes some criticisms of the Crown that I find extraordinary for those days. Here are a few examples: "I tell but one in a thousand cases, and I do not exceed in calling all of them [the Spaniards] great tyrants, no matter whom it touches nor who must suffer for it!" Or again:

---

17. Fabié, app. XXVIII; *DII*, VII, 290-338. See Catalogue, no. 57, for extant manuscript copies.

"The King of Spain sent men there to the Indies . . . whom he might have known by their works had no other intention but falsity or malicious ways or to kill and rob. Violence, wars, robberies, outrages, and killing. . . . is the road by which they entered, commenced, and proceeded up to today. By punishing only the one who discovered the Indies and no other, the Kings of Castile have an intolerable burden on their conscience for which they have not paid much." Near the end, after telling how the Mexican procurators tricked the Emperor and his confessor, Pedro de Soto, into revoking the Law of Inheritance, he comments: "on the day they both die, they will find out in trying to seek their way to heaven what kind of candle they have procured."

Besides this outspokenness, the recommendation for a paid garrison is most striking. From a practical standpoint, an armed force was required to keep in subjection a native population that outnumbered the Spaniards by perhaps a hundred thousand to one. Encomiendas, in a sense, were a device to pay for a militia that would guard the conquered territories, the tribute paid the encomenderos being a tax to support such a force. A number of proposals had been made to the Crown to get rid of the encomiendas and keep a substantial garrison in the Indies instead. Cortés first advanced this scheme, for precisely the same reasons, and Casas himself made the suggestion several times. In fact,, it was proposed in a memorial by some unknown theologian in 1554; this document contains Fray Bartolomé's views and reads as if written by him.[18] Anyhow, Casas emphatically advocated the idea in his long letter of 1555 to Carranza de Miranda.

What was the effect of this "libellus" or tract to the King's confessor? Casas said afterwards that the sale of the encomiendas would have gone through had not Carranza prevented it. Apparently he meant that Philip did not sign a decree while abroad, as the Emperor had done previously. So Casas' big appeal to Carranza de Miranda staved off the immediate danger, but an even more critical episode lay ahead.

THE COUNTEROFFER

Philip began his reign in 1556, remaining in the north and still desperate for funds. Evidently Ribera and his backers redoubled their efforts at this time. For on September 5, the new King wrote to the Council that he wished no further words of caution and that he had finally made up his

---

18. Cf. Cuevas, *Docs.*, 176-180. Casas thought the militiamen could be paid 200 or 300 ducats apiece, with which they could easily make their fortune in the Indies.

mind to grant perpetuity.[19] But the decision was never to be carried out. Bureaucratic obstacles intervened, and Bartolomé de las Casas was able to promote a bold new approach that undercut the financial basis of the whole deal.

Fray Bartolomé switched tactics promptly. Soon after Philip's accession, Casas sent him a blunt memorial advising that the Ribera offer would be matched by the Indian chiefs and enumerating twenty reasons against perpetual encomiendas. Some were the same points he had written to Carranza, but now he stressed practical rather than ethical or legal considerations, insisting that the Peru "Outs" would revolt against perpetuity and the Indies would be lost to the Crown. At the end, he made his climactic proposal. If the King was determined to solve his fiscal troubles by means of the Indians, then "put them at liberty and restore their natural lords . . . and they will buy themselves and will give the millions that this Ribera promises"—the religious can best arrange this, and "we will all help, even from here."[20]

Fortunately for Casas' new plan, there was considerable delay in carrying out Philip's urgent instructions. Though the King wanted a perpetuity commission to leave for Peru no later than January of 1557 to arrange the final terms, the Council of the Indies spent more than two years finding suitable persons. Not till 1559 were instructions finally given to the new viceroy, Count of Nieva, and the commissioners. According to Herrera, they were publicly empowered to grant perpetuity, but secret orders bade them do nothing till they had reported to the King. Herrera adds that, once in Peru, the commission treated the matter not only with agents of the settlers but with the Indians as well, and the latter declared that if they were made direct Crown vassals they would match the Spanish offer and continue their ordinary tribute besides.[21]

---

19. The full text of the royal decision is printed in Silvio Zavala, *La encomienda indiana* (Madrid, 1935), 205-206. Philip was writing from Ghent. Charles, after abdicating, had sailed for home in September 1556. But the new King remained in the North until after the death of his wife Mary, in November of 1558, only returning to Spain the following August.

20. Mariano Cuevas, *Historia de la iglesia en México* (Tlalpam, 1921), I, 468-476. See Catalogue, no. 58, for the dating of this document.

21. Herrera, dec. VIII, lib. X, cap. 18. A report by Francisco López de Caravantes about 1618 or so, on Peru's fiscal affairs since the conquest, says flatly that the Count of Nieva was named viceroy in 1559 to treat of the perpetuity of encomiendas. (*Hispanic American Historical Review*, XXV, 231.) Writing to Philip on February 20, 1559, Casas himself gave a veiled warning about the Peru provisions. (Archivo de

This was the promised counteroffer, and we have the actual documents in which it was presented at court by Casas and Santo Tomás. On July 19, 1559, a number of the most influential caciques executed a general power of attorney, specifically authorizing "Fray Bartolomé de las Casas of the Council of His Majesty . . . and Fray Domingo de Santo Tomás" to request grants, liberties, exemptions, and privileges for them from King and Council, and to obligate them to pay any "services" of gold, silver, etc., thought advisable.[22] At the time, Fray Domingo was already in Spain and staying at the College of San Gregorio de Valladolid. He had arrived, I believe, in 1558, and we can definitely place him there during the next two years: on September 20, 1559, he witnessed the certification of some relics by Casas, and in January 1560, he saw the printing in Valladolid of his *Gramática* and *Vocabulario* of the Quiché language.[23] It was probably in 1560 that he and Fray Bartolomé, by virtue of this power, presented a truly powerful petition to the King.

Speaking on behalf of all the caciques and Indians of Peru, Casas and Santo Tomás began by pointing out that the original Ribera offer had been fraudulent. Moved by false representations and importunities of self-seeking persons, the King had treated or decided to give the Indians' towns in perpetual encomienda to the Spaniards who then held them, in return for a "service" of gold and silver. But the amount promised was so excessive that the encomenderos could not raise it.

Furthermore, should perpetuity be granted, the Indians would be enslaved and exterminated and His Majesty would suffer irreparable losses of his native vassals, his revenue from tribute, his judicial authority; and ultimately his sovereignty would be overthrown by arrogant Spaniards. Nor could he fulfill his duties for the good government and especially the Christianizing of the natives. To prevent all this, the two procurators hereby made the following counterproposal:

Simancas MS, loaned by Dr. Hanke. See Catalogue, no. 60.) Around this same time, Philip was drawing up regulations for the sale of offices and property in the Indies, which resulted in the cedula of June 17. Cf. León, *Tratado,* fol. 118. The sale of public offices had begun under Philip about 1555, and Casas had previously assailed the legality of the custom in his *Erudita et elegans explicatio,* article 16.

22. Hanke, "Festón de Docs.", *Revista Cubana,* XVI, 204-208.

23. On July 29, 1559, Casas received these relics from a convent in Avignon; on September 20, 1559, he executed the certification; on October 19, 1560, a receipt for them was signed by four Dominicans in Santiago de Guatemala. Latin MS in the Conway Collection, see Catalogue, no. 61.

The Indians would top by a hundred thousand ducats any bona fide offer from the Spaniards; and, if no comparison were possible, they would give the King two million ducats in four years. In return, the King must promise, with proper guarantees, to fulfill these conditions: (1) On the death of their present encomenderos, the Indians shall not again be given in encomienda in any part of Peru, nor shall any now under the Crown be so given, but all shall be in Crown towns. (2) Encomenderos, their wives, Negroes, or other servants must forthwith be absolutely prohibited from entering Indian towns. (3) Indians under the Crown, now and hereafter, shall pay only one-half of the present tribute. (4) Whenever Indians are assessed too heavily, by reason of a poor year or dimunition of numbers, their tribute shall be reassessed to what they can reasonably pay. (5) As the encomiendas are extinguished, the lesser caciques shall be placed under the greater, so as gradually to restore the hierarchy of Inca times. (6) When matters of general welfare are to be considered, agents of the Indian towns shall be convoked to give their assent or dissent, as they used to do under the Incas and as is done in the Cortes in Spain. (7) The King shall restore to the chief native lords their ancient immunity from taxes and services, and give them arms and insignia for themselves and their descendants. (8) Lands and waters shall henceforth not be taken from Indian communal holdings or individuals, and those hitherto taken most harmfully shall be restored.

By this plan, all the aforementioned damages would cease and the contrary benefits would ensue. The King would have vassals, tribute, and authority; and the Spaniards would give up their rebellions. For this incorporation of all the Indians under the Crown would be less odious to the majority than perpetual encomiendas, which would satisfy only the minority holding them. Finally, with half the tributes His Majesty would have the means to provide a garrison, which is most necessary in that land; and the Crown Indians, with more leisure and better treatment, could advance in the faith.

At the end, Casas and Santo Tomás added a final financial lure. Referring to the treasures in the many hidden Inca tombs which the caciques do not wish to reveal to the Spaniards, they requested a royal order that no Spaniard may touch these, but that one-third of whatever is found should go to the Crown and the rest to the discoverers.[24]

---

24. Icazbalceta, *Docs.*, II, 231-236; Catalogue, no. 63. Santo Tomás returned to Peru not long afterwards, probably in 1561, since he became the new Bishop of Charcas and was serving in that capacity in 1562.

Needless to say, the caciques' drastic proposal was not accepted, but it ended the fiscal temptation for perpetuity. Soon afterwards the royal commission made its report, recommending all three systems: some perpetual encomiendas for the first conquistadors, some for one lifetime only to be rotated among other settlers, and still others to revert permanently to the Crown. This cautious advice, along with the monetary counteroffer, apparently paralyzed Philip's decision. Though his cedula of June 17, 1559, had authorized the sale of offices and property in the Indies, he commenced only the sale of minor posts but never that of encomiendas.

Bartolomé de las Casas' ten-year struggle against perpetuity had at length succeeded. On three occasions he had served as spearhead for an Indian-friar coalition that blocked a determined drive to buy the Peruvian encomiendas from the King. Where once a bribe had influenced the Emperor to revoke the Law of Inheritance, a similar campaign had failed before the zealous defense of the former Bishop of Chiapa. And Casas, as we have noted, was eighty-five when he finally won this last great policy battle of his career.

DISCOURAGING POSTSCRIPTS

Casas' age, as well as other circumstances, must have raised doubts in his mind as to whether he could go on winning indefinitely. He was already losing some of his staunchest allies, by death and disaster. The Emperor had died two years after retiring; Fray Tomás de San Martín was dead, after serving only briefly as Bishop of Charcas; and in 1559, Archbishop Carranza de Miranda, despite his elevation to the primacy of Spain, had been arrested by the Inquisition and was still held prisoner. Fray Bartolomé, indeed, was facing an even wider loss of moral support in a slackening of reform fervor among friars in the New World.

By now, the Dominican Order in the Indies had begun to look tolerantly on the encomienda system. Partly, this was because of reforms Casas himself had helped bring about, such as conscientious inspectors, tribute reductions, abolition of personal services. Also, there was now a new generation of colonists. No doubt most of the old conquistadors were dead; their heirs held many of their encomiendas and many others had been given to settlers. As for the Indians, their numbers had decreased catastrophically, and probably their present encomenderos treated them somewhat better than the original masters. Even the institution iself had undergone a change. In Guatemala, at least, encomiendas had become virtual pensions of the holders, as the officials collected their tribute and paid it over to them. All told, a different situation had arisen and the friars, who after all were Spaniards, shrank from refusing absolution to a compatriot simply because he held Indians in encomienda.

Naturally, when they wrote these views to the elderly procurator of the Indians, Casas replied with impassioned exhortations about backsliding. We have two of these interchanges, and they are sorrowful postscripts to his long battle against perpetuity.

One such missive actually came from Fray Tomás de San Martín, who had appeared with him at the first perpetuity junta. Back in Peru as Bishop of Charcas, San Martín had written Casas posing a series of questions on restitution. The Peruvian bishop thought conquistadors could not conscientiously hold what they had taken from the Indians and a confessor should insist on restitution. Nevertheless, the Kings of Spain had a clear title to the Indies, having given just orders and possessing the country in good faith. So successors and later settlers presented a different case. They held their encomiendas by royal cedula that transferred the King's tribute to them, and therefore they could enjoy it in good conscience, though oppressors and those collecting excessive tribute had to make restitution.[25]

Casas' lengthy answer virtually rejected this distinction. Conquistadors were indeed liable to restitution, and he spent much space denouncing them. But settlers, and those receiving encomiendas from the King or his subordinates, had only succeeded to the original tyranny since all encomiendas were intrinsically evil and contrary to natural law. San Martín's own list of extortions was fresh evidence. The Spanish King did have a just title to the Indies, for their conversion, but tribute due him could not be assigned to encomenderos.[26]

Fray Bartolomé upheld this same extreme doctrine in an even more heartrending correspondence with the Dominicans of his own old territory of Chiapa and Guatemala. He had sent them a copy of his long anti-perpetuity letter to Carranza, which was virtually a tract against encomiendas. But they had replied with some new rules formulated by their provincial chapters, namely that the ancient tributes obtained by encomenderos were excessive and infernal, but those of today were just and moderate.[27]

---

25. *DII*, VII, 348-362; Fabié app. XXX, first document. This letter must have been written between 1553 and 1557—see next note.

26. *DII*, VII, 362-370; Fabié, app. XXX, second document. See Catalogue, no. 59, for a discussion of the earliest and latest possible dates for this correspondence.

27. I cannot identify these provincial chapters positively, but as there is evidence

Greatly distressed, Fray Bartolomé addressed a long letter to them around 1562 or 1563, beginning "Most reverend and dearly beloved fathers." He challenged their beatific picture of the encomienda, since the information he was receiving constantly, including reports from Fray Tomás de Cárdenas and Fray Tomás de la Torre of their own province, showed that the oppressions were continuing. Above all, he insisted with voluminous Latin citations that encomiendas were tyrannical and illegal.[28]

But the most interesting pages of this letter are those that reveal Casas' own mood of discouragement. He is amazed that the friars contradict his views, when he is by far the most experienced person alive on Indian matters. He tells how the sale of the Peruvian encomiendas was blocked by Carranza de Miranda with the help of his long letter, and vigorously defends his old friend against the charges of the Inquisition—"By the mercy of God, the Archbishop [of Toledo] is no heretic!" He even feels the need of citing the overwhelming approbation of his own doctrines by competent Dominican theologians. Thus, he relates at length how his memorial to Carranza

---

of long delays in the correspondence, two meetings reported by Remesal may be the right ones. In December 1551, before the election of the first provincial, Dominicans from Central America assembled at Santo Domingo de Guatemala with their vicar general, Fray Tomás Casillas, the new bishop-elect. They concluded that holding Indians in encomiendas was no sin if the encomendero saw to their spiritual and practical needs, and that he might in conscience receive their tribute if it was equitably assessed. But confessors should be guided by the doctrines of their masters and the instructions of the Bishop of Chiapa [Casas? Casillas?]. (Rem., II, 279-281, from the notes of Fray Alonso de Noreña. Evidently Torre's diary had been closed, as he was very ill for a long time before his death in September 1567.)

On January 23, 1558, another provincial chapter discussed restitution as applied to the conquest and the descendants of conquistadors. All specific war outrages were condemned, viz., massacres and enslavements of women and children; and total or partial restitution was specified for all increment received in bad faith or after making war in bad faith. But it was held that conquistadors or their families should be preferred in the assignment of encomiendas, as the conquest generally was in good faith [i.e., made in the belief it was a just war]. (Rem., II 385-388, *passim.*) The same provincial chapter found war against the invading Lacandones justified, not for infidelity or cannibalism, but for desecration of churches. This was confirmed by a cedula of March 16, 1558. (Rem., II, 394-395.)

28. Fabié, app. XXVII; see Catalogue, no. 70, for the dating of this letter in the latter part of 1562 or early in 1563. Cárdenas was one of the six friars who finally reached the Dominican province from the large missionary contingent Casas assembled in 1552.

received prior approval from the regents of the College of San Gregorio and Master Cano as superior regent, and then won praise from Carranza himself. He refers to his voluminous writings on the rights of the Indians, and says they were read with approval in the lecture rooms of the universities of Salamanca and Alcalá and his own college. And he tells that Master Domingo de Soto approved all his writings on the Indies, and Carranza and the other judges in the Sepúlveda dispute were all satisfied by the proofs in his *Apología*.[29]

Indeed, Casas' citation of these various approbations makes me wonder if in some way he was implicated in the Inquisition proceedings against Archbishop Carranza de Miranda.[30] Arrested in 1559, Carranza wished to call as defense witnesses Philip himself, several priests, the Duke of Alba, and Bartolomé de las Casas. Apparently, the only one of these who testified was Casas; he is reported by Menéndez y Pelayo to have declared that he always considered Carranza a good Catholic and a preacher of Catholic doctrine.[31] Many of Casas' friends were tried by the Inquisition around this time, including Fray Mancio del Corpus, Fray Juan de Villagarcía (Carranza's companion in England), and Fray Domingo de Soto. All were prosecuted because they were associates of Carranza or had approved his

29. Fabié, app. XXVII, opening four and a half pages.

30. Here it may be noted that Casas was with the court in Toledo, the headquarters of the Inquisition, in 1560. Cf. Fabié, app. XVIII, first item.

31. An account of the trial of Carranza de Miranda may be read in Llorente's *Histoire critique de l'Inquisition d'Espagne*, III, 183-315, and Menéndez y Pelayo's *Historia de los heterodoxos españoles* (Madrid, 1880-1881), lib. IV, cap. VIII. The jealousy of Grand Inquisitor Valdés, who had wanted the primacy, was a main factor. In 1561, the Pope forbade Valdés to pass sentence; and in 1566 he demanded this inquisitor's resignation and Carranza's transfer to Rome, threatening Philip with a papal interdict on the kingdom to force compliance.

Philip's attitude is obscure. Why did he allow this proceeding to begin? No doubt the Lutheran movement had brought a severe reaction against suspected heretics, but throughout the case Philip showed himself personally most anxious to have his archbishop convicted. As Menéndez y Pelayo says, he manifested against Carranza "a blind anger unworthy of a king." The implication seems to me that the accusation of heresy against Carranza was simply one on which to hang some others, in which the Inquisition had no authority. After long imprisonment, Carranza de Miranda was cleared of the most serious charges, ordered to retract certain assertions, and released shortly before his death in 1576. Llorente asserts that Pius V, who died in 1572, had intended to acquit him completely.

Catecismo. Casas was in a like position, though I find no evidence in his writings that he shared Carranza's opinion on justification by faith, which was the main charge against the Archbishop of Toledo.[32] In *Del único modo,* written before he knew Carranza, Casas had gone out of his way to deny this doctrine as a Lutheran heresy; later, in his reply to Sepúlveda, Casas again attacked Luther's doctrines.[33] But certainly Casas did question the rights of kings and the universal sovereignty of the popes; these views were considered heretical and led to his denunciation at one time, and they appear most outspokenly in his lengthy appeal to Carranza.[34] So why was not Casas also prosecuted, or at least involved in the archbishop's trial?

In any event, Carranza's arrest, the death of the Emperor and others, and the waning of the reform spirit among the Dominicans, all added up

---

32. This was the "Lutheran heresy" par excellence. Briefly, Luther announced that man could do nothing by himself to please God, but was saved at once by belief in God's promises. Carranza's writings, notably his famous *Comentarios sobre el catecismo christiano* (Antwerp, 1558), were produced to allege him guilty of this heresy. It was also alleged that Carranza had advised the dying Emperor that he would be saved regardless of sin by his belief in Christ. Cf. Stirling, *The Cloister Life of the Emperor Charles V,* 245.

33. In *Del único modo,* Casas makes the following statement: "Not only faith is necessary but also good works, contrary to the principles of the modern heretics who dare to claim that the dogma of faith alone is sufficient." And again: "Those who are not justified before God and do not work well with the talent they received are thrown to the shades outside, contrary to the doctrine of the most impious Lutherans!" (Cf. 395 and 71.) I have not found any specific allusions to this subject in his writings thereafter, though in the great debate of 1551 (cf. *Aquí se contiene una disputa*) Casas denied that property rights were founded on grace and the faith, a doctrine he claimed had been renewed by Luther. So Casas had imbibed no Lutheran tinge from Carranza de Miranda.

34. I consider Carranza much more of an Erasmian, anyway. We can only wonder whether Casas became slightly infected with Erasmism through his friendship with "Master Miranda" at San Gregorio. I think Casas did have some Erasmian views himself, whether he got them from Carranza or out of the air, so to speak. Carranza was a student of Vitoria's, and that famous Dominican master had studied at Paris and may have come under Erasmus' influence for awhile. To be sure, Casas' limitations on the rights of kings may have been only his own extensions of mediaeval concepts for his special cause. But in his *Erudita et elegans explicatio* he went quite far to demonstrate that the lords of the state were subject to the will of the people. One is reminded that Erasmus once declared a state had the right to dethrone and punish a bad king, and denounced kings who pulled down what the people constructed. Of course, St. Thomas, Erasmus, Vitoria, Casas, and Melchor Cano in his famous *Consulta* of 1555, all denied the temporal power of the Pope.

to a discouraging situation for the eighty-seven-year-old Casas. At his age, besides, he had to look forward to the day when he would no longer be on hand to lead the fight or even to exhort the slackers. What would become of the reform cause that he had championed for nearly half a century? Bartolomé de las Casas was to meet this final challenge to his life's work in a characteristic fashion during his closing years.

LAST TESTAMENT

THE FINAL COLLABORATORS

Casas lived to the amazing age of ninety-two, in failing health but with mind and spirit undiminished. In the time left to him he labored to summarize all his principles in two great farewell treatises for the guidance of the Crown and the inspiration of a new generation of reformers.

Many of them, members of the three mendicant Orders and colonial officials, actually worked with Fray Bartolomé in his closing years. Even as the fire burned out in others, these men were taking up the defense of the Indians, all the way from the tithes question in New Spain to the bloody conquest of Chile and further deliberations at the Spanish court. Perhaps the most celebrated was an Augustinian friar called Veracruz, who became almost Casas' understudy, and whose papers are our main source for the closing chapter of Casas' life.

Fray Alonso de la Veracruz—his real name was Gutiérrez—was born about 1504, making him Casas' junior by thirty years. A noted scholar and missionary, Veracruz had studied letters at Alcalá and law with the famous Vitoria at Salamanca, before joining the Augustinians and going to Mexico where he took his final vows in 1536. Long attached to the province of Michoacán, he was appointed in 1553 to the first chair of theology at the new University of Mexico.[1] Incidentally, Herrera states that Casas was instrumental in recommending the establishment of that institution. As a professor there, Veracruz followed the custom of giving "relectios," or formal lectures, composing in 1555 a significant one entitled *De dominio infidelium*

---

1. See García Icazbalceta's *Bibliografíía mexicana del siglo XVI* for an account of Veracruz's life and published works, especially the much-reprinted *Speculum conjugiorum*. Veracruz died in Mexico in 1584, surviving Casas by some 18 years.

et justo bello.[2] Some of the topics considered—whether the emperor is lord of the known world and has dominion over his subjects' property, whether the pope has supreme power, whether the emperor and king of Castile can wage just war against barbarians, and how the pope can compel infidels to accept the faith—seem to me closely to follow part I of Vitoria's "relectio" *De Indis.*[3] And I find it beyond question that Veracruz embraced Casas' views on the rights of the Spanish kings and their claim to the conquered territories in America.

So this learned Augustinian was admirably fitted to become Fray Bartolomé's associate. Arriving in Spain in 1562, Veracruz stayed on at court, working closely with Casas till the latter's death, and amassing a copious record of his final writings and activities. These papers were later taken back to Mexico by Fray Alonso and afterwards scattered; a number found their way, via Nicolás León, to the John Carter Brown Library in Rhode Island, and others (by some unknown means) to the Bibliothèque Nationale in Paris.[4] All together, they give us a remarkable picture of the ninety-year-old Bishop of Chiapa.

---

2. For the only known manuscript of Veracruz's *Dominación de infieles,* see José Fernando Ramírez' *Adiciones y correcciones* of 1898 to the *Bibliotheca* of Beristain. Consisting of 80 folio leaves, this MS had formerly been in the possession of Vicente de P. Andrade; Ramírez does not specify its subsequent location, though implying he had owned it, but it was not sold with his books in London in 1881. In the manuscript, the major "relectio" is followed by another, wherein Veracruz concludes that Indian neophytes should be exempted from paying tithes.

3. Cf. Vitoria's very similar points: The emperor is not master of the world; the pope is not temporal lord of the universe but has temporal power only in spiritual spheres; the pope does not have and cannot confer a right to war on infidels for not accepting a donation of their lands to Christian rulers or for not accepting the faith. (Part I, 2-55 in Vicente Beltrán de Heredia's edition, Madrid, 1928.) At the outset, Vitoria speaks of 40 years elapsing since the discovery of the Indies, indicating that this was written in 1532. It is therefore no coincidence that his student Veracruz, who left Spain in 1533, so closely echoes what I believe to be Vitoria's earlier views. (For my theory, cf. *supra,* chapter IX, note 37.)

4. Precisely where Dr. León found these papers is uncertain, but I believe Veracruz deposited them in some favorite Michoacán convent, as he did a number of his works. Allegedly Fray Alonso had the largest private library in New Spain, and gave many of his books to the Augustinian College of San Pablo, which he founded in 1577.

The Veracruz papers of the Bibliothèque Nationale contain documentary evidence that they too were in Mexico. A marginal notation on one of the leaves reads: "I, Fray Alonso de la Vera ✝ state that *Doctor Cárcamo, judge for His Majesty in this city of Mexico,* while reporter at court in Spain, heard Crown Attorney Ulloa

Despite his age, Bartolomé de las Casas kept up his work as general representative of the Indians at court. The seat of government had moved permanently to Madrid in 1561 and he now lived at the Dominican convent in that city. He still received reports from friars all over the New World, among them Fray Gil González, a Dominican reformer in Chile, and Fray Nicolás de Witte, a close relative of the Emperor and a prominent member of the Augustinians in Mexico.[5] And he still made miscellaneous appeals to the Council: for royal aid to the church of La Paz in Peru, for a general prohibition against pearl fishing, and so on.[6] Many of these items are pre-served in the Veracruz papers, and we also have details on a most interesting episode in which Fray Bartolomé played an advisory role typical of this period.

Evidently Casas carried on an extensive correspondence with the talent-ed Judge Alonso de Zorita, author of the *Historia de la Nueva España*. A veteran official, Licentiate Zorita had previously served as judge at Santo Domingo, as well as inspector general in Santa Marta. Transferred to the Guatemala audiencia, he had lowered Indian tributes to reasonable rates, which later won him Casas' praise as a "just and God-fearing" man.[7] But it

---

charge . . . that Pizarro had killed more than 20,000 infants taken from the breasts of their mothers, so the women could carry the loads of his expedition." [Italics ours.] This is signed by Veracruz, and written on a manuscript copy of part of Casas' will. (Icazbalceta, *Docs.*, I, cli, transcribed by Ramírez; and II, 512, note, quoted more accurately by JGI himself.) Since Cárcamo was a royal judge from 1572 to 1578, this notation must have been made in Mexico after Fray Alonso's return from Spain in 1573.

There is no clue as to how these papers reached Paris. I first find them men-tioned in 1804, when M. Gregoire read a *Discours* before the Institute, citing a manuscript no. 10,536 which was doubtless one of the Veracruz papers.

5. Fray Gil's letter is in the volume of Veracruz papers in the Bibliothèque Nationale described *infra*, note 13. On August 24, 1555, Fray Nicolás de Witte had written Casas from Mextitlán about how Indians were being oppressed with tithes (Cuevas, *Docs.*, 242-244). Since de Witte was Augustinian provincial when Veracruz was procurator at court, Casas certainly continued to hear from Fray Nicolás.

6. These late petitions illustrate Casas' continuing concern for Indians in all parts of the New World; see the undated texts in *DII*, VII, 161-167 and Hanke, "Festón de Docs.," *Revista Cubana*, XVI, 209-211. Also see Catalogue, nos. 68 and 69, on the La Paz church and a representative for the Indians in Lima; no. 72 on con-ditions in Guatemala; and no. 76 on pearl fishing in the Antilles—where I date them all in Casas' Madrid years.

7. *DII*, VII, 163.

was after Zorita was shifted to New Spain in 1556 that he showed himself a true follower of the teachings of Bartolomé de las Casas.

Once in Mexico, Judge Zorita made a remarkable Casas-style offer to convert and reduce peacefully the Indians to the north. Its genesis appears in a letter from Mexico City on January 10, 1558, where Zorita discloses that the Dominicans and Franciscans were considering sending missionaries to the northerly Indians of Florida and the Chichimecas, and (indirectly) that he himself was in touch with Casas.[8] So the judge may have received his plan directly from Fray Bartolomé, or at least encouragement to try it. Anyway, by 1561 Zorita and the famous Fray Cintos de San Francisco had drawn up concrete proposals that were carried to Spain the following year by a Franciscan, Fray Alonso de Maldonado, who got together with Casas at court.[9]

Zorita's actual scheme—we know it from a letter to the King of July 20, 1561, and a formal petition—had many points resembling the Verapaz experiment.[10] He asked appointment as governor at twelve thousand ducats

---

8. Zorita, *Historia,* app. V—a report to the King. He says that Fray Francisco de Mena, a Franciscan bound for Spain, could give full information on the subject; also that Fray Juan de Torres, Dominican from Guatemala, must already be at court. Both would certainly see Casas, and in other letters Zorita tells of writing to and receiving word from the Bishop of Chiapa.

9. "Cintos," whose real name was Jacinto de Portillo, had come with Cortés and had been active in what is now the state of Durango, as one of the founders of Nombre de Dios. He received two encomiendas in the division of 1522, but gave these up at some early date and joined the Franciscans as a lay brother. For a long time he was porter to the convent in Mexico, and I find no record that he ever took final orders.

Fray Cintos' proposal for the northern territory was made in a letter to the King on July 20, 1561, the same date as Zorita's discussed in my text. It contained almost the same terms, though somewhat scaled down, e.g., half the number of Spaniards. In this letter, Fray Cintos told of leaving Mexico City two years earlier with a couple of companions, in search of New Mexico; they had traveled some 150 leagues northward and found the natives at war with the Spaniards. See Icazbalceta, *Nueva colección de docs.,* II (*Códice franciscano*), 235-247. Also cf. Icaza, *Conquistadores de Nueva España,* no. 1228, for Fray Cintos' 1547 petition that his erstwhile encomiendas be not reassigned.

10. See Zorita, *Historia,* app. VII, the letter describing his services, outlining the plan, and saying he is sending Casas the detailed petition. This was printed in García Icazbalceta's *Docs.,* II, 333-342, from a copy then in his possession and now

with an expedition of one hundred Spaniards on royal salary, to penetrate and settle the north country, entering via the land of the Chichimecas and Culiacán, and then proceeding northward to the new lands discovered by Coronado, New Mexico and Copala. For the conversion, he would take along at least twenty Franciscans, including some who had already visited that country; no clerics or members of other Orders would be allowed. During a ten-year period no Spaniard (except his own men) should be permitted to enter the territory without a license, just like the similar exclusion for the Land of War; and after this had expired, it would be requested for another ten years. His plan was to found Spanish settlements at intervals and attract the natives by gifts, good works, and good examples. So he would not remove the native lords, nor grant any encomiendas, nor make slaves; and he asked a royal guarantee that Christianized chiefs should retain their positions and revenues. Also, converted Indians should be free from tribute for ten years and should pay no tithes, and the cost of churches should be borne by the King. All the expenses of this colonization and conversion would be met from the products of the land, and His Majesty might ultimately expect tremendous revenues from the Indians thus peacefully reduced and from the rich mines to be discovered.

In the main, Zorita's proposal was the Land of War method applied to New Mexico, save for the Spaniards to be taken along, which recalled Casas' old Tierra Firme schemes. It was actually the judge's second plan of the sort, for in his petition he told of drawing up the official instructions for the 1559 Florida expedition and sending Casas a copy. In this new scheme, the extreme ideas on native lords and the cost of conversion clearly incorporated the latter-day views of the Bishop of Chiapa.

Most likely this Zorita petition was presented to the Council of the Indies in 1562 by Fray Bartolomé and Fray Alonso de Maldonado, another collaborator of these later years. We know that they did memorialize the Council jointly and both defended Indian capacity;[11] and this particular petition may be one of those still unpublished in the Bibliothèque Nationale. Anyway, the Casas-Maldonado effort bore scant fruit: a royal cedula auth-

---

in the University of Texas Library. It may well be the same as one presented by Casas and Maldonado in 1562—Catalogue, no. 67.

Zorita also asked the governorship of New Galicia, in order to assemble men, arms, horses, and supplies there, and recommended the suppression of the audiencia in that province.

11. Zorita, *Historia*, 282. Also, Maldonado was one of the three friars who presented Casas' last petition to the Council of the Indies—Icazbalceta, *Docs.*, II, 598.

orized Zorita to try the venture, but only at his own expense, which was impossible.

Yet the event had a certain significance. It was the first of many joint endeavors on behalf of the Indians during the next few years by Casas and a new group of missionaries from Mexico. They had all come to Spain in the latter part of 1561 or the spring of 1562.[12] The contingent included, besides Maldonado, the three Mexican provincials and Fray Alonso de la Veracruz as Augustinian procurator. The provincials had made the trip to protest Philip's revocation of some privileges of the mendicant Orders, but one died shortly after arrival and the other two were appointed to bishoprics. So the work of the mission devolved on Veracruz, who remained at court and became the intimate associate of the nonagenarian Casas and the recorder of his declining years. As they worked together on the defense of the Indians, Veracruz saved copies of important late letters to and from Fray Bartolomé and petitions presented by Casas and Maldonado. Most important of all, he transcribed the final treatises to come from the prolific pen of Bartolomé de las Casas.[13]

"Treasures" and "doubts," a bequest and codicil

When he was nearing ninety, Casas completed his last major writings: a Latin tome *On the Treasures of Peru* and a Spanish *Tract of Twelve Doubts* based upon it. Since they embody his final thinking on the Indies, I shall examine them in some detail.

Both works apparently grew out of problems submitted to him by

---

12. The three provincials reached Spain by 1562; cf. their petition to the King in the Veracruz papers, Bibliothèque Nationale. Before the vessels of that May, there had been no sailings from the port of Veracruz since September 1561, when Maldonado left. See Zorita, *Historia*, lxxxii—his August 30, 1562, letter in response to the disappointing cedula.

13. His Casas miscellany, including the letter to Carranza, is found in a volume of Veracruz's papers in the Bibliothèque Nationale, Paris. This volume was first cited in Eugenio de Ochoa's *Catálogo razonado de los manuscritos españoles existentes en la Biblioteca Real de Paris* (1844), 576, but without mention of all the MSS in it or even of Casas' will. Subsequently, José María Andrade copied the will and some other pieces by Casas from this volume, no. 1588, Fonds St. Germain. These transcripts were printed by García Icazbalceta in 1866, as well as a defective inventory of the Veracruz volume, listing a number of items of Casas interest. (See Icazbalceta, *Docs.*, II, lvi-lviii.) I have cited such items individually, either in my Catalogue as manuscript copies of Casas' writings, or in my notes as manuscripts pertaining to his life. For Veracruz's copies of Casas' treatises, see *infra*, note 18.

Peruvian missionaries. Very possibly this custom had started with the letter of his former co-worker, Fray Tomás de San Martín. Anyhow, the first treatise was addressed to the specific question of who owned the vast treasures found by the colonists in Inca sepulchers. As for the second, the Argument told how a longtime Dominican missionary to Peru, appalled by conditions there, returned to Spain and propounded his doubts to the learned of various faculties, starting with the former Bishop of Chiapa.[14] So Casas probably composed this answer for Fray Domingo de Santo Tomás, who had come from Peru before 1559 to work with him on the caciques' counteroffer and was back there in 1562 as the new Bishop of Charcas.[15]

Yet in content, *The Treasures of Peru* and *Twelve Doubts* are really concluding summaries of Casas' total doctrine—he himself called them his "bequest" and "codicil." Thus, in his dedication to Philip, he said that he had only a little while to live, and in order to complete his mission after fifty years' work he had to divulge an important secret that would correct a dangerous past error:

> This I wrote in Latin, in a treatise entitled *De thesauris,* which I proposed to offer Your Majesty as though I were bequeathing you much wealth in my last testament, if perchance I had the wherewithal to do so. . . . While I was awaiting the time and opportune season to present it . . . a certain friar of the Order of St. Dominic, desirous of learning the justice or injustice of this matter . . . and of serving Your Majesty in the relief of those Indies . . . required me to answer twelve doubts of great importance. . . . So, what I had said in sum in the treatise *De thesauris* in Latin, I explained particularly in Spanish. . . . And it is this [Spanish tract] that can serve almost as a codicil to it.[16]

---

14. See Fabié, I, 337-338, the Argument of *Doce dudas.* "Doubts" of this sort had become customary among Peruvian missionaries. Cf. the conclusions of a Lima council of March 11, 1560, presided over by Archbishop Gerónimo de Loaysa and consisting of provincials and members of the four Orders then in Peru; their 21 points on restitution generally exemplified Casas' doctrine, though the specific question of tomb treasures was not treated. MS in the JCBL.

15. I at first thought the questioner might have been San Martín himself, since the questions posed in his letter (*DII,* VII, 348-362) are quite parallel to those in the *Doce dudas.* But Bishop San Martín died several years before Casas wrote these treatises, and the "doubts" were proposed in Spain and not by correspondence. So I have concluded that the questioner must have been Casas' later Peruvian co-worker, Santo Tomás, following the example of his predecessor. See Catalogue, no. 74, paragraph on *Doce dudas,* for what is apparently the manuscript of the original "doubts."

16. This is from the unpublished portion of *Doce dudas,* fols. 136-137 verso of the MS in the JCBL.

And of this "codicil" he declared further that

> Bartolomé de las Casas . . . resolved twelve doubts . . . concerning the welfare of the consciences of the Kings of Castile and León and of the Spaniards living now and in the future in the Indies, and the spiritual health and good government and preservation of the Indians, native inhabitants of those lands.[17]

So I feel that Casas wrote these works not primarily as Peruvian tracts, but as basic guides for all Indies reformers. In fact, I think he intended his *De thesauris* and *Doce dudas* to be circulated among American friars and select officials, as was his *Del único modo*. The Latin of *De thesauris* suggests a monastic audience, and at least three manuscript copies are known of both works, including several made by or for Fray Alonso de la Veracruz.[18] Perhaps Casas also expected his two last treatises to be read in the lecture halls of the University of Mexico, just as his other books were read in the courses at Alcalá and Salamanca and Valladolid. Anyhow, there is evidence that these final views of his were backed by the new group of Mexican missionaries who worked with him at court.[19]

What was this concluding doctrine on which Casas labored so hard in his great age? *De thesauris* has not been published, and I infer that it contained some material of a historical nature not found in the shorter work. But in *Doce dudas,* as he himself assures us, Fray Bartolomé reiterated all that he had to say on the subject.[20]

---

17. Fabié, I, 336-337, the opening statement of *Doce dudas.*

18. See Catalogue, nos. 73-74, for the manuscripts of both works. The set in the John Carter Brown Library, and the separate *Doce dudas* in the Bibliothèque Nationale, are all Veracruz copies.

A marginal note, added to the JCBL *De thesauris* manuscript, states: "All the writing in this book is in the hand of Fr. Alonso de la Veracruz." But Ramírez reproduces some of the MS of Veracruz's "relectio" of 1555, which he apparently thought was holograph, and the writing is entirely different. So I conclude that the JCBL set belonged to Veracruz, but was not copied by him; this is borne out by an occasional copyist's error.

19. Cf. Catalogue, no. 78, on their presenting his supporting petition. Reformers in America also held identical views, suggesting close communication. Thus, in 1564 Bishop Alburquerque of Oaxaca, a Dominican, asserted that the papal Bull of Donation was solely for conversion, and on the day the Indians had government and the faith, the King would be obliged to leave the Indies to the natives. Cf. the report to the King of Licentiate Jerónimo Valderrama, Inspector General of New Spain. *DII,* IV, 355-372.

20. Llorente, II, 181-335, printing the text only without any of the preliminaries.

The *Twelve Doubts* opens with a scathing review of the Spanish conquest and exploitation of Peru, and a series of questions or "doubts" on the restitution of the wealth thus obtained: Atahualpa's ransom, tributes to encomenderos, gold and silver from the mines, tomb and temple treasures, and so forth. Casas, as might be expected, resolves these doubts by insisting on the restitution to which all, even the King, are bound. He does so by laying down eight guiding principles on Indian rights, Spain's title to the Indies, and her conduct there:

> 1-2. By natural and divine and human law, the Indians—as infidels of the fourth category who never harmed nor were subject to Christians—freely possess and rule their own lands, and no King or Emperor or Pope can make just war upon them.
>
> 3-6. The papal Bull of Donation was issued solely for the conversion of the Indians and did not dispossess the native lords. Rather, the Spanish kings must pay the costs of this conversion, and they need the free consent of the natives to acquire justly the sovereignty granted them over the Indies.
>
> 7-8. From the beginning till now (January 1564), Spain's entire invasion and misgovernment of the Indies has been wrong and tyrannical; and from 1510 on, no Spaniard there can claim good faith as an excuse for wars, discoveries, the slave trade, or the munitions business.[21]

Applying these rules, Casas develops his final doctrine—a reaffirmation of his lifelong views, but brought to their logical conclusion. For instance, he denounces the encomienda system as he did at the start of his crusade in 1515, and he reiterates his continuing opposition to all conquests. But the doctrine of restitution, though dwelt upon in some of his earlier writings, is here carried further than ever, indeed to a point almost entirely impossible of realization.

As before, he insists that all encomenderos are bound to restore tribute collected from the natives. But now he follows this tribute from the encomenderos to their doctors, merchants, wives and children, masons, carpenters, tailors, and even priests who had accepted money to say masses for the souls of the departed. Missionaries alone are exempted; their services in spreading

---

21. It is these eight conclusions that Remesal (II, 109-110) wrongly attributes to the Mexican bishops' junta of 1546, compounding his confusion by stating that they were presented again by some unnamed Dominican at court in January 1564. The chronicler might have seen an abstract of the second or friars' junta of 1546, and a manuscript of *Doce dudas* without the preliminaries, as both of these are in the Veracruz papers now in Paris but probably in Mexico in Remesal's time.

the faith entitled them to some moderate support. But the rest had endangered their souls and should not be absolved until they had made restitution.

I find this unrealistic, though no doubt many were moved over the years by Casas' entreaties and threats. A number of conquistadors did give up their Indians and join monastic Orders; in 1554, one Rebolledo, who had an encomienda in Nata, wrote to Casas that he was making a restitution to his Indians of three thousand pesos worth of cattle. But these were isolated cases, and apparently Casas still hoped to force universal restitution by means of his confessional.

Even more extreme were his final views on the necessity of restitution by the Crown itself. Casas contended that the Spaniards had unjustly deprived the native lords of their sovereignty, and the King was therefore obliged to restore the living heirs of the last Inca ruler to positions of authority over the land and the people. These heirs were hidden in the Andes, but had expressed willingness to become Christians in return for freedom and maintenance. Casas accordingly proposed to send to the Inca Tito a Cuzco priest who knew him, armed with sealed letters from the King. A province where the Incas could live safely was to be assigned to Tito and his followers, and the Inca was to recognize the King of Spain as his overlord. The inhabitants were to be returned to the Inca gradually, Crown towns first and then encomiendas on the death of their holders; and for his part the Inca was to pay an annual royal tribute to the King of Castile, who could thus legally acquire sovereignty.

One doubtful problem in this visionary scheme was how full restitution could be made for the gold and silver taken from the temple in Cuzco and later from the mines and tombs. The Spaniards, of course, had to give back everything. But the King had received one-half or more of the tomb treasures and the royal fifth from war and mining. In view of the impossibility of His Majesty sending back all the wealth shipped to him and his predecessors in Spain, Casas suggested that the Inca remove the entire royal burden of restitution. The King, however, was obliged to pay the cost of missionaries to the Indians, and the natives should not be subjected to church tithes.[22]

---

22. Though a Mexican council of 1555 did not exempt Indians, reformers generally opposed tithing them—cf. Veracruz's second "relectio" and De Witte's letter of that year, and Zorita's peaceful conversion scheme. On April 10, 1557, a cedula was issued not to collect tithes from natives. (Puga, II, 293.) No change seems to have been made before 1558, so perhaps the matter was still pending before the Council of the Indies when Casas wrote.

In this treatise, then, Bartolomé de las Casas set forth the culminating views of his long career. His successive ideas are echoed here—extinction of the encomienda, illegitimacy of conquests, Spanish title based on peaceful conversion and the consent of the governed, full restitution, restoration of native lords—all carried to their logical if extreme conclusion. A few points deal especially with Peru, notably the vast wealth "stolen" from Inca tombs, since the Spaniards had found only negligible amounts in the tombs of New Spain and what is now Ecuador and Colombia. Of course, Casas thought these tomb treasures should be returned to the natives—perhaps he specified the Inca, when elaborating the topic earlier in *De thesauris.* But in general, the questions and conclusions treated here could apply to the Spanish occupation of Mexico or the other territories. So I have no doubt that Casas was here laying down his parting guidelines for the future use of all Indies reformers.

CASAS' DEATH AND WILL

Fray Bartolomé's final writings had a more direct goal, too, though it was not pursued till he lay on his deathbed. By means of them, this venerable old man hoped to instigate one last royal junta to reform the Indies.

Both works were addressed to the King, and there is evidence that Casas finished *De thesauris* in 1563 and *Doce dudas* at the start of 1564.[23] I infer the nonagenarian Bishop of Chiapa became seriously ill around that time, for he drew up his will at the end of February; and on March 17, 1564, he delivered it, sealed and before witnesses, to a notary who came to the monastery.[24] Anyhow, the two treatises were apparently not presented to Philip till 1566. That is my conclusion from a petition of Casas to the Council in the latter year, referring to his two books given "these past days" to His Majesty, and renewing his request that a junta be convoked to consider the principles set forth and take appropriate action.

In his dedication, Casas had asked Philip to summon theologians and jurists to consider his treatises and then end the destruction of the Indies.[25] Now, in this last memorial to the Council, a sort of epilogue to the *Twelve Doubts,* he formally repeats his request. Rehearsing the twofold tyranny whereby Spain has devastated the Indies, i.e., conquests and encomiendas,

---

23. See Catalogue, nos. 73 and 74, for the dating of these two works.

24. See the notary Gaspar Testa's attestation at the opening of Casas' will, Icazbalceta, *Docs.,* II, 509. The date of writing is given in the will itself, *ibid.,* 513.

25. MS of *Doce dudas* in the JCBL, fols. 137-137 verso.

and the duty of restitution that burdens the consciences of King and Council, he begs for the appointment of a junta such as the Emperor used to convoke. Let this commission, he cries, examine the eight conclusions he has prepared for the purpose and proved in the books he gave His Majesty:

1. All the wars called conquests were and are most unjust and truly tyrannical.

2. We have usurped all the kingdoms and lordships of the Indies.

3. The encomiendas or allotments of Indians are most iniquitous, evil per se and therefore tyrannical, as is such a form of government.

4. All who grant them sin mortally and those who hold them are always in mortal sin and cannot be saved unless they give them up.

5. The King our lord, whom God prosper and keep, with all the power God gave him, cannot justify the wars and robberies against these people, nor the said allotments or encomiendas, any more than the wars and robberies of Turks against Christians can be justified.

6. All the gold and silver, pearls and other riches, brought to Spain and traded among Spaniards in the Indies—all is stolen, save perhaps a very little that came from the islands and places we have already depopulated.

7. Those who stole it and today steal it by conquests and allotments or encomiendas, and who participate therein, cannot be saved unless they restore it.

8. The natives in any or all the regions we have invaded in the Indies have acquired right to make just war upon us and erase us from the face of the earth, and this right will last until the Day of Judgment.

If these conclusions are declared valid, confessors in the Indies can be so advised—and thereby Spaniards brought to themselves, the Indians freed, the King made in fact universal lord of the Indies, and Spain spared from divine punishment. "With this supplication to Your Honors at the end and close of my life, and the said conclusions in the two treatises I gave His Majesty, I believe I have fulfilled the mission given me by God."[26]

Indeed, this petition was to prove his very last effort in the cause. Apparently early that year, Fray Bartolomé had been well enough to write to Pope Pius V, newly elected in January, begging for a decree anathematizing all who justified war against the Indians or denied their ownership of their own lands or their capacity to receive the faith! He had even sent the Pope a book proving such views erroneous, and hoped to send him further writ-

---

26. Icazbalceta, *Docs.*, II, 595-598; and see Catalogue, no. 78, for the two MSS of this petition.

ings.[27] But by summer, Casas was too ill to appear in person with this final petition—it was presented to the Council of the Indies on his behalf by Fray Alonso de la Veracruz, Maldonado, and the Franciscan commissary at court.[28] "And a few days afterwards," records Veracruz, "the Bishop of Chiapa, who presented the books and the petition, died on the day of Santa Margarita, June 20 [July 20, 1566] in the monastery of Atocha, Madrid, of the Order of St. Dominic of which the said Bishop was a member."[29]

On July 31, Casas' will was solemnly opened in the presence of his executor, a Dominican named Fray Juan Bautista, the general agent of the College of San Gregorio.[30] And on August 16, a legacy of 1,551 reales was delivered by the notary Testa to Fray Alonso de la Veracruz, who signed a receipt for it.[31] This could hardly have been a personal bequest; before he died Casas must have told Veracruz what to do with it. Unless perhaps the instructions were included in the separate signed and sealed paper packet referred to in the will as containing burial directions. Or perhaps the instructions were in the omitted paragraphs of the will itself, which may have contained other bequests.[32] Anyway I think it most likely that the money was for copying Casas' writings, as the notary apparently also gave Veracruz a

---

27. Icazbalceta, *Docs.*, II 599-600; see Catalogue, no. 77, for verification of the date of this petition. Casas further asks the Pope to order bishops to care for the oppressed Indians and to learn the native languages, and to order restitution by the secular and regular clergy of any treasure they may have taken from the natives. In his introduction to *Del único modo*, Dr. Lewis Hanke makes the plausible suggestion that it may have been the book sent with the petition.

28. See Icazbalceta, *Docs.*, II, 598, for Veracruz's short note at the end of the petition. In a longer note following the JCBL copy (fol. 229), Veracruz adds that it was read aloud by the reporter at a full meeting of the Council of the Indies. See Catalogue, no. 78, for the contents of these two notes.

29. JCBL, Veracruz's long note, fol. 229. Remesal (II, 466) describes Casas' funeral at the Atocha convent and his burial there.

30. Icazbalceta, *Docs.*, II, 509-510, copied from the Veracruz papers in the Bibliothèque Nationale.

31. This receipt is among the notary's papers—Cristóbal Pérez Pastor, *Bibliografía madrileña*, III (1907), 516.

32. E.g., Casas may have left something to relatives or to the college for the scholarships. Where did he get money for a legacy to Veracruz, etc.? I know of only one source, besides his pension, which had been increased in 1563. That same year Casas took steps to collect 149 ducats due him for his services in an arbitration matter. See *DII*, X, 86-87; Catalogue, no. 71.

certified copy of the paragraphs dealing with the assembling of Fray Bartolomé's books and papers.[33]

In these paragraphs of a legal will and testament, Bartolomé de las
Casas spoke his farewell words in the cause he had served so long. They
closely followed the ideas of his last two treatises, his "bequest" and "codicil,"
and the final petition he had been too ill to present to the Council of the
Indies. The faithful Veracruz appended them carefully to his transcript of
that last document. They contain Casas' directions to the college to arrange
his correspondence and preserve his manuscript *History of the Indies*, and
this closing summary of his life's work for the Indians:

> God in His goodness and mercy saw fit to choose me as his minister,
> though unworthy, to plead for all those people of the Indies, possessors of those
> kingdoms and lands, against unheard of and unimagined oppressions and evils
> and injuries received from our Spaniards . . . and to restore them to the
> primitive liberty unjustly taken from them . . . and to free them from the
> violent deaths they still suffer and die as they have died; and by this cause many
> thousands of leagues have been depopulated, many in my presence. And I have
> labored in the court of the Kings of Castile, going and coming from the Indies
> to Castile and from Castile to the Indies many times, for about fifty years, since
> the year 1514, only for God and from compassion at seeing perish such multi-
> tudes of rational men, peaceful, humble, most amenable and simple beings, well
> fitted to receive our holy Catholic faith . . . and to be endowed with all good
> customs. . . . Now therefore I say and hold it certain . . . that all the crimes
> committed by the Spaniards against those people . . . with such perverse
> cruelties, have been against the pure and most righteous law of Jesus Christ,
> and against all natural reason, and to the greatest infamy of His name and the
> Christian religion, and the total obstruction of the faith. . . . And I believe that
> for these impious and ignominious works, so unjustly and tyrannically and bar-
> barously committed . . . God will pour His fury and anger upon Spain if she
> does not perform a great penance. . . . And I fear that she will do this late or
> never, because of the blindness that God has permitted in great and small alike

---

33. Icazbalceta, *Docs.*, II, 509-514. See Catalogue, no. 75, for the two known
manuscripts of these extracts from Casas' will; both copies belonged to Veracruz.
Gaspar Testa, the original notary who had received and opened the will, transcribed
these paragraphs "in this city of Madrid, August 14, 1566. There were present to
see it copied, corrected and compared with the original: Pedro Romero and Juan de
Monesterio, citizens of the town." There are two discontinuous extracts; the text
breaks and resumes with a "Likewise," showing that something has been omitted, and
the notary states he has copied only certain portions and the opening and closing.
The rest of the document seems never to have been published, and may be lost.

... and especially in those who think themselves wise and presume to rule the world . . . a denseness of understanding still so current that seventy years after they started robbing and killing and exterminating those nations . . . even today they have not yet realized that such massacres and captivities . . . and universal desolations have been sins and the greatest injustices.

Thus, virtually with his dying breath,[34] Bartolomé de las Casas concluded the crusade he had carried on with almost superhuman zeal for more than half a century—surely earning for all time that title he had held only briefly in 1517 at the trifling salary of a hundred pesos a year: Universal Procurator or Protector of All the Indians of the Indies.

---

34. He did so with his actual dying breath, too, according to Father Gabriel Cepeda, historian of the monastery of Our Lady of Atocha. Cf. Fabié, I, 239-241.

CONCLUSION:
CASAS' CRUSADE AND PLACE IN HISTORY

"Protector of the Indians" is the title I prefer for Bartolomé de las Casas, not the more widely used "Apostle of the Indies." That designation was popularized by Sir Arthur Helps, but it seems to me a misnomer as Casas was not mainly a missionary.[1] I know that my title can be criticized, too, since it afterwards designated a limited office held by many individuals; but Casas was the first to hold it, and with him it was unlimited.

Universal protector of the Indians he certainly was, from the start of his mission in 1515 until his death more than fifty years later. He set out to relieve the oppression and extermination of the American natives, and in his will he was still at it. The first part of his career, as I see it, sounds much more materialistic than apostolic. Statements of concern for the royal revenues run all through his "community scheme," his many petitions, his efforts to obtain a grant for himself. I doubt if he cared much for the King's revenue, but Fray Pedro de Córdoba had warned him about Ferdinand and he soon learned that this approach was necessary. Casas' early proposals often sound like moneymaking ventures, despite their humanitarian purpose; no doubt they reflect his background as a planter in the islands. When he withdrew from the world after the Cumaná tragedy, he himself wondered if he had "stained" his pure intent by the commercialism of his contract with the Española Conference.

---

1. Helps' *Life of Las Casas, the Apostle of the Indies,* was first published in London in 1868 (extracted and expanded from his famous *Spanish Conquest in America,* 4 volumes, 1855-1861). Thereafter, the "apostle" designation was used by 19th- and 20th-century biographers in Spain, England, and America; more recent writers have called Casas the "Father of the Indians," a term which lacks the active connotation of "protector."

In the next phase of his career, when he had become Fray Bartolomé, I do not see him primarily as a missionary. His first letters, written after his monastic "sleep," show he was eager to be back at court. The Verapaz experiment was a success to a certain extent, but that came afterwards and was due to his brother friars. Certainly Fray Bartolomé had a strong interest in missions, and in the later part of his life he was very active in recruiting friars for the New World. But I would not class him as an "apostle" for a fundamental reason: he never learned the Indian languages well enough to preach in them. Had he lived among his cherished Indians long enough to speak to them fluently in their own tongue, no doubt he could have converted thousands with his persuasive eloquence. As it was, he cannot be compared in this respect with men like Fray Andrés de Olmos, Fray Toribio Motolinía, Fray Bernardino de Sahagún, and Fray Pedro de Gante, who all knew the Mexican language well enough to write in it. But that was not Casas' objective; and his missionary activities, as I have shown, ultimately brought him back to Spain.

It was there Casas' real work lay, not preaching to the Indians in some remote village but pleading for them at court. Only in Spain did he become truly apostolic in the prophetic sense, the Jeremiah of the Spaniards, denouncing injustice and demanding reform. The major mistakes of his career were made when he left court. He should never have attempted the Cumaná colony under impossible circumstances, and after his work for the New Laws it was unwise to accept a bishopric. As Bishop of Chiapa, he was a total failure, because he bickered with the Spanish encomenderos and slaveholders and tried to bring them around to his views. In the end, he returned to court and permanently assumed what I regard as his true role—representative of the Indians with the Spanish government.

So from start to finish he was not the apostle but rather the "protector and procurator" of the Indians, as in his brief official title. The basic relief he advocated did not change during his long crusade—it was simply to take the Spaniards off the backs of the natives. At the outset he hoped to get rid of the encomienda; in his last writings he was still hammering away at the same idea. In 1515 the encomienda had just been given full official status by the allotment of the year before, though it had existed in somewhat inchoate form since 1502, and he himself had held encomiendas in both Española and Cuba. But with his "conversion" he decided to attack it as an abusive system responsible for the "destruction" of the Indians; certainly by then he had seen enough to horrify any save the most insensitive. From then on, the encomienda remained his chief target for half a century, despite modifications he himself helped bring about. In the beginning he sought to replace it with more humane methods of exploitation; during the New Laws period he mounted a frontal attack on the institution itself; late in life he battled the Peruvian settlers when they attempted to buy perpetual encomiendas. Throughout, he insisted that the Indians were free men and should be treated as such.

I find only one major extension of this original drive: his subsequent attack on conquests and Indian slavery and his urging peaceful conversion instead. Here again, Casas himself had served as chaplain in the two- or three-year conquest of Cuba, and he even drew up sworn evidence of those "services." But by 1531, as prior in Puerto de Plata, he preached against the conquest and printed copies of the Bull of Donation. He was now convinced that Spain's title to the Indies rested not on wars but on a papal grant for the conversion of the natives. So in *Del único modo* and the Verapaz experiment he expounded and demonstrated his idea of peaceably converting Indians who would then become tributary vassals of the Crown. Thenceforth, he attacked conquests and the huge traffic in Indian slaves, along with the encomienda. In this first treatise, too, he elaborated the idea of restitution that became prominent in his later writings, notably his *Confesionario* and *Doce dudas*, where he went so far as to assert the King's duty to restore the Inca. Strangely enough, I find no hint anywhere that Casas ever realized the impossibility of full restitution, just as I find no softening in his attitude toward the encomienda.

Such a goal—to free the Indians from encomiendas and slavery—was bound to make Casas obnoxious during his own times to most of the Spaniards in the New World. From the beginning and for a long while thereafter, almost their sole source of wealth was the labor of the natives, in encomiendas, as slaves, in the mines. So the colonists regarded Casas' crusade as an attempt to dispossess them, and he became "the most hated man in the Indies," the object of virulent attacks by interested parties and rivals—Maldonado and Marroquín, Central American town councils, and the famous Motolinía.[2] Casas was charged with everything save actual crimes, but only Fray Toribio's much-quoted diatribe merits any comment. As I have explained fully, it was the "adult baptism" question about Motolinía's missionary labors that led to his grudge. In their controversy, I must side with Casas;

---

2. Cf. the September 10, 1543, letter of the Santiago de Guatemala council to the Emperor, pouring out a tirade of abuse against Casas. Arévalo, *Docs.*, 16-20; Fabié, app. X.

in my *Rise of Fernando Cortés* I have discussed the often superficial character of the mass conversions of Indians.[3] Also, Motolinía had been in Guatemala in 1545, and from some of his remarks I suspect that Bishop Casas had warned him to keep away from the Land of True Peace.[4] All told, therefore, there was ample reason for contemporary hostility toward Casas' objectives.

In later centuries it became the style to admire these aims but to criti-

---

3. See page 461. As I have pointed out, millions of Indians were baptized without in the least understanding the mysteries of the Christian dogma. Their wills were captured by presents, kind treatment, and numerous other devices; their understanding was engaged, but not in the manner proposed in *Del único modo*. For they became only nominal Christians, simply adding a new deity to their already well-filled pantheon. To the Indians, the friars represented the benign spirit of the Christian God, and they flocked to His banner. Essentially, the natives were seeking relief from the brutality of the conquest and the oppression of servitude, and the Christian faith offered some solace. The difficulties of genuine conversion were well illustrated in Casas' own bishopric. One problem was the multiplicity of tongues, thirteen dialects in Chiapa alone (cf. Starr's *Indian Mexico*, 440, and Rem., I, 426). Another was the survival of native cults (cf. Xim., I, 447, on a great idol-burning at Cinacatlán). But the chief obstacle, as Casas pointed out repeatedly, was the bad example of Christian Spaniards: slave raids and oppressive treatment, antagonism towards missionaries, and specific vices.

4. Motolinía had gone to Guatemala with a number of friars in 1544. His correspondence about this interlude reflects the Franciscan-Dominican rivalry that began to be alarming around this time, and reached the proportions of a civil war before the end of the century. Thus, writing to the Santiago council on October 21, 1545, Motolinía alleged that the Dominicans had stated repeatedly that they were sufficient for that province and had made it a matter of conscience to teach the natives. In his diatribe of 1555 to the Emperor, Fray Toribio belittled the peaceful pacification of Verapaz by the Dominicans, asserting that he had been nearby and it was a poor country and very sparsely populated. Cf. Icazbalceta, *Docs.*, I, lxxx and 259.

In general the Franciscans favored the colonists and the Dominicans supported Casas, though there were exceptions on both sides. Casas had Franciscan co-workers, and Motolinía's attack cited a "very public letter" of the Dominican Fray Domingo de Betanzos, chiding Casas for his restless life and the harm caused in Peru by his "Informaciones," and apparently for not completing the China mission errand. Betanzos' letter, presumably written to Casas in Chiapa, is unknown today and there is some mystery about his changeable attitudes as he and Zumárraga had both thanked Casas for the errand. (*DII*, XIII, 531-537.) Stranger still, Betanzos had declared to the Council that the Indians were bestial and God had condemned them to extermination for their sins; this was used as a basis for slaving cedulas, and on his deathbed in 1549 he signed a solemn retraction. See the text in Dr. Hanke's "Pope Paul III and the American Indians," app. I, *Harvard Theological Review*, XXX, 97-98 and cf. 101-102.

cize Casas' methods. The main charges, however, that the *Brevissima relación* was a wild exaggeration and that he was responsible for the introduction of Negro slavery into America—were both unfounded. Casas did indeed increase his estimate of the original number of inhabitants on Española; at first he used the 1,100,000 figure of the Dominicans, but he later raised this to three million after studying the "census" of Bartolomew Columbus. The point seems clear. Casas' absolute figures on native populations are too large, like those of nearly everyone else in that era, but his relative picture is unchallenged. By the close of the sixteenth century not more than ten per cent of the Indians had survived and in many areas the extermination was total, though epidemics were responsible for some of the devastation.[5] But Casas' account of conditions was not overdrawn; as he rightly said, the archives were full of sworn "proofs" describing the most atrocious crimes.[6]

---

5. Possibly Casas did not give enough weight to the tremendous loss of life from the introduction of white men's diseases, to which the natives had no immunity, though some modern writers exaggerate this factor. Thus, the smallpox epidemic of 1520 destroyed innumerable Indians. By then, however, Española was already decimated, and Casas relates in the *Historia* how the epidemic all but wiped out the remnant. Again, in 1545 and 1546, a terrible "cocolistle" [influenza?] epidemic ravaged New Spain. In September 1545, Inspector General Sandoval wrote that at least 200,000 Indians had died, many said more; and around the same time, Jerónimo López wrote that in seven months 400,000 Indians had died within ten leagues of Mexico City, and only about 100 Spaniards. (*Epis. de Nueva España*, IV, 218, 235, and cf. 200.) Yet Casas barely refers to this epidemic in the *Apologética*, though he was in Chiapa and Mexico at the time. Finally, the last great epidemic in New Spain came in 1575-1576, some ten years after Casas' death; and it was not till the following century that the Indian population really began to increase again. By that time, the native races were somewhat inoculated against smallpox and measles which had previously caused so much devastation.

6. Spanish objections are understandably patriotic. But to anyone familiar with the conquest, Casas' narrative is not exaggerated, nor was his the only exposé widely circulated in Europe. About 1541, the Milanese Girolamo Benzoni went to the Indies and served under Benalcázar in what is now Ecuador and Colombia; these campaigns were perhaps even more bloodthirsty and devastating than those of Alvarado and Pedrarias in Central America and Tierra Firme. In 1565, Benzoni published his experiences of 14 years in America, recounting events even more tragic than those in the *Brevissima*.

To my knowledge, however, Casas was the first to point out that the conquest was begun by terroristic methods. (Cf. his *Tratado sobre los indios esclavos*—Llorente, II, 6.) Cortés himself, charged with the murder of innocent Indians at Cholula, finally acknowledged the massacre was meant to instill terror throughout the Aztec region. I think I have demonstrated that he used this method from the start of his

The Negro slavery charge against him was even less substantial. The original controversy merely turned on Herrera's veracity, and the publication of Casas' own *Historia* proved that he did make such a suggestion.[7] I have already pointed out that Casas' Sevillian background was responsible for his initial acceptance of Negro slavery, and his advice had no effect on the course of events. But in view of his strong fight against Indian slavery, it is interesting to see how belatedly Casas realized that Negro slavery was just as evil. In 1531 he repeated his original advice; and when he went to Chiapa as a bishop he had a license to take along four Negro slaves, though I know of only one—the devoted giant Juanillo, who used to carry him across streams. I feel sure someone must have rebuked Bishop Casas about this during the anti-slavery junta he promoted in Mexico in 1546, and he doubtless thought deeply on the subject after his return to Spain, when he apparently added a Third Corollary to his anti-slavery tract. In the end he underwent a total change of heart and made a full and penitent confession in his *Historia*—inserting a long account on the injustice of African slave raids and apologizing humbly for his original suggestion.[8] Why did he take so long to

---

campaign. Yet, as Casas pointed out, not a single one of the arch-criminals was hanged for the atrocities. A few were brought to Spain as prisoners or arrested when they returned there, but the only punishments inflicted were confiscation, fines, or imprisonment.

7. Herrera, dec. II, lib. II, cap. 20, related Casas' original proposal of 1518. With no further evidence, a series of 18th-century writers accused Casas of "introducing" the slave trade—Corneille De Pau in his *Recherches philosophiques,* 1768-1770, Abbé Raynal in his *Histoire philosophique,* 1770, William Robertson in his *History of America,* 1777, and still others. Casas' defenders, a few decades later, had even less to go on. Abbé Henri Gregoire in 1804, the notorious Doctor Servando Teresa de Mier y Terán in 1806, and Juan Antonio Llorente, who reprinted their articles, all defended Casas, mainly on the ground that there was nothing to substantiate Herrera's statement. But as copies of Casas' manuscript *Historia* began to circulate, the source of Herrera's passage was soon recognized. See *Hist.,* IV, 380-381.

Meantime, this controversy had a notable result. In 1822, Llorente brought out his *Obras de las Casas:* free versions of six of the tracts of 1552 and the posthumous treatise, also *Doce dudas* and the letter to Carranza (both MSS discovered by his friend Gregoire who had doubtless interested him in Casas), the whole preceded by a "life" largely drawn from Herrera and Torquemada. Deficient as Llorente's work was, it helped set off the drive to print Casas's writings and documents.

8. For Casas' original suggestion and the real facts about the large-scale introduction of Negro slavery, see *supra,* chapter IV, section on "New colonization proposals"; for his later change of heart, perhaps following the friars' junta of 1546, see chapter XIV, note 29. Also see Muñoz's extracts of documents on Negro slaves in Española prior to Casas' suggestion, and of passages in which Casas first repeated and

see his error? I think it was doubtless because of the overriding singleness of purpose with which he defended the cause of the Indians for so long.

That zeal for half a century is the most conspicuous thing about him. In many ways, Bartolomé de las Casas was gifted with a personality that set him far above most men of his age. His eloquence and persuasiveness were legendary. Sepúlveda, his worthiest adversary, called him "most subtle, most vigilant, most fluent, compared to whom the Ulysses of Homer was dumb and stammering!" In addition, Casas had a remarkable and inquiring mind; he was interested in native customs and beliefs, and in his *Apologética* wrote extensively of the fauna and flora of the islands and parts of the mainland he had seen, perhaps inspired by Oviedo's dissertation on the same subject. Courage he never lacked. I do not think he sought martyrdom, but on the few occasions when danger threatened—in storms at sea or in the presence of an angry mob—fear was not in him, and he went about his business calmly. On the negative side, humility was not one of his virtues. When he made his points or demands, he was insistent almost to the extent of presumptuousness. As Oviedo said of him early in his careeer, "quería mandar": he wanted to direct his reforms in person. Late in life Casas was unbending in the extreme. Though he had a sharp tongue and a ready, biting wit, I believe he lacked a sense of humor—though that was probably an asset. But above all else, his most outstanding trait was his amazing persistence, that unremitting zeal that kept him going for fifty years in his crusade to relieve the oppressed Indians.

So I think it is fair, instead of criticizing either his goal or his methods, to ask bluntly: Did he succeed? Certainly, though he never managed to have his main principles put into full practical operation, he accomplished a great deal of good. His work did bring about an amelioration in the status of the Indians, and a great many protective measures. But as he pointed out repeatedly, no matter how careful the regulations, it was difficult to control the officials to whom they were directed, and still less the colonists at whom they were aimed. Other causes, of course, contributed to a stabilization in the colonies of a more just and equitable government for the natives, so it is difficult to apportion the credit due to Casas and his efforts. But his exposé of conditions, including official corruption, surely influenced these broader factors, too. In the later part of his life he also played a part in the naming

---

then apologized for it. (Quintana, app. VII.) Also cf. *Hist.*, lib. I, caps. 24-27 on the African slave-trade—a late interpolation as it uses material from Juan de Barros' *Asia*, which was not published till 1552. These chapters contain the same kind of remarks that Casas was wont to make about the Indian slave traffic.

of inspectors who watched over the treatment of the Indians, and even had a hand in the transfer of audiencia presidents. And his lifelong role as the leader of the entire reform movement can hardly be overestimated. From the beginning he worked closely with others—he originally traveled to Spain with Fray Antonio Montesino and later with Fray Jacobo de Testera. Throughout his career friars and Indians and even officials sent their complaints to him, and at the close of his life, as I have shown, the reformers of a new generation were his active collaborators.

So I would answer that Casas was successful, but only up to a point. When it came to total reform, he finally faced an obstacle in the Crown itself. At the start of his crusade there was a bare chance that his principles might have been accepted. But as the conquest proceeded, covering larger and larger territory and producing more and more revenue, the prospects of drastic change dwindled. After Charles V brought Spain into the sphere of international politics, his pressing financial needs became all-important. To support his imperialist regime in Europe, he had to have the treasure of the Indies, no matter how it was obtained. In the crucial showdown over the Law of Inheritance, Charles was afraid to thwart the colonists by enforcing an unpopular reform. The rebellion in Peru was too recent; and in New Spain, the sixteenth century was one of constant fear of revolt by the natives. The Emperor needed loyal Spaniards to insure order and maintain control, and to send him ever more shiploads of gold and silver.

Yet if the Crown shied away from total reform, the rulers were generous with partial measures. There was a real contradiction here. All through Casas' writings we can follow the dual motive of the kings of Spain in the subjugation of the Indies: gold and conversion. The royal need for revenue came first, but afterwards there was the obligation to convert the natives. Casas himself, I am sure, was conscious of the antagonism between the two, for he continually played on both, the King's fiscal needs and the royal conscience. And I think he did reach the consciences of both the kings and the regents, again and again. Except at the beginning, when officials in Spain were themselves encomenderos, Casas was able to command the sympathetic ear of the Spanish government. The Emperor certainly had respect for him, perhaps even affection. After all, Charles V did promulgate the New Laws, though perhaps he had his own reasons as well. His officials in the Indies were whittling away the power of the conquistadors with as little pain as possible; Cortés was made Marqués del Valle, and others received similar recognition and honors, such as membership in the military orders— all of which cost money. We may believe that Charles did have good intentions, but reforms like the abolition of personal services not only protected the Indians but enhanced the royal authority. Casas was fully aware of this; he constantly urged the King to reassert his sovereignty in the face of the settlers' arrogance.

In the end, Charles signed the revocation of Casas' "chief remedy, without which all the others are worth nothing." The Emperor simply could not risk further rebellions in his profitable possessions. The colonists argued they had conquered the Indies without the King's help, and demanded the only recompense he would give, the labor of the conquered; otherwise they could not produce revenue for the Crown or maintain themselves. So Charles had to give way. Yet most of the New Laws remained in effect, and in his later years Casas was able to prevent any further erosion in the reform he had helped to enact.

Another man might have been satisfied with these partial accomplishments, but Casas never was. By 1566 the colonial establishment was set; yet in his last petition he was still beating his head against a stone wall, demanding total reform, pointing an accusing finger at the King.[9] I think it was this stubborn persistence that had kept him going all those "fifty mortal years."

What an unbelievable crusade it was! From his first trip to Spain in 1515 till his last breath, Bartolomé de las Casas was pre-eminent among all men having to do with Indian affairs. The very length of his fight was astounding, and so was the roster of rulers he dealt with: the dying Ferdinand, Ximénez, young Charles, the mature Emperor, and Philip. With enemies galore, he always had powerful friends and his influence at court was enor-

---

9. If anything, his final position "hardened": the King himself was to make restitution, Spain had as yet no operative just title to the Indies, the native lords must be restored. All this reflects the approach of death, growing disillusion with the colonists, and some abandonment of optimistic earlier schemes for Europeanizing the natives.

For instance, one of Casas' ideas had been to congregate the Indians. When first discovered, the Indies were apparently populated by people living on the small tracts they cultivated, more or less remote from each other. Casas long advocated bringing in such outlying individuals to a common center, as an aid to their Christianization, which it undoubtedly was. He even tried this himself in Verapaz with a degree of success. But toward the end of his life, he seems to have dropped the plan; perhaps he was convinced that in many ways it was harmful, and on the whole the process was slow and hateful to the Indians. Toward the end of the 16th century, however, the government finally did carry out the policy of congregation. So today, in most parts of Mexico, aside from large haciendas there are only towns, from which the people must walk or ride out some distance to cultivate their farms.

mous, from the Hieronymite mission to the New Laws to the perpetuity battle. His influence was vast in the Indies, too, though he never achieved his goal. And he left behind a prodigious body of writings, of which at least one, the *Historia de las Indias,* has a claim on immortality.

As I review it all, I tend to compare Casas to Charles more and more. Both were men with a lifelong vision and a tremendous career of action. Charles cherished his dream of a dynastically united, Catholic Europe—and lived a life of endless wars and debts and bitter compromises. Casas had his dream of a free America—the native Americans becoming Christian Indians and voluntary vassals of Spain—and his fifty years of endless battles and bitter compromises. Surely these two were the outstanding Spaniards of the sixteenth century, the Holy Roman Emperor and the Protector of the Indians—and, in my opinion, the greater of the two was Bartolomé de las Casas.

NARRATIVE
AND CRITICAL CATALOGUE
OF CASAS' WRITINGS

A MAN OF ACTION, A MAN OF WORDS

In the following pages, I have attempted the first complete and strictly chronological Catalogue of Casas' known writings. These works, as I have shown fully in my biography, were the fruit of an incredible life of action. Yet they also represent a vast literary output that deserves to be surveyed briefly per se before I begin its systematic presentation.

Despite fifty years of almost ceaseless activity, Bartolomé de las Casas was one of the most prolific writers who ever lived, and his writings are as notable for their variety as for their total bulk. They include large formal works which I think he called books, small formal books that he called "tratados" or "tratadillos," memorials, petitions and letters, and investigations, or what were known in his age as "Informaciones." In this last category only one is extant, and his extant letters are mainly addressed to the Council of the Indies or the kings of Spain, with just a few personal ones on subjects of public importance, though he doubtless wrote any number of private letters as well.

For by no means has all of his vast production survived. His shorter "occasional" pieces, whether addressed to the King or to councilors, were doubtless originally filed in the archives of the Council, since it was the voice of the Crown (expressed or implied), and the body through which the rulers carried on practically the entire business of the Indies. We cannot tell if he kept copies of all these reports and representations; only a couple of his own drafts are known to us today. But Casas did have copies of his more formal works, and after his death these copies, too, passed into the government's possession. Herrera had some main items for awhile, and later made a sworn statement that he had returned every document loaned to him for the writing of his history.[1] But this returned material was also placed in the Council archives, where it could be borrowed by councilors, as hap-

---

1. In his will of March 11, 1622, Herrera declared that he had returned, to the same man who delivered them, all Casas' books and the others loaned to him. Rómulo D. Carbia, *La crónica oficial de las Indias Occidentales* (Buenos Aires, 1940), 169, note 63.

pened with the *Historia verdadera* of Bernal Díaz del Castillo, and with time more and more pieces were dispersed and lost.

The main reassembling of Casas' writings was done in the late eighteenth century by Juan Bautista Muñoz. When Muñoz combed the Spanish government's archives and other sources, collecting material for his own history of the New World, he gathered together much by Casas: the *Historia*, the *Apologética*, papers on the Sepúlveda dispute, the rules for confessors, and a great many letters and documents. Some were Casas' own copies of his writings, some were Muñoz's transcripts—though in a number of cases he made only extracts of documents and the originals seem never to have been found again. After Muñoz's death most of his vast collection went to the Real Academia de la Historia in Madrid; it originally filled some ninety folio volumes, plus other sets, if I remember aright, and though a few volumes are missing or found elsewhere, many are still there. The Muñoz Collection has remained the chief source for the activities of Casas and other great characters of the epoch. And it yielded the large mass of Casas' own papers, and the documents about him, that were first published in the nineteenth century: volume VII of the *Documentos inéditos de Indias,* many of the appendices in Fabié's biography, and the Real Academia edition of his great history. Some few pieces were also turned up in the Archives of the Indies, and additional ones have since been found in private collections, in the Veracruz papers, and most recently in various monastic repositories. But I believe that a number of Casas' writings still remain in the archives, buried in out-of-the-way *legajos* (as the bundles are called), or misplaced in Council files originally intended for other material.

Yet incomplete though they may be, Casas' known writings—as I have catalogued them in rigorous chronological order—do form an impressive record of his entire career. This is particularly true of his "minor" or shorter works. When he first went to Spain in 1515 to plead the cause of the Indians, he had surely prepared a memorial of abuses to present to Ferdinand the Catholic; and we have the summary of just such a memorial. Whether the cleric Casas ever read it to the dying King is doubtful, though soon thereafter he did give a similar paper, in Latin and Spanish, to the new Regents. But during the following two or three years he presented a whole series of memorials, most of which have come down to us, starting with the crucial one I have redated and dubbed his "community scheme." All were of the very greatest importance, because in them he first outlined his proposals on the subject of the Indians.

Then, following the tragic end of his own "colony" at Cumaná, Casas retired to the Dominican Order, and no writing of his is extant bearing a date before 1531 (this, too, I have redated). Subsequently, we have but two notable letters written by Fray Bartolomé, in 1534 and 1535. But after 1540, he presented a torrent of memorials and monographs, several of which he printed later. These grew out of the meetings from 1541 to 1543, that resulted in the celebrated New Laws, in which it was generally agreed Casas had a major hand. Named Bishop of Chiapa after their promulgation, he went out to his diocese in 1544, and during his troublous stay there was involved in a series of violent controversies. Much of his correspondence of that period is preserved, and before leaving America he prepared a controversial *Confesionario* to be used confidentially in manuscript, though we know it from the printed version. Upon his return to court, Casas wrote a number of polemical treatises that he also printed afterwards, and from then to the end of his life he presented a ceaseless stream of memorials and petitions as general representative of the Indians. A large number of these have also survived. We even have part of his will, and a paper by him that was read in the Council a few days before his death.

My Catalogue is therefore narrative for these "minor" works, but what of Casas' "major" writings in this rigorous chronological scheme? Here, the results are still more striking. Of course, the distinction between "major" and "minor" is academic; one of his relatively short printed tracts was the *Brevissima relación de la destruición de las Indias,* which has stirred the world for centuries. Furthermore, critical dating discloses that even his very long works—they run to hundreds of tedious pages, sometimes in Latin—were often as topical as his briefest petitions. Thus Casas' first book, *Del único modo,* was connected with his own missionary experiment and written in preparation for his powerful reform effort that provoked the New Laws. His massive *Tratado comprobatorio,* of which the large published tract is but a fragment, was composed under fire to answer specific charges; his huge *Apologia adversus Sepulvedam* was written to be read aloud at a public disputation; his two farewell treatises were addressed to specific Peruvian problems and presented with a request for action. Most of these big books we have *in toto* or in substantial part, though two are still unpublished, and another, about the Jalisco war, was lost in modern times. All of them, save one, were closely related to the events of an impassioned advocacy that covered half a century.

Only the *Historia de las Indias,* written apart from the heat of battle, was different, and only the *Historia* presented difficulties in my cataloguing. Where was one to enter a book at which Casas worked intermittently for almost four decades? Surely not in 1527, when he began it in an interlude of semi-retirement; nor in 1559, when he deeded it to the College of San Gregorio with the request that it be withheld from the public for forty years. Rather, I have placed it in 1561, when he laid down the work substantially as we have it now, though he kept retouching it until a few years before his death. Alone of his works it was not circulated, argued about, discussed, or acted upon in his own lifetime, but definitely meant to be read by posterity, and it stands apart from his other writings as a monumental achievement. I think he "spoiled" it somewhat in the final draft. He did improve it by taking out the descriptive portions on the landscape and the Indian civilizations and making them into a bulky separate volume, the *Apologética historia*. But the endless digressions he added to both works are unreadable today.

Yet the *Historia* remains the most valuable single account of the discovery of the New World and the early Spanish period on the islands and Tierra Firme. Casas was not only an eyewitness of much that he told, and a friend of many chief actors, but a most painstaking historian besides; he used and preserved for us masses of documentary material, the most priceless being the diary of Columbus' First Voyage. The literary merit of his work is another matter. For the most part he tells a straightforward and interesting tale, but the classical "decade" style tends to interrupt his far-flung story. Alas, his history breaks off around 1520, for he was not able to finish it as planned; too much else, especially the fight against perpetual encomiendas, came up to engage his attention in his latter years. But it is fortunate that in such a crowded life of action he did find enough leisure to produce his unfinished masterpiece.

When he died, at the age of ninety-two, Casas left in his cell at San Gregorio a prodigious mass of letters and documents and "my works dealing with the subject of the Indians, in Spanish and Latin, in my handwriting, and my *General history of the Indies,* also written in my own hand."[2] By royal order these were turned over to Juan López de Velasco, the first chief chronicler of the Indies; and afterwards to the chronicler Antonio de Herrera, who borrowed extensively from Casas' *Historia.* In fact in his own *Historia de los hechos de los castellanos* of 1601, Herrera practically printed

---

2. Casas' will of March 17, 1564, Icazbalceta, *Docs.,* II, 597; here he also speaks of many letters from the Indies. Remesal (II, 467) says there were found in his cell "many papers and memorials of importance, investigations, reports, petitions, discoveries, conquests, consultations." There must have been still more at the Atocha convent in Madrid where Casas died.

Casas' entire book in extract.³ I shall discuss this at greater length in my entry on Casas' history, but here I wish to summarize, as it is of considerable interest, the inventory of Casas' manuscripts loaned to Herrera in 1597.

This, plus the nine printed tracts, may be considered the earliest "Catalogue of Bartolomé de las Casas' Writings":

> *General History of the Indies.* 3 volumes folio, the first of 624 leaves.
>
> *On the Treasures found in the tombs of the Indians.* Folio volume in Latin, 192 leaves.
>
> *On the Spiritual Care the Spanish Kings are to take of the world of the Indies, and The Only Way to attract all peoples to the true faith.* Folio volume in Latin, 73 leaves.
>
> *Summary of Doctor Sepúlveda's book against the Indians, and part of a Defense the Bishop of Chiapa wrote against him.* Folio volume, 94 leaves.
>
> *Propositions and Replies that passed between the said Bishop and Doctor Sepúlveda in the junta about the liberty of the Indians,* 12 quires ready for binding, folio, 148 leaves.
>
> In a vellum cover, a packet of loose papers containing drafts of four [sic] treatises:
>
> *On the Legal and Christian Entry and advance of our Kings in the kingdoms of the Indies.* Clean copy, Latin, 61 leaves.
>
> About a *Confesionario* that the said Bishop composed. 32 leaves.
>
> Latin dialogue between an old man and a youth on *The Just Title to the Indies.* Rough draft and clean copy, 115 leaves.
>
> Theological questions, and two or three small treatises. Rough drafts, 37 or 38 leaves.⁴

---

3. Since Casas himself was a character in part of his own narrative, he appears as such in the Herrera chronicle. Indeed, there one can obtain a practical knowledge of Casas' career down to 1522, though after that he reappears only briefly in Herrera's story: e.g., in connection with Governor Contreras in Nicaragua, the conversion of the Land of War, the New Laws, the founding of the University of Mexico, and the abolition of personal services in Peru.

4. Herrera submitted a list of documents in the possession of Juan López de Velasco, evidently with the request that they be turned over to him. Accordingly, on September 24, 1597, a cedula was issued to Velasco to give Juan de Ibarra of the Council of the Indies, in accordance with this list, the books and papers of the Bishop of Chiapa that had been brought from the College of San Gregorio. At the end of the document is a notation that the papers were delivered to Herrera. See Paz, *Catálogo Bib. Nac.,* no. 10. (The earlier 1579 cedula to deliver the papers to Velasco is abstracted in Pérez Pastor's *Bibliografía madrileña,* III, 422.) José Toribio Medina, who examined many documents in the archives, found the 1597 cedula and copied the inventory—*Bib. hisp.-am.,* I, 253.

The next important "Catalogue of Casas' Writings," so to speak, was Remesal's

The Catalogue I have compiled on the following pages will show the reader how greatly this first list has grown. I have been repeatedly astonished at the number of Casas' minor writings, not only those published in modern collections of documents, but a number embedded in early chronicles that have hitherto escaped notice. Both Torquemada and Herrera cite writings by Casas of which no copy is known; Remesal copied four writings by Bishop Casas from government, church, and monastery archives in Central America that have never been listed; and Ximénez also copied a letter by Fray Bartolomé that he saw in the archives of a provincial capital.[5] In entering Casas' larger works, I have been surprised at the number of contemporary manuscript copies and their early use by writers who did not give full credit. Finally, in trying to arrange all of Casas' known writings in chronological order, I have had to blaze new trails of my own. Among major writings, I have re-dated *Del único modo* (to 1539) and the anti-slavery tract (to 1544); and I have supplied positive dates for a number of undated items, such as Casas' last memorial, which closes my list. Negatively, I have avoided glib dating from internal evidence, and outright conjectures; documents to which only a general period can be assigned are placed undated at the end of the appropriate sections (except the last, where an undated document precedes the final two of 1566).[6]

---

in his chronicle of 1619. He spoke of the printed tracts, *passim*, and gave a longer list of Casas' manuscript works in San Gregorio (II, 467-469), saying at the end: "The reverend Bishop wrote many other tracts which have been destroyed by time, or rather, by interested parties to prevent their publication."

5. Those copied by Remesal are no. 30, Bishop Casas' 1545 speech before landing; no. 33, his first petition to the audiencia (extracts); and nos. 39-40, his farewell dispositions for his diocese, the last of particular interest. The one copied by Ximénez is no. 15, which raises the question of Fray Bartolomé's whereabouts in 1539.

6. I have omitted from my list all items that cannot precisely be called writings by Casas. One such category is his clearly oral work at court. Thus, his statement delivered in an audience before Charles in 1519, in contending with Bishop Quevedo, was no doubt carefully prepared. But what Casas gives in quotations, in chapter 149 of the third book of his history, is a short summary of an extemporary speech. Similarly, Casas' representation on behalf of the Trinidad Indians, cited indirectly in the Figueroa instructions of December 9, 1518 (Serrano, *Orígenes,* app. LXXI), was apparently an oral protest against a Council decision on slaving (cf. Casas, *Historia,* lib. 3, cap. 105). By way of contrast, Bishop Casas' speech off Yucatán, no. 30, was read from a manuscript.

I have also excluded perfunctory receipts, contracts, or powers of attorney, where the text is mainly a legal formality. One such is Bishop Casas' June 28, 1544, power to several persons, including Juan Galvarro, Peninsular agent for a number of Ameri-

Of course, in spite of all my efforts at completion, I may have missed some items. But I believe I have provided an orderly and rational framework for the vast writings of Bartolomé de las Casas. And as new works of his continue to be discovered, in the archives and elsewhere, this list will continue to grow over the years, while retaining the shape I have given it in these pages.*

Here, then, is my Narrative and Critical Catalogue of Casas' Writings: his phenomenal literary output completely linked to his phenomenal career, revealing the "Protector of the Indians" as simultaneously a man of action, a man of words.

I. REFORMING CLERIC, 1515-1522

Casas' writings of his early period comprise a series of important memorials—to Ferdinand, Adrian, Ximénez de Cisneros, and Chancellor Gattinara. A number of these, however, are lost. The most significant document, as distinct from his own writings, is the May 19, 1520, contract of Charles with Casas for his settlement on Tierra Firme (signed at La Coruña by Cobos, Adrian, and Fonseca) and its [May 20?] supplement. See *DII*, VII, 65-92.

1. 1515, Santiago de Cuba. "Información" of Casas' services, "ad perpetuam rei memoriam." See his *Historia*, lib. III, end of cap. 81.

    No copy known.

    Casas had this sworn evidence drawn up before a magistrate, prior to leaving Cuba. It covered his "three or four years" of services in that island, confirming that he arrived there early in 1512. He afterwards made use of it in answering the charges drawn up against him by the Council in 1519 (no. 8 of this Catalogue), but I believe he later destroyed it.

2. 1515-1516. Report of Casas to the King about the mistreatment and deaths of the

---

can bishops (*Fondos americanos*, II, app. 14). By contrast, Bishop Casas' grants of powers for his diocese, nos. 39-40, contain daring instructions. Also I have not tried to list Casas' lost letters, only significant ones such as no. 35.

Finally, I have omitted the many documents concerning Casas' career but not written by him; these are fully cited in the footnotes to my text. In the brief headings of each section of my Catalogue, I have merely drawn the reader's attention to the major items of this sort.

* [New items are in brackets and bear the initials of Helen Rand Parish.]

Indians in Cuba and the other islands. See *Hist.*, lib. III, end of cap. 78, and cap. 84.

AGI [Patronato 252, ramo 1, no. 1–HRP]; Rich MSS.

DII, VII, 5-11, followed by related documents, 11-13; [*BAE*, CX,* no. I, 1-5, a new transcript from AGI, but without the ensuing documents–HRP]; *DIU*, VI, 8-11, a Muñoz digest.

The editors of the *DII* printed this from the original summary in the archives, but the last part contains numerous errors not found in the Rich copy. It is not the memorial itself but a résumé, apparently prepared by an official reporter, of Casas' account of the destruction of the Indians in the islands. For next follows "the opinion of some gentlemen who have examined this"—actually the seven-point opinion rendered in 1512 or 1513 in answer to Fray Antonio Montesino's similar relation (cf. *Hist.*, lib. III, cap. 8). And last comes a rebuttal by the Cuban agents, to whom a transcript had been given at their request.

In all probability, this is a summary of the long story Casas first delivered to the dying Ferdinand, who never read it. The original summary might even have been made by the royal confessor. For in the *Historia*, Casas tells how "a man of credit" [himself] wrote to the King about the oppression of the Cuban Indians; how the cleric told the story briefly to Ferdinand in person on December 23, 1515; and how he then presented his written "memoria" to Bishop Fonseca. Furthermore, identical details on the deaths of the children appear in the *Historia* narrative, the Fonseca interview, and the *DII* document. Ferdinand died on January 25, 1516.

That the document was directed to Ferdinand is obvious from the terms of address—V.A. (Vuestra Alteza, as the King was then called) and VV. AA. (Vuestras Altezas, that is Ferdinand and Joanna, King and Queen of Castile). In summarizing Casas' memorial, everything has been put in the third person: "Dice que . . . SS. AA. . . ." But two passages make it doubly apparent that Casas was addressing Ferdinand. In one, Casas charges non-compliance with the laws *made by Their [Your] Highnesses* for the Indians (i.e., the Laws of Burgos). Also, in closing, Casas alleges that if the land had been handled properly *at the beginning*, the King would have had great revenue from it; and he points out twelve causes for the destruction [of the Indians], *from the beginning*, which may be reduced to two: first, excessive labor forced upon them by the cupidity of the Spaniards; and second, maltreatment, namely giving them inadequate food and clothing.

3. 1516. Casas' report to Adrian in Latin of inhumanities towards the Indians of the islands; the same in Spanish to Cardinal Ximénez de Cisneros. See *Hist.*, lib. III, cap 85.

No copy known, but this may possibly be the same report as no. 2 of this Catalogue.

4. 1516 (?) Memorial to Cardinal Ximénez de Cisneros about reforming the government of Española and the other islands, and denouncing abuses. Unsigned. Cf. *Hist.*, lib. III, end of cap. 84.

   DII, I, 253-264; [*BAE*, CX, no. III, 27-31—HRP]; Quintana, app. IV, a Muñoz digest, and *DIU*, VI, 11-12, an extract thereof.

   Beginning with a clause from the will of Queen Isabella, this is chiefly an attack on Conchillos. It tells how Conchillos signed a grant to himself for three hundred Indians in each of the four islands; appointed himself chief notary and obtained numerous other lucrative benefits; and named his men to various offices in the islands, where all of them have enriched themselves and him at the King's expense.

   Muñoz dates this document around 1516 to 1518, and says that some attribute it to Casas and others to Licentiate Zuazo, the judge of inquiry for Española. I have several reasons for dating it 1516 and thinking Casas gave it to the Cardinal Regent. The chief purpose of the memorial is to have the encomiendas taken away from the absentees, and this was actually done early in 1517. And Cardinal Ximénez de Cisneros himself, speaking of the deathbed report to Ferdinand about Indian extermination, refers to a report on the absentee abuse. (*DII*, VII, 442.) Casas, however, did not present any charges till the advent of the regency; he says he was planning to attack Fonseca and Conchillos in the King's presence, but Ferdinand died.

5. 1516. Memorial of Casas to Cardinal Ximénez de Cisneros about remedies for the Indies, viz: the "community scheme" for Cuba, also peasant-Indian companies and miscellaneous suggestions. See *Hist.*, lib. III, end of cap. 85, also opening and closing of cap. 89.

   AGI, in Casas' handwriting [Patronato 252, ramo 2—HRP]; NYPL, Rich MSS. *DII*, VII, 14-65; [*BAE*, CX, no. II, 5-27—HRP]; *DIU*, VI, 6-8, a Muñoz digest.

   This memorial was printed in *DII* under the misleading caption "Relaciones que hicieron algunos religiosos sobre los escesos que habia en Indias, y varios memoriales de personas particulares que informan de cosas que convendria remediar," which obviously refers to a whole bundle of papers. But in the Rich copy, Muñoz says that this particular document has no heading.

   Not only is this a holograph by Casas, but it was addressed to Cardinal Ximénez de Cisneros, as the phrase "Vuestra reverendisima señoría" recurs constantly. This is almost certainly the fundamental memorial drawn up by Casas, with the concurrence of Fray Antonio Montesino and of Dr. Palacios Rubios, who added the "court style"—no doubt the numbering of points, so they can be considered and ruled on separately. For the document coincides exactly with Casas' description of his proposals to the Cardinal Regent, viz., that he gave the plan which was revised for the first part of the Hieronymite instructions, and also suggested peasant emigration. So the editors of the *DII*, copying Muñoz's note, correctly stated that part of these remedies were embodied in the instructions to the commissioners. Since a large portion of this document deals with Cuba, probably Casas had worked it out on that island.

I have fully discussed this memorial and its consequences in the second and third chapters of my text.

6. 1516. Memorial of Casas to Cardinal Ximénez de Cisneros about the class of persons best qualified to carry out the plan drafted from his remedies. See *Hist.*, lib. III, beginning of cap. 86.

No copy known.

7. 1518. Casas' petition to the King, setting forth the advantages to the state of his plans for Tierra Firme and the islands. See *Hist.*, lib. III, cap. 102.

DII, VII, 101-109; Fabié, app. IV; [*BAE*, CX, no. IV, 31-35–HRP].

This is Casas' summary-memorial, discussed in my text. Casas signs himself "Protector de los Indios" and says he has been two and one-half years at court. He first came to court in December 1515, which places the writing around the summer of 1518.

Casas proposes that the King confiscate one-fifth or more of the colonists' property, or take loans from them, to finance the mainland scheme. For the island Indians he now advocates a tribute system, and aided emigration, etc., for the Spaniards.

7A.[1518. Another petition of Casas to the King.

AGI, Panamá 379.

BAE, CX, no. V, 35-39.

In this newly discovered document, Casas deals in more detail with his plan for Tierra Firme. Here he proposes loans as a means of financing. Official comments are included in footnotes–HRP.]

8. 1519. Casas' answer to thirty charges formulated against him by the Council in opposition to his Tierra Firme proposal. See *Hist.*, lib. III, caps 140-141, and Herrera, dec. II, lib. IV, cap. 3.

No copy known. This document was 12 folio leaves, including annexed papers.

Drawn up in Chancellor Gattinara's apartment on four successive evenings, Casas' reply defended his record in Cuba and his role in the Hieronymite mission and the peasant-emigration project; he also offered to give a bond, attacked the activities of Pedrarias in Darien, and defended the mainland Indians against charges of bestial incapacity. To the document he appended the legal proof of his Cuban services (no. 1 of this Catalogue); also his authorization to go to the Indies with the Hieronymites, and his appointment as "Universal Procurator or Protector of the Indians." Cf. *Hist.*, lib. III, cap. 90.

9. 1519. Provisional contract of Diego Columbus and Casas for the Tierra Firme scheme. See *Hist.*, lib. III, cap. 104.

Found in Spain by Henry Stevens in 1854 and printed by him in that year.

This joint offer to the King is signed by Columbus but it was doubtless prepared by Casas, for in the *Historia* he tells how the Second Admiral altered the cleric's draft. Stevens assigned this document to 1520. But Casas discusses the incident in a chapter explicitly devoted to events of the year 1519, and internal evidence supports that date. The final clause regarding caballeros indicates that some concessions had already been made to Casas. But this proposal is for a large territory that was greatly reduced in the final grant of 1520, and many other features were changed as well.

10. 1519, Molins del Rey. Casas' petition to Gattinara about the terms of his grant. Cf. *Hist.*, lib. III, cap. 132, the passage on cutting the territory.

AGI; Huntington Library.

DII, VII, 93-100; [*BAE*, CX, no. VI, 40-43–HRP]; printed by Henry Stevens in 1854, from the copy now in the Huntington, with Gattinara's note at the end.

Casas asks that the province of Cenú be not removed from his territory, for without some gold-producing land he cannot find men to go with him. But if the land is reduced, then the obligations should be cut in proportion. In his note Gattinara directed that they be so cut.

II. Friar and Missioner, 1523-1540

For this transitional interlude, we have a number of significant letters by Casas, some of them quite extensive. His important first book, *Del único modo*, belongs here too; only a portion of it has survived, but it is a large piece.

Main documents about Fray Bartolomé are the hostile "Informaciones" of Governor Contreras made in Nicaragua on March 23, June 30, and August 23, 1536 (*DII*, VII, 116-127, 127-141, and 141-146); and the Tuzulután contract signed by Licentiate Maldonado in Guatemala on May 2, 1537 (*ibid.*, 151-153).

11. 1530 (?) Program by Casas for the method of living of Christian Indians, the feasts they were to keep and the days they had to fast. Cf. Rem., I, 174-176.

No copy known.

Remesal found this document, and felt sure it had been enclosed with a cedula of March 30, 1536, transmitting a draft memorial on religious and civil duties of Indians. Remesal copied the cedula but could find no such memorial. He says however, that Casas in Santiago in 1536 redrafted or reaffirmed his program, which was then approved by Bishop Marroquín and the Bishops of Tlaxcala and Mexico, sent to the Council of the Indies, and forwarded by the Emperor to the Pope. In view of this, the Pope issued "the brief with which this new Indian church is governed, which is the ordinary, and is in the hands of all." Presumably this refers to the bull, "Altitudo divini consilii," of June 1, 1537, which dealt with not only the baptism but also the marriage, fasts, and feasts of Christian Indians.

12. 1531, January 20, Puerto de Plata. Memorial of Casas to the Council of the Indies.
    Real Academia, Muñoz Collection, tomo LXXIX [old numbering], fols. 77-90, copied in 1782; NYPL, Rich MSS.
    Fabié, app. V; [*BAE*, CX, no. VII, 43-55—HRP]; Quintana, app. VII, extract only from the Muñoz transcript, then owned by Antonio Uguina, and now in the NYPL, Rich MSS.
    This is the long and impassioned memorial, written after nearly ten years' "sleep" to the world, in which Fray Bartolomé reiterates many of his earlier ideas. In Fabié's publication, the date within the letter is misprinted 1533. However,1531 is correct, as it appears in Muñoz, Quintana, and Fabié's own caption.

13. 1534, April 30, Santo Domingo. Letter of Casas to the Council of the Indies.
    AGI, Santo Domingo 153 (11).
    Benno M. Biermann, "Zwei Briefe von Fr. Bartolomé de las Casas," *Archivum Fratrum Praedicatorium*, IV, 197-202; [*BAE*, CX, no. VIII, 56-59—HRP].
    In this important letter, Fray Bartolomé describes his visit to Enriquillo and his persecution by the audiencia, thereby correcting for us the old fabulous version of Remesal.

14. 1535, October 15, Granada, Nicaragua. Letter of Casas to a courtier influential in the Council of the Indies.
    Dominican Provincial Archive, Valencia, Spain.
    Biermann, "Zwei Briefe," *Archivum Fratrum Praedicatorum*, IV, 203-219; [*BAE*, CX, no. IX, 59-68—HRP].
    In this key letter, Fray Bartolomé tells his unsuccessful attempt to go to Peru with Berlanga and writes of his Nicaraguan impressions and experiences. See Berlanga's letter of April 26, 1535, from Puerto Viejo (*DII*, XLI, 538). Berlanga left Panama on February 23 and arrived in Casagua on April 9. Casas left Panama at the beginning of February and, after a near shipwreck, reached Nicaragua instead.

15. 1539, [Mexico?] Petition of Casas to the town council of Santiago de Guatemala.
    Town archives, book of letters to the council.
    Ximénez, I, 145-146, with the statement that this petition was included in the *Recordación florida* of Antonio Fuentes y Guzmán.
    Writing as vicar [former vicar?], Casas protests encroachment of the land of the Dominican monastery, left vacant at the time he and the friars departed for Mexico; he gives substantiating details of the former boundaries. Also, he asks that henceforth the boundaries be clearly marked; and that the monastery be given a better and higher piece of land, nearer town and more convenient for catechizing Indians, in place of the present damp unhealthy site.
    Ximénez intimated Casas wrote the petition in Santiago. But all of this

chronicler's interpretations are heavily colored by antagonism to the Franciscan Order and a wish to establish the early presence of Dominicans in Guatemala. In the text, I have discussed my opinion that Casas simply wrote this petition from Mexico City, having received word from Fray Pedro de Ángulo of the unfavorable situation of the monastery. My reasons are twofold: I find that Casas was still in Mexico in the spring of 1540; and I cannot believe that he made the long journey to Santiago de Guatemala and back in this interval, nor is there any evidence he did so.

The petition itself bears neither date nor place. The "decrees" on the reverse merely state it was presented on September 5, 1539, and acted upon the tenth and sixteenth. If my conclusion is correct Ángulo got nowhere with the authorities when he reached Santiago in April, and wrote Casas for his help; it would not be the last time Ángulo had trouble with the same town council.

16. 1539, *Mexico (?) De unico vocationis modo omnium gentium ad veram religionem, fratris Bartholomaei a Casaus, ordinis praedicatorum episcopi quondam civitatis regalis de Chiapa in orbe novo Indiarum.*

Oaxaca, Biblioteca Pública, three chapters only.

This surviving portion—chapters 5, 6, and 7 of book I—was printed in Mexico in 1942, in a transcription made and edited by Agustín Millares Carlo, with a Spanish translation by Antenogenes Santamaría, and an introduction by Dr. Lewis Hanke.

Remesal knew of four copies of the full manuscript: the one in San Gregorio de Valladolid, his own, one in New Spain, and another in the possession of a priest in Guatemala, all in the same handwriting. (Remesal, II, 469.) The San Gregorio copy, in 73 folios, passed into the hands of Antonio de Herrera; it seems to have been the one described by Nicolás Antonio in his *Bib. hispana nova*, Madrid, 1783. Either Remesal's copy or the New Spain copy apparently remained in a Dominican convent in Oaxaca—though mutilated, it is the only one now known. This manuscript was found in the Oaxaca Public Library by Nicolás León and described by him in *Noticia y descripción de un códice del ilmo. D. Fr. Bartolomé de las Casas*, Morelia, 1886, and afterward in his *Anales del Museo Michoacano*, II, 177. Dr. León said the MS bore a brand showing it had belonged to the Dominicans in Oaxaca.

Del único modo was the earliest of Casas' major works—he himself often referred to it by this Spanish title. According to Remesal's summary, given in my text, it outlined Casas' entire doctrine of peaceful conversion. Near the end of the extant text, Casas speaks of finishing the first book, indicating there would be another. But I consider it unlikely that he ever wrote a second book, as it is difficult to see how he could have written more on the subject.

The date of composition is not definitely known. Casas himself said *Del único modo* was the first book he had ever written. This statement does not date it, however, except perhaps to place it before his tracts of 1542—if, that is, he considered these as books. Fabié (I, 143-144) thought Casas wrote it around 1530, i.e., in the monastery at Puerto de Plata; this seems unlikely, for in his Puerto de

Plata Memorial of 1531 (no. 12 of this Catalogue) Casas was still advocating conversion accompanied by forts and Spaniards. Remesal said Casas wrote it some years before coming to Guatemala in 1536, but those are the years for which his chronicle is not reliable. Dr. Nicolás León, in his article, pointed out the "quondam" in the title as evidence that Casas composed the treatise after he resigned his bishopric (1550), but the title might be a later addition. Incidentally, Dr. León also said the handwriting was identical with his copy of Casas' *De thesauris;* the latter MS is now in the JCBL and my comparison indicates that the handwritings differ.

In chapter IX, I have discussed my reasons for believing Casas wrote this book during his first visit to Mexico. The principal ones are the use in the text of the bull "Sublimis Deus," issued in Rome on June 2, 1537, internal evidence that Casas was still a friar at the time of writing, and the fact that this Mexican interlude afforded him both leisure and facilities for composing such a treatise.

17. 1540, December 15, Madrid. Casas to the Emperor.
    Archivo de Simancas, Estado 49.
    Fabié, app. VII, from the holograph MS then in the possession of the Conde de Casa Valencia; *DE,* VIII, 555-556 (from Simancas); [*BAE,* CX, no. X, 68-69– HRP].

This important letter establishes Casas' situation just before the New Laws period. Casas says he had received a letter in Guatemala from the Emperor, directing him to proceed with other friars in the pacification (already commenced) of many provinces which were at war. "It is in good state because the lords thereof already came to see us secretly, and we hope that we are to bring to the knowledge of the faith those countries and many others . . . and increase the dominion and revenue of Your Majesty." But instead, Casas had come to report to the Emperor things of far greater importance for the whole New World, and so had suspended the conversion as delay was not dangerous. Therefore he asks an order to stay on in Spain.

According to Casas' statement at the end, this letter was being carried to Charles by Fray Jacobo de Testera. Fray Jacobo had come to Spain with Casas in 1540, and was subsequently named commisary general of the Franciscans at the general chapter of Mantua in 1541. He returned to America in 1543 with a contingent of missionaries, but died shortly thereafter. See no. 30 of this Catalogue for Casas' accounts of Testera's earlier peaceful conversion of Yucatán.

III. INSTIGATOR OF THE NEW LAWS, 1541-1543

For this crucial period, we have three capital memorials by Casas: his famous *Brevissima relación,* his fundamental Eighth Remedy, and his joint memorial with Ladrada, the cornerstone of his campaign for the Amendment. Two other draft proposals of his have survived from the New Laws period; and attention is also called to his later Latin treatise on the Jalisco campaign (no. 42 of this Catalogue), of which a preliminary version may have been given at this time. Although the printed *Brevissima* has an added Prologue and Supplement directed to Vuestra Alteza (Philip), all of these memorials were addressed to the Emperor, though actually presented to the special commission or the Council of the Indies. Only the "recommendation" (no. 22 of this Catalogue) might have been given personally to Charles.

By contrast, there is a dearth of documents about Casas, as there is about the judicial inspection of the Council of the Indies; and Herrera mentions neither the *Brevissima* nor the *Remedios*.

18. 1542. *Breuissima relacion de la destruycion de las Indias: colegida por el Obispo do[n] fray Bartolomé de las Casas, o Casaus de la orden de Sa[n]cto Domingo. Año 1552.* [From the colophon:] Seville, Sebastián Trugillo, 1552.

4°, 50 unnumbered leaves.

[Separately printed supplement:]

Lo que se sigue es un pedaço de una carta y relacion que escriuio cierto hombre: de los mismos que andaua[n] en estas estaciones: refirie[n]do las obras que hazia & consentia hazer el capita[n] por la tierra que a[n]daua. Seville, Sebastián Trugillo, 1552.

4°, 4 unnumbered leaves.

First Flemish translation appeared in 1578; first French, 1579; first English, 1583; first German, 1597; first Latin, 1598; first Italian, 1626. First Spanish reprint, by Lacavallaria in Barcelona, 1646. Numerous editions in these languages for four centuries. The letter is often reprinted as part of the text.

Fabié, app. XXI; Llorente, I, 100-211; MacNutt, app. I (in English); [*BAE* CX, no. XIV, 134-181, with "Lo que se sigue" included—HRP].

Though he printed it a decade later, Casas' most famous tract, the *Brevissima relación*, is a recasting of the "relation" he read aloud to the special commission in Valladolid in 1542. In chapter X, I have extracted and discussed Santa Cruz's account of the oral presentation; the chronicler begins his sequence of events in 1542. In the printed version, as I have noted, Casas prudently omitted the names of the tyrants.

From the actual text of the *Brevissima*, we obtain more information about the recasting and its date, and the addition of two later postscripts. Casas begins by explaining how he originally wrote this abridgment at the urging of persons impressed by his oral relation, and how the Bishop of Cartagena, Philip's tutor, gave it to the young Prince, but it may have been lost; so he is now, i.e., after a decade, having it printed for Philip's benefit. Then follows the actual "brevissima relacion" of massacres and devastations for region after region; this was completed, Casas says near the end, in Valencia on the eighth day of December 1542. Next, he adds a postscript, written in 1546, about the publication of the New Laws, the civil war in Peru, and non-enforcement. At the end comes the colophon: ". . . Sevilla, en casa de Sebastián Trugillo . . . Año de M.D.Lij."

After this printing, Casas added still another postscript to his 1542 text—a separate supplement done by the same printer: *Lo que se sigue es un pedaço de una carta*. Casas explains that the first page of this letter got lost, but he is printing it anyway as it goes with those already related. The "Carta" concerns atrocities committed by an unnamed captain [Benalcazar] on rejoining Juan de Ampudia in what is now Ecuador and Colombia.

A curious manuscript in the Biblioteca Nacional, Madrid, appears at first sight to contain the omitted portions of both this supplement and the 1542 text: viz., information from the lost part of the letter and the names of the actual tyrants. It bears the title *Istoria sumaria y relación brevísima y verdadera de lo que vió y escribió el reberendo padre Fray Bartolomé de la Peña [sic] de la orden de los predicadores, de la lamentable y lastimosa destruición de las Indias, islas y tierra firme del mar del norte*. Año M. y D. y XL. y IIX [i.e., 1548]. (See Fabié, I, 283-291, a full description, and app. XXI, the entire text.) I have studied this *Istoria sumaria* carefully to see if it might be Casas' earlier version of the *Brevissima*, but a comparison with Santa Cruz's description of that text proves the contrary. In Peña's book, many proper names of places in the Indies are misspelled. The Bishop of Mexico (in Casas' text) has become the archbishop, a post to which Zumárraga was not elevated until 1548; and Fray Jacobo de Testera, a native of Bayonne according to Mendieta, is called "Jacob Lugdunensis," i.e., a native of Lyons. Finally, though the over-all contents are very similar and in many places Casas' exact words are used, the Peña work is arranged in chapters and not by regions, weakening the effct. So I have concluded that this MS is Peña's paraphrase and expansion of a copy of the December 8, 1542, *Brevissima* that had some letters attached—he puts Benalcazar into the story, and gives fuller versions of letters from Fray Marcos de Niza and the Bishop of Santa Marta. Evidently Peña wrote it between 1548 and November 30, 1550, the date at the end.

19. 1542. *Entre los remedios q[ue] do[n] fray Bartolome delas casas: obispo d[e]la ciudad real de Chiapa: refirio por mandado del Emperador rey n[uest]ro señor: enlos ayuntmie[n]tos q[ue] ma[n]do hazer su magestad de perlados y letrados y personas gra[n]des en Ualladolid el año de mill & quinie[n]tos y quare[n]ta y dos: para reformacio[n] delas Yndias. El octauo en orde[n] es el siguie[n]te. Do[n]de se asigna[n] veynte razones: por las q[ua]les prueua no deuerse dar los indios alos Españoles en encomie[n]da: ni en feudo ni en vassallaje: ni d[e] otra manera algu[n]a. Si su magestad como dessea quiere librarlos de la tyrania y perdicio[n] q[ue] padecen como dela boca delos dragones: y q[ue] totalmente no los co[n]suma[n] y mate[n] y q[ue]de vazio todo aq[ue]l orbe d[e] sus ta[n] infinitos naturales habitadores como estaua y lo vimos poblado.* [From the colophon:] Seville, Jacome Cromberger, August 17, 1552.

4°, 54 unnumbered leaves, the last blank.

Llorente, I, 254-358; [BAE, CX, no. XI, 69-119—HRP].

Unlike the *Brevissima*, recast after the promulgation of the New Laws, this tract is a key section from the actual "Remedios" Casas presented to the reform commission in 1542. That is perfectly clear from the elaborate title page to the closing "Protestación" that ends with the words, "Año de mill e quinientos e cuarenta y dos años." In Santa Cruz's sequence, the "Remedios" follow the oral *Brevissima*, which is logical.

Here, a decade later, Casas reprints only the basic Eighth Remedy: the abolition of the encomienda, which he urges for "twenty reasons," legal, moral, and practical. Among them he relates the history of the encomienda system, first introduced by Ovando; Casas had come with Ovando and noted the progressive steps in the institution's development, from personal knowledge as an eyewitness. He also includes the various official declarations on the liberty of the Indians.

20. 1543, February 28, Madrid. Joint memorial of Casas and Ladrada, asking improvements in the New Laws.
    Archive of the Dominican Convent of San Felipe, Sucre, Bolivia.
    Lewis Hanke, "Un festón de documentos lascasianos," *Revista Cubana*, XVI, 156-195; [*BAE*, CX, no. XV, 181-203—HRP].
    I have discussed this joint memorial rather fully in connection with Casas' efforts to have the original ordinances amended. The name of Casas' companion is signed "Fray Rodrigo de Andrada," but he was usually called Ladrada, i.e., del Andrada. The MS bears a notation that Casas delivered it to the Council in Madrid on the last day of February; and another saying that on April 11, 1543, Casas and Fray Rodrigo were directed to submit a further itemized memorial.

21. 1543 (?) Casas [and Ladrada]: "Cerca de los indios. Cerca de la vivienda de los españoles. Cerca de los esclavos. Cerca de las conquistas y descubrimientos."
    Collection of Pascual de Gayangos. Fischer sale, 1869; bought by Sir Thomas Phillipps and sold at his sale in 1919 (no. 123, folio, 5 pp.), possibly Gayangos' copy.
    Fabié, app. XXXI; [*BAE*, CX, no. XII, 120-123, dated 1542—HRP].
    This draft document has no superscription, but begins with the first of the headings. It is signed "Fray Bartolome de las Casas," and Fabié (I, 352-353) thought Casas wrote it after resigning his bishopric. But references to "the remedies we gave" indicate rather that the memorial was written by Casas and Ladrada, and it definitely belongs to the New Laws period.
    Only the short opening section deals with the Indians in encomiendas, and reaffirms Casas' view that they should all be placed under the Crown; this suggests it was presented in 1542 before the New Laws were promulgated. But the majority of the proposals deal with topics in the joint memorial of 1543 (no. 20 of this Catalogue), so this might be the itemized memorial requested. This document strikingly recalls Casas' earlier schemes; cf. nos. 7 and 12 of this Catalogue.

22. 1543, April or May (?) Recommendation of Casas to the Emperor about confiscating goods of conquistadors and preventing rebellions.
    Collection of Pascual de Gayangos, in Casas' handwriting.

Fabié, app., XXIX; [*BAE*, CX, no. XIII, 123-134, dated 1542 like the foregoing, in which cases nos. 21 and 22 of this Catalogue would supplement the
"Remedios" instead of the joint memorial—HRP].

This unsigned draft document is difficult to date. Casas speaks of witnessing
forty-two years of Indies tyranny, and he arrived in America with Ovando in
April 1502. But 1544 is obviously wrong, and Casas sometimes counts fractions
as years, so any date after April 15, 1543, would be in the forty-second year. On
the other hand, in this representation Casas strongly backs administrative changes
that were incorporated in the original ordinances, which seems to place the writing before their promulgation on November 20, 1542. Perhaps, however, this is
personally addressed to the Emperor rather than to the special commission or the
Council, and Casas is urging speed and skill in executing changes already decreed. So I have tentatively assigned this document to 1543, since its emphasis
on conquests resembles the joint memorial. Cf. no. 20 of this Catalogue.

IV. ACTIVE BISHOP, 1544-1547

Casas' letters to Prince Philip are a running commentary on his dis-
heartening experiences as a bishop. Seven have survived and we can reconstruct an eighth. Some were meant for action by the Council, but they were
all addressed to Philip; cf. no. 38 of this Catalogue. Of Casas' episcopal
pronouncements, the most important are his demands on the audiencia and
his sensational "twelve rules" for confessors, known to us from the printed
version.

Prime among documents is the testimonial of Casas' consecration in
Seville on March 30, 1544. See Fabié, app. XXVI; and cf. the end of app.
IX, Muñoz's summary and description of the bulls, on vellum with pendant
seal.

23. 1544 (?) *Este es vn tratado q[ue] el obispo dela ciudad Real de Chiapa do[n]
fray Bartholome de las Casas, o Casaus compuso, por comission del Consejo Real
delas Indias: sobre la materia de los yndios que se han hecho en ellas esclauos.
El qual contiene muchas razones y auctoridades juridicas: que pueden aprouechar
a los lectores para determinar muchas y diueras questiones dudosas en materia de
restitucion: y de otras que al p[re]sente los ho[m]bres el tie[m]po de agora tratan.*
[From the colophon:] Seville, Sebastián Trugillo, September 12, 1552.
    4°, 36 numbered leaves.
    Llorente, II, 3-48; [*BAE*, CX, no. XXVIII, 257-290—HRP].
    In his Argument, Casas explains the genesis of this tract. When he was treat-
ing of the general remedy of the Indians, he insisted, among other things, that all
slaves should be freed as none had been taken justly, and the Council of the
Indies asked him to prepare a written brief on the subject. So he submitted the

following conclusion and corollaries "con sus probanzas." The opening and closing words of the tract show he was a bishop when he wrote it.

This coincides exactly with the situation when Casas was seeking to have the New Laws strengthened, and offered in the joint memorial of 1543 (no. 20 of this Catalogue) to submit just such a brief and "proofs." As he was much occupied shortly thereafter in preparing for his consecration and trip to America, I believe he may not have finished it till 1544.

If so, the tract, as he subsequently printed it, is an expansion of the 1544 brief, recast after 1546. For in his Third Corollary, on the duties of confessors, Casas praises the decision of the anti-slavery junta of 1546, but says the friars did not go far enough. And in the text, he speaks of personal experiences in Guatemala and Nicaragua and of being in Honduras eight years before when coming here (to Spain)—he left Guatemala in 1538. These passages might suggest that Casas wrote the tract after his return to court in 1547. But he could hardly say in his Second Corollary that bishops must "insist and negotiate importunely" before King and Council for the liberation of Indian slaves and "risk their lives" if need be, had he delayed four years or more in presenting his own plea and evidence. It seems far likelier that he renewed his plea with a rewritten brief at the later date.

As a matter of fact, Casas himself, writing to Prince Philip on September 15, 1544—from a stopover at Santo Domingo—positively states that he had written the anti-slavery brief and left it with the Council: "I have already told Your Highness and affirmed various times, that there has not been in all these Indies a single person who has been justly made a slave . . . *as I proved at greater length in the memorial signed by my name that I recently left in that Royal Council.*" DII, VII, 434-435. [Italics ours.]

24. 1544, March 21, Seville. Casas to Philip, telling him that the bulls had not yet arrived.

Fabié, app. IX; MacNutt, 214-216 (in English); [*BAE*, CX, no. XVI, 203-204–HRP].

This letter is definitely addressed to the Prince. Fabié gives the opening as "Muy altos y muy poderosos señores," but the signature is "siervo de vra. al.ª que sus reales manos besa."

Casas says he left court on the fourth and arrived in Seville on the twentieth. There were difficulties with the officials about the passage arrangements and funds. He has no money and asks for the two hundred fifty ducats promised him.

25. 1544, March 21, Seville. Casas to Philip, about his consecration on Passion Sunday.

Fabié, app. IX; MacNutt, 217-219 (in English); [*BAE*, CX, no. VII, 204-206–HRP].

The superscription and signature of this letter are the same as in no. 24 of this Catalogue. Casas was consecrated by Bishop Loaysa (nephew of the Cardinal), Bishop Torres, and the Bishop of Honduras—and he asks that the latter be recompensed for waiting to perform the ceremony.

26. 1544, April 20, Seville. Casas to Philip about his stay in Seville.

   Fabié, app. IX; MacNutt, 222-231 (in English); [BAE, CX, no. XVIII, 206-210—HRP].

   He writes on various topics, particularly the Indian slaves in Seville and An-dalusia, requesting specific steps.

27. 1544, May 4, Seville. Casas to Philip, on missionary and other matters.

   Fabié, app. IX; [BAE, CX, no. XIX, 210-212—HRP].

   He asks help for Franciscan missionaries and the naming of a person to look after the liberation of Indian slaves here.

28. 1544, July 2, San Lúcar. Casas' authorization for Doctor Rodríguez.

   DII, VII, 395, with Muñoz's notes on 394; [BAE, CX, no. XX, 212, without the notes—HRP].

   In this authorization Casas permits an Indian woman servant from Santa Marta to remain in a good home, though he has a "power" to return all free Indians to America.

29. 1544, September 15, Santo Domingo. Casas to Philip about conditions in the Indies.

   Muñoz Collection, tomo LXXXIII; NYPL, Rich MSS.

   DII, VII, 431-437; [BAE, CX, no. XXI, 213-215—HRP].

   He denounces various tyrants and slave raids, praises Licentiate Cerrato, and comments on efforts against the New Laws.

30. 1545, January 5, off Campeche. Speech of Casas to the friars with him about the peaceful conversion of Yucatán.

   Remesal, I, 343-349.

   Fray Tomás de la Torre's diary describes the shipboard occasion when "the reverend Bishop preached us a great sermon" (Xim., I, 296). Remesal, following his practice, copies the entire speech.

   Casas reviews the hardships of the voyage and then relates the missionary venture and tribulations of Fray Jacobo de Testera and his Franciscan com-panions. The story is taken verbatim, but slightly shortened, from the Yucatán section of the Brevissima relación (no. 18 of this Catalogue). A still fuller version, no doubt with names, was given by Fray Bartolomé during the pre-New Laws period, either in the oral Brevissima or as a joint petition with Testera. For Juan de Torquemada, tomo III, lib. XIX, cap. 3, cites an "Información" presented by Casas to the Council of the Indies about the activities of the Franciscans in Yucatán. (Monarquía indiana, Seville [1615], 1723.) Casas' sermon is therefore an abridged retelling of his friend's work, skillfully adapted to the circumstances, as Yucatán was then part of the diocese of Chiapa.

31. 1545, January 9, Campeche. Casas to the Ciudad Real town council, asking for money. See the official answer on February 12, 1545—DII, VII, 211-214, and Fabié, app. XX, 167-169.

   No copy known.

31A. [1545, March 20, Ciudad Real. Casas' proclamation to the faithful in Chiapa. Museo Nacional de Historia, Mexico.

Printed in Benno M. Biermann, "Lascasiana: unedierte documente von Fray Bartolomé de las Casas," *Archivum Fratrum Praedicatorum*, XXVII, 340-344; *BAE*, CX, no. XXII, 215-218.

The Bishop's annual demand for the public denunciation of notorious sins: irregularities in divine services, witchcraft, concubinage, usury, profiteering, and oppression of the Indians. Newly printed, this is the public proclamation, not the "reserved cases" of which a list was given to the confessors—HRP].

32. 1545, July 2. "Información" made by Bishop Casas before the notary Juan Suárez, about the pacification of Tuzulutlán.

DII, VII, 216-231.

Casas entered the province on June 12. At the request of Fray Pedro de Ángulo, Casas examined six witnesses on a set of questions designed to bring out achievements of the peaceful conversion of the Land of War and his own triumphal reception there. Eight of the twelve questions concerned Casas' own trip, and another the excellence of the Cobán church which he admired, so he himself wrote the interrogatory.

33. 1545, [September?] Gracias á Dios. Casas' first petition to the audiencia, requesting protection for the Indians in his diocese, and asking the aid of the "royal arm" against the defiant town authorities.

Archive of the Audiencia of los Confines.

Remesal, II, 56-58.

Remesal copied Bishop Casas' petition from those presented by three Central American bishops. I have given the gist of it in discussing Casas' demands to the audiencia.

34. 1545, [September?] Gracias á Dios. Casas' petition to the audiencia to halt the war parties and slave raids currently destroying the Yucatán Indians and threatening to provoke an uprising in Verapaz. Cf. *DII*, VII, 174-175.

No copy known.

In Point 5 of his final demands (no. 36 of this Catalogue), Casas states he has petitioned the audiencia repeatedly about this.

35. 1545, September 30, Gracias á Dios. Casas to Philip about the diocese of Chiapa, with various requests. See Fabié, app. XIII.

No copy known; no. 32 of this Catalogue was apparently transmitted with this report.

This letter is now lost, but its purport is revealed in the Council's answer of January 15, 1547. Casas had apparently given a long account of the affairs of the province and made a series of requests. He asked that the Audiencias of New Spain and los Confines favor him and his ministers and ecclesiastical persons, so he could better use his pastoral office and gain some fruit in the instruction of the natives. (Suitable cedulas enclosed.) Also, he asked for salaries to be assigned to six clerics (the Prince fixed these at fifty thousand maravedis each); for money to repair the church (the Prince granted him for four years two-ninths of the royal share of the tithes); and for the appointment of a proper dean and chancellor and archdeacon of the cathedral (to be granted). He further stated that the officials did not pay the Bishop of Nicaragua's assigned salary of 500,000 maravedis in good gold, besides which his living cost him a hundred thousand maravedis more than his salary (an order was being sent). For the Land of War, Casas wanted a five-year extension of the exclusion of Spaniards, the territory to be officially renamed "Verapaz," and the royal officials of Guatemala or Chiapa to provide wine for the monasteries out of the royal funds (all granted). Finally, Philip also granted Casas' request to provide ecclesiastical constables with staffs of office.

The rest of Casas' letter required consultation with the Emperor, and accordingly had been forwarded to him. Possibly Casas had complained about President Maldonado or suggested the partition of the Chiapa diocese; both topics would require such referral, and they do appear in his further reports to the Prince from Honduras.

36. 1545, October 22, Gracias á Dios. Casas' final demands on the audiencia.

Huntington Library, the original, signed by Casas; AGI, the official audiencia transcript with the audiencia's October 26 reply [Indiferente General, 1381—HRP]; Bancroft Library, Squier MSS, XXII, 141-142, the audiencia's answer, a Muñoz extract.

Printed by Henry Stevens, 1854, Casas' demands only. Printed with the reply in DII, 172-180; also in Fabié, app. XII; and in [BAE, CX, no. XXIII, 218-222—HRP].

I have discussed these climactic demands fully in my text.

37. 1545, October 25, Gracias á Dios. Casas and Fray Antonio de Valdivieso to Philip, about the audiencia and their tribulations.

Archivo Historio Nacional, in Casas' handwriting, five sheets and cover, cf. Fabié, I, 191, note 1; Bancroft Library, Squier MSS, XXII, 118-124, a Muñoz transcript.

Cartas de Indias, no. IV, 14-27; [BAE, CX, no. XXIV, 222-229—HRP].

They describe the rebellious state of affairs and the Yucatán slave trade, the dean's defiance and the hostility of the other bishops, and their own poverty.

38. 1545, November 9, Gracias á Dios. Casas to Philip, reviewing his hopeless situation.

Archivo Histórico Nacional, in Casas' handwriting. The original of this and of no. 37 of this Catalogue were acquired by the Ministerio de Fomento in 1876, in a large group of autograph letters from the Indies, and may therefore be in the AHN. There is also another copy in NYPL, Rich MSS, a Muñoz transcript.

Cartas de Indias, no. V, 28-37, and facsimile D; [BAE, CX, no. XXV, 229-234—HRP].

The cover is addressed "Al muy alto y muy poderoso señor, el Príncipe, nuestro señor, para Consejo de las Indias." In this final letter from Honduras, Casas reports his October brush with the audiencia, bad news from Ciudad Real, Soconusco, and Oaxaca, and petty persecutions by the royal judges. He wishes to return to court and to give up all the provinces of his bishopric save Verapaz.

39. 1546, November 9, Mexico. Casas' appointment of Juan de Perera as vicar general of the Diocese of Chiapa, with instructions and an interdict against Ciudad Real in case of disobedience.
    Remesal, II, 160-163.
    Remesal transcribed this "escrito . . . que vi autorizado." The most interesting clauses are those directing Perera how to handle the excommunicated cases and prevent raids against Indians, and the concluding sanctions. In this document, Casas also confirms his grant of general powers to Fray Tomás de le Torre, who had been interim vicar general.

40. 1546, November 10, Mexico. Casas' nomination of confessors in Chiapa, forwarding "twelve rules" for the reserved cases, with instructions for their use.
    Remesal II, 164-165.
    Remesal mistakenly states that these rules had been agreed to by the junta of confessors in Mexico. Instead, they were Casas' own rules; see no. 41 of this Catalogue.

41. 1546, Mexico. *Aqui se co[n]tiene[n] vnos auisos y reglas para los confessores q[ue] oyeren confessiones delos Españoles que son, o han sido en cargo a los Indios delas Indias del mar Oceano: colegidas por el obispo de Chiapa don fray Bartholome d[e]las casas, o casaus de la orden de Santo Domingo.* [From the colophon:] Seville, Sebastián Trugillo, September 20, 1552.
    4°, 16 unnumbered leaves.
    Muñoz Collection, tomo XLIV.
    A curious manuscript copy of this, possibly with additions, was made in 1598 by M. Hieronimo Campot—no. 28 in Phillipps' sale of 1913 at Sotheby's, London.
    [*BAE*, CX, no. XXVI, 235-249—HRP].
    In the text, I have identified the "twelve rules" that Casas sent to his diocese from Mexico on November 10, 1546 (cf. no. 40 of this Catalogue) with these which he afterwards printed. Remesal thought he had prepared them earlier; but in the Argument, Casas merely says he drew them up at the request of friars who would have to hear confessions, and to provide for his diocese. The printed rules show signs of having been actually written in Mexico that year— rule 8 refers to the bishops' junta "*now* past or celebrated, the year 1546" [italics ours] but not to the subsequent friars' junta.
    The Addition to the First and Fifth Rules in the printed tract was written after Casas' return to Spain (cf. his foreword to no. 43 of this Catalogue), presumably when his *Confesionario* came under fire in 1548. He closes his Argument with the names of the six theologians who approved the enlarged formulary.

Cf. José Fernando Ramírez' article on Motolinía, in Icazbalceta, *Docs.*, I, xcii-xciii, for an account of Casas' *Confesionario* and the original in Muñoz's papers.

42. N.d. "Sobre el hacer los esclavos de la segunda conquista de Jalisco que mandó hacer don Antonio de Mendoza virrey de la Nueva España año de 1541." The Latin title was "Quaestio circa bellum per Hispanos anno 1541 contra incolas Indos de Xalisco."

Latin manuscript of 272 leaves, folio, in the College of San Gregorio, Valladolid. Cf. Remesal, II, 469.

No copy known.

Navarrete, I believe it was, stated that Muñoz saw this treatise in 1784, when he found five folio volumes of Casas' papers in the office of the Secretaría General de Indias. Cf. Fabié, I, 330; Muñoz Collection, tomo XCII, fol. 128.

It is difficult to tell when Casas wrote this lost book. I have found only an indirect reference to its subject matter in a letter to Casas from Licentiate Ceynos, dated at Zamora, April 4, 1555; Ceynos seems to be answering a question on the procedure of the audiencia, of which he was then a member, regarding slaves branded after the Mixtón War. (*DII*, VII, 338-340.) This suggests it might have been a late work; yet it is not among the Veracruz papers from Casas' later years, in the Bibliothèque Nationale, Paris. But Casas surely gathered material for the Jalisco treatise during his second stay in Mexico in 1546, when he convoked a friars' junta that discussed Indian slavery and these particular slaves. So he might have written it then. See no. 56 of this Catalogue for his subsequent acquaintance in Spain with the Mixtón warrior chief, Tenamaztle.

V. Polemicist at Court, 1548-1552

From the production of these years we have a torrent of theoretical works by Casas: his two "just title" treatises; his voluminous writings in the controversy with Sepúlveda, of which only a portion has been published; and his two treatises on the authority of kings. For the eight tracts Casas had printed in 1552, see this Catalogue, nos, 18, 19, 23, 41, and this section, nos. 43, 44, 48, 49; also no. 50, the posthumous one. The original eight tracts are available in a facsimile edition—Casas, *Colección de tratados, 1552-1553,* Buenos Aires, 1924.*

The major document of this period is Casas' July 21, 1551, contract to live permanently in the College of San Gregorio—printed in Narciso Alonso

---

* [A very elaborate facsimile edition has been issued for the quadricentennial: *Tratados de Fray Bartolomé de las Casas,* with introductory essays on the tracts and on Casas' activities in 1552-1553 by Lewis Hanke and Manuel Giménez Fernandez, transcriptions by Juan Pérez de Tudela Bueso (from *BAE,* CX), translations of the Latin tract and passages by Agustín Millares Carlo and Rafael Moreno, an appendix with the Bulls of Donation, and an index of proper names. 2 vols., Mexico and Buenos Aires, 1965.—HRP]

Cortés' "Fray Bartolomé de las Casas en Valladolid," *Revista de Indias*, I (1940), no. 2, 105-111.

43. 1549 (?) Valladolid. *Aqui se co[n]tiene[n] treynta proposiciones muy juridicas: en las quales sumaria y succintamente se toca[n] muchas cosas pertenecie[n]tes al derecho q[ue] la yglesia y los principes christianos tienen, o puede[n] tener sobre los infieles de qualquier especie que sean. Mayormente se assigna el verdadero y fortissimo fundamento en que se assienta y estriba: el titulo y señorio supremo y vniuersal que los Reyes d[e] Castilla y Leon tienen al orde de las que llamamos occide[n]tales Indias. Por el q[ua]l son constituydos vniuersales señores y Emperadores enellas sobre muchos reyes. Apunta[n] se tambien otras cosas co[n]cernientes al hecho acaecido en aq[ue]l orbe notabilissimas y dignas d[e] ser vistas y sabidas. Colijo las dichas treynta p[ro]posiciones El obispo do[n] fray Bartholome de las Casas, o Casaus: Obispo q[ue] fue d[e]la ciudad Real de Chiapa: cierto Reyno delos dela nueua España. Año 1552.* From the colophon: Seville, Sebastián Trugillo.

    4°, 10 unnumbered leaves.

    Llorente, I, 369-394; [*BAE*, CX, no. XXVII, 249-257—HRP].

    In his Argument and Prologue, Casas explains that he composed this abbreviated treatise in haste to answer the charge that his *Confesionario* denied the King's title to the Indies.

    Near the end he says he has seen the "mal hecho" in the Indies for forty-nine years and studied the "derecho" for thirty-four. This is one of many passages where Casas uses dual points of reference—his knowledge of the Indies and his work for the Indians—which are difficult to pinpoint. His arrival in America may date roughly from near the turn of the century (*Hist.*, Prologue, next to the last paragraph), or precisely from April 1502, with a fraction for the last year; his mission may date from his conversion in August 1514, when he pondered the "hecho" and "derecho" of the rights of the Indians, or from his arrival at court late in 1515. In this instance, we know when his *Confesionario* came under fire: the cedula to collect manuscript copies in New Spain was issued on November 28, 1548 (Rem., II, 165). So he might have written *Treinta proposiciones* in 1548, thirty-four years after his "conversion." But as that was late in the year, I believe he may not have finished it till 1549. The alternative date of 1551 is impossible, in view of the haste.

44. 1549, Valladolid. *Tratado co[m]probatorio del Imperio soberano y principado vniuersal que los Reyes de Castilla y Leon tienen sobre las indias: compuesto por el Obispo don fray Bartholome d[e] las Casas, o Casaus de la orden d[e] Sancto Domingo. Año 1552.* [From the colophon:] Seville, Sebastián Trugillo January 8, 1553.

    4°, 80 unnumbered leaves. According to Sabin this contains 84 leaves, but Medina says the copy in the British Museum has only 80, as does also that in the JCBL. In a copy sold by the estate of Sir Thomas Phillipps in London on November 25, 1946, a printed slip of two lines was pasted at the bottom of folio 6.

    [*BAE*, CX, no. XXXIII, 350-423—HRP].

Casas should have completed this treatise in 1549. In a Prologue to Philip he recalls his *Treinta proposiciones* dashed off in haste to be sent to the Emperor (no. 43 of this Catalogue), and how he afterwards wrote the corroboration. Here he is printing only an abridgment: the supporting proofs of the fundamental Propositions 17 and 18, "taking it from a larger work wherein each is more particularized." In addition, he refers to his long eyewitness knowledge of the Indies, the years whereof now exceed fifty ("pasan de cincuenta"). This gives a date of around 1552, not for the original writing of the treatise but for its presentation to Philip in this short form. If Philip wishes it published abroad, Casas will give it in Latin, but little will be lost if it is not published in Spanish or Latin, "because I only had it printed so Your Highness can read it more easily."

Casas ends the tract by submitting it and himself to the judgment of the Holy See, since he has discussed the papal power and jurisdiction. The lost treatise *De juridico et christiano ingressu et progressu Regum nostrorum in regna Indiarum*, 61 leaves, included in Herrera's inventory of 1597, may well be a Latin version of this work.

45. 1548-1550, Valladolid. *Apología [contra Sepúlveda]*. The Latin translation of this work bears the title: *Apologia R.mi Domini Fratris Bartholome a Casaus, Episcopi quondam Chiapensis adversus Genesium Sepulvedam theologum cordubensem*. Cf. Fabié, II, 578, and note 4, for the Spanish and Latin versions, and the discovery of the Latin manuscript by Morel Fatio.

Bibliothèque Nationale, Paris, a Latin MS of about five hundred pages; also Library of Congress, photostat. No copy known of the Spanish work, which had about one hundred folio leaves.

Fabié, app. XXIV, Latin Argumentum only; an official Spanish summary of the entire work is printed in no. 48 of this Catalogue.

This treatise was Casas' answer to Sepúlveda's *Democrates alter*, which upheld the conquest. I have entered it with two dates because Casas may have written a shorter version as early as 1548, and completed a longer one in 1550.

In his brief Latin Argumentum, Casas says he composed this "apologia" to answer Sepúlveda's "Spanish summary of his work" because at the time he could not get hold of the book itself. Afterwards Alcalá ruled against Sepúlveda's work; and then Charles named a junta, before which Sepúlveda first appeared, and then Casas read "all this *Apología* seriatim" for five days. In a longer foreword to no. 48 of this Catalogue, Casas gives a more elaborate sequence: upon returning to court in 1547, he learned of Sepúlveda's book; and owing to his intervention, *Democrates alter* was referred to Salamanca and Alcalá, which ruled against it; then Sepúlveda wrote an *Apología* that was printed in Rome and seized in Spain. "*And because the said doctor wrote [time unspecified] a Spanish Sumario of his book, the said Bishop of Chiapa decided to write an* Apología, *also in Spanish, against it.*" [Italics ours.] Finally, after many events which afterwards occurred, the Emperor convoked a junta in 1550: Sepúlveda appeared for a few hours and gave a summary of his work [from his *Sumario?*]. But Casas "in five continuous days read his entire *Apología*."

From these two accounts I infer that: (1) Casas originally wrote his *Apología* perhaps the year after his return to court, as he twice says that some time elapsed before the Emperor convoked the junta. (2) The *Apología* that Casas read to the judges in 1550 was probably expanded from the first draft, for Sepúlveda was not prepared for it, and requested a copy of the official résumé in order to reply. I conclude that the Latin translation was made later.

Remesal (II, 256-257) quotes a portion of the Spanish text: what Casas had to say about Fray Luis Cáncer's martyrdom, in answer to Sepúlveda's observations.

46. 1549(?) Valladolid. Petition of Casas to the Council, opposing a Guatemalan agent.
AGI.
DII, VII, 167-172; Fabié, app. XIX; [*BAE*, CX, no. XXIX, 290-292—HRP].
This relates the coming of a representative from Santiago, to beg for revocation of President Cerrato's liberation of Indian slaves and reassessment of tributes in compliance with the orders of His Majesty. Casas says such agents deserve to be punished. He protests the suggestion that Bishop Marroquín be allowed to revise the tributes, and asks the building of roads to spare Indian carriers.

Mainly through Casas' efforts, Cerrato had been sent as the new president of the Audiencia de los Confines in 1548. Casas opens his petition as "El obispo de Chiapa" and signs it with the same title, presumably indicating that he had not yet resigned his bishopric.

47. 1550. Casas to Diego Hurtado de Mendoza, imperial ambassador at Rome, and Rodrigo de Mendoza, empowering them to resign his bishopric. Cf. Fabié, app. XVII.
No copy known.
Transmittted in the Emperor's letter to his ambassador from Augusta on September 11, 1550, naming Fray Tomás de Casillas as Casas' successor.

48. 1550-1551, Valladolid. *Aqui se contiene vna disputa, o controuersia: entre el Obispo do[n] fray Bartholome de las Casas, o Casaus, obispo q[ue] fue de la ciudad Real de Chiapa, que es enlas Indias parte de la nueua España y el doctor Gines de Sepulueda Coronista del Emperador nuestro señor: sobre q[ue] el doctor contendia: q[ue] las conquistas delas Indias contra los Indios eran licitas: y el obispo por el co[n]trario d[e]fendio y affirmo auer sido y ser i[m]possible no serlo: tiranicas, injustas & iniquas. La qual questio[n] se ve[n]tilo & disputo en presencia d[e] muchos letrados theologos & juristas en vna co[n]gregacion q[ue] mando su magestad juntar el año de mil & q[ui]nie[n]tos y cincue[n]ta en la villa de Ualladolid. Año 1552.* [From the colophon:] Seville, Sebastián Trugillo, September 10, 1552.

4°, 62 unnumbered leaves, the last blank. JCBL has another edition, a different original printing.

Llorente, I, 416-487; reprinted in Madrid in 1908 by the Marqués de Olivart; [*BAE*, CX, no. XXXI, 293-348—HRP].

Casas' Argument is of the greatest interest, as it gives his version of the dispute

with Sepúlveda. The tract proper consists of the official summary by Fray
Domingo de Soto, resuming Casas' *Apología* and Sepúlveda's statement of the
points in *Democrates alter* (see no. 45 of this Catalogue), followed by Sepúlveda's
and Casas' rebuttals. At the end of his rebuttal, Casas says he has had experience
[of the Indies] from fifty years back, and started working at court thirty-five
years ago. As the first session of the judges was in 1550, according to the title
page, this runs the rebuttals into 1551.

49. 1552. *Principia queda[m] ex quibus procedendum est in disputatione ad mani-
festandam et defendendam iusticiam Yndorum. Per Episcopu[m] F. Bartholo-
meu[m] a Casaus ordinis predicatoru[m], collecta. [Certain principles from
which to proceed in disputation in order to reveal and defend the rights of the
Indians. Collected by Bishop Fray Bartolomé de Casaus of the Order of Preachers.]* [From the colophon:] Seville, Sebastián Trugillo, n.d.

    4°, 10 unnumbered leaves, caption title.

    Like the use of Latin, the title of this tract seems designed to conceal rather
than reveal its subject matter—viz., limitations on the authority of the king.
Inferentially, Casas is attacking the right to grant encomiendas, see no. 50 of
this Catalogue. [See *Tratados de Fray Bartolomé de las Casas*, II, 1234-1273, for
a page-by-page translation into Spanish.—HRP.]

50. 1552. *D. Bartholomaei de las Casas, episcopi chiapensis, viri in omni doctrinarvm
genere exercitatissimi, erudita & elegans explicatio quaestionis vtrum reges vel
principes iure aliquo vel titulo, & salua conscientia, ciues ac subditos à regia
corona alienare, & alterius domini particularis ditioni subjicere possint? Antehac
nunquam ab vllo doctorum ita luculenter tractata.* Edita cura & studio Wolff.
Griestetteri. Cum gratia & priuilegio Caesareae Maiestatis. Francofvrti ad Moe-
num, M.D. LXXI. [*By D. Bartolomé de las Casas, Bishop of Chiapa, a man most
proficient in all kinds of doctrine, a Learned and Elegant Explanation of the
Question: whether Kings and Princes, by any right or title, and with a sound
conscience, can alienate citizens and vassals from the royal Crown and subject
them to the sovereignty of another private master? Never before treated so
lucidly by any of the doctors.* Edited under the care and study of Wolfgang
Griestetter. With the grace and privilege of the Imperial Majesty. Frankfurt
on the Main, MDLXXI.] [From the colophon:] By George Corvin, at the
expense of Hieronymus Feyerabend, 1571.

    4°, 67 pp.

    Later editions have somewhat different titles. Cf. Fabié, I, 321, and Nicolás
Antonio, *Bibliotheca hispana nova sive hispanorum scriptorum*, Madrid, 1783
[8], I, 193.

    Llorente, II, 49-111, a Spanish translation; also a French translation in his
Oeuvres of Casas.

    This longer treatise, on the topic broached in no. 49 of this Catalogue, was
the one that the Inquisition had Casas deliver to it in manuscript; there was, however, no trial. In the text, I have discussed both of these books and endeavored to
reconstruct what is known of the episode.

51. N.d. Casas to Dr. Sepúlveda.

Holograph letter of 2 pp., folio, closely written, present location unknown. Sale of Fischer's books, London, 1869, bought by Sir Thomas Phillipps.

No extract of this letter's contents is given in the sale catalogue, but "JGI" was stamped on it, like the stamp on many of Icazbalceta's documents. This creates a mystery. How did Fischer obtain the letter from him, and why did Icazbalceta not mention it in any of his writings? The letter was sold to Sir Thomas Phillipps, and may have remained in his possession. It seems to be entirely unknown.

I have wondered if this was Casas' answer to the Inquisition charge. There is no telling precisely what the letter may have contained or when Casas wrote to Sepúlveda, but it must have been after his return to Spain and in connection with their controversy.

52. N.d. A dialogue in Latin, apparently between an old man and a youth, on *"The Just Title to the Indies."* Cf. Medina, *Bib. hisp-am.*, I, 253.

115 leaves, part draft and part recopied. No copy known.

This work was one of the items delivered to Herrera in 1597. The dialogue form, the young and old interlocutors, and the presumed subject matter, all bear a striking resemblance to Sepúlveda's *Democrates alter*. At first sight, it might be taken for Casas' copy of that work. But the fact that it is partly a draft suggests that it was indeed a writing by Casas in answer to Sepúlveda.

VI. General Representative, 1552-1560

In his latter years, Casas served unofficially as general representative or "universal procurator" at court, not only for the Indians but for missionary affairs. A number of his petitions are concentrated here, including a memorable one for a chief from Nochistlán; earlier and later ones are in this Catalogue. See nos. 46, 68, 69, 72, and 76.

We also have in this period three significant writings of his against perpetual encomiendas: appeals to the royal confessor and to Philip himself, and the counteroffer on behalf of the Peruvian caciques.

Among the many powers of attorney Casas received, the broadest and most notable was from these chiefs, dated at Lima on July 19, 1559. AGI, Indiferente General, 1580; printed in Lewis Hanke's "Festón de docs.," *Revista Cubana*, XVI, 204-208.

53. 1552, before May 17, Valladolid. Casas to the King concerning dispatches of missionaries for the Indies.

DII, X, 87-88, also XIX, 533-534; [*BAE*, CX, no. XXX, 292-293, correcting the misprinted addressee to Vuestra Alteza, i.e., Philip—HRP].

Casas asks renewal of the dispatches that were issued for him to present to last year's general chapter of the Dominican Order, so he may take them to this year's chapter. He signs as bishop, but the endorsement on the back calls him "obispo que fué." Since Casas was prominent at the 1551 chapter (Rem., II, 282-283), this undated letter must have been written in 1552.

54. 1552, October 25, San Lúcar. Casas to the Council about difficulties in embarking missionaries to the Indies.
    AGI.
    Fabié, app. XVI; [BAE, CX, no. XXXII, 348-350—HRP].
    Casas complains of the ten-month delay in the sailing of the fleet. Of the thirty or so missionaries he assembled, all but fourteen have gone back to their monasteries and he does not know how many can wait it out. He has spent seven hundred ducats of his own money taking care of them.

55. 1552. Casas to the Audiencia of Lima, transmitted by Fray Domingo de Santo Tomás. Cf. Herrera, dec. VIII, lib. VII, cap. 3.
    No copy known.
    Casas complains that the royal judges have not yet executed the order about personal services of the Indians. The consequences of this letter are discussed in my text.

55A.[1553, Valladolid. Casas' itemized complaint to the Council of the Indies on Audiencia President Cerrato's assignment of Indians: an illegal encomienda, encomiendas to relatives, excessive encomiendas.
    AGI, Indiferente General 1093.
    Marcel Bataillon, "Las Casas et le licencié Cerrato," Bulletin Hispanique, V, 79-87; BAE, CX, no. XXXIV, 424-425.
    This is another illustration of Casas' attention to the work of the audiencias. Instead of Bataillon's "1552 (?)" conjecture, this recently printed document can now be dated more precisely. One of Casas' Guatemala informants at court did not leave Santiago till after July 1, 1553; and Casas' bill-of-particulars is part of the background of the September 17, 1553, cedula ordering the judicial investigation of Cerrato and the royal judges. Cf. Catálogo de la colección de don Juan Bautista Muñoz, II (Madrid, 1955), nos. 1,426 (2) and 1,546 (55)—HRP.]

56. 1553 (?) Valladolid. Petition of Don Francisco Tenamaztle, cacique of Nochistlán in Jalisco [but now in Spain], to the Council of the Indies—drafted and written for him by Casas.
    AGI, México 205.
    Lewis Hanke, "Festón de docs.," Revista Cubana, XVI, 196-203.
    This Indian chief had been sent to Spain by Viceroy Velasco as a prisoner for having been implicated in the Mixtón War. Here Casas tells his story for him. The petition is in Casas' handwriting and in his typical style: first a long tale of crimes committed by the Spaniards, then a remedy whereby Tenamaztle will undertake a peaceful conversion venture.

Tenamaztle begins by reciting the outrages committed by Nuño de Guzmán against him and his subjects. This gave him a perfect right to make war on the Christians, but instead he received them well, and then Guzmán put them in an encomienda. "Soon the Franciscans came to teach us about God in the heavens and the just and pious King of Castile." Tenamaztle was converted and baptized with many other lords and commoners, but Guzmán's cruelties continued. Finally, Alvarado came with five hundred soldiers and lodged in the province, committing fresh outrages. To escape, Tenamaztle and his people fled to the forests and fortified themselves, to defend their lives and their women and children. For nine years he hid where no Spaniard could find him. At length, he came back alone to his own country, to offer his services to Bishop [Pedro Gómez de Malaver] and seek friendship with the Spaniards. This bishop sent him to Viceroy Mendoza, but when he reached Mexico he found that Mendoza had gone and Velasco was in his place. At this time the bishop died and Tenamaztle wished to return home, but the viceroy detained him without any just reason. "They put irons on me, took me to Veracruz, and brought me here a prisoner."

Tenamaztle concludes by asking for a bishop and a number of friars: they would go to the wild Indians who had never known God or obeyed the King and tell them of His Majesty's good wishes and grants, especially an amnesty. "Let Your Highnesses give me a letter and royal provisions for safe conduct, as strong as possible, so that I may bring all those people to peace, and by my industry they may come soon to the royal Crown of Castile." At the end of the document is a note by Casas asking for funds to buy the chief some clothing and other necessities.

This petition could not have been written much later than 1552, as Tenamaztle's bishop died in that year. At first I thought it had been used by Santa Cruz in his *Crónica*, IV, 215-216. But he must have drawn upon a different document as he tells of Tenamaztle's escaping from Spanish hands at Mixtón Rock and then fleeing after the battle. See no. 42 of this Catalogue for Casas' interest in the Mixtón War.

56A.[1555, Valladolid. Casas' petition to the Council of the Indies for support of the missionary penetration of Pánuco.

   AGI, Indiferente General 1373.

   Benno M. Biermann, "Lascasiana," *Archivum Fratrum Praedicatorum*, XXVII, 349-351; *BAE*, CX, no. XXXVIII, 450-451, with the favorable response of the Council.

   Like the Tenamaztle petition, this newly printed document verifies Casas' earlier interest in the matter later developed in no. 67 of this Catalogue—HRP.]

57A.[1555, June 20, Valladolid. Casas to Philip in England, presenting an agent from Española and saying he has written separately about that island.

   AGI, Indiferente General 737.

   Benno M. Biermann, "Lascasiana," *Archivum Fratrum Praedicatorum*, XXVII, 354-355; *BAE*, CX, no. XXXVII, 429.

This agent also carried a letter from Casas to Carranza, shortly prior to no. 57 of this Catalogue—HRP.]

57. 1555, August, Valladolid. Casas' "letter or treatise" to Carranza de Miranda against perpetual encomiendas.

Bibliothèque Nationale, Paris, MS Esp. 277, fols. 98-134, and MS Esp. 325 (Veracruz papers), fols. 151-170; Biblioteca Nacional, Madrid, MS X-153.

Llorente, II, 117-174 (also in French, too free a translation of the later MS 277); Fabié, app. XXVIII (Veracruz); *DII*, VII, 290-338 (Bib. Nac.); [*BAE*, CX, no. XXXVII, 430-450—HRP].

This is Casas' specific answer to Carranza's of June 6, which took a month and a half to reach him. Despite their previous correspondence, including a recent letter, Casas deems this of the greatest urgency.

In the text, I have discussed this important document. Casas wrote it to block the granting of perpetual encomiendas in Peru, then being proposed to the Crown by Antonio de Ribera in exchange for a cash consideration. Casas uses specific arguments, a virtual tract against the encomienda, and direct appeals to the royal conscience; the letter is one of the most outspoken he ever wrote, especially as it was obviously intended for the King himself.

Casas sent a copy of this letter to the Dominicans of Chiapa and Guatemala, and probably to other friars also, in view of the number of extant copies.

58. 1556, Valladolid. Casas to King Philip II in England, against perpetual encomiendas.

AGI, Indiferente General 1093.

Mariano Cuevas, *Historia de la iglesia en México,* I (Tlalpam, 1921), 468-476; [*BAE*, CX, no. XLI, 453-460—HRP].

This is the second of Casas' important memorials in the perpetuity fight. It follows Philip's accession and marks a change in tactics—see my text for a full analysis. Here Casas says a counteroffer will be forthcoming from the caciques and he will help to arrange it.

The letter is dated internally, with a reference to the start of his mission: "As all the world knows, I have worked at this for forty-one years till today, which is the year 1556."

59. Between 1553 and 1557, Valladolid. Casas' answer to an opinion on restitution by Fray Tomás de San Martín, Bishop of Charcas.

AGI.

DII, VII, 362-370, and cf. San Martín's opinion, 348-362; Fabié, app. XXX, San Martín's opinion and Casas' answer; [*BAE*, CX, no. XXXV, 425-429, Casas' answer only—HRP].

Contrary to San Martín's distinction, Casas insists on restitution not only by conquistadors but by later encomenderos as well. Their interchange is difficult to date, despite many possible indications, because of the lack of authentic information on San Martín.

Casas begins by referring to two letters from San Martín about the fortune brought by Lope de Mendieta "whom God forgive." This Mendieta is elusive: On January 15, 1550, he had sent money from Peru to his uncle Diego de Zárate, and on October 14, 1551, he was in Seville, paying over 448 pesos that someone in Peru had sent to a relative. (*Fondos americanos,* IV, no. 980, and cf. pp. 142-143.) But the prayer suggests he was dead now, and in his conclusion Casas speaks of "the estate of Lope de Mendieta" and says that the restitution has to be made in Peru.

Internal evidence suggests only the earliest and latest dates for the correspondence, which I have given. Near the end, Casas says he would be pleased "if Your Reverence would also look at my *twenty printed reasons* which are circulating there." This is a reference to his printed tract against the encomienda—*Entre los remedios: el octavo: donde se asignan veynte razones.* The printing of Casas' eight tracts was not completed till 1553, but they might not have reached Peru till 1554. As the San Martín opinion is entirely a guide to "the discreet confessor," I believe he wrote it after seeing the printed copy of Casas' *Confesionario.*

Finally, in *his* opening, San Martín states that he has composed "an abbreviated chapter of what I have seen in the Indies, in the space of twenty-five years, of the injuries committed against the natives of those provinces." The passage, however, is ambiguous. If, as Remesal asserts, San Martín came originally with Pizarro and Valverde, he might be writing this in 1557, though not in 1558, as efforts to name a new bishop began then; and San Martín might have died a few years before that. But it is not certain that San Martín did come to Peru with Valverde. He might have come with Berlanga, and as I have pointed out he may have been in the islands earlier.

60. 1559, February 20, Valladolid. Casas to the King on behalf of the island of Española.

Archivo de Simancas, Estado 138, fol. 360, holograph MS. Photostat kindly loaned by Dr. Lewis Hanke.

[Benno M. Biermann, "Lascasiana," *Archivum Fratrum Praedicatorum,* XXVII, 355-356; *BAE,* CX, no. XLIII, 463-464—HRP.]

The Española agent, who has come again, will tell in greater detail "all that I have noted." Here, Casas begs the King to settle the island with peasants, which would cost about fifteen to twenty thousand ducats a year, for no more than ten years. He also recommends relieving the citizens of import duties.

In the opening and close of this petition, Casas alludes in veiled language to the pending struggle over perpetuity. He insists on his own services to the Crown; and if [Carranza de] Miranda were still at court and not archbishop, he would write further. But for now he warns the King to place a master over the Indies and to "be very careful in the matter of the provisions for Peru, as they have not been made as befits the service of Your Majesty." Doubtless Casas is referring to the viceroy's recall and the instructions for the perpetuity commission.

61. 1559, September 20, College of San Gregorio, Valladolid. Casas to the fathers of the Dominican province of San Vicente de Chiapa y Guatemala, sending relics.

Collection of G. R. G. Conway, MS in Latin, signed by Casas.

Casas says that some of the items had been seen by Fray Domingo de Santo Tomás of the province of San Juan Bautista in Peru. At the top end of the document is a receipt for the relics, dated at Santiago, Guatemala, October 19, 1560, and signed by four friars: Fray Tomás de Cárdenas, Fray Tomas de la Torre, prior, Fray Jaime de San Esteban, and Fray Vicente López, master of novices.

Remesal (II, 405) says that these relics were brought from Spain by Fray Domingo de Azcona, along with related papal documents, and received in Santiago with a great public celebration, including Indian dances.

62. 1559-1560, Valladolid. Casas' memorial to the Council about fresh oppressions of the Indians in New Spain.

   University of Texas, original, according to JGI.

   Icazbalceta, *Docs.*, II, 228-230; [*BAE*, CX, no. XXXIX, 451-452—HRP].

   This is undated and signed "El obispo que suplica"; but a notation says "Del obispo de Chiapa que fué."

   Casas has letters from New Spain advising him of fresh "inventions" to extort tribute from the Indians. These devices are the joint work of the audiencia and the encomenderos. While he labors at court to get Indians put under the Crown, with unscrupulous officials their lot in Crown towns is worse than before. Indians have been "recounted" to raise the number of tributaries. Furthermore, by means of the cedula obtained here through false information, Indian villages have been deprived of their small reserves for community needs. Most aggrieved have been the Crown towns of Guaxocingo [Huejotzingo] and Tepeaca, which have appealed and are appealing for relief, but to no avail, because of the opposition of the royal attorney.

   This precise situation is described in a detailed report by Judge Zorita. He explains how an *October 3, 1599, cedula,* obtained by false information, has halted the reserving of one fourth of the tribute for needs of the Indian communities; also, pursuant to an order for retaxing certain Crown towns reassessed by Diego Ramírez, Guaxocingo and Tepeaca have had their tributes drastically raised, despite sharp population losses. See Zorita, *Historia,* app. VI—his June 10, 1560, letter to the King.

   The retaxing evidently took place in 1558. For on January 21 of that year, Accountant Ibarra forwarded a summary of Ramírez' tribute reductions for Crown towns (*Epis. de Nueva España,* VIII, no. 455). Full Guaxocingo records show that the town's levy, substantially commuted from cash to maize by the viceroy in 1556 after a drought, was so drastically increased that it became the subject of litigation between the Indians and the royal attorney in 1558. The Guaxocingo villagers finally lost their appeal on September 6, 1560, when the audiencia ruled that their tenants must be counted as tributaries. *Epis. de Nueva España,* IX, no. 510.

   Casas' petition was therefore presented late in 1559 or in 1560. Since the full Guaxocingo records were abstracted on April 3, 1562, his efforts at court may have led to a reopening of the case.

63. 1560 (?) Valladolid. Memorial of Casas and Fray Domingo de Santo Tomás to the Council of the Indies.

University of Texas, original MS.

Icazbalceta, *Docs.*, II, 231-236, printed by JGI from the original then in his possession; [*BAE*, CX, no. XLVI, 465-468–HRP].

Casas and Santo Tomás apparently presented this petition with the power of attorney issued to them by the Peruvian caciques on July 19, 1559.

This is the counteroffer that I have discussed in my text. García Icazbalceta was of the opinion that Casas did not write it but simply signed his name, the implication being that Santo Tomás was the author. My opinion is quite the contrary. As early as 1556 (no. 58 of this Catalogue), Casas promised the King to promote precisely such a counteroffer, and the whole document is in line with his ideas. Doubtless Santo Tomás, who was in Valladolid by September 20, 1559 (cf. no. 61 of this Catalogue), made the arrangements with the caciques in Peru and contributed many concrete details.

On the cover of the MS is a note about transmitting the memorial to the viceroy of Peru and the commissioners; this was actually done by a cedula of February 7, 1561. Cf. Zavala, *La encomienda indiana*, 209-210.

VII. HISTORIAN AND ANTHROPOLOGIST, 1560-1561

Since I have devoted a chapter to Casas' *Historia* and *Apologética*, I shall confine myself here to examining the holograph and contemporary manuscripts of these works, and the early chroniclers who used them. The writing of the final drafts covered a decade, and Casas began the project in 1527, but I have entered the two books in the years when I believe he "finished" them.

Easily the most important document of his activity as a historian is a transcript made by him: the only extant copy of the diary of Columbus' Voyage of Discovery. As it is in Casas' writing, I shall discuss it at the close of this section.

64. 1560, Valladolid. *Apologética historia sumaria cuanto a las cualidades, dispusición, descripción, cielo y suelo destas tierras, y condiciones naturales, policías, repúblicas, maneras de vivir e costumbres de las gentes destas Indias occidentales, y meridionales, cuyo imperio soberano pertenece á los Reyes de Castilla.* [From the Argument: Escribió esta historia] Fray Bartolomé de las Casas ó Casaus, fraile de Santo Domingo y Obispo que fué de la Ciudad Real de Chiapa.

Muñoz Collection, holograph manuscript, originally in the College of San Gregorio, Valladolid, 830 folio leaves.

First partial printings: 52 selected chapters in 1876 (with no. 65 of this Catalogue); portions relating to Peru, by Marcos Jiménez de la Espada, as *De las antiguas gentes del Perú*, Madrid, 1892. First printed in full from the holograph MS, by Manuel Serrano y Sanz, Madrid, 1909, as vol. XIII of the Nueva Biblioteca de Autores Españoles.

The holograph MS and its date: According to Serrano, the manuscript is entirely in Casas' hand and contains numerous emendations by him; the struck-out passages are printed as footnotes in Serrano's edition. These are mostly minor changes, except for the first ones which show how Casas separated this work from his larger history. I have already discussed the evidence that he did so at a quite late date.

As we have it, the *Apologética* is a complete book: a formal title; an Argument stating the author's purpose; 267 chapters with careful headings, carrying this out as promised; an Epilogue; and a closing "A Dios sean dadas graçias para siempre jamas." The separate *Apologética* was evidently in this shape before Casas finished the final draft of his history (no. 65 of this Catalogue), as the second half of that work contains a number of references to it. The most striking occurs in the *Historia*, lib. III, near the end of cap. 12, where Casas says that "Lic. Gregorio did not know the distinction of the four different kinds of barbarians, as we explain *at the end* of our *Apologética historia*." [Italics ours.] I have entered the *Apologética* under 1560, the last date of writing that can be established in the text.

Contemporary MSS and their users: Unlike Casas' other big books—*Del único modo*, the *Historia*, and *De thesauris* (nos. 16, 65, and 73 of this Catalogue)—no contemporary manuscript copies of the *Apologética* are now extant. But there certainly were a number, and the manuscript work was used by at least three chroniclers in the sixteenth century.

According to Dávila Padilla, the library of the Dominican province in Mexico City had a copy which Fray Domingo de la Anunciación had had transcribed from an "original" in the hands of the Dominicans in Chiapa: it comprised a ream of paper and bore the abbreviated title, *Del bien y favor de los indios*. Fray Jerónimo de Mendieta saw this manuscript and used it in his *Historia eclesiástica indiana*. He calls it an *Apología* "in defense of the Indians"; and on page 42 he states that it was in the Dominican convent in Mexico, and had not been printed and never would be. Relating the attempts of the Franciscans and Dominicans to settle the Pearl Coast, Mendieta says that only Casas tells the true version of the affair; he then proceeds to quote it in his chapter 9, copying it verbatim from chapter 246 of the *Apologética*. Mendieta also quotes other passages from Casas' *Apologética*, and his description and use of the MS (cf. also page 536 *et seq.*) proves conclusively that it was the same one described by Dávila Padilla as *Del bien y favor de los indios*. Doubtless there were other copies, besides these two in Mexico and Central America, but I have not been able to identify any.

A friar in Spain, who borrowed very extensively from the *Apologética*, may have had access to the original. This was the Augustinian Jerónimo Román, who published a two-volume *Repúblicas del mundo* in Medina del Campo in 1575. (See Pérez Pastor, *Imprenta en Medina del Campo*, Madrid, 1895.) Román's "Repúblicas de Indias" occupy three books in his second volume, and in 1897 the portion on Mexico and Peru was reprinted in Madrid. Curiously, Román merely includes Casas among many sources, speaking in an opening list (page 9, this edition) of the "Papeles del Santo varón don Fray [Bartolomé de las Casas] obispo de Chiapa," and at the end naming the Bishop of Chiapa among various "conquistadores y cronistas" whose works he has consulted; only twice (187 and 220 of part I) does he cite Casas' *Apología*. From these scant references one would never guess that nearly all of his account of the Indians in New Spain, Guatemala, Honduras, and Española is copied almost word for word from Casas' *Apologética* —that is to say, the first 313 pages of part I of the reprint. Only a small bit is taken from Gómara. But generally speaking, practically everything in these three books of his, except his account of the customs and rites of the Peruvians, is lifted bodily from Casas' work.

Where and when did Román see the manuscript? His book was licensed by the Madrid provincial in 1573, so it was before that date. In his second volume (lib. X, cap. 13), he praised Spanish universities and especially the colleges in Valladolid. Is this a hint that the College of San Gregorio, which held Casas' papers, had allowed him to consult the *Apologética*? Quién sabe?

Anyway, it seems the college did retain the manuscript. For the *Apologética* was *not* on the list of writings delivered to Antonio de Herrera in 1597—those that had been taken from the College of San Gregorio and were in Velasco's possession. The inference is that neither Velasco nor Herrera wished to use it; the encyclopedic data on Indian civilizations could hardly fit in with Herrera's assignment to defend the conquest. Furthermore, in the seventeenth century, Remesal describes the holograph MS of the *Apologética* as still among those "in the trust" of San Gregorio—"830 folio leaves of Casas' own close and small writing, almost without margin." Cf. Rem., II, 467.

Remesal definitely did use the *Apologética* in his chronicle, making quotations and borrowing incidents from it. Did he have his own copy, as he did of *Del único modo*, or did he consult those in the New World? There is only a hint, but it suggests rather that he too used the San Gregorio copy. Speaking of the Land of War Indians, he cites a passage in [Román's] *Repúblicas del mundo* that he had not believed until he read the same in chapter 236 of Casas' *Apologética* and the four following, "which occupy 16 folio leaves in his writing that is very abbreviated and small." Cf. Rem., I, 215.

Several later manuscript copies are known. For instance, Sir Thomas Phillipps owned one formerly belonging to Lord Kingsborough (see Phillipps' sale of 1919, no. 320). But both of Lord Kingsborough's copies had no doubt been transcribed from the original in the Real Academia.

Publication: Despite Mendieta's prediction, Casas' *Apologética historia* finally was printed in 1909, as noted, by Serrano y Sanz, though without introduction, notes, or index. [The *Apologetica* has been reprinted from the holograph MS, by Juan Pérez de Tudela Bueso, in Biblioteca de Autores Españoles, CV-CVI, Madrid, 1958, with an introduction on Casas' anthropology and an index of proper names—HRP.]

65. 1561, Madrid. *Historia [general] de las Indias*. [From the Prologue: El autor es] D. Fray Bartolomé de las Casas o Casaus, fraile de Santo Domingo y obispo de la Ciudad Real, que se dice de los llanos de Chiapa.

Biblioteca Nacional, Madrid, holograph MS, books I, II, and III; sixteenth-century copy, book III only. Real Academia de la Historia, Madrid, Muñoz Collection, duplicate by a copyist, with corrections in Casas' handwriting, books I and II only.

First printed in 1875-1876—from a transcript checked with the Academia manuscript—by the Marqués de la Fuensanta del Valle and José Sancho Rayón, in five volumes (selected chapters from the *Apologética* in volume V).

Original MSS. This is Casas' most important writing and is preserved in two manuscripts:

According to Julián Paz's catalogue of American MSS in the Biblioteca Nacional, Casas' holograph original is in three books: the first of 14 preliminary leaves and 496 folios, the second of 194 folios, the third of 495 folios, or a total of 1,199. This MS was delivered to Herrera in 1597, according to a notation on the last page signed by Licentiate Baltodano, a member of the Council of the Indies from 1589 to 1612. Afterwards, Casas' MS was apparently not returned to the archives or the King's library in the Escorial, for it was not until 1904 that the Biblioteca Nacional finally purchased it from a private individual.

The Real Academia manuscript is a copy "en limpio" of libs. I and II, with marginal corrections by Casas himself. The companion volume of lib. III is in the Biblioteca Nacional, but has no corrections. Up till 1843, the Biblioteca Nacional possessed an identical copy of lib. III, which has since disappeared. But its existence shows there were originally at least three contemporary copies of Casas' history, including the one in his own hand.

Dating: I have chosen to date the work at Madrid, rather than at the College of San Gregorio de Valladolid, because Casas completed his final revision in the new capital. His November 1559 letter of donation to the college may have been written in anticipation of moving with the court, as he went along to Toledo in 1560 and apparently to Madrid in 1561. (For the holograph "carta dedicatoria," which precedes lib. I and lib. II, see the Academia edition of the *Historia*, I, vii and 1, also II, vii and facsimile.)

Although *Historia de las Indias* is apparently the title on the "clean copy" Casas himself revised, in his will made at Madrid in 1564 (no. 75 of this Catalogue) he calls it his *Historia general de las Indias*. Casas evidently had the work with him in his last years at Madrid, for the next to the last paragraph of the Prologue was revised in 1563, though this date cannot be inferred in any passage of the text. As I have explained in detail, I consider the *Historia* an unfinished work, since it has only three "books" or decades instead of the six announced in the Prologue. In addition, many chapters have blank spaces for headings to be put in, and there is no formal closing. So I have entered it in 1561, the date when Casas finished book III, presumably the last he wrote. He closes with these words about the obtuseness of an audiencia president: "But that ignorance and blindness had its first origin in the King's Council . . . and please God that today, which is the year that is ending of '61, the Council may be free of it. And with this imprecation, and the glory and honor of God, we conclude this third book. *Deo gratias*."

Herrera's use of the manuscript: Casas' MS *Historia* had an early and decisive influence on the writing of American history. Although he had expressed his wish, in the "carta dedicatoria," that the manuscript remain in the possession of the fathers of San Gregorio and not be seen by laymen for forty years, Casas had not counted on Philip. The King was determined to have somebody write a history of the Indies and appointed different people to perform the task—and they, in turn, got hold of Casas' work.

When López de Velasco was appointed chief cosmographer and chronicler of the Indies in 1571, it seems apparent that some if not all of Casas' papers were removed from the college and turned over to him; just when he received them is not certain, but he had them in 1579. Velasco wrote a *Geografía y descripción de las Indias* that was finished about 1574. I do not know whether he borrowed anything from Casas' *Historia,* but I recall no reference to Casas in it.

From López de Velasco's hands, the *Historia* passed in 1597 into those of the chronicler who made the most extensive use of it—Antonio de Herrera, named chief chronicler the year before. Herrera had Casas' manuscript copied at a cost of 49,800 maravedis (see the documents printed by Cristóbal Pérez Pastor, *Bib. madrileña,* II, 337, note). That seems to be proof positive that Herrera had the whole work transcribed; it would be definitely established if an examination of the holograph manuscript showed it had *not* been marked off at portions Herrera wanted transcribed (as happened to the MS of Cervantes de Salazar). Yet Herrera did not by any means insert the whole of Casas' text in his own *Historia general,* though he did use a very substantial part of it. His printed acknowledgment, like Román's for the *Apologética,* was sparing. When Herrera published the second part of his history in 1615, he enumerated many of his authorities and included Casas among them; and in his text he occasionally cites him as an "autor de mucha fe" and the "Santo Obispo de Chiapa." But now that we have Casas' own *Historia de las Indias* we can see that Herrera borrowed a great deal, though he made very judicious selections. He omitted entirely the numerous digressions and philosophical and moral diatribes, copying only Casas' facts and apparently placing great reliance upon them.

Herrera's example was followed by many later writers, using manuscript copies of Casas' work—a number of these copies, made from about 1790 onward, are still in existence. Servando Mier y Terán, in the introduction to his 1821 reprint of the *Brevissima,* said he saw the MS *Historia* in Muñoz's power and afterwards the three volumes were removed to the Secretaría de Gracias y Justicia de las Indias. Sir Arthur Helps had a portion of the work transcribed for his use. William H. Prescott had a manuscript copy and used it extensively, though it covers only a small part of the conquest of Mexico. In recent years, two manuscript copies have been included in the sales of Sir Thomas Phillipps' books: in 1913 the Rothsay copy, recently acquired by the JCBL; and in 1919 the Kingsborough copy, whose present whereabouts are unknown to me.

Publication: Despite the obvious historical value of Casas' book, first recognized by Herrera, his *Historia* was withheld from publication for three centuries. The authorities and then the Real Academia seemed to think that publication would injure Spain's credit abroad, though the *Brevissima* had been widely reprinted ever since the sixteenth century. Casas had asked that his history be withheld from publication for forty years; it finally appeared in 1875-1876, a long 310 years after his death, in an edition without introduction, notes, or an index. A life and works by the academician Antonio María Fabié, commissioned as a prologue, did not appear till 1879, though by then Fabié had amassed a supplementary volume of documents. But Casas' *Historia de las Indias* still awaits an adequate edition.

[Two recent printings of Casas' *Historia* have been based on the holograph manuscript:

Agustín Millares Carlo's edition, 3 vols., Mexico and Buenos Aires, 1951— with his analytical index incorporating essays on printed and manuscript sources cited in the text, and an introductory monograph by Lewis Hanke on Casas as a historian.

Juan Pérez de Tudela Bueso's edition, Biblioteca de Autores Españoles, XCV-XCVI, Madrid, 1957—with his introductory monograph on Casas' life and works, an index of proper names, and the transcription partly by Emilio López Oto—HRP.]

66. N.d. Bartolomé de las Casas, abridged transcript of Columbus' log of his Voyage of Discovery to America.

Biblioteca Nacional, Madrid, MS in Casas' handwriting.

In 1791, Navarrete found this document—together with Casas' copy of Columbus' report of his Third Voyage—in a volume belonging to the Duke of Infantado. Navarrete printed both in tomo I of his *Colección de viages* (1825).

As with many documents, Casas made this priceless transcript of the Columbus log for his own use in writing the *Historia;* much of the text consists of verbatim extracts, though there is some abridgement. No other manuscript is known to have survived.

Casas uses the First Voyage log extensively in book I of his history, from chapters 35 through 75—quoting extracts, frequently changing Columbus' personal account into indirect narrative, and interpolating digressions of his own. At the end he states that he has taken the Discoverer's words "from the book that Columbus made for the Kings of his first navigation to and discovery of the Indies." (*Hist.,* lib. I, beginning of cap. 75.) Casas does not say when or where he made the copy, but Menéndez y Pelayo thought it was in the Dominican monastery of San Pablo de Sevilla, at the time Hernando Columbus' books and papers were deposited there.

In his account of the Third Voyage, starting with chapter 127 of his book I, Casas again makes extracts from Columbus' log, now lost, but uses other sources as well, notably his aforementioned copy of the report Columbus sent the monarchs from Española.

VIII. NONAGENARIAN, 1561-1566

These years, following Casas' move to Madrid, mark the final phase of his career. Though he turned ninety in 1564, he continued to work as procurator, and we have a number of his petitions as well as his last memorial and a part of his will. But his chief labor was the composition of two farewell treatises, both of which have survived.

The most important document relating to the close of Casas' life was the posthumous order to deliver his papers to the chief cosmographer and chronicler of the Indies. (Pérez Pastor, *Bibliografía madrileña*, III, 422.) López de Velasco's relinquishment of them was accompanied by the inventory with which I opened this Catalogue.

67. 1562, Madrid. Petition of Casas and Fray Alonso de Maldonado, offering Judge Zorita's proposal for the peaceful reduction of Pánuco and New Mexico.
    Bibliothèque Nationale, Paris, copy evidently among the Veracruz papers.
    Zorita's draft capitulation (Icazbalceta, *Docs.*, II, 333-342) was carried to Spain by Maldonado. It was to have been presented by Casas and the Franciscan provincial, but the latter left as Bishop of Yucatán.

68. 1562 (?) Madrid. Casas' petition to the Council of the Indies for the repair of the church at La Paz.
    AGI, Charcas 135.
    Hanke, "Festón de docs.," *Revista Cubana*, XVI, 211; [*BAE*, CX, no. XLIX, 477–HRP].
    He transmits sworn evidence from the Bishop of Charcas to the effect that the church was falling apart and mass had to be said in a thatched hut. This bishop was therefore Fray Domingo de Santo Tomás, who returned to Peru in 1562 to look after the see, vacant and neglected since the death of San Martín.

69. 1562-1563 (?) Madrid. Letter of Casas to the Council, recommending Diego de Ocampo as agent in Lima for the Peruvian Indians.
    AGI.
    DII, VII, 161-162; [*BAE*, CX, no. XL, 453–HRP].
    This was undoubtedly the result of a suggestion made by Fray Domingo de Santo Tomás in his letter to Casas in *DII*, VII, 371-387; cf. particularly 382-385. The letter is undated, but it can definitely be placed after Santo Tomás' return to Peru as Bishop of Charcas, for he speaks of the conquest of Chile having been completed quite some time ago.

70. 1562-1563, Madrid. Casas to the fathers of the Dominican province of Chiapa and Guatemala, exhorting them about the evil of encomiendas.
    Huntington Library, MS signed by Casas but not in his hand. Acquired in

1925 from Charles Sessler of Philadelphia, this is probably the copy formerly
in the possession of Pascual de Gayangos.

Printed by Henry Stevens in 1854, from the copy now in the Huntington.
Fabié, app. XXVII, from a copy then in the possession of Gayangos; [*BAE*, CX,
no. XLVIII, 469-477—HRP].

From the text it appears that this is the third letter of a prolonged two-way
correspondence. Casas had sent these friars a copy of his anti-encomienda "letter
or tract" to Carranza (no. 57 of this Catalogue). In reply, they expressed the view
that encomiendas, as now modified and regulated, were held lawfully. Casas
contradicts this opinion, citing his long experience, continuing oppression, and
theoretical reasons. The last portion of his letter is entirely in Latin, as it speaks
of the royal authority.

Though the letter bears no date, this can be fixed approximately from internal
evidence. Near the beginning, Casas makes two successive statements using his
usual dual points of reference (cf. no. 43 of this Catalogue). It has been sixty-one
years since he saw these tyrannies begin, and forty-eight years that he has been
"working to inquire and study and clearly extract the *derecho.*" The forty-eight
years refer specifically to his "conversion" in August of 1514, so I place the writing of this letter in the latter part of 1562 or early in 1563. For external evidence,
we know only that this communication had not yet been *received* some time in
1563—cf. Fray Tomas de la Torre's letter in that year, Fabié, app. XX, 201-203.

71. 1563, March 3, Madrid. Casas' letter to the King about payment of 149 ducats
due him for serving as arbitrator between two noblemen.

DII, X, 86-87 and XIX, 534-535; [*BAE*, CX, no. XLVII, 468-469, correcting
the misprinted addressee to "vuestra merced," i.e., not the King—HRP].

72. 1563 (?) Madrid. Memorial of Casas about mistreatment of Indians and persecution of friars in Guatemala.

AGI.

DII, VII, 162-167; [*BAE*, CX, no. XLII, 460-462—HRP].

Casas asks reforms in the tribute assessments and modification of the hiring-
out system of forced native labor. He cites the misdeeds of a Guatemalan
royal judge, "Doctor Megías," concerning personal services of the Indians, and
persecution of the Dominicans (about which a report has already been given) and
he requests this man's suspension till a judicial investigation can be made.

Though this is undated, the references to Mexía fix the approximate time of
writing. Remesal (II, 403-404) gives details on the persecution of the Guatemala
Dominicans instigated by Mexía in the years immediately following the 1560
chapter, the information to His Majesty, and the June 5, 1565, cedula issued
"algunos años despues" to prevent any recurrence of such a situation.

73. 1563, Madrid. *De thesauris qui reperiuntur in sepulchris indorum.* [*About the
Treasures that are Found in the Tombs of the Indians.*]

Vellum bound MS, 192 folio leaves, according to the original inventory of

Casas' papers, Medina, *Bib. hisp.-am.*, I, 253. Extant MS copies have variant titles. JCBL; Biblioteca Nacional, Madrid; and another, whereabouts unknown.

[Bartolomé de las Casas, *Los tesoros del Peru,* ed. by Angel Losada, Madrid, 1958.

Biblioteca de Palacio, MS II-938—copyist's manuscript with corrections in Casas' handwriting.

Published after nearly four centuries, this edition contains, besides the Latin text of the codex discovered by Losada, his introduction describing the MSS and summarizing the treatise, and his Spanish translation and classified indices.

Losada concludes (xxi) that Casas completed the treatise on August 30, 1562, but the passage he cites (294, 295) says 1561 (a misprint?) and occurs less than two-thirds of the way through the text. So Casas may have finished it later in the year—HRP.]

For a discussion of this work, see no. 74 of this Catalogue.

74. 1564, January, Madrid. *El muy ilustre y reverendísimo Sr. D. Fray Bartolomé de las Casas, obispo de Chiapa, declaró y dió resolucion á las doce dudas en este tratado contenidas. . . .*

JCBL; Biblioteca Nacional, and Biblioteca de Palacio, Madrid; Bibliothèque Nationale, Paris; and two others, whereabouts unknown.

Llorente, II, 181-335, free text without opening note, Argument, or annexed documents; Fabié, I, 232-234, note and Argument only (Bib. Palacio), and I, 336-338, same (Bib. Nac.); [*BAE,* CX, no. L, 476-536, tract with note and Argument, checked with Bib. Nac. The dedication is still unpublished—HRP.]

I shall discuss here both this and the preceding work because their existing manuscripts are so often bound together that it would be unintelligible to describe them separately. In addition, the two treatises are intimately related, as Casas himself explains in the unpublished dedication of *Doce dudas* to Philip II, which I have quoted in my text:

"De thesauris," he says, *was written first, in Latin, and he was offering it to Philip as his testament or bequest.* Directed ostensibly to the question of the ownership of the vast Inca tomb treasures, it begins "In regnis que communi vocabulo dicuntur del Peru": In the kingdoms of Peru there have been and are daily being found, in the most ancient tombs, so-called Guacas: gold and silver, vessels and objects thereof, precious stones, etc.; and the grave question is, do they belong to those who find them, with or without license of the Spanish authorities? (JCBL MS, fol. 1.) Undoubtedly this is answered by elaborating and then applying general principles.

"Doce dudas," he himself says, *was written afterwards, using the same basic doctrine, but recast to answer "twelve doubts" of a Dominican friar—and Casas was offering it to the King as his codicil.* I have identified this friar as probably Domingo de Santo Tomás, and the British Museum has a manuscript entitled "Ciertas dudas y conclusiones que puso un frayle de la Orden de Santo Domingo los quales se embiaron ha (*sic*) Alcalá al P̄ᵉ. maestro Deça, al Maestro Juan Açor y al P̄ᵉ. Alonso de Montoya de la Compañía de Jesús, con la respuesta de cada uno de ellos." Cf. Pascual de Gayangos, *Catalogue of Spanish Manuscripts in*

the British Museum (London, 1877), II, 386, no. 32. Since Casas himself says that the Dominican also proposed his doubts to the learned of various faculties, it would appear that this is the original document to which Casas' tract of *Doce dudas* was the reply.

According to a note written on the JCBL copy of *De thesauris,* Casas composed it in 1563. *Doce dudas* is dated internally, at the beginning of Principio VII, where Casas says "today we are at January, the year of 1564." Casas himself states that he wrote the second tract while awaiting an opportune occasion to present the first to the King.

I have located or identified the following manuscripts of these two works:

John Carter Brown Library, a dual set. This is perhaps the most interesting because of provenance and annexed documents. Evidently it belonged to Fray Alonso de la Veracruz, Casas' final co-worker, though my investigation does not bear out the note in the margin which says the volume is entirely in his writing. The codex contains: *De thesauris,* without title or Argument, fols. 1-134; *Doce dudas,* without the preliminary entitling note, but beginning with a half-page Argument and a five and one-quarter page dedication to Philip, fols. 134 verso-226 verso; Casas' last memorial to the Council, and Fray Alonso de la Veracruz's long note which includes clauses from Casas' will (nos. 78 and 75 of this Catalogue), fols. 227-230 verso. This manuscript volume was found by Dr. Nicolás León in Mexico before 1886; as Veracruz was in Michoacán early, and afterwards disposed of some of his books to monasteries in that province, Dr. León may have found it in one of them. He wrote an account of it that year, and in 1889 published another in the *Anales del Museo Michoacano.* From his hands it passed to the JCBL.

Biblioteca Nacional, a dual set. According to the Julián Paz catalogue, no. 36, this volume contains the two works in 131 numbered leaves, plus an unnumbered leaf with some verses at the beginning; it appears to lack all the additions of Veracruz. The codex consists of: *Doce dudas,* prefixed by a short note evidently in the form of a title, and an Argument, fols. 1-95 verso; *De thesauris,* with the title "Singularis tractatulus reuerendissimi domini D. F. Bartolomei a Casaus Episcopi quondam Chiapen super quodam quae sito ad nouum Indiarum orbem attinenti," fols. 96-131. I do not believe Casas wrote this title, as so far as I know he did not put such headings on his memorials. It was probably from this "Singularis tractatulus" that Henri Ternaux had the one made which he attached to Casas' nine printed tracts, now in the JCBL, although from the difference in the number of folios it appears that this copy is only an extract.

Phillipps' copy, a dual set. In London in 1869, at the Behrendt sale (Agustín Fischer's books), no. 2952 was bought by Sir Thomas Phillipps. The catalogue entry reads as follows: "Respuesta de Don Fray Bartholome de las Casas a la Consulta que se le hizo sobre los sucesos de la Conquista del Peru, en 1564. 140 folio leaves." Following was: "Argumentum hujus tractatulus. In regnis . . . 182 folios." Said to have been in seventeenth-century handwriting, the volume was sold in Sir Thomas Phillipps' sale at Sotheby's in 1919. The present whereabouts of this codex is unknown to me.

Copies of Doce dudas *alone.* The Bibliothèque Nationale manuscript of *Doce dudas* was used by Llorente for his defective publication in 1822; it apparently bears the same title as the Phillipps copy, "Respuesta, etc.," and is presumably among the Veracruz papers. Fabié (I, 232) cites and prints the note and Argument from a manuscript copy of *Doce dudas* in the Biblioteca de Palacio. He says it originally came from the "Biblioteca del colegio mayor de Cuenca"; but of the Biblioteca Nacional copy he also says (I, 336) that it came from the "biblioteca del mayor de Cuenca." Finally, Salvá in his *Catálogo* of 1872 says he had seen in London a manuscript of Casas in 274 pages quarto, with the following title: "Solución de doce dudas acerca de la oppressión y servidumbre que padecen los Indios del Perú."

75. 1564, March 17, Madrid. Will of Casas, authorized on this date.
      Bibliothèque Nationale, Paris, Veracruz papers. JCBL, following the MS copy of *Doce dudas,* but lacking the notary's attestations.
      Icazbalceta, *Docs.,* II, 509-514, from the Paris Veracruz papers; [*BAE*, CX, no. LII, 538-541—HRP].
      This is not the whole will, drawn up at the end of February. Rather, these are extracts of those passages where Casas speaks of his mission, and his writings and papers, also the opening and closing paragraphs.

76. N.d. Petition of Casas to the Council, asking prohibition of pearl fishing.
      AGI, Patronato 195, ramo 27.
      Lewis Hanke, "Festón de docs., *Revista Cubana*, XVI, 209-210; [*BAE*, CX, no. XLV, 464-465—HRP].
      There is no internal indication of when Casas wrote this, except a reference to the Emperor, "may he be in heaven." But its extreme brevity for such a subject, only two paragraphs, suggests that it may have been written between 1564 and 1566, when I have conjectured that Casas was ill.

77. 1566, Madrid. Petition of Casas to the Pope [Pius V], asking a papal decree on behalf of the Indians.
      Bibliothèque National, Paris, Veracruz papers.
      Icazbalceta, *Docs.,* II, 599-600; [*BAE*, CX, no. LIII, 541-542—HRP].
      Apparently written after Pius V's election in January 1566, but before Casas' fatal illness. Prompt word of the new Pontiff's election had been transmitted to Casas from Rome on January 7 by the Chiapa precentor—*DII*, VII, 245.

78. 1566, July, Madrid. Casas' last memorial to the Council, referring to the presentation of his two farewell treatises and urging a junta to reform the Indies.
      Bibliothèque Nationale, Paris, in the Veracruz papers, with a short note; JCBL, following the MS of *Doce dudas,* with a long note.
      Icazbalceta, *Docs.,* II 595-598, from the Paris Veracruz papers, with the short note; [*BAE*, CX, no. LI, 536-538, with the short note—HRP].
      In this, Casas begs for the examination of the eight conclusions that he has

demonstrated; the list is not to be confused with the eight principles he used for resolving the *Doce dudas*—no. 74 of this Catalogue.

Fray Alonso de la Veracruz's long note, in the JCBL manuscript, adds sufficient information to the short one, printed by García Icazbalceta, to establish the positive date of this petition. As Casas was ill, it was presented in his name by Veracruz, Maldonado, and Fray Hernando de Barrionuevo (short note), the Franciscan commissary general, and read aloud by Licentiate Santander in the full Council of the Indies—and "a few days later" Casas died in the Dominican monastery of Our Lady of Atocha on Saint Margaret's Day, July 20, 1566 (long note).

LIST OF LOCATIONS AND ABBREVIATIONS

The following list will locate, in archives, libraries, private collections, manuscript catalogues, or printed sources, all items entered in my Catalogue of Casas' Writings with their corresponding numbers. As it incidentally identifies the main abbreviations used in my footnotes, I have also included here the few other chronicles and document collections cited in abbreviated form. [HRP additions to the Catalogue are in brackets.]

Apologética or *Apol.* Casas, Fr. Bartolomé de las. *Apologética historia* . . . Nueva Biblioteca de Autores Españoles, XIII. Madrid, 1909.
> No. 64.

AGI. Archivo General de Indias, Seville.
> Nos. 2, 5, [7A], 10, 13, 36, 46, 54, [55A], 56, [56A], [57A], 59, 63, 68, 69, 72, 76.

Archivo Histórico Nacional, Madrid.
> Nos. 37, 38.

Archivo Provincial, Valencia. See Dominican Provincial Archive.

Archivo de Simancas.
> Nos. 17, 61.

Archivum Fratrum Praedicatorum. See Biermann.

Arévalo, *Docs.* Arévalo, Rafael, ed. *Colección de documentos antiguos del archivo del ayuntamiento de la Ciudad de Guatemala.* Guatemala, 1857.

[*BAE*, CX. Casas, Fray Bartolomé de las. *Obras escogidas, V: Opúsculos, cartas y memoriales.* Juan Pérez de Tudela Bueso, ed. Biblioteca de Autores Españoles, Continuación, CX. Madrid, 1958.
> Nos. 2, 4-5, 7, 7A, 10, 12-14, 17-29, 31A, 36-38, 41, 43-44, 46, 48, 53-54, 55A, 56A, 57A, 57-61, 63, 68-72, 74-78.]

Bancroft Library, Berkeley, California. See Squier MSS.

[Bataillon, Marcel. "Las Casas et le licencié Cerrato," *Bulletin Hispanique,* V (1953), 79-87.
> No. 55A.]

Biblioteca Nacional, Madrid.
> Nos. 57, 65, 66, 73-74.

Bibliothèque Nationale, Paris.
> Nos. 45, 57, 67, 72, 74, 75, 77, 78.

[Biermann, Benno M., O.P. "Lascasiana: unedierte documente von Fray Bartolomé de las Casas," *Archivum Fratrum Praedicatorum*, XXVI (1957), 337-358.
> Nos. 31A, 56A, 57A, 60.]

Biermann, Benno M., O.P. "Zwei Briefe von Fray Bartolomé de las Casas," *Archivum Fratrum Praedicatorum*, IV (1934), 197-202.
> Nos. 13, 14.

British Museum.
> No. 44.

[*Bulletin Hispanique*. See Bataillon.]

Cartas de Indias. Madrid, 1877.
> Nos. 37, 38.

Casa Valencia, Conde de. Private collection.
> No. 17.

Casas, Bartolomé de las: Abbreviations, collections of works, see: *Apol.*; [*BAE, CX*]; Casas, *Colección de tratados* and *Tratados* . . . ; Fabié; *Hist.*; Llorente.

[Casas, Fr. Bartolomé de las. *Colección de tratados, 1552-1553*; facsimile edition. Emilio Ravignani, ed. Biblioteca Argentina de Libros Raros Americanos, III. Buenos Aires, 1924.
> Nos. 18, 19, 23, 41, 43, 44, 48, 49.]

Casas, Fr. Bartolomé de las. *Tratados de Fray Bartolomé de las Casas*, facsimile and transcribed edition, with Latin translated. Lewis Hanke, Manuel Giménez Fernández, Juan Pérez de Tudela Bueso, Agustín Millares Carlo, and Rafael Moreno, eds. and collabs. Biblioteca Americana, XLI-XLII, serie de Cronistas de Indias. 2 vols. Mexico and Buenos Aires, 1965.
> Nos. 18, 19, 23, 41, 43, 44, 48, 49.

Conway, G. R. G. Private collection.
> No. 61.

Cuevas, *Docs.* Cuevas, Mariano, ed. *Documentos inéditos del siglo XVI para la historia de México*. Mexico, 1914.

Dávila Padilla. Dávila Padilla, Fr. Agustín. *Historia de la fundación y discurso de la Provincia de Santiago de México*. Madrid, 1596.
> No. 64.

DE. *Colección de documentos inéditos para la historia de España*. 113 vols. Madrid, 1842-1895.
> No. 17.

Díaz, *Historia verdadera*. Díaz del Castillo, Bernal. *Historia verdadera de la conquista de la Nueva España*. Genaro García, ed. 2 vols. Mexico, 1904.

DII. Colección de documentos inéditos relativos al descubrimiento, conquista y organización de las antiguas posesiones españolas de América y Oceania. 42 vols. Madrid, 1864-1884.

Nos. 2, 4, 5, 7, 10, 28, 29, 31, 32, 34, 36, 46, 53, 57, 59, 69, 71, 72.

DIU. Colección de documentos inéditos relativos al descubrimiento, conquista y organización de las antiguas posesiones españolas de Ultramar. 25 vols. Madrid, 1885-1932.

Nos. 2, 4, 5.

Dominican Convent of San Felipe, Sucre, Bolivia.

No. 20.

Dominican Provincial Archive, Valencia, Spain.

No. 14.

Epis. de Nueva España. Paso y Troncoso, Francisco del, ed. *Epistolario de Nueva España.* 16 vols. Mexico, 1939-1942.

Fabié. Fabié, Antonio María. *Vida y escritos de fray Bartolomé de las Casas, obispo de Chiapa.* 2 vols. Madrid, April 1879. Also printed in *DE,* LXX-LXXI, March 1879. N.B. My citations of documents, e.g., app. IV, can be verified in either edition; page references are to the April edition, which has text in vol. I and documents in vol. II.

Nos. 7, 12, 17, 18, 21, 22, 24, 25, 26, 27, 31, 35, 36, 45, 46, 47, 54, 57, 59, 70.

Fernández de Oviedo. See Oviedo.

Fischer, Agustín. Sale of his books at Sotheby's, London, in 1869. N.B. It is not certain that the following items actually belonged to Fischer. As they appeared in a separate section at the end of the catalogue, they might have been Dr. C. H. Behrendt's; the fact that one item had belonged to García Icazbalceta reinforces the possibility that this was a separate lot.

Nos. 21, 51, 73, 74.

Fondos americanos. Catálogo de los fondos americanos del Archivo de Protocolos de Sevilla. 5 vols. Seville, 1930-1937. Vol. IV was issued as: *Documentos americanos del Archivo de Protocolos de Sevilla.* Madrid, 1935.

García Icazbalceta. See Icazbalceta, University of Texas Library.

Gayangos, Pascual de. Private collection.

Nos. 21, 22, 70.

Gómara, *Historia.* Gómara, Francisco López de. *Hispania victrix. Primera y segunda parte de la historia general de las Indias.* [Zaragoza, 1552.] Enrique de Vedia, ed. Biblioteca de Autores Españoles, XXII, 155-355. Madrid, 1852.

Hanke, "Festón de docs." Hanke, Dr. Lewis. "Un festón de documentos lascasianos," *Revista Cubana,* XVI (July-December 1941), 150-211.

Nos. 20, 56, 68, 76.

Herrera. Herrera y Tordesillas, Antonio de. *Historia general de los hechos de los castellanos en las islas i tierra firme del mar océano.* 4 vols. Madrid [1601-1615], 1726-1730.
　　Nos. 8, 52, 55, 64, 65.

Historia or *Hist.* Casas, Fray Bartolomé de las. *Historia de las Indias.* 5 vols. Madrid, 1875-1876.
　　Nos. 1, 2, 3, 4, 5, 6, 7, 8, 9, 65.

Huntington Library. Henry E. Huntington Library, San Marino, California.
　　Nos. 10, 36, 70.

Icazbalceta, *Docs.* García Icazbalceta, Joaquín, ed. *Colección de documentos para la historia de México.* 2 vols. Mexico, 1858, 1866.
　　Nos. 60, 63, 75, 77, 78.

Icazbalceta, *Nueva colección de docs.* García Icazbalceta, Joaquín, ed. *Nueva colección de documentos para la historia de México.* 5 vols. Mexico, 1886-1892.

JCBL. John Carter Brown Library, Providence, Rhode Island.
　　Nos. 44, 48, 65, 73, 74, 75, 78.

León, *Tratado.* León Pinelo, Lic. Antonio de. *Tratado de confirmaciones reales de encomiendas, oficios y casos en que se requieren para las Indias Occidentales.* Madrid, 1630.

Library of Congress, Washington, D. C.
　　Nos. 45 and 66 (photostats).

Llorente. Llorente, Juan Antonio. *Colección de las obras del venerable obispo de Chiapa, don Bartolomé de Las Casas, defensor de la libertad de los americanos.* 2 vols. Paris, 1822. Also in French: *Oeuvres de don Barthélemi de Las Casas, évêque de Chiapa, défenseur de la liberté des naturels de l'Amérique.* 2 vols. Paris, 1822. N.B. All citations are to the Spanish edition.
　　Nos. 18, 19, 23, 43, 48, 50, 57, 74.

López de Gómara. See Gómara.

MacNutt. MacNutt, Francis Augustus. *Bartholomew de las Casas. His Life, His Apostolate, and His Writings.* New York and London, 1909.
　　Nos. 18, 24, 25, 26.

Medina, *Bib. hisp-am.* Medina, José Toribio. *Biblioteca hispano-americana, 1493-1907.* 7 vols. Santiago de Chile, 1898-1907.
　　No. 52.

Muñoz Collection, in the Real Academia de la Historia, Madrid. Juan Bautista Muñoz's 90-odd volume collection of original manuscripts, transcripts, and digests. See also *DIU*, Quintana, Rich MSS, Squier MSS.
　　Nos. 12, 29, 41, 42, 64, 65.

[Museo Nacional de Historia, Mexico.
  No. 31A.]

NYPL. New York Public Library. See Rich MSS.

Oaxaca, Biblioteca Pública.
  No. 16.

Oviedo. Oviedo y Valdés, Gonzalo Fernández de. *Historia general y natural de las Indias, islas y tierra firme del mar océano.* [Parte I, 1535, 1547. Parte II, lib. XX, 1557.] 4 vols. Madrid, 1851-1855.

Paz, *Catálogo Bib. Nac.* Paz, Julian. *Catálogo de manuscritos de América existentes en la Biblioteca Nacional.* Madrid, 1933.
  Nos. 65, 73, 74.

Phillipps, Sir Thomas. Sales of his books in London, 1913 and 1919; sale by his estate, 1946.
  Nos. 21, 41, 44, 51, 64, 65, 73, 74.

Puga, *Cedulario.* Puga, Vasco de. *Prouisiones, cedulas, instrucciones de Su Magestad, ordenanças de difuntos y audiencia para la buena expedicion de los negocios y administracion de justicia y gouernacion de esta Nueua España y para el buen tratamiento y conseruacion de los indios, dende el año 1525 hasta el presente de 63.* 2 vols. Mexico, [1563], 1878-1879.

Quintana. Quintana, Manuel Josef. "Fr. Bartolomé de las Casas," in his *Vidas de españoles célebres,* III, Madrid, 1833. N.B. This exceptional monograph was based on papers then in the hands of Antonio Uguina, no doubt copied by Muñoz. For Muñoz is named in app. VI, and the extant portion of the Uguina Collection consists of Muñoz transcripts. See Rich MSS.
  Nos. 4, 12.

Real Academia de la Historia, Madrid. See Muñoz Collection.

Remesal or Rem. Remesal, Fray Antonio de. *Historia general de las Indias Occidentales, y particular de la gobernación de Chiapa y Guatemala.* [Madrid, 1619.] Biblioteca "Goathemala" de la Sociedad de Geografía e Historia, IV-V. 2 vols. Guatemala, 1932. N.B. All citations are to this second edition.
  Nos. 11, 16, 30, 33, 39, 40, 42, 45, 64.

Revista Cubana. See Hanke.

Rich MSS, New York Public Library. These copies and digests of documents, made by Juan Bautista Muñoz, were formerly in the possession of Uguina. They were sold by Obadiah Rich to James Lenox, and thus found their way to the NYPL.
  Nos. 2, 5, 12, 29, 38.

Santa Cruz, *Crónica.* Santa Cruz, Alonso de la. *Crónica del emperador Carlos V.* 5 vols. Madrid, 1920-1925.

Serrano y Sanz, *Orígenes*. Serrano y Sanz, Manuel. "El gobierno de las Indias por frailes Jerónimos, años 1516 a 1518," in his *Orígenes de la dominación española en América*. Nueva Biblioteca de Autores Españoles, XXV. Madrid, 1918.

Squier MSS, XXII, Bancroft Library, The University of California, Berkeley, California. This volume of digests and transcripts comprises Central American material from tomos LXXXIV, LXXXV, and LXXXVII of the Muñoz Collection. It was evidently no. 743 of the Squier sale in New York in 1876.
    Nos. 36, 37.

Stevens, Henry, Publications of separate documents, London.
    Nos. 9, 10, 36, 70.

Uguina, Antonio. Private collection. See Rich MSS, Quintana.

University of Texas Library, Austin, Texas. Collection of García Icazbalceta.
    Nos. 60, 63.

Ximénez or Xim. Ximénez, Fray Francisco. *Historia de la provincia de San Vicente de Chiapa y Guatemala de la orden de predicadores*. Biblioteca "Goathemala" de la Sociedad de Geografía e Historia, I-II. 2 vols. Guatemala, January, 1929-1930.
    Nos. 15, 30.

Zorita, *Historia*. Zorita, Lic. Alonso de. *La historia de la Nueva España*. Manuel Serrano y Sanz, ed. Colección de Libros y Documentos Referentes a la Historia de América, IX. Madrid, 1909.
    No. 67.

INDEX

N.B. For Casas' writings, a single consolidated entry gives handy reference to all main text and Catalogue discussions, with Catalogue pages in *italic* type. All *titles* by Casas are also indexed separately, with full citations; however, his many letters, memorials, petitions, etc., are not indexed individually, since they are so listed in the Catalogue, with complete cross-reference in the notes. The vexing problem of Spanish composed personal names has been solved by the new Anglo-American cataloguing rules: *all* persons are listed with the first surname first; but persons appearing in the text by their second surname are so listed *also*—and when their own preference for the second surname is emphatic, as in their writings (e.g. Oviedo), the main entry appears sensibly under the preferred name.